THE
GRAMMAR OF
CONDUCTING

THE
GRAMMAR OF CONDUCTING

A COMPREHENSIVE GUIDE TO BATON TECHNIQUE AND INTERPRETATION

Max Rudolf

Third Edition
Prepared with the Assistance of
Michael Stern

SCHIRMER
CENGAGE Learning™

Australia • Brazil • Japan • Korea • Mexico • Singapore • Spain • United Kingdom • United States

The Grammar of Conducting: A Comprehensive Guide to Baton Technique and Interpretation, Third Edition
Max Rudolf

For product information and
technology assistance, contact us at **Cengage Learning
Customer & Sales Support, 1-800-354-9706**

For permission to use material from this text or product,
submit all requests online at **www.cengage.com/permissions**
Further permissions questions can be emailed to
permissionrequest@cengage.com

Library of Congress Control Number: 93-12310

ISBN-13: 978-0-02-872221-4

ISBN-10: 0-02-872221-3

Schirmer
20 Channel Center Street
Boston, MA 02210
USA

Cengage Learning is a leading provider of customized learning solutions with office locations around the globe, including Singapore, the United Kingdom, Australia, Mexico, Brazil, and Japan. Locate your local office at **www.cengage.com/global**

Cengage Learning products are represented in Canada by Nelson Education, Ltd.

To learn more about Schirmer, visit
www.cengage.com/schirmer

Purchase any of our products at your local college store or at our preferred online store **www.ichapters.com**

Printed in the United States of America
9 10 11 12 13   15 14 13 12 11

FD346

Contents

Part Two. APPLICATIONS

Preface to the Third Edition

Habent sua fata libelli is an ancient saying that implies that there is a story behind every book. The story behind *The Grammar of Conducting* covers a span of fifty years. It began soon after my arrival in America when, while looking for a job, I did not wish to idle away so many free hours and decided to write a text on conducting. So it came that I, a conductor who had never had a conducting lesson, would undertake to write a voluminous book on the subject! My project was encouraged by my old friend, George Szell, who not only lent his advice but brought my finished script to the attention of G. Schirmer, during the brief period in 1945 when William Schuman was the firm's director of publications. He was strongly in favor of publishing my book. Yet, due to editing and other preparatory steps, it was not until January 1950 that copies of the *Grammar* appeared in the stores.

The first edition carried the subtitle "A Practical Study of Modern Baton Technique," and its thirty chapters, proceeding from simple to more complicated beat patterns, were organized to explain conducting techniques as fully as possible for the purpose of self-study or as a workable system for classroom instruction.

Reactions from educators were favorable, though slow in coming, until the *Grammar* was given broad publicity by Virgil Thomson's review in the *New York Herald Tribune*. It concluded with the words: "all musicians need access to it and many amateurs will find it fascinating. I fancy it will remain the basic text on its subject for many years to come."

The first edition included only occasional references to musical interpretation. When time came for a second edition it seemed the right moment to expand the *Grammar*'s usefulness by treating questions of style and interpretation as well as rendering advice related to the preparation of orchestra parts. Extending the scope of my text had been favored by my students at the Curtis Institute of Music in Philadelphia. Their lively interest in performance practice, an interest shared nowadays by most younger musicians, justified the addition of chapters dealing with interpretational questions and providing guidelines for further study.

Aside from being augmented by new chapters, the *Grammar*'s second edition, published by Schirmer Books, underwent a general revision, which involved updating the musical examples and other textual changes. The very favorable reception by the book's users indicated that I had been on the right track and now gives me the hope that the third edition will meet with similar approval.

Those familiar with the former versions will notice, just by looking at the new table of contents and index, that the Grammar's setup has been substantially altered. While planning the present volume, my thinking was to a great part influenced by "feedback," which came from three different directions.

First, from reports by teachers and students, I had increasingly become aware of the fact that the course of study suggested in my book was not necessarily identical with the one preferred in a classroom situation. In other words, class assignments are given in an order that best suits an instructor's own teaching method. Consequently, the *Grammar*'s essential function is no longer seen as a "primer" but rather as a general guide and source of pertinent information. Actually, some chapters in the second edition have been judged to be suited as reading material for advanced students.

Second, a significant impulse came from a group of prominent teachers who, having been consulted as to the merits of a new edition, recommended changes. I wish to thank them here and express my sincere appreciation. Their comments and criticisms made me rethink some of my views, including questions of terminology.

To help orient the reader the text is now divided into four main parts, and the chapters have been placed in a completely different order for this edition. Much of the text, especially in Part Four, has been rewritten, and new material has been added. Some chapters have been combined, others eliminated; yet all the essential information has been retained by transferring it to other suitable places. In reorganizing the material my goal was to facilitate a flexible plan of study and to strengthen the book's value as a reference source on individual topics.

Out of a total of thirty-five chapters, thirteen are in Part One, "Basic Techniques," in which most of the beat patterns are explained and illustrated. In Part Two, "Applications," modifications of the basic patterns are discussed, and a long chapter is devoted entirely to the proper handling of fermatas and breaks. Part Three, "Execution and Performance," covers a broad spectrum of a practicing conductor's work and presents an advanced level of study. "Interpretation and Style" are treated in four extended chapters in Part Four.

During my years in Philadelphia, continuing to the present day, I have put in writing—in the form of articles published in diverse professional journals —the results of my investigations into various topics of musical interest. Throughout the present volume, but especially in Part Four, I have tried to incorporate some of these ideas. The concluding chapter, a confessional summary of "Recollections and Reflections," was an afterthought suggested to me by friends who believed that readers would welcome a personal account of my experiences and thoughts.

An explanation is due why I have seen fit to retain a number of technical exercises meant to enable the student to concentrate entirely on mechanical problems. In my teaching experience I have found them essential for testing a student's absolutely secure feeling of a given pulse. These exercises must be practiced at different metronomic speeds, a method that could not be applied to "real" music.

The book's format will make it more convenient for use on a piano or music stand. Furthermore, measure numbers or rehearsal figures, lacking in the second edition, have been added to facilitate placing the musical examples in the context of the full scores. The musical examples themselves are now numbered within each chapter to simplify cross-referencing through-out the book. A new appendix has been added to discuss Weber's *Oberon* Overture in context of the complete opera. Some of the former appendices have been revised.

Finally, and most important, in preparing this new edition I was assisted by my colleague, Michael Stern, a skilled conductor and knowledgeable musician, who had been intimately familiar with the *Grammar* since his student days. The aim of our close collaboration was to produce a text that, without impairing the book's original intent, combines all old and new materials within a newly designed system.

I would also like to express gratitude to Mr. Robert Axelrod of Schirmer Books, who has given the *Grammar's* new edition his firm support, fully understanding our problems and making many valuable suggestions.

With this book I extend to all conductors, but especially to my young colleagues, greetings of good will, and I wish them the best of luck. At the risk of being judged a curmudgeon, I still see some conductors satisfied with "keeping things together," others whose gestures may be meaningful for the audience but not for the players, and again others who never made an effort to explore, realistically, the exact relation between gesture and response. We should not forget that musicians, once they know "what the conductor wants," will adjust to even the most awkward gestures! There has been no change, however, in the feeling that I expressed at the end of my preface to the *Grammar's* first edition: "If my book will contribute to the education of genuine conductors and diminish the number of time beaters, I shall feel amply rewarded."

Max Rudolf
Philadelphia
Spring 1993

Introduction

Directing an Orchestra Is a Complex Job

The conductor must be a trained musician, must know how to work with people in a group, and must be able to convey musical intentions to players by means of gestures.

A conductor's training must have included courses in composition, and the conductor must have gained insight into all the questions of interpretation, such as structural analysis, style, and performance practice. Most important, a conductor must be a competent performer on at least one instrument, aside from possessing a working knowledge of all instruments used in an orchestra. The ability to read an orchestral score and, if necessary, play it on the piano is a vital part of the conductor's faculties. While absolute pitch is not a prerequisite, the conductor's ear should be keen enough to recognize inaccuracy in pitch and to maintain the proper balance. The mastery of all these elements will give the conductor the authority to be a genuine leader.

But musicianship and thorough study of scores will help little unless a conductor knows how to talk to people, work with them, and get results in a quick and direct manner. Knowledge of the principles of group psychology is of great value in rehearsing efficiently and in stimulating the players to a good performance.

Musicianship and knowledge of psychology, however, still do not make a conductor. There is a technique of conducting just as there is a technique of playing an instrument.

The Technique of Conducting

The technique of conducting involves the use of the right arm in wielding the baton, the left arm in lending support, and the eyes as a means of communication. The most elementary gestures are used to set the tempo of the music, to indicate when to start and stop, and to indicate holds and interruptions. These gestures are indispensable but are in themselves hardly more than traffic signals to keep the orchestra together. To obtain an artistic result the conductor must be able to communicate nuances in dynamics, phrasing, articulation (legato and staccato), and general expression. For this, mere time beating is not enough; the appropriate gesture to elicit from the players the desired response must be mastered before we can actually speak of *conducting.*

If you watch closely, you will be impressed by the natural unity and coherence of an accomplished conductor's gestures. They seem to be such a simple and direct means of evoking musical expression that you may not realize their carefully planned and purposeful nature. These motions constitute a technique for conveying to the orchestra a large number of musical details. In order to teach this technique, this book will analyze and discuss the various gestures that the conductor uses. You may wonder why an activity that appears so easy and natural must be dissected. You may also doubt whether all conductors have worked out their techniques as methodically as this book proposes to do. Actually, if they have not done so, they have attained the same end only by a prolonged process of trial and error.

Whether you study in the manner proposed by this book, or whether your technique evolves in the course of experience alone, you will have to pass through a stage of development in which you become acutely conscious of technical problems. Most musicians rely at first on their natural feelings and may work for some time with little to guide them but their instinct. But presently they realize that technical control is indispensable to artistic mastery. Once attained, such control gives the artist the expressive simplicity that is the goal of all artistic performance. This means that gestures become second nature and the conductor's involvement can be entirely with the music.

The Use of the Baton

A conductor with a fractured left arm would still be able to exercise complete control of the orchestra, thanks to an efficient baton technique. Therefore, a large part of this book will be devoted to advising the student how to handle the baton, the conductor's most efficient tool.

The handiest kind of baton is about twenty inches long and fairly light in weight. It should not be so thin that the point is shaky, making it hard to beat distinctly. The choice of a baton with or without a handle depends upon the individual. You must also decide for yourself which grip is the most convenient. You must be able to control the baton completely and feel perfectly at ease; this is the test of a good grip. The most advisable way to hold the baton is with the thumb, the first and second fingers, and with the butt against the palm of the hand. You will feel more secure in the energetic beats if you use an even fuller grip.

Conducting Without a Baton

Conducting without a baton has one obvious advantage in that there are two expressive hands instead of one. But even though the baton takes some of the expressiveness from the right hand, there are advantages in using it. Remember that the player's attention always shifts from music stand to conductor. It is much easier for the player to follow the baton, especially in accompaniments, or if the music is unfamiliar or the part is technically difficult. The baton is even more important when there is a large ensemble, for then many of the players are quite a distance from the conductor's stand. In the interest of clarity, therefore, the student should learn to conduct with a baton. Nevertheless, the figures in this book can be studied without one.

General Explanation of the Figures

Because of the two-dimensional nature of the figures, different beats along the same line can be indicated only by slight separations of the beat lines. Straight lines that run close together on the figures coincide in actual practice.

All counts are marked so that the played beat coincides with the written count: The baton is at ① when the first beat sounds and moves so as to arrive at ② at the start of the second beat. The following symbols are used in the figures, and they appear here with brief explanations of their meanings.

○   The baton passes through without stopping

▢   The baton stops at this point

ATT   Position of attention

There are four kinds of lines in the diagrams:

indicates the field of beating

indicates deliberate, controlled movement

indicates very quick movement

indicates bouncing

PART ONE

BASIC TECHNIQUES

CHAPTER 1

The Neutral-Legato Pattern (4-Beat)

GENERAL TRAINING OF THE RIGHT ARM

In directing music the tip of the baton describes certain patterns that represent the rhythm. There is a different pattern for each rhythm, and the patterns are modified according to the musical expression. The movements of the baton are: up, down, left, right, and their various combinations, as shown in figure 1.1. This figure shows the up-down line and the left-right line used in beating. The general area covered by these lines is called the field of beating, and the lines are the axes of the field. The size of the field of beating may vary widely from one situation to another. Preliminary exercises will help to develop the dexterity needed to control the motions of hand and arm.

Practice the up—down and left—right motions with the wrist alone, first slowly, then rapidly. Be sure that the forearm does not move. Avoid tension in the wrist and make as large a gesture as possible.

There are two positions of the wrist: palm downward and palm sideways. Practice with both positions. In practicing the left—right movement you may find the palm–downward position stiff. If so, do not try to force it on the wrist; just practice the palm-sideways position. In actual conducting it is most

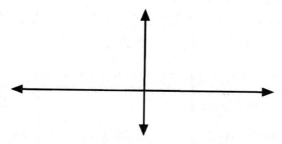

Fig. 1.1. Up-down and left-right lines in beating field

convenient to use a position halfway between the two or to change smoothly from one to the other.

In adding the forearm motion to the wrist motion, you must be aware of a general rule: The motion increases with the distance of the moving part from the body. Thus, the tip of the baton travels farther than the hand, which in turn moves farther than the forearm. To prevent any motion of the upper arm, use the left hand to hold the arm above the elbow while practicing with the forearm. In slow tempo, precaution should be taken in order to achieve smooth coordination of all parts: The hand motion should always be a little behind that of the forearm. This necessitates a turn of the wrist each time the forearm changes direction.

For the third preliminary exercise, a slight motion of the upper arm is added. Work for a smooth motion in which all parts of the arm blend their movements so that no one part sticks out awkwardly. Think of the baton as an extension of the arm; its motion should be smooth and steady. Remember: The elbow must not be raised and must remain relaxed and motionless so as not to distract from the tip of the baton as the clear point of orientation!

Figure 1.2 shows five swinging movements. Practice each with wrist alone, then with wrist and forearm. Vary the size and the speed of your beat, from a snap of the wrist to a slow turn.

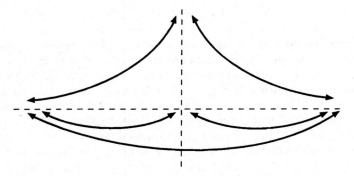

Fig. 1.2. Swinging movements for practice in beating field

In addition to these preliminary exercises the student should use a warming-up routine familiar to string players and pianists: shaking the hands freely, lifting the arms and letting them drop suddenly, and so on.

THE NEUTRAL-LEGATO PATTERN (4-BEAT)

The first four chapters deal only with music that requires four beats in a measure. Several patterns of beating this rhythm will be shown, beginning with the neutral-legato pattern.

The neutral-legato beat is a plain, continuous motion. It is neutral in character and therefore uses mostly straight

lines. It is not large in size and is done with no intensity in the forearm motion.

Figure 1.3, like all figures in this book, is drawn at one-fourth scale: The lines are roughly one-fourth of the distances that the tip of the baton travels from one count to another. Keeping this in mind, you should restrict the field of beating within reasonable limits, not forgetting that clarity remains of the essence and that an unnecessary extension of size must be avoided.

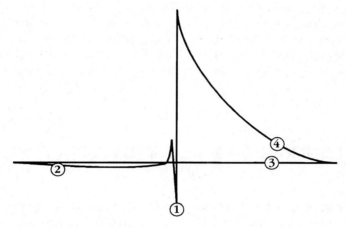

Fig. 1.3. 4-beat; neutral-legato

When practicing with the help of this figure, first count aloud (without beating) *One, Two, Three, Four* in moderate tempo ($\quarternote = 66$). When you feel that the tempo is established, continue to count aloud and start moving the baton, following the lines exactly so that the point of the baton passes through the number corresponding to each count. Try to achieve a smooth motion and avoid stopping on the counts.

A wrist motion is sufficient for this pattern. However, many students will find that they cannot use the wrist alone without feeling some strain. Since it is of utmost importance to feel at ease while beating time, a slight forearm motion may be used in addition to the wrist motion. In this case it should always be remembered that the point of the baton moves more than the hand, the hand more than the forearm. The elbow should be held still but relaxed. With practice you will gradually develop the ability to use the wrist alone. For an effective handling of the baton, a flexible wrist is as indispensable as for a string player's masterly use of the bow. It is to be regretted that in recent times some teachers of conducting, favoring an inflexible wrist, have tried to force their own questionable technique on their students. As an undesirable consequence, arm movements become unduly large, and worse, the elbow moves steadily up and down. Thus, it has sometimes happened that orchestra players inquired of a conductor: "Do you want us to follow your stick or your elbow?"

Richard Strauss, whose masterly conducting style was rightly admired, once stated: "The left hand and *both arms* are dispensable, a good wrist is sufficient." This need not lead to unreasonably small gestures. In fact, a skillful use of the wrist allows for a surprisingly ample field of beating.

You will observe that on the first count the baton is carried upward before it is turned to the left. This upward movement on the first count is called the rebound. You will also notice that the distance between the counts is not uniform. The distance between ③ and ④ especially is smaller than the others, while the distance between ④ and ① is much larger. Nevertheless, you will soon learn to adjust your beat automatically so as to keep it even and smooth.

When you are sure that you can follow this pattern without the help of the figure, check yourself by using a large mirror. Now start beating, watching yourself to see that no part of your body is moving except wrist and forearm. Your whole body should be relaxed and calm. Be sure to keep the elbow quiet, but do not press it against your side. Watch your beat, keeping it clear and steady!

THE PREPARATORY BEAT AT THE START

It is a general rule that the conductor gives one extra beat, strictly in time, before the music actually begins.

In other words, to start playing on the first count you must start beating one count earlier—that is to say, on *Four*. However, this beat of preparation (which is shown in figure 1.4) is not merely the regular fourth beat, for it starts from the position of "attention" and has the quality of an invitation. It is equivalent to lifting the bow in the string instruments and to taking a breath in

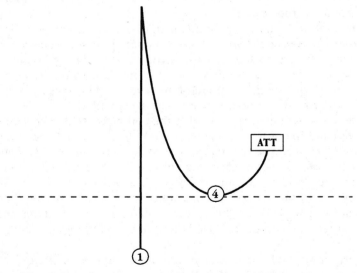

Fig. 1.4. 4-beat; start on the first count (legato)

the winds. It enables the conductor to get a clean and unified attack. In general, refer to this figure for starts on the first count.

Practice the preparatory beat in the following manner, without using the left arm. Point the baton to the attention space ATT on figure 1.4 and count aloud the previous *One, Two, Three, Four.* Just before Four, let the baton move so that it passes through ④ as you count Four. Keeping strict tempo, follow the line until you reach ①, where the music presumably begins. Having mastered this, return to the mirror with both arms down and relaxed. Lift the baton and assume the position of attention. Try to feel that by doing this you would really gain the attention of your group. This will be still more effective if you lift elbow and forearm slightly. Count—this time to yourself—and give the preparatory beat. When you reach ①, continue beating as you did with figure 1.3 and beat for several bars. Repeat this several times, starting each time from a completely relaxed position with the arm at the side.

APPLYING THE GESTURES TO MUSICAL EXERCISES

Since it is a good habit for the conductor to watch his players, you should always memorize the first few bars before starting.

Face your colleague at the piano and take the position of attention. Concentrate on the tempo and be sure that you know exactly how fast you are going to beat. Then, using what you have learned so far, conduct examples 1.1a–c. Repeat them several times in each of the tempos indicated by the metronome markings. To end the last note in each of these exercises, stop the fourth beat decisively at the center of the field on the next *One.* (A detailed explanation of cutoff gestures is given on pp. 191 and 196.) Be sure that the pianist is playing strictly in time. Do not hesitate to correct your accompanist; develop the habit early of knowing exactly what you want and getting it.

In class work, examples 1.1a–c should be not only played on the piano but also sung by the group while you conduct. Here you will have to

Ex. 1.1. Exercises

coordinate the actions of several people, exactly as you will have to do when you conduct an orchestra. Your preparatory beat will work much better if you take a slight breath simultaneously. Many exercises in this book lend themselves to singing, with or without piano accompaniment. Whenever possible, the class should sing the melody in those exercises.

Examples 1.2 and 1.3 are to be played on the piano or can be arranged for a small instrumental ensemble. Example 1.3 is marked $\frac{2}{4}$, but use four beats in a measure because of the slow tempo.

Ex. 1.2. Exercise

Ex. 1.3. Exercise

So far you have conducted these exercises *p* or *mp*. Now repeat them *mf*. To do this, you will have to enlarge the size of your beat. Make your gestures about a third larger than those used for *p*, but do not change their proportions. Keep checking the smoothness and clarity of your beat with the mirror. For the larger beat, use the forearm in addition to the wrist, but without moving the elbow!

EMPHASIZING THE BEATS BY "CLICKING"

In examples 1.4a–c you will find that you want to indicate some counts more emphatically because of the dotted rhythms and syncopations. Especially in slow tempo, the beats will have to be emphasized; this is done by "clicking." This is a sharp, quick wrist motion that speeds up the movement of the baton just before you reach a count. Immediately after the count, the

Ex. 1.4. Exercises

motion continues at normal speed. This technique can be applied only when the forearm participates in moving the baton. Remember that clicking serves the purpose of emphasizing the beat and must not be used where a smooth beat is sufficiently clear.

Use figure 1.5 for practice (♩ = 66). The first count is now located on the left–right line, to allow space for you to continue the motion in the same direction after the click. While practicing clicking on all four counts, you will feel that each beat is emphasized. Learn to do it with ease and certainty, but do not get into the habit of clicking continually!

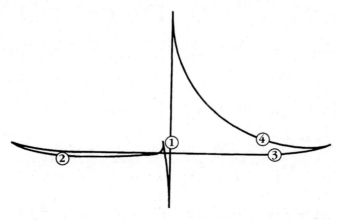

Fig. 1.5. 4-beat; neutral-legato with clicking on the counts

APPLYING THE NEUTRAL-LEGATO PATTERN TO MUSICAL EXAMPLES

By learning the neutral-legato beat first, you start your conducting without any emotional bias and you concentrate upon a clear presentation of the rhythm. But aside from its educational value, you will need it in actual conducting.

In practicing examples 1.5–1.9, it is a good habit to hum a few bars of the melody before starting to beat. This will fix the tempo firmly in your mind and enable you to give the preparatory beat strictly in time. Otherwise, the preparation might not be in the same tempo as the succeeding beats; the players will be confused and the rhythm will be rather shaky.

Ex. 1.5. Bizet, *Carmen,* Act III, Entr'acte, mm. 1-6

Ex. 1.6. Verdi, *La Traviata,* Act I, No. 1, Preludio, mm. 1-4

Do not use the left hand in directing these examples; its use will be discussed in later chapters.

The metronome markings are those of the original scores—except for those in parentheses, which are merely suggestions.

For example 1.5, the harp needs only a clear indication of the rhythm; the quiet flute solo certainly requires no dramatic gestures (see p. 314). In example 1.6, indicate the accent in measure 3 with a slightly larger Three, putting emphasis on Four without slowing down. You will feel that the enlarged third beat is a preparation for the accented fourth. Since the orchestra has nothing but **pp** accompaniment in example 1.7, the neutral-legato beat is quite adequate (see pp. 303 and 314). For example 1.8, a minimum of gesture will be sufficient to indicate the tempo for the English

Ex. 1.7. Beethoven, Violin Concerto, first movement, mm. 329-35

Ex. 1.8. Dvořák, Symphony No. 9, "From the New World," second movement, mm. 7-10

Ex. 1.9. Mendelssohn, *Fingal's Cave* Overture, mm. 1-6

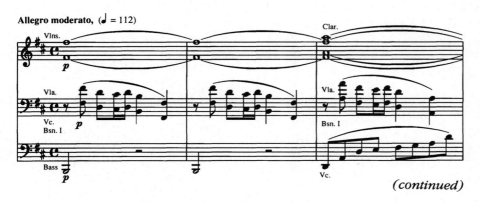

(continued)

Ex. 1.9. *Continued*

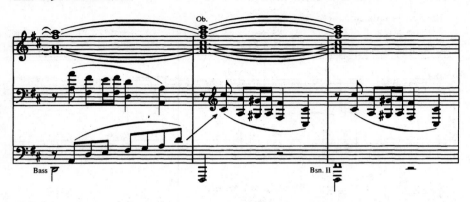

horn accompanied by the string section. Here is a good chance to practice keeping the baton in continuous motion in very slow tempo. The opening bars of *Fingal's Cave* Overture (example 1.9) set an atmosphere for the entire piece—more color than expression. For this you need the unemotional neutral-legato beat.

Additional examples for the study of the neutral-legato pattern (4-beat):

Beethoven: Piano Concerto No. 5, 2d movement, mm. 16-24
Haydn: *The Creation,* No. 12 (Recitative), mm. 1–3
Mahler: Symphony No. 1, 1st movement, beginning
Nicolai: Overture to *The Merry Wives of Windsor,* mm. 1–3, 6, 7
Shostakovitch: Symphony No. 1, 3d movement, beginning (the solo
  oboe needs no special direction)
Tchaikovsky: *Romeo and Juliet* (Overture-Fantasia), beginning
Verdi: Prelude to *Aïda,* mm. 18-23
Wagner: *Tristan und Isolde,* "Liebestod", mm. 1–5

CHAPTER *2*

Staccato Patterns
(4-Beat)

LIGHT-STACCATO

The light-staccato beat is a quick, straight motion with a stop on each count. The gestures are small.

The light-staccato beat, as shown in figure 2.1, is done by the wrist alone. In this pattern there is no rebound on the first count. Point the baton to 4 and set the tempo at ♩ = 126 in your mind. Then start beating: Stop at each count and move very quickly between the counts. Avoid any tension, especially in the forearm. Check your appearance in the mirror to be sure that your shoulder and elbow are not moving. Practice light-staccato also at ♩ = 108 and ♩ = 160.

Use figure 2.2 for the start. The motion with which you reach 4 must be very quick and decisive: a snap of the wrist. The preliminary beat is a little larger than the other beats. Since this preparation indicates not only the

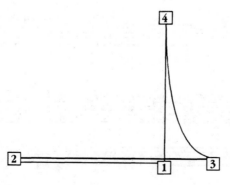

Fig. 2.1. 4-beat; light-staccato

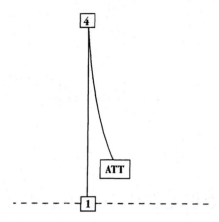

Fig. 2.2. 4-beat; start on the first count (light-staccato)

tempo but the staccato quality, you must be sure to make a definite stop at 4 and not leave it until just before the downbeat.

Examples 2.1–2.6 will give you practice in using this beat. Light-staccato

Ex. 2.1. Exercise

Ex. 2.2. Exercise

Ex. 2.3. Exercise

Ex. 2.4. Rossini, *Semiramide,* Overture, mm. 112-19

Ex. 2.5. Wagner, *Die Meistersinger von Nürnberg,* Prelude, mm. 122-25

Ex. 2.6. Mozart, Symphony No. 35, K. 385, second movement, mm. 17-21

(continued)

Ex. 2.6. *Continued*

is generally used with tempos of ♩ = 100 or faster (for more on exx. 2.4 and 2.6, see p. 315).

Additional examples for the study of the light-staccato pattern (4-beat):

Beethoven: Symphony No. 8, 2d movement (see ex. 25.2)
Grieg: *Peer Gynt,* Suite No. 1, 4th movement, beginning
Haydn: Symphony No. 99, 1st movement *(Vivace assai),* beginning
Mozart: *Le Nozze di Figaro,* No. 1 (Duettino)
Mussorgsky-Ravel: *Pictures at an Exhibition,* No. 3 "Tuileries"
Shostakovitch: Symphony No. 1, 1st movement, #8
Tchaikovsky: *The Nutcracker Suite,* "Danse Chinoise" (the solo flute needs no special direction)
Tchaikovsky: Symphony No. 6, 1st movement *(Allegro non troppo),* after the introduction

FULL-STACCATO

The full-staccato beat is a quick, slightly curved motion with a stop on each count. It is snappy and energetic, with a characteristic "bouncing" on the downbeat. The size may vary from small to large.

Bouncing, a special form of the rebound, is done by a wrist motion. First, practice bouncing without the baton. Lift your forearm slightly and jerk it downward, stopping abruptly at about the left–right line. The wrist must be completely relaxed so that when the forearm stops, the hand continues downward and snaps up again immediately. This bouncing of the hand is a natural muscular reaction and must not be hindered by any tension in the wrist.

Practice figure 2.3 at ♩ = 80 and ♩ = 100. Execution in **p**: The beat is slightly larger than for light-staccato. The first count is at the bottom of the bounce, and the stop immediately after is on the left—right line. Use very little forearm for the second and third beats; a slight twist will make them snappier. On the fourth beat, whip up the arm immediately after the count.

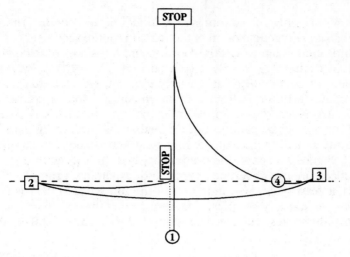

Fig. 2.3. 4-beat; full-staccato

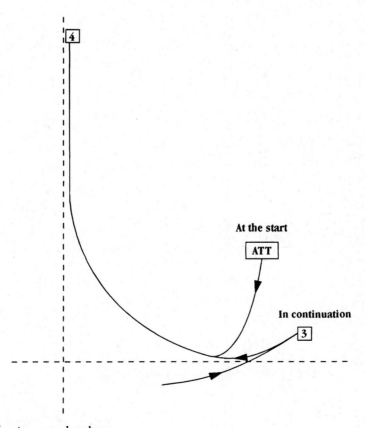

Fig. 2.4. Accented upbeat

Execution in *f*: Since the pattern is now about one and one-half times as large as in *p*, use an energetic motion of the forearm for the second and third beats.

As indicated in figure 2.3, the fourth count does not coincide with STOP at the top, though ④ is only a split second from STOP. By making the experiment of beating *Four* at the very top, you will see that it involves a special effort and thus indicates an accent on the fourth count *(accented upbeat)*. However, this is an exceptional case (see fig. 2.4) and must be avoided in the regular pattern. But remember that, in the light-staccato, the fourth count actually comes on the highest stop because of the limited size of that beat. Figure 2.5 shows the preliminary beat in full-staccato.

Practiced in the different speeds and dynamics, example 2.7 (to be repeated at least once) will train you in the full-staccato. You will help the players by beating very sharply on the rests so that they can enter precisely on the small-value notes. Full-staccato is applied in examples 2.8–2.10.

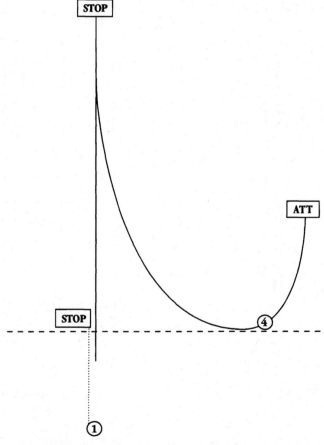

Fig. 2.5. 4-beat; start on the first count (full-staccato)

Ex. 2.7. Exercise

Ex. 2.8. Tchaikovsky, 1812 Overture, mm. 77-79

Ex. 2.9. Meyerbeer, *Le Prophète,* Act IV, No. 24, mm. 1-5

Ex. 2.10. Mahler, Symphony No. 3, fifth movement, mm. 1-7

Additional examples for the study of the full-staccato pattern (4-beat):

Bach: "Brandenburg" Concerto No. 3, 2d movement

Bizet: *L'Arlésienne* Suite No. 1, 1st movement, beginning

Brahms: *Academic Festival* Overture, *L'istesso tempo, un poco maestoso*

Haydn: *The Creation,* No. 3 (Recitative), *Allegro assai*

Mahler: Symphony No. 6, 1st movement

Mendelssohn: *Fingal's Cave* Overture, passage starting with m. 76 (one bar before B)

Roussel: *Bacchus et Ariane,* Suite No. 1, beginning

Tchaikovsky: Violin Concerto, 1st movement *(Moderato assai),* after E

Vivaldi: Concerto Grosso in A Minor, Op. 3 No. 8 (RV 522)

CHAPTER 3

The Expressive-Legato Pattern (4-Beat)

The expressive-legato beat is a curved, continuous motion.
It is done with a certain feeling of intensity in the forearm.
The degree of intensity as well as the shaping of the curves
vary with the emotional quality of the music. The size may
be anywhere from fairly small to quite large.

In figure 3.1, start with the preparatory beat shown in figure 1.4, but a little larger and with more sweep. Practice with the metronome at ♩ = 72, using wrist and forearm. Since the purpose of this pattern is to express a more or less emotional melodic line, you should feel the intensity in the forearm—without too much muscular tension!—and the baton should move as if it were encountering some resistance, a motion similar to the intense drawing of the violin bow in a lyric passage.

Remember that only the tip of the baton offers a clear point of orientation to the players, and movements of wrist and arm are subordinate to those of the baton. The shoulder must remain still but never tense.

There are many degrees of expression between neutral-legato and expressive-legato (*molto espressivo*), and you should have a wide enough variety of beats to indicate all the shades of intensity. It is therefore important to realize that the expressive-legato beat is a development of the neutral-legato beat. For *poco espressivo,* for instance, the pattern of the lines will be bent only slightly, as suggested in figure 3.2; figure 3.1 indicates more intensity, and figure 3.3 is still more expressive. Practice before the mirror; start with **𝒑** neutral-legato and, referring to figures 3.2 and 3.3, work up gradually to **𝒇** *molto espressivo.*

The relatively neutral patterns of the first two chapters appear quite similar with different conductors. The espressivo beat, however, is more individual; its execution will differ from one conductor to another, but the freedom you gain must not be misused. The orchestra will be confused unless you indicate

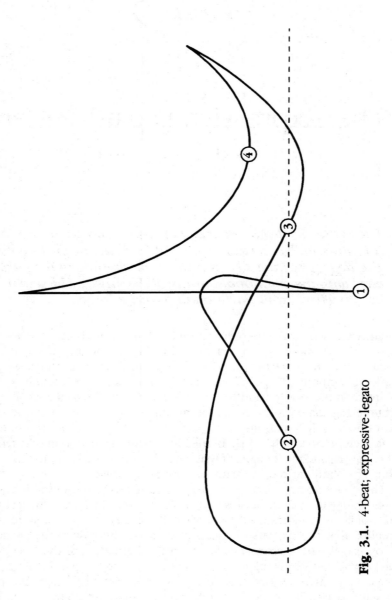

Fig. 3.1. 4-beat; expressive-legato

the counts clearly. There will be occasions when you will need clicking with this beat, especially in slow tempo. The *locations* of ①, ②, ③, and ④ remain the same, even though the manner of connecting them depends on the musical interpretation. The connecting gestures must be flexible and varied to express the melodic line's nuances, which sometimes change from beat to beat in the same bar.

Since the execution of this pattern must be well balanced and graceful, a conductor with very long arms will have to be more careful than one with relatively short arms to control the size of the beat.

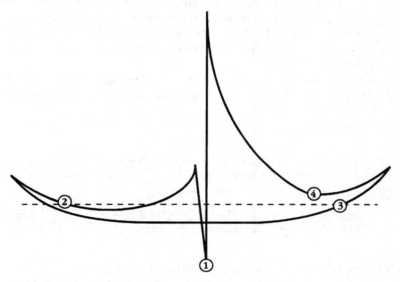

Fig. 3.2. 4-beat; expressive-legato (alternate style)

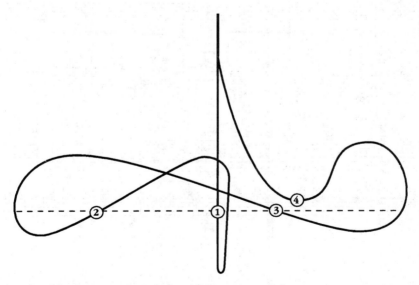

Fig. 3.3. 4-beat; expressive-legato (alternate style)

The skill you gain by practicing the same music at different speeds will prove invaluable in your conducting experience. It is worthwhile to take great pains with the preparation; students have a tendency to rush the preliminary beat in very slow tempo and to drag it in fast tempo.

The last measure in example 3.1 needs special attention. The sustained note does not require an *espressivo* beat; neutral-legato is sufficient. When playing f, however, a gesture of the left hand is needed to prevent the orchestra from playing $f \mathbin{>}$. The palm faces upward or inward, and the fingers are somewhat bent. The quality of demand contained in this gesture can be intensified by a slight shaking of the forearm. In other words, while the right hand just beats time (neutral-legato) in this bar, the gesture of the left hand maintains a steady f.

By starting example 3.2 with a somewhat larger beat than the usual p, you will be able to build the musical phrases. Then you will express the

Ex. 3.1. Exercise

Ex. 3.2. Verdi, *La Traviata,* Act I, Preludio, mm. 18-25

Ex. 3.3. Haydn, Symphony No. 92, second movement, mm. 1-4

decreasing intensity of the measure 19 by the decreasing intensity of your gesture. *Four* in measures 19 and 21 has the function of a preliminary beat, preparing the following phrase. The emphasized third beat in measure 24 should also be prepared (without delaying the tempo!): Carry the second beat farther to the left, and you will naturally give more expression to the third beat. In measure 2 of example 3.3, use a very small gesture for *Three*—then on Four prepare for the next bar. The intensity in the forearm, usually characteristic of the *espressivo* beat, would be too heavy for this graceful music. Therefore, lead the melody with a light forearm, *poco espressivo*. In example 3.4, the conductor must devote as much attention to the counterpoint in the cellos as to the melody. All the beats must reflect a singing line and the intensity of the gesture should express the rise and fall of the melody. While guiding the strings in example 3.5 with an *espressivo* beat, the conductor must not lose sight of the triplets in the brass. For an accurate indication of the rhythm, emphasize the counts whenever needed. The crescendo in measure 122 requires an increasing gesture. The character of the music in example 3.6 indicates a light and graceful gesture. Here, again, you should not "feel" your forearm.

Additional examples for the study of the expressive-legato pattern (4-beat):

Berg: *Lulu* Suite, "Rondo"
Brahms: Symphony No. 3, 2d movement, passage starting at F
Delius: *A Song of Summer,* passage starting at m. 48
Elgar: *Enigma* Variations, Op. 36, Variation No. 5, beginning
Franck: Symphony in D Minor, 1st movement, Lento
Ives: Symphony No. 4, 3d movement
Mahler: Symphony No. 4, 3d movement
Rachmaninoff: Symphony No. 2, 3d movement
Tchaikovsky: Symphony No. 6, 1st movement, *Andante* in D major
Verdi: Overture to *La Forza del Destino, Andante mosso,* at C

Ex. 3.4. Wagner, *Lohengrin*, Act II, 44 measures before Scene 3

Ex. 3.4. *Continued*

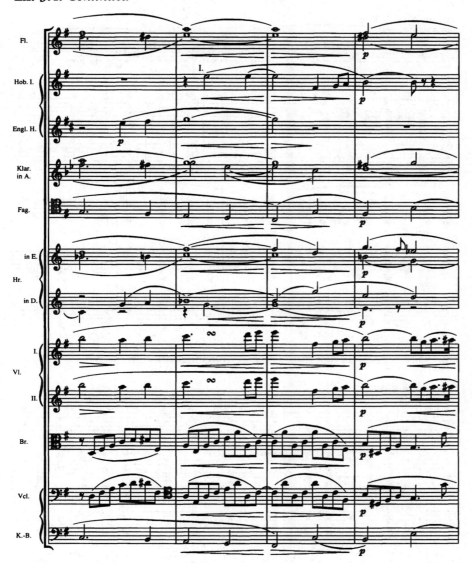

Ex. 3.5. Bizet, *L'Arlésienne* Suite No. 1, Overture, mm. 119-26

Ex. 3.6. Borodin, *Polovtsian* Dances, Introduction, mm. 31-34

CHAPTER *4*

Starting on Counts Other
Than the First Count

According to the rule discussed in the first chapter under "The Preparatory Beat at the Start," you are supposed to give one extra beat, strictly in tempo, before the first "played" beat. Thus, if the music starts on the fourth count, start beating on *Three*; if it starts on the third count, start beating on *Two*; if it starts on the second count, start beating on *One*. Your preparation must also include the dynamics: A larger gesture prepares $\boldsymbol{f}$, a smaller gesture $\boldsymbol{p}$.

STARTING ON THE FOURTH COUNT

It has been pointed out that the preliminary beat, because of its quality of invitation, is not identical with the regular pattern. As shown in figure 4.1,

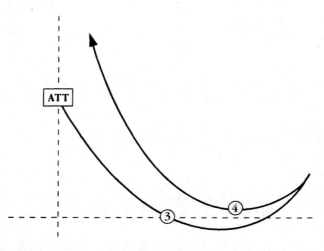

Fig. 4.1. 4-beat; start on the fourth count (legato)

even in neutral-legato this motion is slightly curved, unlike the usual straight line. The more expressive the music, the more expressive the preparation should be. Do not, however, give too much weight to the preliminary beat, which is always gentler than the first played beat. Apply these ideas to your practice of example 4.1. In all staccato beats, as shown in figure 4.2, use a snappy and decisive motion in the preparation. You can indicate the tempo clearly only by making a definite stop at ③; otherwise the staccato quality is lost and the players do not get a precise feeling of the tempo. Keep this in mind while practicing example 4.2. Conduct example 4.3 using a small beat, *poco espressivo.* The metronome marking, ♩ = 60, follows Carl Czerny's suggestion (see p. 397). Usually, this movement is performed at a slightly slower pace, ♩ = 54–56. For the very energetic start in example 4.4, raise the

Ex. 4.1.   Exercise

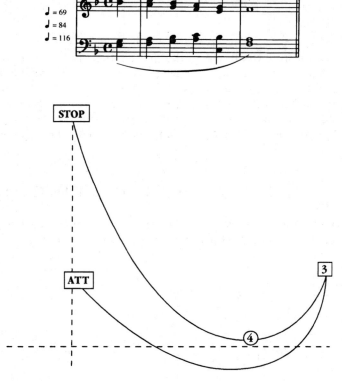

Fig. 4.2.   4-beat; start on the fourth count (staccato)

Ex. 4.2.   Exercise

Ex. 4.3. Beethoven, Violin Concerto, second movement, mm. 1-2

Ex. 4.4. Bizet, *Carmen,* Act II, No. 14, mm. 1-2

whole arm on the preparatory beat (the baton pointing downward!), while the elbow may go slightly backwards to increase the impetus of the start. Check in the mirror to be sure that the gesture appears convincing but not too frantic. Beat staccato *ff*. The beginning of example 19.13 should be handled in similar fashion, accenting the start in a similar but less aggressive manner. Although the first phrase of example 4.5 is slurred, the theme does not have legato character, therefore beat staccato (see the remark at the end of this chapter).

Ex. 4.5. R. Strauss, *Der Rosenkavalier,* Overture, mm. 1-3

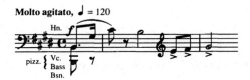

STARTING ON THE THIRD COUNT

In practicing figures 4.3 and 4.4, you will feel that the change of direction from left to right included in the preparation gives the quality of invitation to the beat. Apply this in examples 4.6 and 4.7. Beat full-staccato in example 4.8. In example 4.9, beat in four in spite of the time signature ₵, but compare the comment on p. 390. The first two notes are detached, the rest legato; beat accordingly. Your preparatory gesture should be very gentle, to match the graceful music.

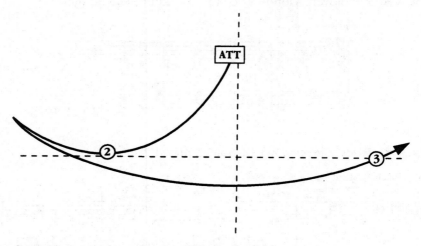

Fig. 4.3. 4-beat; start on the third count (legato)

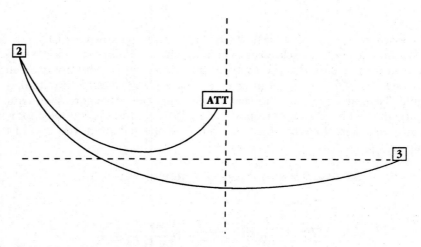

Fig. 4.4. 4-beat; start on the third count (staccato)

Ex. 4.6. Exercise

Ex. 4.7 Exercise

Ex. 4.8. J.S. Bach, Easter Oratorio, No. 11 (Chorus) mm. 1-3

Ex. 4.9. Mozart, *Eine kleine Nachtmusik,* K. 525, second movement, mm. 1-2

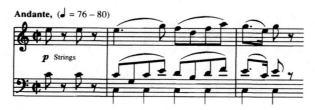

STARTING ON THE SECOND COUNT

In figures 4.5 and 4.6, the change of direction again leads the players into their attack. The staccato preparation in this case requires a large bounce but should be very elastic and by no means heavy. Lifting the forearm slightly on the rebound will emphasize the introductory character. In light-staccato, however, use the wrist only. The gesture then is considerably smaller. For training, use examples 4.10 and 4.11. Start example 4.12 **p** legato, then crescendo to **f**. After a large downbeat (**fp**), make the second beat much smaller and crescendo again. This introduction is often done with subdivision (see p. 131). The quarter rest on One, in both examples 4.13 and 4.14, does not affect the manner of preparation (do not prepare One!). Conduct **p** legato, *poco espressivo.* In example 4.15, beat **f** staccato, but not too sharp, since the music is solemn and the bowing should not be too detached.

Keep in mind the various positions of attention! Once you lift the baton, do not leave the position of attention until you give the preparatory beat.

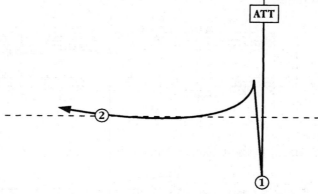

Fig. 4.5. 4-beat; start on the second count (legato)

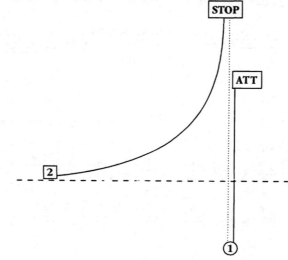

Fig. 4.6. 4-beat; start on the second count (staccato)

Before lifting the baton, be sure where to point it. Remember this simple rule: When the attack is on the first count, point the baton to the right; to start on the other counts, point it to the center. There is one exception. For a spectacular attack on the fourth count, point the baton to the left. This position allows a very large preliminary beat (whole-arm gesture). Try it, but do not use it too often.

Ex. 4.10. Exercise

Ex. 4.11. Exercise

Ex. 4.12. Brahms, Symphony No. 1, fourth movement, mm. 1-2

Ex. 4.13. Shostakovich, Symphony No. 5, third movement, mm. 1-2

Ex. 4.14. Gluck, *Iphigénie en Aulide,* Overture, mm. 1-2

Ex. 4.15. Handel, Concerto Grosso, Op. 6, No. 8, second movement, mm. 1-2

Additional examples:

Starting on the Fourth Count

Beethoven: Symphony No. 3, 2d movement
Brahms: Symphony No. 2, 2d movement
Haydn: *The Creation*, No. 24 (Aria)
Mahler: Symphony No. 4, 4th movement
Mozart: *Die Zauberflöte*, No. 21 (Finale)
Puccini: *Madama Butterfly*, Act II, beginning
Verdi: *Il Trovatore*, Act II, No. 4 (Chorus)

Starting on the Third Count

Gershwin: *Porgy and Bess*, Overture, mm. 1, *ff*
Haydn: *The Seasons*, No. 34 (Cavatina)
Mozart: *Così fan tutte*, No. 25 (Rondo; often conducted with subdivision)
Prokofiev: "Classical" Symphony, 3d movement

Starting on the Second Count

Bach: Cantata No. 21 (*Ich hatte viel Bekümmernis*), No. 3 (Aria for soprano)
Bach: Cantata No. 106 (*Gottes Zeit ist die allerbeste Zeit*), No. 4 (Coro)
Bartók: Piano Concerto No. 3, 2d movement
Rachmaninoff: Symphony No. 2, 1st movement
Verdi: *Falstaff*, Act I, beginning
(For more examples of "Starting on the Second Count," see Chapter 6.)

CHAPTER *5*

The 3-Beat

NEUTRAL-LEGATO AND EXPRESSIVE-LEGATO

For figure 5.1, apply the same procedure as for figure 1.3. To start on the first count, use figure 1.4 (changing the figure ④ to ③) and practice before the mirror at different tempi. Conduct example 5.1 using the neutral-legato pattern. The explanations of chapter 3 apply to the pattern shown in figure 5.2. Figures 5.3 and 5.4 show *poco espressivo* and *molto espressivo*. Enlarge these according to dynamics.

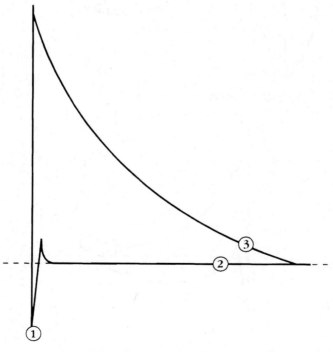

Fig. 5.1. 3-beat; neutral-legato

Ex. 5.1. Exercise

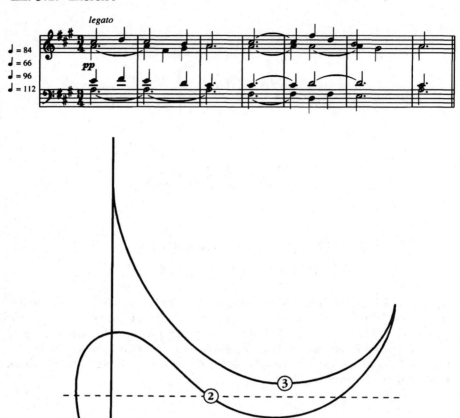

Fig. 5.2. 3-beat; expressive-legato

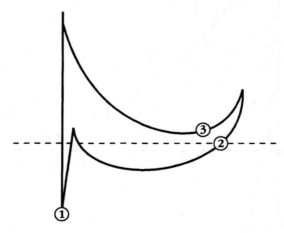

Fig. 5.3. 3-beat; expressive-legato (alternate style)

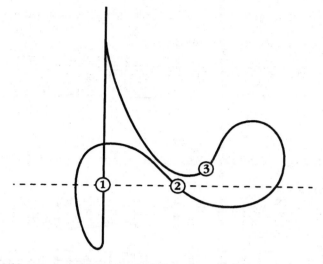

Fig. 5.4. 3-beat; expressive-legato (alternate style)

Practice example 5.2 with *poco espressivo* to *molto espressivo*. In example 5.3, beat in three, indicating each ♩ with one beat. Use neutral-legato. A very small neutral-legato should be applied in example 5.4. Conduct example 5.5 *molto espressivo*.

Ex. 5.2. Exercise

Ex. 5.3. Vaughan Williams, *A London Symphony*, mm. 1-3

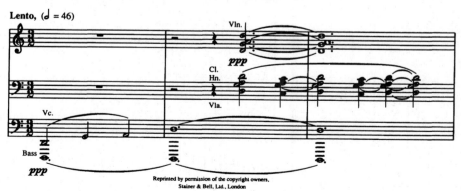

Reprinted by permission of the copyright owners,
Stainer & Bell, Ltd., London

Ex. 5.4. Schubert, Symphony No. 7, "Unfinished," first movement, mm. 1-5

Ex. 5.5. Mascagni, *Cavalleria Rusticana,* Intermezzo, mm. 20-27

LIGHT-STACCATO AND FULL-STACCATO

For figures 5.5 and 5.6, compare the explanations of chapter 2. For the start, apply figure 2.2 (light-staccato) and figure 2.4 (full-staccato), changing the figure ④ to ③. Practice at different speeds.

Fig. 5.5. 3-beat; light-staccato

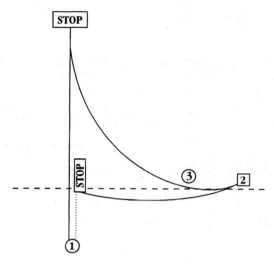

Fig. 5.6. 3-beat; full-staccato

For training in 3-beat staccato use examples 5.6 and 5.7.

Conduct light-staccato in example 5.8. The legato in the flutes (m. 4) does not affect the beat, which remains staccato. Staccato patterns are often applied to fast passages when slurring is primarily a matter of articulation and a strong feeling for the rhythm prevails (see p. 315). The first two bars of example 5.9 are full-staccato (not too large), followed by two bars of light-staccato. A large gesture, full-staccato, is used for example 5.10. In example 5.11, beat light-staccato. Make your preparation sufficiently fast. Here, as in the first two measures of example 5.8, the strings are playing pizzicato, which often requires staccato beating.

Ex. 5.6. Exercise

Ex. 5.7. Exercise

Ex. 5.8. Bizet, *Carmen,* Act II, No. 12, mm. 1-6

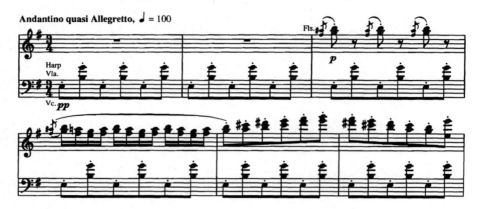

Ex. 5.9. Bizet, *Carmen,* Act II, No. 12, mm. 39-42

Ex. 5.10. Ravel, Bolero, at #16

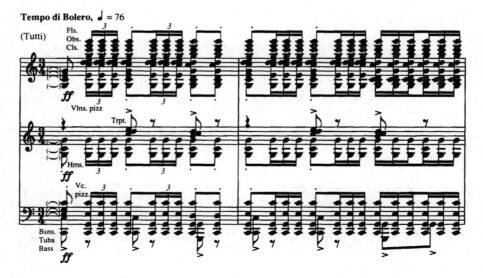

Ex. 5.11. Grieg, *Peer Gynt* Suite No. 1, "Anitra's Dance," mm. 3-7

STARTING ON THE SECOND AND THIRD COUNTS

Use figures 5.7 and 5.8 for the start on the second count, figures 4.1 and 4.2 for the start on the third count (changing figures as usual). Practice examples 5.12–5.15. The full-staccato in example 5.16 should not be too large! The quiet beginning of example 5.17 needs a neutral-legato beat.

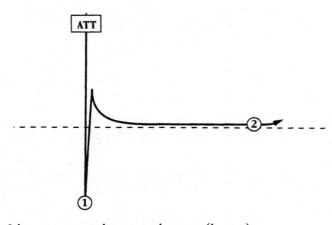

Fig. 5.7. 3-beat; start on the second count (legato)

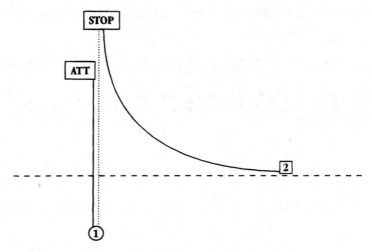

Fig. 5.8. 3-beat; start on the second count (staccato)

Ex. 5.12. Exercise

Ex. 5.13. Exercise

Ex. 5.14. Exercise

Ex. 5.15. Exercise

Ex. 5.16. Gluck, *Orphée et Euridice,* Chaconne, mm. 1-2

Ex. 5.17. Mendelssohn, *A Midsummer Night's Dream,* Nocturne, mm. 1-8

In some of the Beethoven excerpts there are two sets of metronome markings: the one printed in the score and, in parentheses, the one that is now often used. Beethoven's metronome markings, discussed in chapters 32 and 34, are an important source of information. Only minor modifications are suggested.

In example 5.18, beat *poco espressivo* and always legato. The staccato on the eighth note C serves the phrasing and must not be reflected in the beat, which is concerned with a continuous melodic line.

The following two examples are both full-staccato but not too large. Your preparation must be very precise to indicate the correct tempo: *Allegretto* in example 5.19, *Allegro* in example 5.20. All turns are to be played before the beat. Regardless of the beat pattern a conductor chooses, *Menuet* movements of this type, marked *Allegretto*, and certainly thoses marked *Allegro*, ought to be "felt" in *One* (see p. 389).

Ex. 5.18. Beethoven, Symphony No. 5, second movement, mm. 1-4

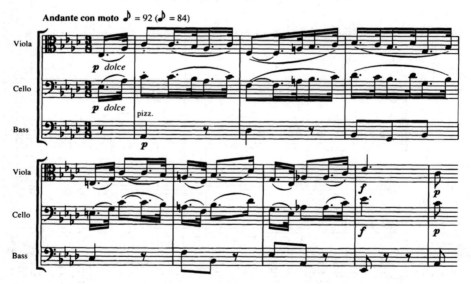

Ex. 5.19. Haydn, Symphony No. 88, third movement, mm. 1-4

Ex. 5.20. Haydn, Symphony No. 102, third movement, mm. 1-4

Additional examples for the study of 3-beat:

Neutral-Legato

Beethoven: Symphony No. 5, 2d movement, mm. 39–46
Elgar: *Enigma* Variations, Variation No. 9, beginning
Rimsky-Korsakov: *Capriccio Espagnol,* 2d movement, beginning
Stravinsky: *L'Oiseau de feu* (Suite), Finale, beginning

Expressive-Legato

Bizet: Symphony in C Major, 2d movement
Fauré: *Pelléas et Mélisande* Suite, 1st movement
Grieg: Piano Concerto, 2d movement
Nielsen: Symphony No. 4, 1st movement
Prokofiev: Symphony No. 5, 1st movement until #6; 3d movement at
    #60
Tchaikovsky: *Manfred,* 1st movement *(Andante)*
Tchaikovsky: Serenade for Strings, 3d movement
Wagner: Overture to *Tannhäuser,* mm. 17–31

Light-Staccato

Dukas: *L'Apprenti sorcier,* three measures before #2 (Vif)
Haydn: Symphony No. 97, 3d movement, Trio
Rossini: Overture to *La Gazza Ladra, Allegro*
Stravinsky: *Feu d'artifice,* beginning
Tchaikovsky: *The Nutcracker* Suite, Danse Arabe, beginning

Full-Staccato

Brahms: Symphony No. 4, 4th movement, passage starting at C
Mussorgsky: Polonaise from *Boris Godunov*
Offenbach: *Les Contes d'Hoffmann,* Act II, Minuet in A major

Shostakovitch: *The Golden Age,* 1st movement, starting at #2
Strauss, Richard: *Salomé,* "Dance of the Seven Veils", beginning
Tchaikovsky: Symphony No. 3, 5th movement

Starting on the Second Count

Ravel: *Rapsodie Espagnole,* beginning

Starting on the Third Count

Beethoven: Symphony No. 8, 3d movement
Brahms: *Ein deutsches Requiem,* 2d movement
Franck: Symphony in D Minor, 2d movement
Handel: *Messiah, Aria,* "The Trumpet Shall Sound"
Mahler: Symphony No. 7, 3d movement
Schumann: Symphony No. 1, 2d movement

CHAPTER *6*

The 2-Beat

NEUTRAL-LEGATO AND EXPRESSIVE-LEGATO

Follow the diagram in figure 6.1 exactly! Do not slip into a habit that is confusing to the players—namely, to use almost identical gestures for the first and second beats. Avoid carrying the rebound of the first beat too far up, as shown in figure 6.2. The position of ② must be on the left–right line, not below! It will help you in practicing to imagine that you are lifting something off the left–right line with the point of the baton at ②.

Use the preliminary beat of figure 1.4 for the start on the first count. Practice example 6.1.

Fig. 6.1. 2-beat; neutral-legato (the correct pattern)

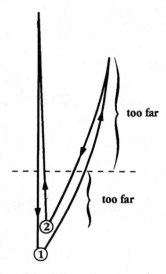

Fig. 6.2. 2-beat; neutral-legato (the incorrect pattern)

Ex. 6.1. Exercise

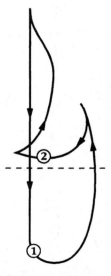

Fig. 6.3. 2-beat; expressive-legato

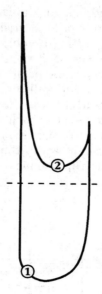

Fig. 6.4. 2-beat; expressive-legato (alternate style)

Use the pattern in figure 6.3 for slow and very expressive music. The double curve looks almost like a subdivided second beat *(Two, and)*, but there is no rhythmic subdivision here; the double curve gives you more space to execute the second beat smoothly and fluently. Figure 6.4 is used often, especially in a tempo faster than ♩ = 60. Figure 6.5 is recommended for *molto espressivo*.

All of these figures, both neutral-legato and expressive-legato, can be applied only in slow and moderate tempi.

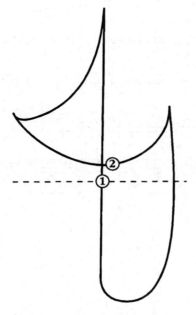

Fig. 6.5. 2-beat; expressive-legato (alternate style)

Practice examples 6.2 and 6.3. For the latter you need the start on the second count shown in figure 6.6. Most violinists perform the *Andante* in example 6.4 at a speed of ♪ = 96. (Joseph Joachim, who studied the concerto with the composer, suggested ♪ = 92.) Still, beating six counts to the measure would be contrary to the nature of this quiet beginning. Use a 2-beat, neutral-legato, with calm and well-controlled gestures. (In the course of this movement, the 2-beat alternates with 6-beat subdivision.) Conduct example 6.5 *poco espressivo*. In Offenbach's original score the tempo is marked *Allegretto*. In example 6.6, beat expressive-legato. Clicking on the counts may be used to maintain a firm rhythm for the triplets played by the winds. Start on the second count in example 6.7; use a very intense expressive gesture (see p. 272).

Ex. 6.2. Exercise

Ex. 6.3. Exercise

Ex. 6.4. Mendelssohn, Violin Concerto Op. 64, second movement, mm. 1-4

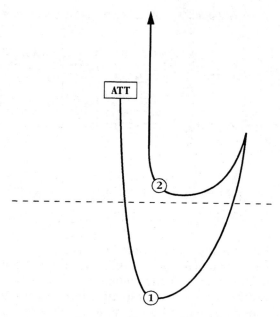

Fig. 6.6. 2-beat; start on the second count (legato)

Ex. 6.5. Offenbach, *Les Contes d'Hoffmann,* Act III, No. 17, mm. 3-6

Ex. 6.6. Tchaikovsky, Symphony No. 4, second movement, mm. 166-73

Ex. 6.7. Puccini, *La Bohème*, Act IV, twelve measures after #2

LIGHT-STACCATO AND FULL-STACCATO

Figures 6.7 and 6.8 show the patterns for staccato.

Use example 6.8 for practicing light-staccato and full-staccato. Example 6.9 starts on the second count. On the preliminary beat (as shown in fig. 6.9), lift the forearm swiftly with the hand turned downward at the lower STOP. Thus, the baton points down and gives more impetus to the *f* attack. For light-staccato the size is smaller. Use full-staccato, energetic gestures in example 6.10. A sharp second beat in the second bar of the example will get a good trombone entrance strictly in time. Beat *One* in the fourth measure similarly, and emphasize the second beat in the fifth measure, after which the horns and violas come in. The violins play the entire passage on the G string.

Ex. 6.8. Exercise

Ex. 6.9. Exercise

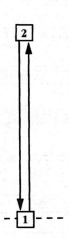

Fig. 6.7. 2-beat; light-staccato

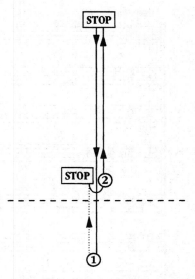

Fig. 6.8. 2-beat; full-staccato

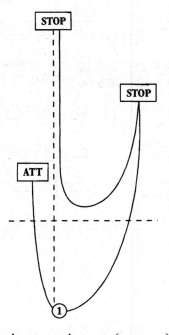

Fig. 6.9. 2-beat; start on the second count (staccato)

Ex. 6.10. Rimsky-Korsakov, *Capriccio Espagnol,* fourth movement, "Scena e canto gitano," six measures before N

Ex. 6.10. *Continued*

(continued)

Ex. 6.10. *Continued*

In example 6.11, beat light-staccato. Your small but distinct movements should be seen equally well by the first violins playing the theme and the second violins playing the staccato counterpoint. Beginning in measure 6 of example 6.12, use full-staccato (see p. 187). In example 6.13, beat light-staccato, in spite of the legato marking. Conduct example 6.14 with full-staccato, example 6.15 with light-staccato. Both following examples start on the second count; example 6.16 in full-staccato, example 6.17 in light-staccato. Beat the preparation in the correct tempo! The metronome speed suggested for Bach's Gavotte conforms to the style of late Baroque (see p. 384).

Ex. 6.11. Beethoven, Symphony No. 7, second movement, mm. 183-87

Ex. 6.12. Britten, *Four Sea Interludes,* No. 2, "Sunday Morning," mm. 1-8

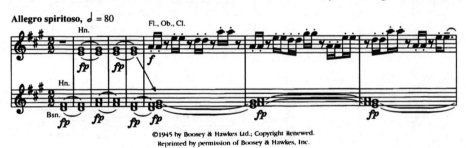

©1945 by Boosey & Hawkes Ltd.; Copyright Renewed.
Reprinted by permission of Boosey & Hawkes, Inc.

Ex. 6.13. Ravel, *Le Tombeau de Couperin,* I, Prélude, beginning

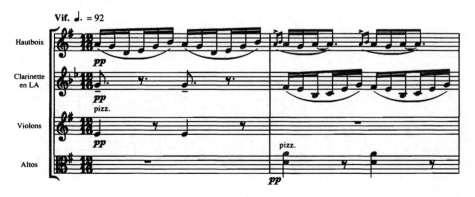

(continued)

Ex. 6.13 *Continued*

Ex. 6.14. Bizet, *Carmen,* Act I, Prelude, mm. 1-4

Ex. 6.15. Bizet, *Carmen,* Act I, Prelude, mm. 17-20

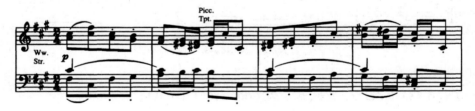

Ex. 6.16. J. S. Bach, Suite No. 3 in D Major, Gavotte, mm. 1-5

Ex. 6.17. Haydn, Symphony No. 88, fourth movement, mm. 1-8

Additional examples for the study of 2-beat:

Neutral-Legato

Bruckner: Symphony No. 4, 1st movement, beginning

Dvořák: Symphony No. 7, 1st movement, beginning

Strauss: *Tod und Verklärung,* passage beginning eighteen measures after L

Stravinsky: *L'Oiseau de feu* (Suite), "Ronde des princesses", beginning and last nineteen measures

Tchaikovsky: Serenade for Strings, 4th movement, beginning

Expressive-Legato

Borodin: Symphony No. 2, 2d movement, passage starting at F

Brahms: Symphony No. 4, 1st movement (see Appendix A, No. 5)

Janáček: Sinfonietta, 3d movement.

Mascagni: *Cavalleria Rusticana,* Santuzza's aria, "Voi lo sapete", introduction

Rachmaninoff: Piano Concerto No. 2, 3d movement *(Maestoso),* second theme

Smetana: *The Moldau,* passage starting at m. 40

Verdi: Overture to *I Vespri Siciliani,* passage starting at I (mm. 185–99).

Light-Staccato

Beethoven: Symphony No. 6, 4th movement, beginning

Mendelssohn: Overture to *A Midsummer Night's Dream*

Mozart: Overture to *Le Nozze di Figaro,* beginning
Prokofiev: Symphony No. 5, 4th movement, at #80.
Rimsky-Korsakov: *The Flight of the Bumble-Bee*
Rossini: *Il Barbiere di Siviglia,* Act II, "Tempest Music"
Tchaikovsky: *The Nutcracker* Suite; "Ouverture miniature" and "Danse des mirlitons"

Full-Staccato

Bach: "Brandenburg" Concerto No. 1, 3d movement
Berlioz: *La Damnation de Faust,* "Marche Hongroise" ("Rakóczy March")
Berlioz: *Symphonie fantastique,* 4th movement
Brahms: Symphony No. 2, 4th movement, passage starting at A
Dvořák: *Carneval* Overture
Franck: Symphony in D Minor, 1st movement *(Allegro non troppo)*
Rimsky-Korsakov: *Capriccio Espagnol,* passage starting at M
Roussel: Suite in F Major, 1st movement (see ex. 14.11)

Starting on the Second Count

Bach: Suite No. 2 in B Minor, Badinerie
Beethoven: Symphony No. 8, 4th movement
Gluck: *Orphée et Euridice,* Act II, Scene 2, *Cet asile* (*Grazioso* $\frac{6}{8}$)
Gounod: *Faust,* Act I, Scene 2, No. 3 (Chorus)
Haydn: Symphony No. 103, 1st movement (*Allegro con spirito*)
Mozart: *Don Giovanni,* Act I, No. 2, Duet, "*Fuggi crudele*"
Rachmaninoff: *Rhapsody on a Theme of Paganini,* beginning

CHAPTER 7

The 1-Beat

When the tempo of a piece of music is very fast, the conductor will be unable to give all the beats without confusing the players. In many Classical scherzos, the written tempo of $\frac{3}{4}$ is so fast that it is much more convenient to give only one beat in a measure. The same is true for most waltzes. Many Classical pieces with the time signature $\frac{2}{4}$ are also done in this way, as are a number of modern pieces written in 4-time and even 6-time (Sibelius, Symphony No. 2, 3d movement in $\frac{6}{8}$—see ex. 20.31; Stravinsky, *L'Oiseau de feu*, *"Danse infernale"* in $\frac{6}{4}$).

NEUTRAL-LEGATO

The diagram in figure 7.1 shows that the downward movement is quicker than the upward movement. Avoid any stop at the top of the beat. For the start,

Fig. 7.1. 1-beat; neutral-legato

use figure 7.2 or figure 1.4; the choice between the two is a matter of personal preference. Practice using example 7.1.

EXPRESSIVE-LEGATO

The pattern shown in figure 7.3 implies a subdivision into 3-time; when that is not desired, use figure 7.4. In any case, do not stress any part of the beat except ①. Since the execution of the beat depends upon the individual gesture and the character of the music, feel free to vary the pattern, which is only one of several possibilities; apply this advice to example 7.2.

Fig. 7.2. 1-beat; start (legato)

Ex. 7.1. Exercise

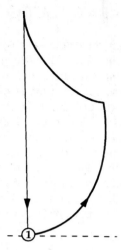

Fig. 7.3. 1-beat; expressive-legato

Fig. 7.4. 1-beat; expressive-legato (alternate style)

Ex. 7.2. Exercise

STACCATO

Figure 7.5 covers both light-staccato and full-staccato. For full-staccato the size is larger and the bounce sharper, with more arm movement. The intensity of the beat depends upon the speed with which you snap the baton up. If this movement is moderately slow, the staccato is rather gentle; if you make a special effort to whip the baton up, the orchestra will play very sharply. In practicing the start in figure 7.6 (also in figs. 2.2 or 2.4), remember that the preliminary beat must express the type of staccato you want from the players. Examples 7.3 and 7.4 give you varied practice. In example 7.5, a graceful *espressivo* beat is recommended. The neutral-legato 1-beat pattern would be too dull, while beating three beats in a measure would be too agitated. A flexible *espressivo* beat is needed in example 7.6 to build up the melodic line. In examples 7.7 and 7.8, use a very small but precise light-staccato. Apply

Fig. 7.5. 1-beat; staccato

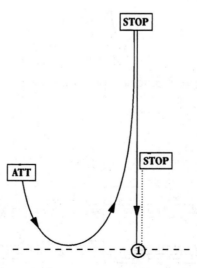

Fig. 7.6. 1-beat; start (staccato)

Ex. 7.3. Exercise

Ex. 7.4. Exercise

Ex. 7.5 Mozart, *Eine kleine Nachtmusik,* K. 525, third movement, mm. 16-24

full-staccato in example 7.9. Do not be too quick with the diminuendo, since the orchestra is apt to quiet down too suddenly. Because of the strong rhythmic element in example 7.10, beat staccato, first gently, but with full-staccato at *ff* (see p. 381). In example 7.11, beat four bars legato, two bars full-staccato, then change suddenly to light-staccato. Start full-staccato in example 7.12, but not too heavily. (Save a more aggressive gesture for the *ff* in the eighth measure!) For measure 2, use a rather small light-staccato beat with the character of an upbeat leading into measure 3. The beat remains light-staccato for measures 5–7 but is carried upwards in measure 7 to prepare the full-staccato (*ff*).

Ex. 7.6. Tchaikovsky, Suite No. 3, second movement, mm. 282-85

Ex. 7.7. Mendelssohn, *A Midsummer Night's Dream,* Scherzo, mm. 1-8

Ex. 7.8. Barber, *Essay for Orchestra,* nine measures after #6

Ex. 7.9. Bizet, *Carmen,* Act IV, Entr'acte, mm. 1-17

Ex. 7.10. Beethoven, Symphony No. 5, first movement, mm. 83-96

Ex. 7.11. J. Strauss, *Emperor* Waltz, No. 2, mm. 27-34

Ex. 7.12. Beethoven, Symphony No. 2, third movement, mm. 1-8

Additional examples for the study of 1-beat:

Neutral-Legato

Beethoven: Symphony No. 5, 3d movement, passage starting at m. 324
Bizet: Symphony in C major, 3d movement, passage at #38
Brahms: *Variations on a Theme by Haydn,* Variation No. 8
Chausson: Symphony Op. 20, 1st movement (also expressive-legato and staccato)
Delius: *Brigg Fair,* passage at #2
Dvořák: Scherzo Capriccioso, mm. 7–16

Expressive-Legato

Bruckner: Symphony No. 7, 3d movement, Trio.
Gounod: *Faust,* Ballet No. 1 (A major), starting at the double bar
Ravel: *La Valse,* passage at No. 30 (also dynamic changes)
Strauss, Johann: *Emperor* Waltz, No. 1
Verdi: Overture to *La Forza del Destino, Allegro agitato* $\frac{3}{8}$
Weber-Berlioz: *Invitation to the Dance,* passage starting at #7

Staccato

Beethoven: Symphony No. 9, 2d movement
Bruckner: Symphony No. 9, 2d movement
Dukas: *L'Apprenti sorcier,* starting at #6
Dvořák: Symphony No. 9, 3d movement
Elgar: *Enigma* Variations, Op. 36, Variation No. 4
Handel: Concerto Grosso, Op. 6, No. 5, 3d movement (*Presto* $\frac{3}{8}$)
Rossini: *Il Barbiere di Siviglia,* Act I, Finale I, *Allegro* $\frac{3}{4}$ in E-flat major
Schubert: Symphony No. 2, 4th movement
Schubert: Symphony No. 6, 3d movement

CHAPTER *8*

Dynamics and Articulation

In the opening chapters it has already been pointed out that the dynamics of the music can be expressed by the size of the gesture. There are two other ways of indicating volume of sound, and all three will be discussed in this chapter, for both sudden and gradual changes.

CHANGING THE SIZE OF THE BEAT FOR DYNAMIC CHANGES

In examples 8.1 and 8.2, you must avoid overemphasizing the last *p* beat (preparing for the *f*) by using a field of beating in the *p* bars that is higher than the normal. You will then have ample room for a large *f* downbeat. The transition from *f* to *p* (in the repeats) is done simply by a sudden diminution of the downbeat. Use neutral-legato for *p* and *espressivo* for *f*. The preliminary gesture is small in example 8.1, large in example 8.2.

The last *p* beat in example 8.3 must be somewhat larger to prepare for the *f*, but without indicating a crescendo. On the rest in measure 4, beat *p* to prepare the repeat. For *p* staccato, use light-staccato; for *f*, full-staccato. Maintain your tempo, do not speed up in *f*, and do not slow down when changing back to *p*! In example 8.4, beat *f* on the rest in the fourth measure to prepare the repeat.

Ex. 8.1. Exercise

Ex. 8.2. Exercise

Ex. 8.3. Exercise

Ex. 8.4. Exercise

These exercises offer practice in the sudden change of dynamics on the first count in a measure. Changes on the other counts, which are less difficult to execute, are directed in a similar manner.

CHANGING THE SIZE OF THE BEAT IN CRESCENDO AND DECRESCENDO

As the dynamics gradually increase or decrease, your gesture changes its size. If there is a crescendo from *p* to *f* in one measure, the second beat will be markedly larger than the first, the third still larger, and the fourth will indicate *f*. But if you have two or more measures at your disposal, the increase of size is sometimes so gradual *(crescendo poco a poco)* that the change from beat to beat is hardly noticeable. The same applies to decrescendo.

Practice first before the mirror, beating in four and three (♩ = 80) and indicating *p* ◁ *f* in one measure, then in two measures, finally in three or more measures. In legato, start neutral-legato or *poco espressivo.* As a rule, the neutral-legato pattern is not suited for very large gestures because it would look awkward. Therefore, do not carry this straight beat too far in crescendo,

Ex. 8.5. Exercise

Ex. 8.6. Exercise

Ex. 8.7. Exercise

but change to *espressivo*. This also applies to light-staccato, which should change gradually to full-staccato. Practice similarly *f* ⟩*p*.

Now use examples 8.5–8.8. Each of these has four different dynamic markings. Thorough practice will make your beat flexible and improve your control considerably. Be economical in the use of your arm and avoid exaggerated gestures. To direct *p* ⟨ ⟩*p*, it is often sufficient to add some forearm motion to the wrist movement used to lead the *p*.

Ex. 8.8. Exercise

USING THE LEFT HAND

It has already been demonstrated how to indicate *f* with the left hand (see p. 24). For the gesture that expresses *p*, the palm of the hand, fingers together, faces the orchestra. These two gestures do not take the place of indicating dynamics with the beat but are supporting gestures. (The one exception is in a *f* passage with sustained notes, as in ex. 3.1, where a large and cumbersome baton motion can be avoided by a *f* gesture in the left hand.)

Repeat examples 8.1–8.4, using the left hand. The *f* gesture of the left hand must come exactly on the first *f* beat; the *p* gesture, however, should come a little ahead of the *p* beat. In other words, the left-hand gesture, immediately following the last *f* beat, indicates a sudden warning before the *p* passage begins. Practice turning your left hand quickly on the last eighth note of the measure.

In staccato, use the left hand to indicate the change to *p* only and not for the change to *f*. Strictly avoid time beating movements in the left hand!

USING THE LEFT HAND IN
CRESCENDO AND DECRESCENDO

Crescendo is indicated by lifting the left hand, palm facing upward, from the level of the hip to eye level. The hand is held up as long as you want to maintain *f*. For decrescendo, turn the hand slowly so that the palm faces the players; then start dropping the hand gradually, the palm still toward the orchestra, until it reaches the starting position. (The reason for turning the left hand slowly is that a sudden turn would indicate sudden *p* instead of decrescendo!)

Practice these movements by allowing yourself first one measure, then two, then three or more measures for crescendo. Count aloud in four and in three. Practice decrescendo the same way. Take great care not to make any time beating movements with the left hand. The up-and-down motions must be absolutely smooth and continuous. Students sometimes have trouble in achieving this smoothness in the left hand while the right hand is beating time. Practice the coordination of both hands and check in the mirror.

In applying the left-hand gestures to examples 8.5–8.8, you should realize that they constitute very strong support. Therefore, you will not need beats as large as those you used with the right hand alone. Try to balance the movements of both hands and avoid exaggerations. Crescendo in staccato does not need the expressive left-hand gesture. However, the left hand is considerably more effective than the right in securing a diminuendo or *p* subito in both legato and staccato.

An effective application of these techniques is closely linked to the reaction of the orchestra. Many players have a tendency to play loudly at once when they see *cresc.* and softly when their parts indicate *decresc.* or *dimin.* On the other hand, the orchestra does not easily give all its strength to the climax of a crescendo unless stimulated by the leader. Therefore, you will have to be fairly restrained at the beginning of a crescendo but very energetic at the climax.

The conductor must not yield to the temptation to increase the tempo when directing a crescendo or to slow down during a diminuendo passage.

In order to indicate the dynamics exactly as they occur in example 8.9, your mind must always be ahead of your hand. Practice example 8.10 first with the right hand alone, then support with the left hand.

For example 8.11, most editions show the time signature **C** for this movement. However, both Beethoven's manuscript and the first print have **₵**.

Ex. 8.9. Exercise

Ex. 8.10. Exercise

Ex. 8.11. Beethoven, Piano Concerto No. 5, second movement, mm. 1-13

Moreover, Carl Czerny, who performed the work under the composer's supervision, pointed out that this *alla breve* movement must not drag.

Still, the *Adagio un poco moto* is directed with a 4-beat (Czerny suggested ♩ = 60). During the measure 8, lift the left hand halfway to indicate *f* espressivo in measure 9, while the beat increases in expressiveness. The pauses must not interrupt the flow of the melodic line. Turn the palm during the first beat of measure 10 and drop the hand slightly. With the first beat in

Ex. 8.11. *Continued*

Ex. 8.12. Verdi, *La Traviata,* Act III, Scene 8, mm. 25-31

(continued)

measure 11, the left hand moves back to indicate $\boldsymbol{f}$; it is turned again during the third beat and dropped slowly. The right hand uses the fourth beat in measure 8 (quarter rest) for a fairly large preparation for the following $\boldsymbol{f}$. In measure 10, use small gestures for the second and third beats but a large preparatory beat to attack the second $\boldsymbol{f}$ entry. Measure 12 requires restrained gestures (see p. 192 and p. 206).

Ex. 8.12. *Continued*

Beat *espressivo* in example 8.12. In measure 27, gradually put the left hand into action. After the climax in measure 29, there follows a strong diminuendo, which requires convincing gestures of both hands. In example 8.13, increasing intensity of the gestures indicates the increase in the volume and sonority of the string orchestra. A strongly contrasted motion is needed for the *p* subito.

In a case such as example 8.14, do not enlarge your beat for the crescendo in the drums; it is much more effective to save the first large gesture for the preparatory beat (full-staccato) needed on Three for the *ff* attack on *Four*. Small beats will do to start the drum players, who are "on their own." In example 8.15, use full-staccato. It is not advisable to use beats that are overly large in staccato when the tempo is lively, because gestures would become too hectic. Instead, indicate the crescendo by increasing the intensity and sharpness of the staccato beat.

Beat *poco espressivo* in example 8.16. Increase the size of the beat in the 5th bar only slightly and gradually; then use the left hand to indicate the sudden *p* in measure 7. Keep your gestures small and graceful.

When Beethoven transcribed this symphony for piano trio he marked this movement *Larghetto quasi Andante*. His metronome indication seems to

Ex. 8.13. W. Schuman, Symphony No. 3, Part II, mm. 53-59

Ex. 8.14. Rossini, *La Gazza Ladra,* Overture, mm. 3-5

Ex. 8.15. Tchaikovsky, Symphony No. 6, first movement, mm. 238-43

Ex. 8.16. Beethoven, Symphony No. 2, second movement, mm. 1-7

support a flowing pace. Moreover, there is information that he expected the movement to be played at varying speed; for instance, for the passage beginning with measure 73 (also with measure 237), Beethoven asked for an *Allegretto*. For this, a metronomic speed of ♪ = 92 appears entirely convincing, although most conductors prefer to begin the movement at a somewhat calmer pace.

Start beating neutral-legato in example 8.17 with restrained gestures, and indicate the three small crescendos (mm. 123–27) with slightly enlarged beats. For the crescendo starting in measure 128, use the methods you have learned, but be economical with your gestures! If you have exhausted your resources by measure 134 (*f*), nothing is left to build up the climax in measure 146. This *ff* requires a special preparation, made by beating the last beat in measure 145 full-staccato with Three on STOP. This is the accented upbeat mentioned on p. 18 (see fig. 2.4, adapted to 3-beat, and comments on pp. 315). The most up-to-date catalogue of Schubert's works (Bärenreiter, 1978) lists the "Unfinished" as Symphony No. 7; for a discussion of the numbering of Schubert's symphonies, see p. 404.

Example 8.18 offers an excellent opportunity to practice the coordination of both hands. In measures 42 and 43, use the right hand alone. In measure

Ex. 8.17. Schubert, Symphony No. 7, "Unfinished," first movement, mm. 122-50

Ex. 8.18. Grieg, *Peer Gynt* Suite No. 1, Allegretto Pastorale, mm. 38-47

(continued)

Ex. 8.18. *Continued*

Ex. 8.18. *Continued*

(continued)

Ex. 8.18. *Continued*

44, use the left hand again. Apply the pattern of figure 6.4, with clicking on the accented beats. In measures 118 and 122 of example 8.19, the first beat is large, the second small.

A general remark may be appropriate. The detailed suggestions made in this and the following chapters are largely a matter of individual interpretation. They do not constitute the only right way of execution, for there are several "right" ways to conduct a particular piece of music. Nevertheless, it is important for the student to be shown at least one right way in order to start on the road that leads away from mere time beating and to begin to acquire the ability to convey artistic intentions to the musicians in the orchestra.

Ex. 8.19. Tchaikovsky, Symphony No. 5, first movement, mm. 116-23

MOVING THE RIGHT HAND NEARER TO OR FARTHER AWAY FROM THE BODY

The right hand may beat close to the body, or it may move away from it. To emphasize a f beat, the right hand may move suddenly forward. Likewise, a sudden retreat of the hand close to the body makes the change to p more effective.

For applying the various techniques, practice examples 8.20–8.23 without using the left hand. Support by the left hand and motion by the right hand as described are rarely used together. Their combination is a very powerful dramatic gesture and should be reserved for great climaxes.

Ex. 8.20. Beethoven, Piano Concerto No. 5, first movement, mm. 13-16

Ex. 8.21. Franck, Symphony in D Minor, first movement, mm. 64-67

Ex. 8.22. Kodály, *Háry János* Suite, fifth movement, Intermezzo, mm. 31-34

CHANGING FROM LEGATO TO STACCATO AND VICE VERSA

Experiment by having a pianist play example 8.24 (♩ = 66) while you are beating the first bar staccato and the second legato, contrary to the music. The player will neither feel comfortable in the legato line nor be sure of the rhythm of the staccato chords. This experiment, better than a long explanation, proves the necessity of articulating the beat in agreement with the music—in spite of certain exceptions already mentioned and others to be discussed later.

As to the execution of the transitions, you will not find it difficult to go from legato to staccato. Just begin to beat staccato on the count at which the detached playing begins; if this is the first count, use "bouncing." To change from staccato to legato, beat staccato as usual on the last staccato count, but instead of waiting on the STOP during the count, let the hand *immediately* continue in a legato motion to the next count. Practice this technique in slow tempo until you feel able to apply it to the faster metronome markings.

For all the beat patterns, practice all the transitions in examples 8.24–8.30 from legato to staccato and vice versa by doing all the repeats.

Generally speaking, there are different ways of performing staccato: from very short and sharply attacked notes to moderately detached playing; from a vigorous *f* staccato to a very gentle touch. You can make the players understand what kind of staccato you want by the beat alone.

Furthermore, learn to articulate so distinctly that, when playing some simple passage such as a scale, your assistant at the piano will know when to play legato or staccato just by following your baton. For this very useful exercise, you will have to think ahead; if you are not sure of what you want, your gesture will not convince the player.

For the sudden *p* in measure 15 of example 8.31, put up the left hand just in time to announce the change without affecting the last *f* eighth note. After the legato beat in measures 13–15, change to a gentle staccato, becoming somewhat sharper with the gradual crescendo. Reverse this procedure for the diminuendo. (For a discussion concerning the choice of tempo, see p. 398).

Ex. 8.23. Beethoven, Symphony No. 1, second movement, mm. 52-56

(continued)

Ex. 8.23. *Continued*

Ex. 8.24. Exercise, 4-beat

Ex. 8.25. Exercise, 4-beat

Ex. 8.26. Exercise, 4-beat

Ex. 8.27. Exercise, 3-beat

Ex. 8.28. Exercise, 3-beat

Ex. 8.29. Exercise, 2-beat

Ex. 8.30. Exercise, 1-beat

Ex. 8.31. Beethoven, Symphony no. 6, first movement, mm. 13-19

For the articulation in example 8.32, see example 8.31. In a passage such as this, it helps to think of the structure of the music. (periods of four bars each) in building up a gradual crescendo. Do not forget the cues! Beating example 8.33 in three would disturb the smooth flow of the melody; therefore, a 1-beat is always used here. Beat the first eight bars legato to neutral-legato, and the following accompanying figure staccato, very gently.

Ex. 8.32. Beethoven, *Leonore* Overture No. 3 , mm. 45-65

Ex. 8.32. *Continued*

Ex. 8.33. Bizet, *Carmen*, Act I, No. 10, mm. 1-12

Additional examples for the study of sudden dynamic changes and crescendo and decrescendo:

4-Beat

Beethoven: Symphony No. 6, 2d movement
Bizet: *L'Arlésienne* Suite No. 1, 1st movement, last ten measures
Bruckner: Symphony No. 7, 2d movement, at H and S
Debussy: *Sirènes* (also *p* subito)
Dvořák: Symphony No. 9, 2d movement, after #4
Haydn: Symphony No. 101, 2d movement, mm. 11–12
Mozart: Symphony No. 39, K. 543, 2d movement
Beethoven: Symphony No. 5, 2d movement
Mozart: Violin Concerto No. 5, K. 219, 2d movement
Sibelius: Symphony No. 2, 2d movement, passage starting at D
Tchaikovsky: Symphony No. 5, 1st movement, introduction
Tchaikovsky: Symphony No. 5, 4th movement at C and nine measures
    after C
Tchaikovsky: Symphony No. 6, 1st movement at O
Verdi: *Messa da Requiem*, No. 1 (Kyrie eleison)
Wagner: *Tristan und Isolde*, "Liebestod", mm. 44–46, 54

3- Beat

Bartók: Divertimento for String Orchestra, 1st movement, mm. 59–60

Beethoven: Symphony No. 2, 2d movement

Berlioz: *La Damnation de Faust,* "Menuet des Feux-Follets"

Brahms: *Ein deutsches Requiem,* 2d movement.

Brahms: Symphony No. 2, 1st movement (see ex. 20.16)

Haydn: Symphony No. 92, 1st movement *(Allegro)*

Hindemith: Symphony *Mathis der Maler,* 3d movement
  (Sehr lebhaft $\frac{9}{8}$)

Mendelssohn: Elijah, No. 21 (Aria, "Hear ye, Israel")

Puccini: *Manon Lescaut,* Act IV, mm. 1–4

Ravel: *Daphnis et Chloé,* Suite No. 2, from #156 to #170

Rimsky-Korsakov: *Capriccio Espagnol,* Variazioni, sixteen measures
  before the end

Saint-Saëns: *Samson et Dalila,* Act II, Dalila's aria, "Amour, viens
  aider"

Tchaikovsky: Symphony No. 4, 1st movement, five measures after B
  and at E

Wagner: Overture to *Tannhäuser*

2-Beat

Beethoven: Symphony No. 4, 1st and 4th movements

Berlioz: Overture, *Le Carnaval Romain, (Allegro vivace)*

Berlioz: *Symphonie fantastique,* 1st movement, *Allegro* section

Bizet: *Carmen,* Act I, Prelude

Falla: *Three-Cornered Hat,* Suite No. 2, "Danse du Meunier" and
  "Danse final"

Haydn: Symphony No. 88, 4th movement

Mozart: Overture to *Le Nozze di Figaro*

Rossini: Overture to *William Tell (Allegro vivace $\frac{2}{4}$)*

1-Beat

Beethoven: Symphony No. 5, 3d movement

Berlioz: *Symphonie fantastique,* 2d movement ("Un Bal")

Dvořák: Slavonic Dance in C Major, Op. 46, No. 1

Mahler: *Das Lied von der Erde,* 1st movement

Schubert: Symphony No. 8, "Great", 4th movement

Schumann: Symphony No. 1, 3d movement, Trios 1 and 2

Strauss: *Burleske* (also neutral-legato, expressive-legato, and staccato)

Tchaikovsky: *The Nutcracker* Suite, No. 3 ("Valse des Fleurs")

CHAPTER 9

Starting After the Count

If the music does not start on the count but on a fractional value, ignore the fraction in your beating and give the same rhythmic preparation that you would if the music began on the next full count. Do not try to beat the fractions, but rather feel them within the regular preparatory beat.

In class work, examples 9.1a—m should be sung. There is a risk that the singers may not enter correctly, even if the beat is right. However, the valuable experience gained by the student as a result of direct contact with the group is easily worth the time spent in interrupting and repeating.

In examples 9.1a—g, give the preparation as though the music began on the first count; in 9.1h—j as though it began on the second count; in 9.1k and 9.1l prepare the third count; and in 9.1m, the fourth. If you have a firm feeling for the rhythm, you can give a convincing preparation, and then the fractional values will come out correctly and automatically. Each of these short exercises should be repeated immediately in different tempi.

Ex. 9.1. Exercises

Examples 9.2 and 9.3 show an eighth note before the first count. The preliminary beat is **pp** legato in example 9.2 and **f** staccato in example 9.3.

The two openings in examples 9.4 and 9.5 are similar. But while the attack works easily in fast tempo, it is more difficult in slow tempo. The attack of example 9.5 can be handled in several ways: (1) Strictly according to rule—the staccato preparation has the value of a quarter note (do not wait for the ♪, but keep going without hesitation!); (2) the preliminary beat has the value of an eighth note; (3) free style—make the preparation as though the ♪ were on *One;* this technique is successful if all the players have a definite feeling for the short–long rhythm. (See also the comment for ex. 26.11.)

Some musicians believe that the Baroque practice of shortening the notes, regardless of the music's tempo, applies to these kinds of double chords even in post-Baroque music.

When applying such double dotting to the passage in example 9.6, the

Ex. 9.2. Mendelssohn, *Elijah,* Ouverture (I), mm. 1-5

Ex. 9.3. Handel, Concerto Grosso, Op. 6, No. 6, fourth movement, mm. 1-3

Ex. 9.4. Offenbach, *Orphée aux Enfers,* Overture, mm. 1-2

Ex. 9.5. Cimarosa, *Il Matrimonio Segreto,* Overture, mm. 1-7

Ex. 9.6. Mozart, *Die Zauberflöte,* K. 620, Overture, mm. 97-102

best manner in which to direct the winds is simply to beat *One, Two, Three* in straight gestures and let the players attack the chords without hesitation. ("Waiting" or trying to "help" with extra gestures like subdivision would merely create confusion.) In example 9.7, the *Allegro* section follows a pause and starts after the third count. The technique of preparing the new attack is the same as that used at an opening start. During the pause, point the baton to the left to get a clear preliminary beat on Three. The downbeat should express the solemn diginity of the music in example 9.8, while the preparations for examples 9.9 and 9.10 are a very snappy full-staccatos. (To conform to Baroque practice, the eighth note in example 9.8 must be shortened. The same applies to the sixteenth notes.) Conduct example 9.11 *poco espressivo,* legato. Apply light-staccato in example 9.12, *f* and full-staccato in example 9.13. A sharp upbeat secures a precise ♪ at the attack in example 18.12. Similar techniques are used in examples 7.5, 9.14, 9.15, and 9.16, with contrasting tempi. In example 9.17, use a very energetic staccato. Examples 9.18 and 9.19 have the same rhythm, with different tempos and dynamics. The preparation for both has the character of an upbeat.

Ex. 9.7. Rossini, *L'Italiana in Algeri,* Overture, mm. 26-28

Ex. 9.8. Handel, *Messiah,* No. 5, mm. 1-2

Ex. 9.9. Milhaud, Piano Concerto, third movement, mm. 1-3

Copyright © 1933 (Renewed) G. Schirmer, Inc.

Ex. 9.10. Shostakovich, *The Golden Age,* Introduction, mm. 1-2

Ex. 9.11. Mendelssohn, Symphony No. 4, third movement, mm. 1-2

Ex. 9.12. Haydn, Symphony No. 94, fourth movement, mm. 1-4

Ex. 9.13. Haydn, *The Creation,* Chorus (No. 13), mm. 1-4

Ex. 9.14. Rimsky-Korsakov, *Scheherazade,* third movement, mm. 1-2

Ex. 9.15. Dvořák, Symphony no. 7, third movement, mm. 1-3

Ex. 9.16. Mozart, *Don Giovanni,* K. 527, Act I, Scene 5, "Giovinette che fate all'amore", mm. 17-20

Ex. 9.17. Smetana, *The Bartered Bride,* Overture, mm. 1-3

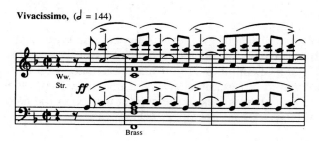

Ex. 9.18. Schubert, Symphony No. 2, third movement, mm. 1-4

Ex. 9.19. Beethoven, Symphony No. 3, "Eroica," third movement, mm. 1-5

Ex. 9.20. Haydn, Symphony No. 92, fourth movement, mm. 1-4

Conduct examples 9.20 and 9.21 with 1-beat in $\frac{2}{4}$ time. Example 9.20 requires light-staccato, example 9.21 full-staccato. The preparatory gesture again has the character of an upbeat. (In example 9.20, the second violin may not be authentic.) In examples 9.22, 9.23, and 19.25, the entrance occurs immediately after the downbeat. Proceed in strict tempo and without hesitation from the first downbeat to the next. Do not wait unnecessarily for the notes in the first bar to be played, or the tempo will drag. The preparation here does not feel like an upbeat but has the solidity of an actual strong beat.

USE OF AN EXTRA BEAT

Because of the difficulty of executing certain starts after the count, especially in fast tempo, conductors sometimes give an extra beat to secure precision. Thus, in example 9.24 you may beat One, Two to establish the tempo with certainty. In example 9.25, you may beat Two, One, but a very small Two, no more than a flick of the wrist at the top of the field of beating, followed by a large staccato downbeat *(One).*

Ex. 9.21. Schubert, Symphony No. 8, "The Great," fourth movement, mm. 1-7

Ex. 9.22. Puccini, *La Bohème,* Act I, mm. 1-6

Ex. 9.23. Elgar, *Enigma Variations,* Var. 7, mm. 1-4

Ex. 9.24. Mozart, *Eine kleine Nachtmusik,* K. 525, fourth movement, mm. 1-2

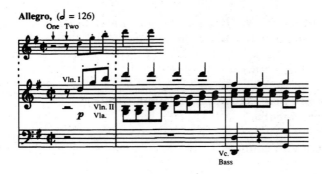

Remember: Use the extra beat only if you cannot get a satisfactory result without it. If you want to use the extra beat, you have to inform the players.

Occasionally the left hand can be used for extra beats to set up the tempo for tricky attacks. For the start in example 9.19, for instance, small left-hand

Ex. 9.25. R. Strauss, *Don Juan*, mm. 1-3

motions may indicate *One, Two, Three, Four,* each motion at the pulse of one measure. Exactly on *Four,* the baton gives the upbeat.

Earlier in our century such extra beats were hardly ever used. In fact, they were considered unprofessional, an expedient for amateur groups. In our days, however, even master conductors do not hesitate to make use of them as a safety device to ensure precise attacks.

Additional examples for the study of the start after the count:

4-Beat

After the first count:

Bach: Cantata No. 31 *(Der Himmel lacht, die Erde jubilieret)*, No. 2 (Coro); No. 6 (Aria)
Beethoven: *Fidelio*, No. 5 (Terzett)
Schumann: Overture to *Manfred*
Verdi: *Aïda*, Act IV, scene 2
Weber: *Der Freischütz*, No. 9 (Terzett)

After the second count:

Bach: Cantata No. 80 *(Ein feste Burg ist unser Gott)*, No. 4 (Aria)
Haydn: Symphony No. 86, 4th movement

After the third count:

Brahms: *Ein deutsches Requiem*, 5th movement
Stravinsky: *Ragtime*

After the fourth count:

Enesco: Roumanian Rhapsody No. 1
Handel: Concerto Grosso, Op. 6, No. 8 *(Allemande)*
Haydn: Symphony No. 59, 1st movement
Haydn: Symphony No. 83, 4th movement
Rossini: *Il Barbiere di Siviglia*, Act I, Finale 1

3-Beat

After the first count:

Bach: *St. Matthew Passion,* No. 49 (Chorus)
Vivaldi: Concerto Grosso in D Minor, Op. 3, No. 11 (RV 565)

After the second count:

Bach: Suite No. 4 in D Major, "Réjouissance"
Haydn: *The Seasons,* No. 21, Introduction (Autumn)
Rossini: *Il Barbiere di Siviglia,* Act I, Rosina's cavatina
Weber: *Der Freischütz,* No. 2 (Terzett mit Chor)

After the third count:

Barber: Overture to *The School for Scandal*
Handel: *Messiah,* Part II, Aria (Thou Art Gone Up on High)
Respighi: *Feste Romane,* beginning
Wagner: *Die Walküre,* Act III, "Ride of the Valkyries"

2-Beat

After the first count:

Bach: Cantata No. 31 *(Der Himmel lacht, die Erde jubilieret)* No. 1
  (Sonata)
Mendelssohn: Overture to *Ruy Blas (Allegro molto)*
Mozart: *Così fan tutte,* No. 22 (Quartetto)
Rachmaninoff: Symphony No. 2, 2d movement
Tchaikovsky: Symphony No. 4, 2d movement
Tchaikovsky: Suite No. 3, Scherzo
Verdi: *Messa da Requiem,* No. 3 (Offertorio)
Wagner: Overture to *Der Fliegende Holländer,* six measures before L
  (after the general pause)

After the second count:

Beethoven: Symphony No. 2, 4th movement
Brahms: Symphony No. 4, 1st movement
Dvořák: String Serenade Op. 22, Finale
Haydn: Symphony No. 80, 4th movement (with syncopation)
Haydn: Symphony No. 85 *(La Reine),* 4th movement
Mozart: Piano Concerto No. 14, K. 449, 3d movement
Mozart: *Così fan tutte,* No. 8 (Coro); No. 12 (Aria); No. 15 (Aria); No.
  28 (Aria)
Puccini: *La Bohème,* Act III, beginning

1-Beat

Beethoven: Symphony No. 5, 3d movement
Brahms: Serenade No. 1 in D Major, Scherzo 1
Dvořák: Symphony No. 8, 3d movement
Elgar: *Enigma* Variations, Variation 2
Mahler: Symphony No. 6, 2d movement
Mozart: *Così fan tutte,* No. 13 (Sestetto, at Allegro $\frac{3}{4}$)
Schubert: Symphony No. 3, 3d movement
Schubert: Symphony No. 6, 3d movement
Stravinsky: *Pulcinella* Suite, at No. 53 (to set the tempo for the "Tarantella," $\maltese$ = 88, a 2-beat, $\maltese$ = 176, can be used for the first measure)
Tchaikovsky: Serenade for Strings, 2d movement

10

The 6-Beat

The most common style used in beating 6-time is the so-called German style, although some conductors prefer to alternate between the German and Italian styles according to the musical context. These two styles differ mainly in regard to the motion that leads from the third to the fourth counts: in the German style it is a sidewise motion, whereas in the Italian style the motion goes upward. The former lends itself to music at a moderate speed with an expressive melodic line, while the Italian style is handier in quick tempo. Especially in operatic conducting, the economy of gesture gives the Italian style the advantage.

GERMAN STYLE

In figure 10.1, think of ② and ⑤ as being interpolated into the 4-beat pattern. Use the wrist alone for these two "added" beats except in very expressive passages. For the expressive pattern, see figure 10.2. Practice before the mirror in a fairly slow tempo; then use example 10.1.

Figures 10.3 and 10.4 show the staccato beat. Practice with example 10.2.

To start on the	apply figures
1st count	1.4, 2.2, and 2.4
2nd count	7.2 and 7.6
3rd count	4.5 and 4.6
4th count	4.3 and 4.4
5th count	4.3 and 4.4 (slightly farther to the right)
6th count	4.1 and 4.2

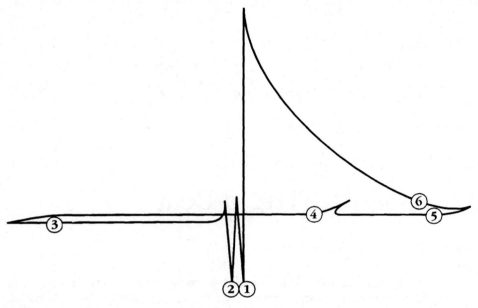

Fig. 10.1. 6-beat (German style); neutral-legato

Ex. 10.1. Exercise

Ex. 10.2. Exercise

ITALIAN STYLE

The pattern shown in figure 10.5 is fairly close to a subdivided 2, which means that the first and fourth counts are considerably more marked than the others. By adding curves to the lines, you can easily work out the expressive-legato pattern. Figures 10.6 and 10.7 demonstrate the staccato.

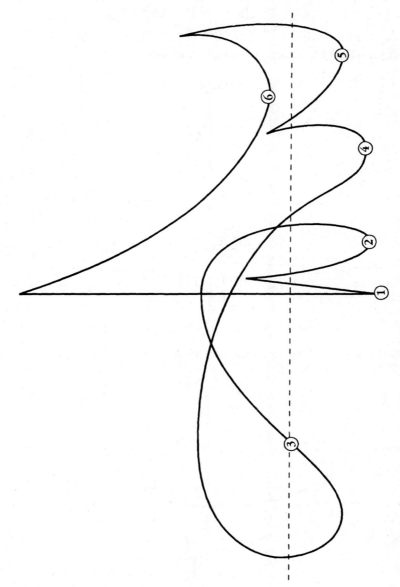

Fig. 10.2. 6-beat (German style); expressive-legato

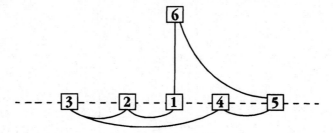

Fig. 10.3. 6-beat (German style); light-staccato

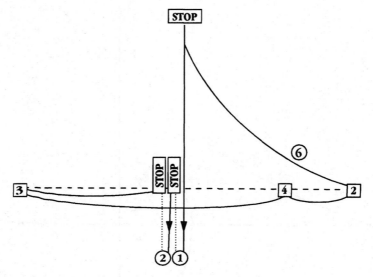

Fig. 10.4. 6-beat (German style); full-staccato

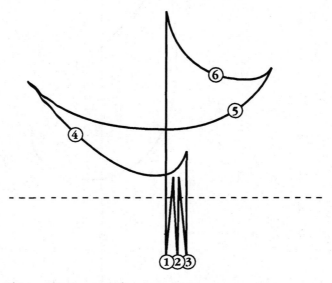

Fig. 10.5. 6-beat (Italian style); neutral-legato

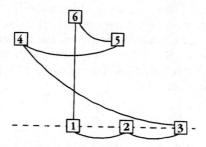

Fig. 10.6. 6-beat (Italian style); light-staccato

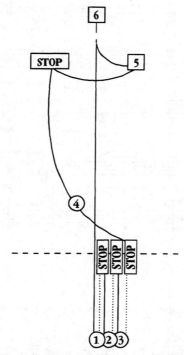

Fig. 10.7. 6-beat (Italian style); full-staccato

Both the German and Italian styles are applicable in the following examples. Start example 10.3 with an intense beat, not too large; with the diminuendo, change to neutral-legato. In example 10.4 use full-staccato, accented upbeat on 6 in measure 1 (for more on this upbeat, see the comment for ex. 8.17). Example 10.5 is conducted *molto espressivo*, legato. The woodwind entry in example 10.6 requires a certain emphasis on One in measure 2; then beat neutral-legato very quietly. The fifth beat in measure 3 is used for a cutoff (as discussed on p. 191). For the legato *poco espressivo* in example 10.7, the gesture must be very graceful. In example 10.8, there is a gentle staccato for the strings; use the third beat to prepare the entrance of the

winds (neutral-legato). (The two wind chords are spurious. Mozart's autograph does not include them at the beginning of the duet.) To accompany the
singer in example 32.3, a neutral-legato beat leads the sustained wind chords
beginning in measure 40. When the same theme is played in the overture of
the opera, as shown in example 32.4, a more expressive gesture is needed for
the crescendo and decrescendo.

Ex. 10.3. Brahms, Symphony No. 4, second movement, mm. 1-6

Ex. 10.4. Brahms, Symphony No. 4, second movement, mm. 83-85

Ex. 10.5. Brahms, Symphony No. 4, second movement, mm. 88-91

Ex. 10.6. Wagner, *Tristan und Isolde,* Prelude, mm. 1-3

Ex. 10.7. Haydn, Symphony No. 95, second movement, mm. 1-4

Ex. 10.8. Mozart, *Die Zauberflöte,* K. 620, Act I, Scene 7, Duet, "Bei Männern," beginning

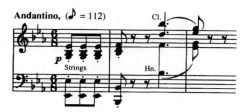

Ex. 10.9. J.S. Bach, Mass in B Minor, "Qui sedes ad dextram Patris" (No. 10), mm. 1-4

Start after the count in example 10.9. Give the preparation as though the music would start on the sixth count.

Additional examples for the study of 6-beat:

Neutral-Legato

Berlioz: *Symphonie fantastique,* 3d movement (also expressive-legato, staccato, and dynamic changes)
Brahms: Symphony No. 1, 1st movement, 1st and 2d measures after A
Debussy: *La Mer,* beginning
Mozart: Piano Concerto in A major, K. 488, 2d movement (also *poco espressivo)*
Verdi: *Aïda,* Act III, Aïda's aria starting at D

Expressive-Legato

Debussy: *Nuages*
Hindemith: *Sinfonische Metamorphosen (Andantino)*
Massenet: *Manon,* Act I, Prelude (Andante sostenuto)
Mendelssohn: *Elijah,* No. 37 (Arioso)
Puccini: *Madama Butterfly,* Act I, #116 to #118 (alternating with subdivided $\frac{3}{4}$); *Largamente* before #135 to #136
Schubert: Symphony No. 5, 2d movement (also neutral-legato)
Verdi: *Messa da Requiem,* No. 2 ("Quid sum miser") at No. 24 *(poco espressivo)*
Wagner: *Die Meistersinger von Nürnberg,* Act III, Scene 4, Quintet

Staccato

Bach: Cantata No. 62 *(Nun komm, der Heiden Heiland),* No. 1 (Chorale)
Britten: *Spring* Symphony, "The Driving Boy"

Kodály: *Psalmus Hungaricus,* passage starting at #25

Liszt: *Mazeppa,* beginning

Mozart: *Don Giovanni, K.527,* No. 15 (Terzetto)

Mozart: *Die Zauberflöte, K.620,* No. 16 (Terzett; for this lively tempo, use fig. 10.6)

Rossini: Overture to *Semiramide,* passage starting at the twentieth measure of *Andantino,* $\frac{6}{8}$

Tchaikovsky: *Capriccio Italien,* at B

Dynamic Changes

Brahms: Symphony No. 1, 1st movement, passage starting at m. 9

Delius: *On Hearing the First Cuckoo in Spring*

Dukas: *La Péri*

Haydn: Symphony No. 96, 2d movement

Mozart: Symphony No. 38, K.504 ("Prague"), 2d movement

Reger: Variations on a Theme by Mozart, Variation 8

Verdi: *Aïda,* Act I, Scene 1, Radames's aria, starting at B

CHAPTER *11*

Subdivision

When the music is so slow that the regular beat would not give the conductor enough control or intensity, the beat is divided into fractional parts. This chapter deals mainly with the execution of the subdivided patterns; their application will be discussed in greater detail in chapter 12.

The general principle is that, unless the musical expression demands otherwise, the main beats are larger and receive more stress than the subdivisions. To start in subdivided time, always give the preliminary beat in terms of the smallest unit that you are actually beating.

EIGHT BEATS IN A MEASURE

In figure 11.1, the weaker beats ②, ④, and ⑥ are usually done with wrist motions only. Conductors differ in their manner of beating ⑦ and ⑧. Some always beat ⑦ at the top of the field. The main reason for not doing so is that it emphasizes the seventh beat and destroys the smooth flow.

The various patterns (staccato, *espressivo,* etc.) can be deduced easily from figure 11.1. Sometimes the musical context makes it advisable to click on the main counts: ①, ③, ⑤, and ⑦. In example 11.1, conduct neutral-legato; the preliminary beat has the value of an eighth note. Conduct the strings as accompaniment, but know exactly what is going on in the oboe solo. The conductor must be able to deal with fractional values very easily in order to correct the players. The study of Bach will train the conductor's mind to recognize these small values quickly, even in the most complicated passages. (Bach's violin sonatas afford especially good practice.) In example 11.2, the composer's metronome refers to quarter beats, but subdivision is needed to lead the violas securely and to coordinate the xylophone entry in measure 9. For the start of example 11.3, see example 9.5. (Rossini did not write an overture to *Il Barbiere di Siviglia.* The piece exists in different versions. Scholars give preference to the original one, the overture to *Aureliano in Palmira,* but not all conductors agree. See also p. 192)

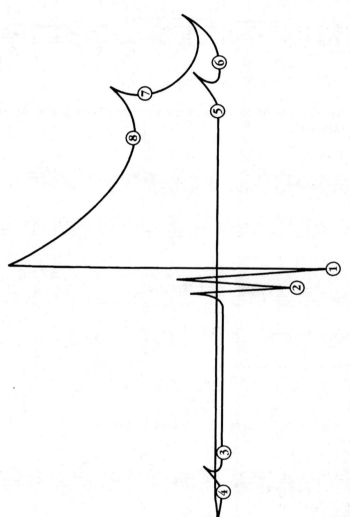

Fig. 11.1. 4-beat subdivided in 8

Ex. 11.1. J.S. Bach, Cantata No. 21, Sinfonia, mm. 1-2

Ex. 11.2. Bartok, *Music for Strings, Percussion, and Celesta,* third movement, mm. 6-9

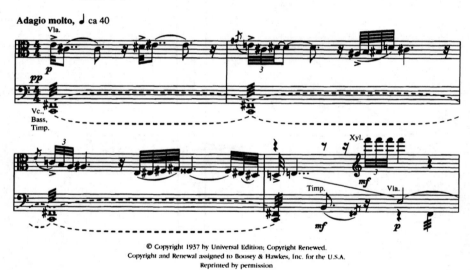

© Copyright 1937 by Universal Edition; Copyright Renewed.
Copyright and Renewal assigned to Boosey & Hawkes, Inc. for the U.S.A.
Reprinted by permission

Ex. 11.3. Rossini, *Il Barbiere di Siviglia,* Overture, mm. 1-6

FOUR BEATS AS A RESULT OF SUBDIVISION

Beating in 2-time with subdivision is shown in figures 11.2 and 11.3. The style shown in figure 11.3 is especially recommended for transitions from a 4-beat to a 2-beat (see also p. 179). The first bar of example 11.4 requires a regular 4-beat; then use a subdivided $\frac{2}{4}$ ($= \frac{4}{8}$) to lead the melody. In the third through the fifth measures of the example, the subdivision should be hardly noticeable; use it in the last two measures. In example 11.5, subdivision applies only to measures 132 and 133. Here it helps to bring out the sf and to lead the thirty-second groups with a decisive beat. In example 11.6, subdivision starts with the ff; it controls the accented ritenuto (see p. 253). The most effective way of directing the allargando in example 15.5 is to subdivide the beat.

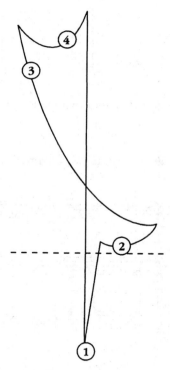

Fig. 11.2. 2-beat subdivided in 4

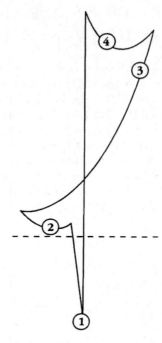

Fig. 11.3. 2-beat subdivided in 4 (alternate style)

Ex. 11.4. Puccini, *La Bohème,* Act I, "Mi chiamano Mimi," at #35

Ex. 11.5. Beethoven, Symphony No. 9, first movement, mm. 124-33

Ex. 11.5. *Continued*

Ex. 11.6. Smetana, *The Bartered Bride,* Act I, Scene 5, Polka (Finale), mm. 1,377-1,384

TWELVE BEATS IN A MEASURE

Figure 11.4 shows 4-time with each beat subdivided triply. Now it is even more important to keep the main beats—①, ④, ⑦, and ⑩—clear and distinct, to avoid any misunderstanding on the part of the players.

Use slightly curved motions for the graceful music of example 11.7. The restrained mood of example 11.8 requires small neutral beats. Example 11.9 should be sung and the various entries indicated precisely by the conductor.

Ex. 11.7. J.S. Bach, *St. John Passion,* Aria (No. 20), mm. 1-2

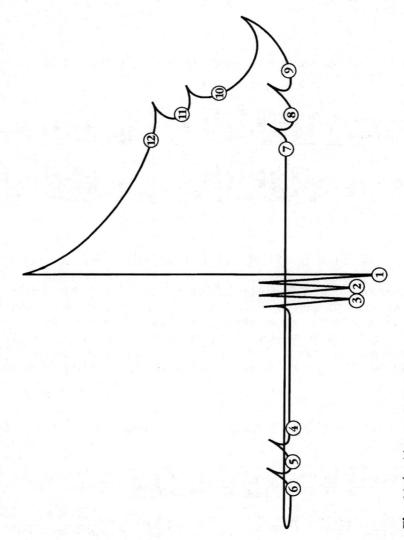

Fig. 11.4. 4-beat subdivided in 12

Ex. 11.8. Stravinsky, *L'Oiseau de feu*, Introduction, mm. 1-2

Ex. 11.9. Verdi, *Il Trovatore*, Act IV, No. 14, "Parlar non vuoi?" mm. 19-21

NINE BEATS IN A MEASURE

The pattern in figure 11.5 is 3-time with each beat subdivided triply. In example 11.10, although the composer's metronome indication reads ♩. = 48, the final measures of this movement are best directed with a 9-beat. Clear gestures are needed to coordinate the pizzicato chords in the last bar (*a tempo!*). Measure 101 of example 11.11 requires nine beats, legato.

Ex. 11.10. Walton, Viola Concerto, first movement, final measures

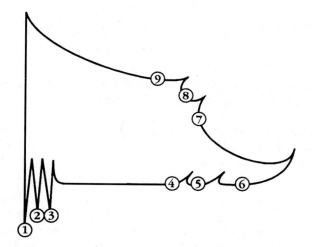

Fig. 11.5. 3-beat subdivided in 9

Ex. 11.11. Debussy, *Prélude à l'après-midi d'un faune,* mm. 100-102

SIX BEATS AS A RESULT OF SUBDIVISION

Conducting 6-beat resulting from subdivision is different from regular 6-beat; it is 3-time or 2-time subdivided. (1) The pattern for 3-time subdivided is shown in figure 11.6.

In example 11.12, the subdividing gestures must not disturb the feeling of three pulses per measure (see the comments on Mozart's tempi on p. 390). Subdivision serves to lead the thirty-second notes in the melody and to prepare the *f* chords.

Begin in example 11.13 with neutral-legato; on the second eighth beat in measure 2, suddenly enlarge the gesture, which then becomes smaller while you direct the diminuendo. In the first measure of example 11.14, use strong gestures for the main counts while the subdivided beats serve as preparation. The character of the music in example 11.15 requires emphatic motions on each of the six beats, but keep the pattern unmistakably clear.

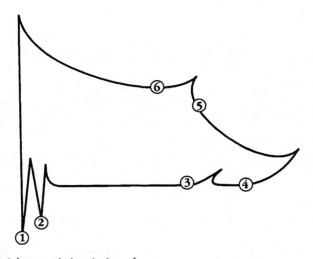

Fig. 11.6. 3-beat subdivided in 6

Ex. 11.12. Mozart, Symphony No. 41, K. 551, second movement, mm. 1-6

Ex. 11.13. Berlioz, *Harold in Italy,* first movement, mm. 1-3

Ex. 11.14. W. Schuman, Symphony for Strings, second movement, mm. 1-2

Ex. 11.15. W. Schuman, Symphony for Strings, second movement, mm. 58-59

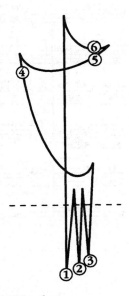

Fig. 11.7. 2-beat subdivided in 6

The pattern for **2-time** with each beat **subdivided** triply is shown in figure 11.7 (compare the different Italian pattern for 6-beat, fig. 10.5).

In example 11.16, the time signature is $\frac{6}{4}$. This music is best directed with a regular 6-beat. A regular 6-beat in example 11.17, especially in the German style, would be too academic and would not conform to the pulsation of the music. Start with relatively small gestures and bring out the crescendo. Start beating example 11.18 in two; with the first (optional) *rallentando,* subdivide, and at *rall. molto* use the 6-beat pattern (Italian style). Return to beating two beats for a *tempo*.

Ex. 11.16. J.S. Bach, Cantata No. 147, No. 1 (Chorus), mm. 1-3

Ex. 11.17. Puccini, *Tosca,* Act II, three measures after #29

Ex. 11.18. Mascagni, *Cavalleria Rusticana,* 7 measures after #10

1-BEAT WITH SUBDIVISION

Subdivided 1-beat occurs only in fairly fast 3-time when the regular 3-beat would be awkward and the regular 1-beat would lack distinctness or intensity. It can be done in three different ways.

First, as a special case of 3-beat, the gesture is very small, and the second beat, instead of going to the right, goes upward at a very small angle (see fig. 7.4). This pattern is useful when an occasional indication of the three beats is needed, although the rhythm is felt primarily as one pulse to the measure.

Having led measures 149–52 of example 11.19 with firm 1-beat gestures, the conductor may switch to subdivision for the double hemiola in measures 153–56, using small, yet clear beats (wrist!). This will help the string players to maintain a steady rhythm. Some conductors choose to direct this 4-measure period as though it were notated in $\frac{3}{2}$ meter, using altogether six beats: $\frac{3}{2}$ ♩♩♩| ♩♩♩. No matter what your preference, you must return to 1-beat in measure 157.

Ex. 11.19. Bach, Brandenburg Concerto No. 4, first movement, mm. 149-59

Ex. 11.20. Mozart, Symphony No. 40, K. 550, third movement, mm. 15-27

Second, when the pulsation felt is *One, Two (three)*, apply figure 7.3. The gesture indicating the third count is not only very small but weak as well. The outline of each bar is practically a 2-beat in 3-time, in which each bar can be considered as | ♩ ♩ |.

Third, when the pulsation felt is One, (two) Three, you may apply a regular 2-beat with the feeling | ♩ ♩ |.

In example 11.20, neither a regular 3-beat nor a regular 1-beat would do justice to this music, both being too academic. *One (two), Three* is felt in measures 15–22, *One, Two (three)* in measures 23–6; beat accordingly.

Additional examples for the study of the subdivided pattern:

Twelve Beats in a Measure

Bach: *St. Matthew Passion,* No. 47 (Aria)
Debussy: *Prélude à l'après-midi d'un faune,* at #3
Messiaen: *L 'Ascension,* 1st movement
Prokofiev: Violin Concerto No. 2, 2d movement
Verdi: *Rigoletto,* No. 14, Duetto finale, passage starting with the twenty-fifth measure of *Andante* in D-flat major (subdivision helps to coordinate the off-beat notes of the first lines with the pizzicato of the second violins)

Nine Beats in a Measure

Brahms: Symphony No. 1, 1st movement, m. 8
Dukas: *La Péri,* at No. 1 and after #6
Saint-Saëns: Symphony No. 2, 2d movement, at S
Strauss: *Also sprach Zarathustra,* at No. 18 (9/4, ♩ = 160 change to 3-beat, ♩. = 54, once the rhythm has been established)
Wagner: Prelude to *Parsifal,* passage starting at *Sehr gehalten*

Eight Beats in a Measure

Bach: Cantata No. 12 *(Weinen, Klagen, Sorgen, Zagen),* Sinfonia
Bartók: Divertimento for String Orchestra, 2d movement
Handel: Concerto Grosso Op. 6, No. 12, 1st movement
Haydn: Symphony No 104, 1st movement, introduction
Hindemith: *Nobilissima Visione,* beginning
Rossini: *Il Barbiere di Siviglia,* Act II, Quintet
Schoenberg: Piano Concerto Op. 42, mm. 297–325
Schubert: Symphony No. 2, 1st movement, *Largo*

Six Beats in a Measure (3-time)

Beethoven: Symphony No. 4, 2d movement
Brahms: *Academic Festival* Overture, Maestoso 3/4

Copland: *A Lincoln Portrait,* beginning
Haydn: *The Creation,* No. 29 (Recitative), Prelude to Part III
Prokofiev: *Romeo and Juliet* Suite No. 2, "Romeo and Juliet before parting" (No. 5), at #42
Rachmaninoff: Piano Concerto No. 2, 2d movement, mm. 13, 16, etc.
Sibelius: Symphony No. 3, 1st movement, seventh measure after #4, second measure after #12, etc.

Six Beats in a Measure (2-time)

Brahms: Piano Concerto No. 1, 1st movement, mm. 175–225
Enesco: Roumanian Rhapsody No. 1, passage starting at No. 7, *Posato*
Mascagni: *Cavalleria Rusticana,* Prelude bars 20–27.
Wagner: Overture to *Der fliegende Holländer,* passage of third measures at *Un poco ritenuto* (four times)

Four Beats in a Measure (2-time)

Britten: *Sea Interludes,* No. 1, "Dawn" (the intended tempo is indicated by $\textteight = 44$ and confirmed by the composer's recording; use subdivision whenever needed for coordination, but do not alter the pace of the music)
Haydn: Symphony No. 104, 2d movement
Schoenberg: *Kammersymphonie,* mm. 75–79.
Schubert: Symphony No. 2, 2d movement
Tchaikovsky: Serenade for Strings, 1st movement, m. 8
Verdi: Overture to *I Vespri Siciliani, Allegro agitato* (start beating two but subdivide whenever necessary to lead the sixteenth-note passages and the syncopations; the subdivision ends seven measures before D but is resumed at E)

One-Beat with Subdivision

Bizet: *L'Arlésienne* Suite No. 1, 2d movement, middle section
Debussy: *Ibéria,* beginning
Debussy: *La Mer,* 2d movement, passage beginning at #16
Dvořák: Symphony No. 9, 3d movement, after the double bar
Falla: *The Three-Cornered Hat,* Suite No. 2, "Danse Finale" at #11, (Giocoso)
Prokofiev: Piano Concerto No. 3, 3d movement
Strauss, Johann: *Tales from the Vienna Woods,* Waltz No. 1, at *poco ritenuto*

CHAPTER 12

Number of Beats in a Measure

GENERAL CONSIDERATIONS

The conductor cannot always rely upon the time signature to indicate how many beats to use in a measure because composers do not necessarily think of beat patterns when setting the time signature. Metronome markings can also be misleading: One would not use 1-beat for the fourth movement of Beethoven's Eighth Symphony, although the metronome refers to the whole bar as the rhythmic unit (Beethoven marked it **o** = 84, because his metronome did not provide a notch for a pulse beyond 150). Regardless of the music's meter, clear direction may demand that priority be given to technical considerations. The following examples will show how the beat patterns that have been discussed in previous chapters are best applied to music of various styles. Additional beat patterns, including techniques needed for the performance of twentieth-century music, will come up for discussion in chapter 13.

Three main factors are to be taken into consideration: the tempo of the music, the players' need for rhythmic security, and the degree of intensity you desire on the weak counts or in the smaller rhythmic values. The last is more a question of style and interpretation than of technique.

The speed of the music sets a limit to the number of possible beats in a measure. Thus, in *Presto or Allegro molto* in $\frac{4}{4}$, a 4-beat would often be uncomfortable for the conductor and confusing to players. The musical pulsation, moreover, may demand an *alla breve* beat rather than a stroke on every written count, as in Mendelssohn's "Wedding March" (see ex. 15.6) or *Allegro vivo* in Rossini's Overture to *Il Barbiere di Siviglia* (see ex. 19.27). On the same principle, examples 9.20 and 9.21 need 1-beat, although marked $\frac{2}{4}$.

On the other hand, some slow movements written in $\frac{2}{4}$ or $\mathcal{C}$ have to be directed in four, for otherwise so much time would elapse between beats that the rhythm would no longer be clear (see exx. 2.6, 3.3, 4.9, 20.1, and 20.2). In these movements, even though the musical pulse may be felt in two, a 4-beat or a subdivided 2-beat pattern serves a better definition of the rhythm, giving the musicians the security they expect from the beat. In example 12.1, despite of the metronome marking and the composer's indication "very moderate

Ex. 12.1. Berg, *Wozzeck,* Act I, Scene 1, mm. 7-9

Sehr mässige Viertel, ♩ = 60

quarter notes,'' the players would feel uneasy unless the conductor used subdivision.

A subdivided 2-beat is often practical when neither 4-beat nor 2-beat can be applied continuously, as in the second movement of Schubert's Symphony No. 8 (see ex. 17.7) or the *Andante più tosto Allegretto* of Haydn's Symphony No. 103 ("Drum-roll"). In these movements, the alternating use of the regular and subdivided 2-beat allows the conductor to adjust the gesture to the pulsation of the music. If the transition from one pattern to the other is performed with ease and flexibility, the change, sometimes even from bar to bar, will not upset the clarity of the beat. Similarly, subdivision is often applied to slow movements in $\frac{4}{4}$ time.

If you try to beat four in example 12.2, you will find that the first half of measure 1 may turn out satisfactorily, but both the continuation of the melody and the triplets in the accompaniment demand eight beats in a bar.

In example 4.12, at a pace as slow as ♩ = 46–50, a 4-beat might be impractical. Subdivision helps to coordinate double bassoon and low strings.

The problems that arise in triple time are treated similarly. In its straight or subdivided form, 1-beat is often used for fast movements in 3-time. In slow 3-time, use subdivision with six beats or, when triplets occur on each count, nine beats in a measure. However, two beats in a bar may be used for fast 6-time, three beats for 9-time, and four beats for 12-time.

The metronome marking in example 12.3 suggests two beats in a measure, but it would be difficult for the flutists to coordinate their playing unless the conductor indicates the eighth notes. Use a subtle subdivision (see fig. 11.7).

In all cases, the choice of beats must not affect the choice of tempo. Do not drag when using more beats than indicated in the time signature; do not hurry when using fewer beats.

Aside from the music's tempo, interpretive considerations may determine the number of beats in a measure. It may happen that there is a choice between two ways of beating, both technically correct but having different effects on the players' responses. The rule, sometimes taught, that no more beats should be used than are necessary to mark the time, may be good for time beaters but is never followed in artistic conducting. Obviously, by beating the smaller rhythmic values, even though this may not be "necessary," the weak beats are played with more intensity. On the other hand, the indication of fewer strokes result in a broader flow of the music. Thus, the mode of beating may have a marked influence on the meter of the music, which in turn can affect the interpretation of a whole piece. It is self evident

Ex. 12.2. Mozart, Violin Concerto No. 3, K. 216, second movement, mm. 1-2

Ex. 12.3. Ravel, *Daphnis et Chloé* Suite No. 1, at #74

that examples 6.5 and 10.9 require a different number of beats, though both are marked $\frac{6}{8}$ and are played at a moderate speed. For the lilting melody of the Barcarolle, 2-beat is adequate, while 6-beat is needed to bring out the polyphonic interweaving in the example from Bach.

The overture shown in example 12.4 is usually directed in 2-beat. It has been conducted in 4-beat without altering the tempo significantly. The shape of the theme, however, is quite different in the two cases, because of the subaccent on the third quarter in 4-beat. The *tenuto* signs must be observed by the players, but they are not reflected in the beat. A special gesture would be fussy and might lead to an accent.

There are many cases in which stylistic considerations should determine the number of beats in a measure. A particular feeling for rhythm may be an essential characteristic of a composer's style, and failure to do justice to it may result in a performance that either lacks intensity or is overemphatic.

The music in example 12.5 has been conducted with four beats in a bar and with twelve. Aside from the question of tempo, the difference is that in the latter case the eighth note values receive more stress. Such emphasis does not conform to the best traditions of performing Bach (see p. 385).

That baton technique can be closely related to the musical language of different composers may be seen by comparing certain passages from the works of Verdi and Wagner. Verdi's music often demands a beat that gives to the smaller time values that intensity that is characteristic of Italian feeling for the rhythm. For Wagner, on the other hand, an *alla breve* beat is often used to bring out the broad line of the music, even when the time signature is $\frac{4}{4}$.

Outside of Italy the music of example 12.6 may be heard conducted *alla breve*. Such treatment loses the dramatic effect of the music and makes the melody sound rather banal.

In examples 12.7 and 12.8, typical of Verdi's style, the composer's metronome markings indicate half beats; but most Italian conductors use four

Ex. 12.4. Beethoven, *Coriolanus* Overture, mm. 15-19

Ex. 12.5. J.S. Bach, Concerto for Two Violins, second movement, mm. 1-2

Ex. 12.6. Verdi, *Rigoletto,* Act II, "Si, vendetta" (No. 10), mm. 1-4

Ex. 12.7. Verdi, *Il Trovatore,* Act II, Scena e racconto, (No. 5), mm. 103-7

Ex. 12.8. Verdi, *Il Trovatore,* Act III (No. 11), "L'onda de'suoni mistici," mm. 23-26

strokes, generally with the subdivided pattern. This results in a more exciting performance and at the same time secures better rhythmic control. Thus the violins will play the descending figure in example 12.7 clearly, whereas the passage is apt to be muddy when directed *alla breve*. In Ex 12.8, the syncopated rhythm will hardly come out distinctly unless the conductor indicates four beats in a bar.

In example 12.9, the section marked **C** requires an *alla breve* beat, although the string passages look as though they need 4-beat. The latter, however, would not bring out the grandeur of the melody (see p. 407).

SIMULTANEOUS DIFFERENT RHYTHMS

Other situations in which the conductor must determine how many beats to use in a measure occur when different rhythms are played simultaneously

Ex. 12.9. Wagner, *Die Walküre*, Act I, Scene 3, mm. 231-37

by various groups of the orchestra. The principle to be followed is simple: avoid gestures that would disturb the rhythm of any group. This is best done by weakening or omitting such disruptive beats.

The melody in example 12.10 is in triplet quarter notes against the $\frac{4}{4}$ rhythm of the accompaniment. A change to *alla breve* is not recommended, because triplets can easily be played against the regular 4-beat, provided *Two* and *Four* are somewhat weakened. This will accommodate the triplet figure without confusing the accompanying instruments. In the first measure of example 12.11, six beats are needed for clear direction of the various groups. In the next bar only slight subdivision is recommended, so as not to interfere with the smooth execution of the triplet. Do not subdivide in the third measure; then you may return to subdivision.

Since in example 12.12 the rhythmic figures in the woodwinds and trumpets are predominant, continue beating two in measure 21. Violins and horns thus play their $\frac{3}{4}$ rhythm as a syncopation.

Ex. 12.10. Tchaikovsky, *Capriccio Italien,* mm. 203-5

Ex. 12.11. Griffes, *The White Peacock,* seven measures before E

Ex. 12.12. Harris, *When Johnny Comes Marching Home*, mm. 19-24

In example 12.13, in spite of the composer's metronome indication ($\quarternote$ = 132) for the quadruplet in measure 186, the 3-beat ($\quarternote$ = 100) continues. The players carrying the melody must coordinate the four notes with the 3-beat. Changing the pattern would confuse the ensemble.

For the quintuplet in the third measure of example 12.14, use 1-beat; in the sixth and seventh measures, use 2-beat with weakened *Two*. For the entrance of the first violins, it is advisable to indicate a sharp *Two* with the left hand, a gesture that does not interfere with the brass figure. Be sure that the 1-beat is strictly in time, $\quarternote$ = 63.

Mentioned in Berlioz's *Traité d'instrumentation*, the passage in example 12.15 has become a classic example of simultaneous different rhythms. As Berlioz points out, the *Allegro* movement in the violas is maintained in the *Allegretto* by subdividing the third measure. The fourth bar, however, is not subdivided, for this would disturb the rhythmic feeling of the solo melody.

In example 12.16, the $\frac{8}{8}$ and $\frac{7}{8}$ against $\frac{3}{4}$ cannot both be included in the beat. Use 3-beat, but with weakened second and third beats, which facilitates the synchronizing of the odd rhythms with the beat. Apply similar technique to the third and fourth measures.

In many instances, the choice of beat takes into consideration which players are most in need of direction, while others can coordinate their divergent rhythmic patterns without difficulty.

In example 12.17, the flute and clarinet players calculate for themselves where their notes coincide with the 4-beat. Their triplets will be sufficiently well established and will allow a smooth execution in measure 11, even

Ex. 12.13. Schoenberg, *Five Pieces for Orchestra,* No. 2, mm. 185-87

Ex. 12.14. Stravinsky, *Le Sacre du Printemps,* "Danse Sacrale," two measures before #251

though the rhythmic figures do not always coincide with the beat. However, the conductor may find it necessary to help the flutes and clarinets by indicating six beats in a measure with the left hand while beating four with the baton. (This procedure is recommended as an interesting exercise to achieve independence of the two hands!)

Ex. 12.15. Berlioz, *Harold in Italy,* third movement, forty-nine measures after #35

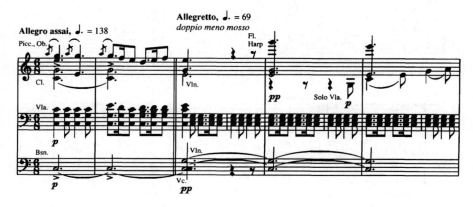

Ex. 12.16. Stravinsky, *Petrouchka,* 1er Tableau, one measure before #4

Additional examples for the study of passages in which different rhythms occur simultaneously:

Barber: *Second Essay for Orchestra,* passage starting at #19

Brahms: Variations on a Theme by Haydn, finale

Bruckner: Symphony No. 5, 2d movement

Debussy: *La Mer,* 1st movement, passage beginning two measures before #1

Debussy: *Nuages,* passage starting at the 7 seventh bar after #2

Hindemith: Symphony *Mathis der Maler,* 3d movement, passage starting five measures before #25

Rimsky-Korsakov: *Scheherazade,* 4th movement, at *Vivo* $\frac{2}{8}$ ($\frac{6}{16}$, $\frac{3}{8}$)

Schoenberg: *Five Pieces for Orchestra,* #1

Sibelius: Violin Concerto, 1st movement, passage beginning six measures after #3 (*Largamente*); 4-beat and 6-beat alternate, because the conductor's main concern is with clarinet and bassoons; it is practical to change to 2-beat ten measures after #3

Tchaikovsky: *1812* Overture, passage starting at m. 188

Ex. 12.17. Wagner, *Parsifal,* Act I, Vorspiel, mm. 9-11

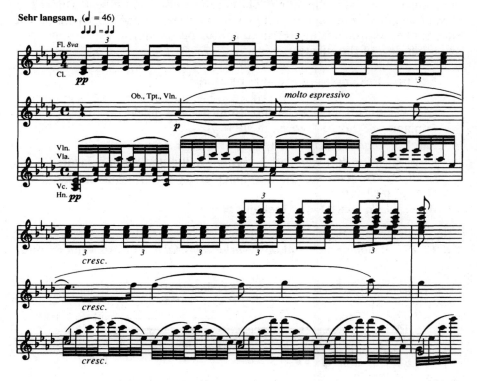

Ex. 12.18. Rimsky-Korsakov, *Scheherazade,* second movement, mm. 162-63

IRREGULAR MEASURES

Sometimes a composer includes more counts in a measure than are allowed by the time signature. The treatment of such measures depends on the musical context.

Beat the first three counts in example 12.18 distinctly, stopping at *Three* while the strings continue playing. Listen to the solo clarinet and synchronize the preparatory gesture so that the attack on measure 163 will not interfere with the steady pizzicato. Whether to use a free or an eighth beat preparation depends on individual experience. In example 12.19, use *Two* for the cutoff and preparation, with the strings playing the G on the off-beat. Direct the remaining notes of the figure with two or three small extra strokes on the left side of the field of beating. (The third can be omitted if this results in a smoother flow of the rubato.)

Additional examples of irregular measures:

Bartók: Concerto for Orchestra, 4th movement, m. 143
Copland: *A Lincoln Portrait,* m. 183
Ravel: *Rapsodie Espagnole,* 1st movement, at #6 and #8
Respighi: *Pini di Roma,* Part 2 (*Lento* $\frac{4}{4}$), fifth and ninth measures
Verdi: *La Traviata,* Act II, Germont's aria ("Di Provenza il mar"), fourth measure
Verdi: *Otello,* Act III, one measure before Q

Ex. 12.19. Hindemith, Symphony *Mathis der Maler,* third movement, mm. 1-2

CHANGING THE NUMBER OF BEATS FOR ONE OR MORE MEASURES

It sometimes becomes necessary in the middle of a piece to change the number of beats in a measure. This situation can be caused by a change in the rhythmic structure of the music, as, for instance, by the appearance of triplets in duple or quadruple time. Another cause is the occurrence of intricate rhythms or rapid passages that may be played indistinctly unless the conductor exercises firm control over the players. This technique may be compared to the routine of counting "one-and, two-and," familiar to all instrumentalists as an aid in the precise performance of rhythmically tricky passages.

Whether to beat the smaller values or not may also depend upon the ability of the particular orchestral group; experienced and technically superior musicians may not need such help. In slow or moderate tempo, the regular strokes often will not allow sufficient indication of intensity. In such a situation you may feel that your gestures are becoming purely mechanical, instead of "being with the orchestra," and that only by adding more beats to the bar can you regain close contact with the players. Or else, in lively tempo, you may sense that there is too much excitement in your gestures and that only by reducing the number of beats can you make the music flow more calmly.

As far as baton technique is concerned, such changes require an especially clear beat that leaves no doubt about your intention. This is particularly true when the change is not marked in the players' parts. A change from four to two beats or vice versa can be the cause of trouble if it is not executed properly. It is dangerous to use curved expressive gestures during such a change because the orchestra may be unable to see "where the conductor is." The main counts should be easy to recognize, while smaller gestures should be used for the weak beats. Subdivided patterns lend themselves readily to temporary changes. They are also used to achieve a gradual transition, applying the technique discussed on p. 179 ff., except that now the speed is not changed.

The triplets in the fifth measure of example 12.20 may require a change from 4-beat to 2-beat. The change should be marked in the parts. In example 12.21, change to 1-beat in the third measure and return to 2-beat at *rallentando*.

Ex. 12.20. Puccini, *Madama Butterfly,* Act I, at #79

Ex. 12.21. Puccini, *Tosca,* Act I, seven measures after #3

Because of the slow tempo in example 12.22, the triplet in measure 48 (*breit*) is directed with three strokes, applying a regular 3-beat. The structure of the music in example 12.23 calls for a change of beat. Measures 37 and 38 are directed with four strokes; subdivide in the second half of measure 36 to get an effective preparation for the *ff*. Return to 2-beat in measure 39, at the same time giving a clear indication of the sudden *p*. The fourth bar in example 12.24 requires 3-beat if the traditional *ritenuto* is made.

Ex. 12.22.   Bruckner, Symphony No. 4, fourth movement, mm. 43-49

Ex. 12.23.   Beethoven, *Fidelio,* Overture, mm. 35-41

Ex. 12.24.   J. Strauss, *Emperor* Waltz, No. 4, mm. 1-7

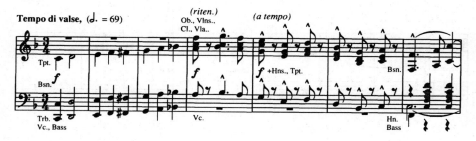

Because of the slow pace (*rit.*) in example 12.25, the syncopated passage in measure 6 must be directed with eight beats in a measure, or the violins will not feel secure. In example 12.26, the first three sixteenth notes of the *precipitando* (m. 132) are held back slightly; the others are played quickly and forcefully. Hence, subdivide the first half of the measure with sharp gestures, but use only one stroke for the second half. The following bar is legato.

The conductor must know to what extent the orchestra needs help in examples 12.27 and 12.28 for a flawless rhythmic execution. Subdivision may not be necessary when the players are thoroughly familiar with the music and have strong rhythmic feeling of their own. If this is not the case, the conductor will prefer to subdivide for the triplet figure in example 12.27, measures 19 and 20, either by using six small beats (fig. 11.7) or by beating *One, Three, Four, Six* with downward gestures for *One* and *Three,* upward gestures for *Four* and *Six.* Beat legato in measures 17 and 18 and then change to staccato.

Ex. 12.25. Elgar, *Enigma Variations,* Var. I, mm. 4-7

Ex. 12.26. Mascagni, *Cavalleria Rusticana,* "Regina coeli," mm. 130-34

Ex. 12.27. Brahms, Symphony No. 3, first movement, mm. 17-20

(continued)

Ex. 12.27. *Continued*

Ex. 12.28. Brahms, Symphony No. 3, first movement, mm. 31-35

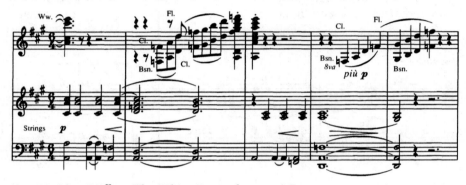

Ex. 12.29. Griffes, *The White Peacock,* mm. 1-7

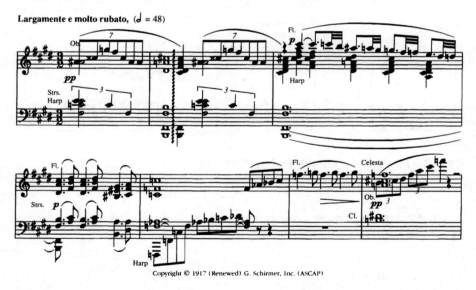

In example 12.28, measure 32, use 6-beat neutral gestures but with staccato on Six; return to 2-beat in measure 33. Measures 34 and 35 need no subdivision.

Direct the opening of example 12.29 (which is a start on the third count) with a very calm 3-beat. In measure 2, however, change to subdivision to lead the flute passage and the harp chords. In the next bar, return smoothly to the calm 3-beat.

Although the music in example 12.30 is marked *alla breve,* 4-beat is advisable, even for the best orchestras, to secure precision in the violin and viola passages. Change to 2-beat in the fifth measure.

In example 12.31, though conductors differ in the way they lead the $\frac{12}{8}$ section of this movement (four or twelve beats in a measure), there is no doubt that, in measure 151, the beat must be subdivided.

Ex. 12.30. Wagner, *Tristan und Isolde,* Act I, Scene 1, mm. 33-38

Ex. 12.31. Beethoven, Symphony No. 9, third movement, mm. 150-53

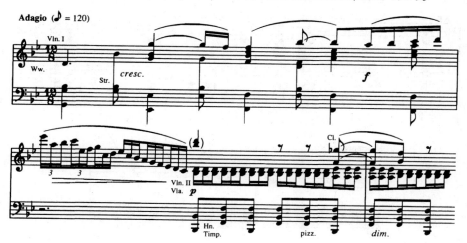

The violin run in measure 50 of example 12.32 will be muddy in many orchestras unless directed with six beats, light-staccato (see fig. 11.7). Return to 2-beat legato in the next measure.

The rhythmic figure in example 12.33 requires eight beats in a measure. In measure 4, change to a calm 4-beat, but return to subdivision on the 4th count in measure 5.

In example 12.34, as the metronome marking indicates, this music is directed with 1-beat. However, the first violin section may need your help to coordinate the thirty-second notes; subdivide the first bar (see fig. 7.3).

Although the metronome marking in example 12.35 suggests eight beats in a measure, most conductors find that continual subdivision would upset the calmness of the line. Use a sixteenth beat as preparation and subdivide for the beginning, then only when needed, as for the staccato chords. Subdivision is essential for the horn entry (in older scores this entry is printed one count too late).

Ex. 12.32. Rimsky-Korsakov, *Scheberazade,* third movement, mm. 48-51

Ex. 12.33. Verdi, *Les vêpres siciliennes,* Overture, mm. 1-6

Ex. 12.34. Prokofiev, *Peter and the Wolf,* 2 measures after #2

In example 21.13, in case the off-beat accents (mm. 79, 82, etc.) lack precision, skillful subdivision on the preceding counts may give satisfactory results.

Mozart's time signature, in example 12.36, is **C**, but 2-beat is recommended for most of the movement. Some passages fare better when conducted with subdivision, as the rhythmic figure in measures 33 and 34. Resume the *alla breve* in measure 35 for the natural flow of the music. In example 12.37, again, subdivision is not mandatory, but the use of six beats in the second and fourth measures underlines the expression of the melodic line.

Ex. 12.35. Dvořák, Symphony No. 9, "From the New World," first movement, mm. 1-5

Ex. 12.36. Mozart, Symphony No. 35, K. 385, first movement, mm. 31-36

Ex. 12.37. Puccini, *La Bohème*, Act III, seven measures after #21

The entire movement from which the passage in example 12.38 is taken requires frequent change from regular to subdivided 3-beat, partly for technical reasons, partly for the sake of expressiveness. In measure 27, the eighth note values must be indicated to secure a smooth execution of the dotted rhythm. Start to subdivide unobtrusively on the first count in that bar. In measure 29, the subdivision is hardly noticeable since the rhythm is now established. In the next bar, however, subdivision helps greatly to give intensity to the sixteenth notes.

In example 12.39, start subdividing in measure 50 (still in tempo!) and

Ex. 12.38. Brahms, Symphony No. 1, second movement, mm. 24-30

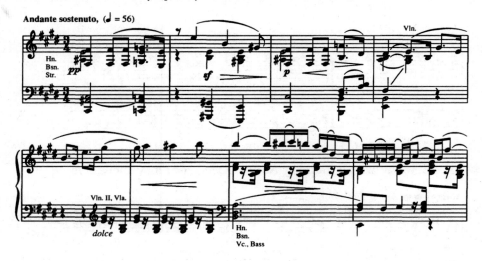

Ex. 12.39. Beethoven, Symphony No. 8, first movement, mm. 47-55

use a 3-beat in the next bar. Some conductors continue to beat three at *a tempo.* However, this **pp** section achieves its quality of lightness and suspense when directed with a small 1-beat. This entire movement demands flexibility on the part of the conductor; the interpretation is brought to life with a skillful mixture of 1-beat and the subdivided pattern *One (two), Three.*

Additional examples for the study of passages in which the conductor usually changes the number of beats for one or more measures:

Berlioz: Overture *Le Carnaval Romain, Andante sostenuto* $\frac{3}{4}$; whether and where to subdivide the 3-beat depends on interpretation. Most conductors subdivide at #3 for clear definition of the rhythm—*Allegro vivace* $\frac{6}{8}$; 1-beat is recommended for the **pp** passage with three-measure phrase groups (which passage begins two measures after No. 14), but 2-beat should be resumed at #15.

Brahms: Symphony No. 1, 4th movement; for the introduction see ex. 4.12 (including the comment above, p. 131) and ex. 14.8. Subdivision is applied to the passages with thirty second notes. Whether to return to 4-beat third measures before B is a matter of interpretation. Some conductors increase the tempo in these measures noticeably, although such a change of speed is not indicated by the composer and might make it difficult for violins and violas to execute the sextuplets correctly. Brahms's careful notation of the timpani rhythm before and after letter B seems to mark a tempo relation between the *Adagio* and the *Più Andante,* often disregarded in performances (see the composer's remark on "free artistic interpretation," quoted on p. 408). In the *Allegro non troppo,* several passages require a 2-beat, for instance at *animato* (eight measures after E), but a 4-beat must be resumed whenever necessitated by the musical context.

Dvořák: Symphony #9, 4th movement. Use 4-beat at the start, but change to 2-beat in m. 10; resume the 4-beat at #2. Similar changes are applied to the rest of this movement.

Puccini: *La Bohème,* Act I, Rodolfo's aria. In the *Andante lento,* subdivision is applied to the measure before the $\frac{2}{4}$ measure.

Strauss: *Also sprach Zarathustra;* passage beginning at #31. Subdivide whenever the rhythm needs clear definition and should be emphasized.

Tchaikovsky: Symphony No. 6, 3d movement; change to 2-beat for the concluding section. With "virtuoso" orchestras, the entire movement may be directed with 2-beat, using subdivision for passages that require rhythmic emphasis. In the 4th movement, the beat changes frequently from regular to subdivided 3-beat.

Verdi: *Aïda,* Act I, Scene 1. In Aïda's aria ("Ritorna vincitor") 2-beat is used at *Cantabile,* with subdivision for the triplet at *tremendo.* Return to 4-beat after the fermata.

Wagner: Overture to *Der fliegende Holländer.* In the *Andante,* change from 6-beat to 2-beat at *Animando un poco.*

SUBDIVIDING A SINGLE COUNT

Subdivision of single counts has been discussed as a means of directing ritardando. It may be used occasionally, even though the tempo does not change, either for secure playing or for the sake of intensity. The skillful application of this technique adds vitality and expression to the interpretation. Indeed, to use it without interrupting the flow of the musical line or upsetting the clarity of the beat is the mark of a master. However, young conductors are warned against too frequent subdivision of this kind, especially in *espressivo;* many curved gestures in a bar are hard to follow if they are not used in a completely convincing way. When accompanying instrumental or vocal soloists, it is often better to trust the players' attention than to confuse them by uncalled-for subdivision.

On the other hand, subdividing single counts can be very useful in slow passages with dotted rhythm when a small note value follows a larger one, as in example 26.10. Beginning on *Four* in measure 89, use subdivision to secure correct playing of the thirty-second notes; subdivide only on the counts on which the dotted rhythm occurs.

In example 12.40, subdivide on *Four* in measures 9 and 10; subdivision can also be applied to the first two counts in measure 11, to control the triplets. Should there be any difficulty in example 12.41 with the afterbeat of the trill in flutes and violins, a skillful subdivision of the third count in measure 118 will keep the instruments together. The gesture must be small and precise, without any delay.

Ex. 12.40. Wagner, *Faust* Overture, mm. 8-12

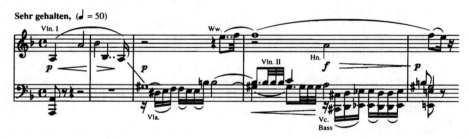

Ex. 12.41. Mendelssohn, *A Midsummer Night's Dream,* Nocturne, mm. 117-19

In example 12.42, subdivision on *Two* in the fifth measure leads the violins (C and D flat played with two up-bows!) to indicate the tender expression of the phrase.

The triplet in the second measure of example 12.43 is subdivided (composer's note: "Die Triole ausschlagen"). It is advisable to subdivide also on the third count for the accented D sharp. The singers enter on the third triplet note, which should be conducted as an accented upbeat for the *Luftpause* (see ex. 19.75).

Ex. 12.42. Puccini, *La Bohème,* Act I, "Che gelida manina," seven measures before #31

Ex. 12.43. Mahler, Symphony No. 8, first movement, two measures before #38

CHAPTER 13

5-Time, 7-Time, and Other Asymmetric Time Patterns

There are two ways of beating these odd counts. If the tempo is not too fast, each count receives one beat. When the tempo is so rapid that this cannot be done distinctly, several counts are included in one gesture. The techniques to be applied depend on the rhythmic structure of the music.

5-TIME WITH BEATS ON EACH COUNT

Several patterns may be used, depending on the way the groups of notes fall within the bar. A $\frac{5}{4}$ signature may stand for continual alternation of $\frac{2}{4}$ and $\frac{3}{4}$, in which case figure 13.1a or 13.1c is applicable (the figures indicate staccato; other types of gestures can easily be deduced from them). Some conductors actually alternate 2-beat and 3-beat in the same size, but the 5-beat pattern shown in figure 13.1a has this advantage: By keeping the second group (*Three, Four, Five*) smaller and toward the top of the field of beating, the downbeat on *One* stands out, and the orchestra has a definite point of orientation.

For example 13.1, apply figure 13.1a. The entire third movement of the symphony follows this beat. However, once the rhythm is established, beats can be lightened or skipped (except the downbeat) to shape the expressive undulation of the melodic line.

The notation in example 13.2 indicates $\frac{3}{4}$ + $\frac{2}{4}$; apply figure 13.1b or 13.1d. In example 13.3, no division of the 5-group is apparent. The pattern of figure 13.1c ($\frac{4}{4}$ + $\frac{1}{4}$) is the best because it is close to the 4-beat of the preceding and following bars. In the third measure of example 13.4, the rapid pace necessitates a modification of the 3 + 2 pattern. The first third counts are directed with a subdivided 1-beat, while *Four* and *Five* are done with a small

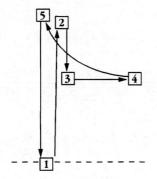

Fig. 13.1a. 5-time: 2 + 3

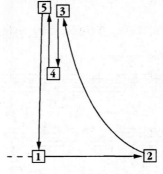

Fig. 13.1b. 5-time: 3 + 2

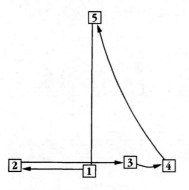

Fig. 13.1c. 5-time: 4 + 1
(also alternate 2 + 3)

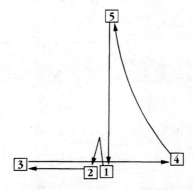

Fig. 13.1d. 5-time: alternate 3 + 2

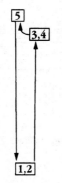

Fig. 13.1e. 5-time: $\frac{2}{8} + \frac{3}{8}$

Fig. 13.1f. 5-time: alternate $\frac{2}{8} + \frac{3}{8}$

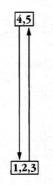

Fig. 13.1g. 5-time: $\frac{3}{8} + \frac{2}{8}$

Fig. 13.1h. 5-time: alternate $\frac{3}{8} + \frac{2}{8}$

Ex. 13.1.   Tchaikovsky, Symphony No. 6, second movement, mm. 1-4

Ex. 13.2.   Barber, *Medea's Meditation and Dance of Vengeance,* at #32

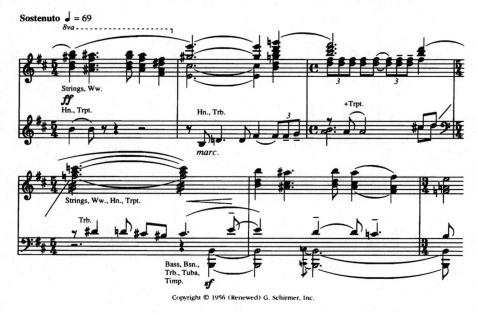

Ex. 13.3.   Shostakovich, Symphony No. 5, fourth movement, two measures before #106

Ex. 13.4. Wagner, *Tristan und Isolde*, Act III, Scene 2, mm. 30-33

2-beat at the top of the field of beating. (A subdivided 1-beat also applies to the first and second measures; see ex. 22.10.)

Additional examples for the study of the 5-beat patterns:

2 + 3 Beats

Barber: *Second Essay for Orchestra*, 3d measure after #25

Bartók: *Music for Strings, Percussion, and Celesta,* 3d movement, mm. bars 54–58

Britten: *War Requiem*, Agnus Dei, $\frac{5}{16}$, $\eighthnote$ = 80 (2 + 3 alternating with 3 + 2)

Griffes: *The White Peacock,* passage starting at m. 7 (alternating patterns; apply fig. 13.1a, 13.1b, or 13.1c according to the rhythmic structure)

Mahler: Symphony No. 8, 1st movement, #23 to #28

Mussorgsky-Ravel: *Pictures at an Exhibition,* all Promenade passages

Rimsky-Korsakov: Overture, *Russian Easter,* beginning, $\frac{5}{2}$ with subdivision, $\halfnote$ = 84 (for each bar, combine figs. 11.2, 11.3, and 11.6 with relatively small gestures except for a fairly large downbeat)

3 + 2 Beats

Bartók: *The Miraculous Mandarin,* passage beginning at #26 (alternating with 2 + 3)

Berg: *Lulu* Suite, Variations, Variation 3

Copland: Orchestral Variations, Variations 4 and 6

Ravel: *Daphnis et Chloé,* Suite No. 2, passages beginning at #194 and #198

Respighi: *Pini di Roma,* Part 2, m. 13; also at *Ancora più mosso* (here the pattern 4 + 1 can be applied)

Strauss: *Salome,* passage starting at #15

Strauss: *Salome,* "Salome's Dance," from F to K

Stravinsky: *Agon, Four Duos,* beginning with m. 521

4 + 1 Beats

Bartók: *The Miraculous Mandarin,* 2 measures before #31
Mahler: Symphony No. 7, 2d movement, one measure before #72
Shostakovitch: Symphony No. 1, 2nd movement, m. 2

5-TIME WITH ONE, TWO, OR THREE BEATS IN A MEASURE

When the tempo is too fast to beat clearly and easily on each count, fewer beats are used in a measure. In figure 13.1e there are three beats: the first includes *One* and *Two,* the second *Three* and *Four,* and the third, with a small turn of the wrist, indicates *Five,* which has a preparatory quality. There are only two beats in figures 13.1f and 13.1g, resulting in a lopsided pattern. Which pattern to use depends on the music's rhythm and, to a certain extent, upon what turns out to be the most practical gesture. Using a wrist motion on *Three,* you may prefer figure 13.1h for bars in which *Four* is accented. Direct the fourth measure in example 13.5 according to figure 13.1e, since the feeling is $\frac{2}{4} + \frac{1}{8}$. In example 13.6, the $\frac{5}{8}$ rhythm in the fourth through the seventh measures seems to conform to figure 13.1e or 13.1f.

For example 13.7 (the second, third, and fifth measures), figures 13.1f or 13.1g could be used; if the pattern 13.1f is used, the *ff* figure ♪♫ is felt as a syncopation, while with the pattern 13.1g the upbeat coincides with the attack of that figure (see below, pp. 163 and 165 and p. 285).

If the music moves very quickly, it becomes necessary to use 1-beat. This requires a definite feeling on the part of the conductor for the five small note

Ex. 13.5. Walton, Viola Concerto, second movement, at #31

Ex. 13.6. Barber, *Second Essay for Orchestra,* seven measures before #6

Ex. 13.7. Stravinsky, *Le Sacre du Printemps,* Part II, one measure before #120

values within each beat. The following exercises are recommended for developing a secure feeling for five notes played on one beat.

(1) Set the metronome at 50. Count aloud, starting with *One* for each tick, and repeat several times. Then double the count, counting *One, Two* on every tick. Continue to increase the count one at a time, up to five counts for each tick. The sequence of counts within each tick must be kept smooth and continuous. In this way you learn to alter the rhythmic unit while the beat for the measure remains fixed.

(2) For the next exercise set the metronome at 208. Start with two ticks per beat, then use three and four. With five ticks per beat the metronome is not fast enough for a convenient 1-beat. Dispense with the metronome and increase the tempo until 1-beat becomes convenient in 5-time.

Examples 13.8a–b serve the practice of (1) maintaining a steady beat in spite of changing units or (2) adjusting the beat to an even flow of constant units.

The $\frac{5}{8}$ measures in example 13.9 are conducted with 1-beat (see p. 285–86). Beginning with the second bar in example 13.10, the sixteenth note unit ($\flat$ = 252), which is derived from the metronome marking $\flat$ = 126, remains constant. The preparation after the fermata is timed as a whole measure ($\frac{2}{16}$). The $\frac{2}{8}$ measures are directed with a regular 2-beat, but the $\frac{5}{16}$ measure requires a lopsided beat (fig. 13.1g). The downbeat in the twelfth bar (timpani) must be very incisive for the syncopated tutti *ff* entry.

Ex. 13.8.   Exercises

Ex. 13.9.   Stravinsky, *Petrouchka* (1911), 1er Tableau, at #7

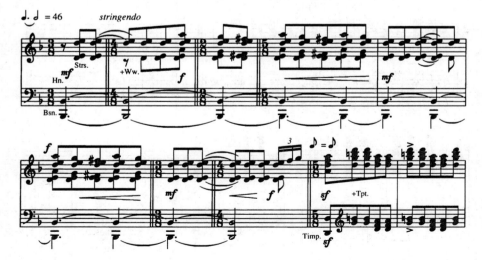

Ex. 13.9. *Continued*

Ex. 13.10. Stravinsky, *Le Sacre du Printemps,* II, 1 measure before #142

Additional examples for the study of 5-time with one, two, or three beats in a measure:

1-Beat

Bartók: *Music for Strings, Percussion, and Celesta,* 2d movement, mm. 260–290 (there may be a choice between 1-beat and lopsided 2-beat; most of the time a 1-beat is more practical)

Britten: *War Requiem,* "Requiem Aeternam" (Each quarter beat is a quintuplet within slow $\frac{4}{4}$ time, $\quarternote$ = 42–46. The players must maintain an even distribution of five units on each count with the pattern | 𝄾♪ 𝅘𝅥𝅮♪ 𝅘𝅥𝅮♪ 𝅘𝅥𝅮𝅘𝅥𝅮 | 𝅘𝅥𝅭 .

Stravinsky: Variations, mm. 11, 68, 75, 76 ($\frac{5}{16}$).

Lopsided 2-Beat: 2 + 3 (fig. 13.f)

Barber: *Medea's Meditation and Dance of Vengeance,* starting at #20
Bartók: *Dance* Suite, 2d and 3d movements (also 3 + 2)
Copland: *Music for the Theatre,* No. 2, "Dance"
Stravinsky: Variations, mm. 41–43, 66

3 + 2 (fig. 13.1g)

Bartók: Concerto for Orchestra, 4th movement (also 2 + 3)
Copland: *Appalachian Spring,* between #31 and #33
Prokofiev: Violin Concerto No. 2, 3d movement, at #77
Stravinsky: *Le Sacre du Printemps,* numerous places (also 2 + 3)

Lopsided 3-Beat

Stravinsky: *Dumbarton Oaks* Concerto, 3d movement, at #57 and after #58 (fig. 13.1e)
Stravinsky: *Variations,* m. 7, ♪ = 160 in $\frac{5}{8}$ (fig. 13.1h)

7-TIME WITH BEATS ON EACH COUNT

Figures 13.2a–h show different methods of execution depending on the grouping within the measure. Figure 13.2a combines 4-beat with 3-beat. In figure 13.2b the 3-beat precedes the 4-beat. Figures 13.2c–d are used for combinations of 2-beat and 3-beat patterns.

For example 13.11, apply figure 13.2a. For example 13.12, apply figure 13.2b. In example 13.13, the composer has indicated the grouping by two alternating patterns, 3 + 2 + 2 and 2 + 2 + 3. Use figures 13.2c and 13.2d.

Ex. 13.11.   Hindemith, Concerto for Orchestra, fourth movement, mm. 1-2

Hindemith CONCERTO FOR ORCHESTRA
Copyright 1925 B. Schott's Soehne, Mainz   Copyright Renewed
Used by permission of European American Music Distributors Corporation,
sole U.S. and Canadian agent for B. Schott's Soehne

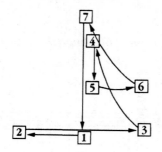

Fig. 13.2a. 7-time: 4 + 3

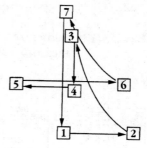

Fig. 13.2b. 7-time: 3 + 4

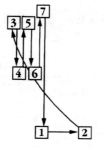

Fig. 13.2c. 7-time: 3 + 2 + 2

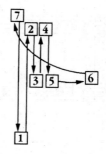

Fig. 13.2d. 7-time: 2 + 2 + 3

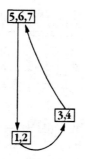

Fig. 13.2e. 7-time: $\frac{2}{8} + \frac{2}{8} + \frac{3}{8}$

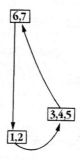

Fig. 13.2f. 7-time: $\frac{2}{8} + \frac{3}{8} + \frac{2}{8}$

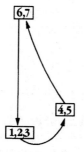

Fig. 13.2g. 7-time: $\frac{3}{8} + \frac{2}{8} + \frac{2}{8}$

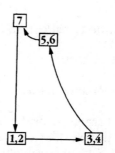

Fig. 13.2h. 7-time: $\frac{3}{4} + \frac{1}{8}$

Ex. 13.12. Barber, *Medea's Meditation and Dance of Vengeance,* two measures before #12

Ex. 13.13. Stravinsky, *L'Oiseau de feu,* Suite (1919), Finale, at #17

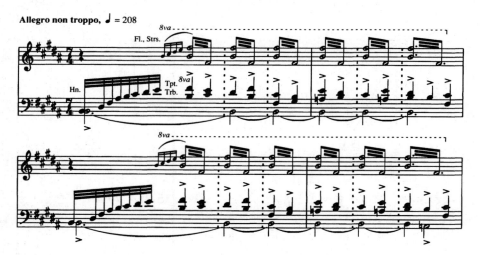

Additional examples for the study of the 7-beat patterns:

4 + 3 Beats

Barber: *Medea's Meditation and Dance of Vengeance,* passage before #13

Barber: *Second Essay for Orchestra,* eleventh measure after #21

Britten: *War Requiem,* "Dies Irae," at #17 (in spite of the rapid pace, ♩ = 160, use figure 13.2a at least for the start; once the rhythm is firmly established, figure 13.2e may be applied)

Delius: *A Song of Summer,* the first fifteen measures

Griffes: *The White Peacock,* 2 measures before A

Mussorgsky-Ravel: *Pictures at an Exhibition,* "Promenade" before No. 5 ("Ballet of the chicks in their shells")

3 + 4 Beats

Barber: *Medea's Meditation and Dance of Vengeance,* at #12

Berg: *Lulu* Suite, Variationen, Variation No. 4 (3 + 4 and 4 + 3 alternate)

Stravinsky: *Le Sacre du Printemps,* 2d movement, second measure after #106 (the 3 + 4 pattern is recommended because of the **sf** in the horns)

7-TIME WITH THREE OR FOUR BEATS IN A MEASURE

Figures 13.2e—h show various patterns. Their application is guided by considerations similar to the ones discussed in connection with 5-time patterns. The fourth bar of example 13.7 is best handled with figure 13.2e. For the second and fifth measures of example 13.14, use figure 13.2e; for the sixth measure use figure 13.2f. The fourth measure ($\frac{5}{8}$) is best done with figure 13.1f.

In example 13.15, although the metronome refers to eighth notes, the second measure is best directed with a $\frac{2}{8} + \frac{2}{8} + \frac{3}{8}$ pattern. Use figure 13.2e at the speed of $\downarrow$ = 80. Figure 13.2h is an alternate.

Ex. 13.14. Stravinsky, *L'Histoire du soldat,* Little Concert, one measure before #7

Ex. 13.15. Bartók, *The Miraculous Mandarin,* four measures after #31

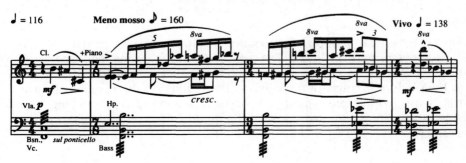

Additional examples for the study of 7-time with 3 or 4 beats in a measure:

2 + 2 + 3 (fig. 13.2e)

Bartók: *Dance* Suite, 2d movement, passage between #17 and #18 (changing patterns)

Bartók: *Music for Strings, Percussion, and Celesta,* 1st movement (the tempo allows for marking all the counts in the several $\frac{7}{8}$ bars; use figs. 13.2e and 13.2g for subdivision)

Copland: *Orchestral Variations,* Variation 15

Stravinsky: *Agon,* mm. 452–462 (sequence of $\frac{6}{16}$, $\frac{5}{16}$, and $\frac{7}{16}$)

Stravinsky: Variations, m. 95 ($\frac{7}{16}$, $\quarternote = 160$)

2 + 3 + 2 (fig. 13.2f)

Bartók: Concerto for Orchestra, 4th movement, mm. 47 and 55

Prokofiev: Violin Concerto No. 2, 3d movement, at #52

3 + 2 + 2 (fig. 13.2g)

Bartók: Concerto for Orchestra, 4th movement, m. 59

Bartók: Divertimento for String Orchestra, 1st movement, m. 30

Dallapiccola: Variazioni, Variation No. 6, mm. 5 and 10 (mm. 2 and 7 are done with figure 13.2e)

2 + 2 + 2 + 1 ($\frac{3}{4}$ + $\frac{1}{8}$, fig. 13.2h)

Dallapiccola: Variazioni, Variation 8, m. 33

Stravinsky: *Dumbarton Oaks* Concerto, 3d movement, three measures after #55 (as indicated by the composer)

VARIOUS ASYMMETRIC TIME PATTERNS

Asymmetrical grouping of counts within a measure is part of the contemporary musical idiom. For the conductor, it means that time signatures now refer to a greater variety of beat patterns than found in scores written before the turn of the century. Depending on the number of rhythmic units, beats are shortened or lengthened, thus producing lopsided conducting patterns, similar to the figures that were discussed in this chapter.

8-TIME WITH LOPSIDED 3-BEAT

In 8-time, three asymmetrical patterns are possible: 3 + 3 + 2; 2 + 3 + 3; or 3 + 2 + 3. Practice these three forms of a lopsided 3-beat, first by counting the units. When you have gained a firm feeling for the rhythm, dispense with counting.

In example 13.16, use 3 + 3 + 2; the metronome speed (equivalent to ♪ = ca. 200) precludes subdivision. A graceful yet clear beat is needed to bring out the lilt of the music. If a small string group is available, the first movement of Bartók's Divertimento should be conducted in class.

Additional examples:

Bartók: *Dance Suite,* 4th movement
Bartók: *Music for Strings, Percussion, and Celesta,* 1st movement
Copland: *Orchestral Variations,* Variation 16
Copland: Symphony No. 1, passages beginning at #18 and #27
Dallapiccola: Variazioni, Variation #4
Stravinsky: *Agon,* "Gailliarde," $\frac{8}{4}$

9-TIME WITH LOPSIDED 4-BEAT

Four patterns are possible: 3 + 2 + 2 + 2; 2 + 3 + 2 + 2; 2 + 2 + 3 + 2; or 2 + 2 + 2 + 3. Two of them are shown in examples 13.17 and 13.18. In example 13.17, the pattern for measure 176 is 2 + 3 + 2 + 2, which means that the second beat is extended to $\frac{3}{8}$. Subdivide the preceding *alla breve* and conduct the $\frac{9}{8}$ measure with a lopsided 4-beat at ♩ = ca. 138. In example 13.18, the extended beat falls on *Four:* 2 + 2 + 2 + 3.

In the context of the passage in example 13.7, the $\frac{9}{8}$ measure can be directed either with a regular 3-beat or with a lopsided 4-beat (2 + 2 + 2 + 3). In the first instance, each of the three strokes must conform to ♩ · = 96, the equivalent of the composer's marking ♪♩ = 144.

In the first movement of Britten's *Spring* Symphony ("The Driving Boy," four bars before #16), the composer requests that measures with the time signature $\frac{9}{8}$ be conducted with 4-beat, 2 + 2 + 2 + 3.

Ex. 13.16. Bartok, Divertimento for Strings, first movement, mm. 25-26

Ex. 13.17. Rochberg, Symphony No. 2, mm. 175-178

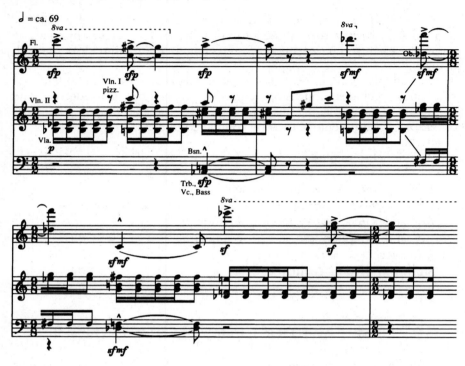

Ex. 13.18. Rochberg, Symphony No. 2, m. 753

10-TIME WITH LOPSIDED 4-BEAT

Out of six possible patterns in 10-time, four are found in the first movement of Bartók's *Music for Strings, Percussion, and Celesta:* 3 + 3 + 2 + 2; 3 + 2 + 3 + 2; 3 + 2 + 2 + 3; and 2 + 2 + 3 + 3.

An extended passage based on the pattern 3 + 3 + 2 + 2 occurs in Roussel's *Bacchus et Ariane,* Suite #2, beginning four measures before # 111.

11-TIME

The best-known and, technically speaking, simplest example of 11-time is the $\frac{11}{4}$ measure that introduces the section "Glorification de l'elue" in Stravinsky's *Le Sacre du Printemps* (#104). The tempo allows a stroke on each of the eleven counts, using any beat pattern that suits the conductor.

The $\frac{11}{8}$ measure in Bartok's *Music for Strings, Percussion, and Celesta* (seven bars before the end of the first movement) calls for a 4-beat, 3 + 3 + 3 + 2. It is followed by an $\frac{8}{8}$ measure with the 3-beat pattern 3 + 3 + 2.

In Dallapiccola's Variazioni, there occurs an $\frac{11}{16}$ measure occurs (Var. 1) that requires a lopsided 5-beat with an extended *One* at the speed of $\flat = 84$: $\frac{3}{16} + \frac{4}{8}$.

13-TIME

The second movement of Janáček's Sinfonietta contains several measures with the time signature $\frac{13}{8}$. A 6-beat is used with the pattern 2 + 2 + 2 + 2 + 2 + 3. Asymmetrical rhythms of this kind present no problem to a conductor who has learned to apply precise gestures to a rapid succession of small units, no matter whether each beat stands for two or three constant units.

PART TWO

APPLICATIONS

CHAPTER *14*

Ritardando and Accelerando

Just as gradual changes in dynamics require well-controlled gestures, so do gradations in the speed of music. In order to obtain the desired results in speeding up and slowing down, your mind must be ahead of your hand. The way you *lead into* the count on which the change starts should prepare the players. If you do not think of the change until you are on the count, it will be sudden and awkward instead of gradual and smooth. However, this preparation must not start the change prematurely; it only warns the players that one is coming. It is helpful to use a slightly larger beat before a ritardando and a slightly smaller beat before an accelerando.

A quick change in the size of the beat is also very effective for indicating *a tempo*. For *a tempo* after ritardando, use a smaller beat; after accelerando, use a larger beat.

Once a tempo change has been started, it gains a certain momentum of its own, and you must be careful not to cause an exaggeration by indicating too much on the subsequent beats. Know exactly how fast or how slow you want to be when the change is completed, and you will achieve a smooth and continuous gradation.

Practice ritardando and accelerando, with return to tempo on all counts and in different rhythms. Have the pianist improvise simple chords while following your beat. Practice the changes in varying degrees from *poco ritard.* to *molto ritard.* and similarly with accelerando. The following should be remembered:

4-beat

To start a ritard on the	wait slightly before moving
1st beat	to the left
2d beat	to the right
3d beat	to the left
4th beat	up

3-beat

To start a ritard on the	wait slightly before moving
1st beat	to the right
2d beat	to the left
3d beat	up

2-beat

1st beat	up rebound
2d beat	up

1-beat

Beat	up

By practicing ritardando and accelerando according to these suggestions, you avoid the spasmodic gestures that mar the conducting of inexperienced leaders and disturb the security of the players. The following suggestions should be helpful.

In example 14.1: (1) No preparation is required for *poco rit.* within an entire bar. (2) Since you have only two beats for the *ritard.*, prepare it. (3) Prepare; subdivide for eighth notes. (4) Ritard very gradually. (5) Use a small,

Ex. 14.1. Exercise

Ex. 14.2. Exercise

Ex. 14.3. Exercise

1)		poco rit.	
2)			molto rit.
3)		accel.	rit.
4)	rit.		a tempo
5)		molto rit.	a tempo

Ex. 14.4. Exercise

1)	accelerando	rit.	a tempo	rit.
2)		molto rit.	animando	poco rit.	molto rit.	a tempo
3)			molto rit.	animando	poco rit.

Ex. 14.5. Exercise

1)		animando	rallent.
2)		molto rit.	a tempo
3)	rit.		accel.
4)	accel.		a tempo

exact beat on *Three* in measure 2 (*a tempo*). In example 14.2: (5) Be sure to return to the exact tempo—no faster! In example 14.3: (5) The last two chords are *a tempo*; wait on *One* in measure 4, then beat the eighth rest and the two chords strictly in time.

Only by painstakingly following the markings in examples 14.4 and 14.5 can you get the full benefit of these exercises. In example 14.6, subdivide in measure 46; *lento* is twice as slow as the first tempo. In measure 47 a beat on Two is superfluous; cut off with a small gesture to the right (see p. 196).

In example 14.7, observe the gradual ritard. in the second through the fifth measures, then *a tempo* immediately in the sixth measure. For the *meno* in the eighth, stop the beat on *One* and use the second beat to prepare *Three* in the new tempo.

Ex. 14.6. Nicolai, *The Merry Wives of Windsor,* Overture, mm. 44-50

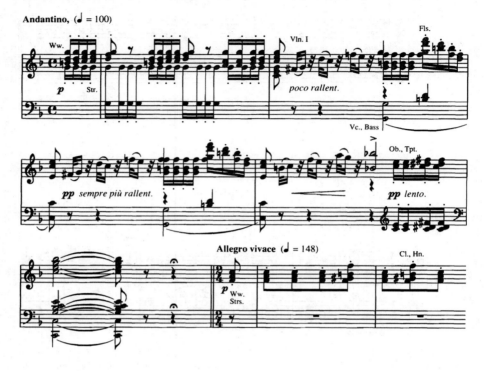

Ex. 14.7. Dvořák, Symphony No. 9, "From the New World," fourth movement, twenty-two measures after #12

In example 14.8, conduct two bars strictly in tempo (conductors who prefer a tempo slower than ♩ = 50 subdivide this passage). There should be a well-planned gradual stringendo with complete stop on the **ff**, then subdivide *One* (m. 12), using the rest for an eighth note preparation in the original tempo.

Despite the large orchestration in example 15.2, a heavy and large beat is not required. On the contrary, a small energetic beat for *animando* keeps the brass instruments well under control. Do not do much for the *rit.* or the orchestra will overdo it. In example 14.9, start subdividing in the sixth measure, using the rest in the next measure for preparation, as in example 14.8.

Ex. 14.8. Brahms, Symphony No. 1, fourth movement, mm. 6-13

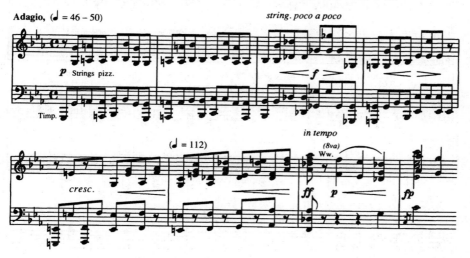

Ex. 14.9. Bizet, *Carmen,* Act I, No. 7, final fourteen measures

You get the full advantage of example 14.10 by following a singer in his individual rendering of Pagliaccio's lament. Subdivide in measures 25–9. In this case, subdivision is used to control the sustained chords of the accompaniment, but the subdivisions should be unobtrusive.

For example 14.11, use 2-beat, full-staccato. For the first bar, the gesture must not be too large, to allow for larger beats in the second and third bars in order to lead the ritard. Subdivide in the fourth bar, with incisive beats on the third and fourth quarters for slowing down the eighth notes. Return to 2-beat

Ex. 14.10. Leoncavallo, *Pagliacci,* Act I, "Vesti la giubba," mm. 17-34

Ex. 14.11. Roussel, Suite in F, five measures after #6

Ex. 14.12. Tchaikovsky, Serenade for Strings, second movement, mm. 16-36

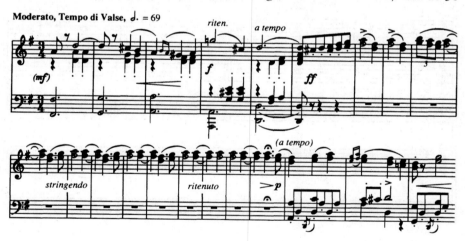

(*Tempo I*) with a vigorous downbeat. In example 14.12, subdivide for the first *ritenuto.* After the *stringendo* use a larger beat to start *ritenuto* (the composer undoubtedly meant *rallentando*) and slow down, first by subdividing, then changing to a 3-beat (see p. 234).

The *accelerando* in the third measure of example 14.13 is rather marked. A clear beat on *Two* in the sixth measure brings the basses in with the harp, which plays very slowly. The notes marked *rubando* are quite fast; wait on *Six,* then give an eighth note preparation, as though the 6th count were subdivided.

Ex. 14.13. Puccini, *Tosca,* Act III, Six measures before #11

Additional examples for the study of ritardando and accelerando

4-Beat

Barber: Overture to *The School for Scandal,* ninth measure after F
Brahms: Variations on a Theme by Haydn, nine measure from the end
Gershwin: *Rhapsody in Blue,* four measures before #12 (For this type
  of preparation, see Ex. 4.4)
Prokofiev: *Peter and the Wolf,* passage starting at #54
Prokofiev: Symphony No. 5, 2d movement, #50 to #51
Tchaikovsky: *1812* Overture, *poco a poco rallentando* (m. 340)

3-Beat

Bizet: *Carmen,* Act II, No. 12, ("Gypsy Song")

Brahms: Symphony No. 2, 1st movement, passage starting fifteen measures after M

Tchaikovsky: Symphony No. 4, 1st movement, *Ritardando,* fourth measure after E

2-Beat

Bartók: *Dance* Suite, 2d movement, mm. 23, 26, 59

Berlioz: *Symphonie fantastique,* 1st movement, *Allegro agitato e appasionato assai*

Copland: *Tender Land* Suite, 1st movement

Dvořák: Slavonic Dance in A-flat Major Op. 46, No. 3

Liszt: *Les Préludes,* passage starting at E

Mendelssohn: Overture to *A Midsummer Night's Dream,* end of the development section

1-Beat

Bartók: Concerto for Orchestra, 1st movement, mm. 470–88, with subdivision ($\frac{3}{8}$ and $\frac{4}{8}$) in mm. 474 and 475 (see Appendix A, No. 9)

Beethoven: Symphony No. 9, 2d movement, eight measures before *Presto* (see p. 398)

Dukas: *L'Apprenti sorcier, Vif* $\frac{3}{8}$, several passages

Mahler: Symphony No. 1, end of 2d movement

Mahler: Symphony No. 6, 2d movement, #84 to #85

Sibelius: Symphony No. 5, 1st movement, beginning *Allegro moderato* after N; tempo increases from ♪• = 80 to ♪• = 138

TEMPO TRANSITIONS BY CHANGING THE NUMBER OF BEATS IN A MEASURE

When a ritardando or accelerando is not temporary—that is to say, when it leads to a slower or faster section—it is often necessary to change the number of beats in a bar. If you are using 2-beat, a slower section may require 4-beat or 6-beat, whereas for a faster section 1-beat may be useful. Frequently, subdivision serves as an intermediate step. The conductor, however, must be sure that a change of the number of beats in a measure is clearly understood by the players—even when it is marked in the parts, but especially when it is not.

First indicate the change of tempo by slowing down or speeding up for a few counts, without changing the number of beats; then switch to the new rhythmic pattern.

Practice the tempo transitions in example 14.14. (1) A smooth transition can be achieved by emphasizing *One* and *Three* in the third measure, changing to subdivision in the fourth or fifth measure. *Two* and *Four* become weaker and almost disappear, which makes for a smooth transition to the 2-beat in measure 6 (for this change of beat, $\frac{4}{4}$ to ₵, fig. 11.3 is best suited). (2) Start subdividing in measure 5 to lead easily into $\frac{4}{4}$. Figure 11.2 or 11.3 will work. (3) The changes are more sudden and require a more concentrated beat.

Practice similarly the changes of tempo in example 14.15: (1): For the *accelerando* first weaken *Two,* then *Three,* until they disappear. (2) *Three* reappears first in the *ritardando,* then *Two.*

In example 14.16, subdivide in the third measure and change to 2-beat.

Ex. 14.14. Exercises

Ex. 14.15. Exercises

Ex. 14.16. Verdi, *Aïda,* Act I, No. 3, three measures after U

Ex. 14.16. *Continued*

In example 14.17, you have nine bars for accelerando with change from 2-beat to 1-beat. Beat Two with less and less emphasis until it disappears altogether, but without losing control over the rhythm, and arrive at *Presto* without any last-second adjustment.

Do not subdivide in example 14.18 until the fourth measure; subdivision in the third measure would exaggerate the *ritardando*.

Ex. 14.17. Beethoven, Symphony No. 5, fourth movement, mm. 350-65

Additional examples for the study of tempo transitions that involve a change of the number of beats in a measure:

Changing from 4-Beat to 2-Beat

Grieg: *Peer Gynt* Suite No. 1, 4th movement
Liszt: Piano Concerto No. 1, 1st movement (use 2-beat at *animato* after B)

Ex. 14.18. Offenbach, *Orphée aux enfers*, Overture, mm. 147-52

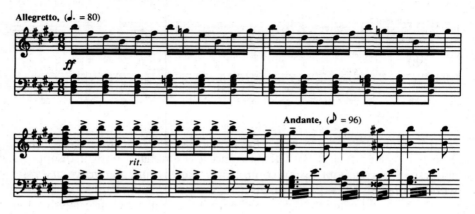

Strauss: *Also sprach Zarathustra*, after #11 and after #17
Strauss: *Tod und Verklärung*, at F (or two measures earlier)

Changing from 2-Beat to 4-Beat

Schoenberg: *Kammersymphonie*, mm. 79–84
Tchaikovsky: *Romeo and Juliet*, after the 2-beat at *Allegro* (five measures after C) return to 4-beat at *Molto meno mosso*

Changing from 3-Beat to 1-Beat

Strauss: *Also sprach Zarathustra*, at #26 (*Etwas zurückhaltend* requires a subdivided 3-beat)
Stravinsky: *L'Oiseau de feu* (Suite), "Danse infernale," at #29 or earlier

Changing from 1-Beat to 3-Beat

Barber: *Essay for Orchestra*, sixth measure after #21
Puccini: *Madama Butterfly*, Act II, ten measures after #35 and five measures after #36
Strauss, Johann: *Emperor* Waltz, Coda, several measures before *Tempo di Valse*

Changing from 2-Beat to 1-Beat

Falla: *El Sombrero des tres picos*, Suite No. 2, 2d movement, at #10
Tchaikovsky: *Capriccio Italien*, the 1-beat begins at *Presto* before F; the preceding 2-beat (*stringendo molto*) follows a 6-beat

Changing from 1-Beat to 2-Beat

Bartók: *Dance Suite*, Finale, mm. 100–110
Sibelius: Violin Concerto, 1st movement; after the 1-beat (which

usually begins fifteen measures before #11), return to 2-beat four measures before #11 in preparation for the *Allegro molto vivace,* whose attack needs an incisive upbeat to coordinate the solo violin with the orchestra.

RITENUTO

A special technique is used for a sudden, marked slowing down of the tempo. In ritenuto there is no gradual change; one beat is in tempo and the very next is much slower. The beat used for this is in effect a wait on the count without stopping the motion.

This technique is especially useful in accompaniment, where the more or less unpredictable vacillations on the part of the soloist might force the conductor to wait on a certain count. A sudden complete stop would confuse the players, but the flexible ritenuto beat keeps the orchestra under control.

The heavy black line in figure 14.1 indicates an extremely slow and very intense movement, as though the baton were being drawn through a strongly resisting substance. The length of time you can keep moving the baton while still on the count will surprise you. The point where the heavy line changes back to the medium line (normal speed) must be distinct in the beat, for the release at this point leads to the next count. Practice first on all counts without music.

The solo part in example 14.19 may be either sung or played. First practice with the conductor indicating the ritenuto and a tempo. Then have the soloist take liberties in rhythm and lead the accompaniment only.

Ex. 14.19. Exercise

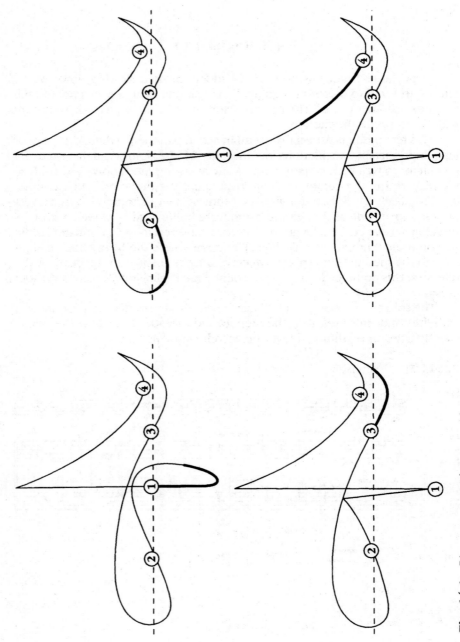

Fig. 14.1.   Ritenuto on each count, 4-beat

CHAPTER *15*

The Marcato Pattern

*The marcato beat is a heavy motion with a stop on each
count. It is forceful, sometimes aggressive in character, and
medium to large in size. The gestures connecting the counts
are slower than in staccato; they are either straight or
curved.*

There are two types of marcato, both done with a strong and vigorous gesture.
For the first type, which uses straight lines to connect the counts, apply figure
2.1. Since marcato is used only in loud dynamics (*mf* to *ff*), the size will have
to be about three times that of the light-staccato pattern. Also, remember that
you must not move too quickly. The beat 4 is at the top of the field of beating,
characteristic of this type of marcato. To gain the impetus needed for a start on
the first count, use the accented upbeat of figure 2.5. Start on the other counts
with a full-staccato preliminary beat.

Figures 5.5 and 6.7 are applied in a similar manner for marcato in 3-beat
and in 2-beat. Figure 15.1 shows the execution of 1-beat marcato. It is
characterized by an intense holding on 1 and a quick but energetic up–down
motion that gives the impetus for the next marcato attack.

Example 15.1 is a good example for practicing marcato with straight lines.
Conduct the entire "Hallelujah." Try to find a few instrumentalists to assist the
class, which sings the chorus. Conduct legato, beginning with the words "The
kingdom of this world"—seven and one-half measures in all.

The marcato with curved lines (the second type of marcato) is used for
rather slow music of passionate intensity and strong rhythm. It combines the
expressiveness of the legato beat with the rhythmical decisiveness of the
staccato. In 4-beat, apply figure 3.1 or 3.3, making a full stop on each count.
Apply figures 5.2, 6.3, and 7.3 for this type of marcato in 3-beat, 2-beat, and
1-beat, respectively.

In example 15.2, the curved-line marcato beat expresses the sweep of the
melody and at the same time maintains a steady rhythm for the sixteenth notes
(see p. 175).

In example 15.3 there is a gradual intensification from neutral-legato

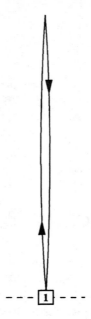

Fig. 15.1. 1-beat; marcato

Ex. 15.1. Handel, *Messiah,* "Hallelujah" Chorus, mm. 1-4

Ex. 15.2. Tchaikovsky, Symphony No. 5, second movement, mm. 142-45

Ex. 15.2. *Continued*

Ex. 15.3. Verdi, *Rigoletto,* Act I, Preludio, mm. 11-19

(**pp**) to marcato (**ff**). Start with a fairly small gesture; gradually increase both the size and the accentuation of each beat until measure 15. Use the straight-line marcato. Do not wait for the sixteenth notes in the brass; only a strict beat precludes dragging.

Example 15.4 is similar to example 15.2 but in 3-beat. The advantage of marcato in such cases over *espressivo* (even with clicking) is that it keeps the heavy brasses from dragging, as they are otherwise likely to do. In example 15.5 the heavy brass chords and syncopated strings demand the marcato (see p. 115).

In each of the first five measures of example 6.12 the downbeats are best directed with marcato gestures. In these measures *Two* serves as preparation; use the same preparatory beat as you would in staccato. With the entrance of the woodwinds, the beat changes to full-staccato.

Though the time signature is $\frac{4}{4}$, the music in example 15.6 lends itself to *alla breve* (2-beat). Experiment by beating legato; try it again staccato. You will not feel comfortable either way, and only the marcato beat will give you firm control.

Conduct example 15.7 with 1-beat. The heavy chords starting with the measure 196 require a strong marcato beat. In measures 210–14, decrease not only the size but the heaviness of the beat until you reach **p** neutral-legato. The 1-beat marcato used in example 15.8 should have a very lively connecting motion.

Ex. 15.4. Flotow, *Martha,* Overture, mm. 336-41

Ex. 15.5. Sibelius, *Finlandia,* at O.

Ex. 15.6. Mendelssohn, *A Midsummer Night's Dream,* Wedding March, mm. 112-19

Ex. 15.7. Beethoven, Symphony No. 5, first movement, mm. 195-222

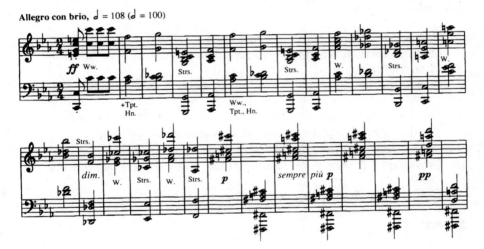

Additional examples for the study of the marcato pattern:

4-Beat

Bach: "Brandenburg" Concerto No. 1, 1st movement
Liszt: *Les Préludes, Andante maestoso* **12/8**
Shostakovich: Symphony No. 5, 3d movement, passage starting at #89
Wagner: "Funeral March" from *Götterdämmerung,* ***ff*** passages

3-Beat

Brahms: *Ein deutsches Requiem,* 2d movement, thirteen measures after B
Britten: *The Young Person's Guide to the Orchestra,* theme

Ex. 15.8. J. Strauss, *Emperor* Waltz, No. 3, mm. 52-60

Handel: Concerto Grosso Op. 6, No. 6, 3d movement ("Musette"), passage starting at m. 81 (see Appendix A, No. 1)

Prokofiev: Symphony No. 5, 1st movement, at #23; 3d movement, at #71

Puccini: *Tosca,* Act I, beginning

Sibelius: Symphony No. 2, 4th movement, three measures before B (Pesante)

2-Beat

Beethoven: Symphony No. 5, 4th movement, beginning

Liszt: Hungarian Rhapsody No. 2, fourth measure from the end (*Andante*)

Mendelssohn: Symphony No. 5, 4th movement, last nineteen measures

Rachmaninoff: Piano Concerto No. 2, 1st movement, beginning

Rimsky-Korsakov: *Scheherazade,* 1st movement, beginning

Saint-Saëns: Symphony No. 3, 2d movement, at T

Stravinsky: *L'Oiseau de feu* (Suite), Finale, five measures beginning at #20

Verdi: *Messa da Requiem,* No. 2 (Dies Irae), beginning

1-Beat

Brahms: Piano Concerto No. 2, 2d movement, passage starting thirty-eight measures after C

Mahler: Symphony No. 1, 2d movement, beginning; (if played not faster than indicated by the composer, ♩• = 66, the marcato beat emphasizes the half notes; in the revised edition, the second note in violins and violas was changed from an eighth to a sixteenth)

Mussorgsky-Ravel: Pictures at an Exhibition, No. 10 ("The great gate of Kiev"), at #115

6-Beat

Bach: Cantata No. 11 (*Lobet Gott in seinen Reichen),* No. 11, (Chorale)

Saint-Saëns: Symphony No. 3, 2d movement, *Maestoso* after R

Wagner: Prelude to *Parsifal,* passage for brass instruments, ⁶⁄₄

CHAPTER *16*

Rests

Proper handling of rests is part of conductorial skill. There are three different uses for beats where no music is sounding: (1) to cut off the tones preceding the rest when necessary; (2) to indicate counts during the pause; (3) to prepare the next attack.

The cutoff is used only after a sustained tone, not after a detached one. However, not every sustained tone followed by a rest needs a cutoff; use it only when a unified release needs control. This occurs more often in slow tempo than in fast and more often in loud passages than in soft. You may cut off with the baton alone, either by clicking or by making a definite stop on the rest. The left hand may also be used. Some conductors move the forearm in toward the body, palm inward, closing the hand simultaneously. Another effective motion is a quick downward turn of the left hand, signaling "be quiet."

To count during a pause, a small neutral-legato beat is usually sufficient to indicate the rests when neither cutoff nor preparation is needed.

When a rest is followed by an attack, use the rest for preparation, especially if it is the last of several in succession. In most cases the preparatory gesture will not have to be as emphatic as at the start, since the rhythm is already established.

In example 16.1, the first rest is for cutoff (in slow tempo), the second for a slight preparation. In the third measure, cut off on *Two,* mark the time on *Three,* and prepare on *Four.* Follow this procedure throughout the example and do not forget that the half note in measure 5 ends exactly on *Four.*

No cutoff is needed in example 16.2a because of staccato. Do not yield to

Ex. 16.1. Exercise; rests in legato

the temptation of beating staccato on the rests, except of course when a rest serves as preparation. Example 16.2b is the same in 2-beat; for handling measures 2 and 4, see p. 262.

The fourth beats in measures 7 and 8 of example 8.11 must indicate a clear release and, at the same time, maintain a continuous crescendo. In example 11.3, use the left hand, which supports the *ff*, for an incisive cutoff, allowing the right hand to find the most convenient position for the light-staccato that follows. Use the rests in the second bar for preparation. In measure 3, beat the first two eighth rests small, neutral-legato; beat the following (preparatory) eighth sharply and further to the left, to make room for a large gesture to attack the *ff* chord. Review example 11.12, applying what you have just learned.

In example 16.3, the tempo marking *Allegro con brio* and the movement's thematic structure clearly indicate that this music is to be "felt in *One*." As far as beat patterns are concerned, most conductors alternate between 1-beat, subdivided 1-beat, and 3-beat (see ex. 26.7). As to the handling of the rests in the initial measures, the full-staccato beat for the first chord is followed by a very small gesture, a mere flick of the wrist, to indicate *Two*. An accented upbeat on *Three* prepares the second measure. Three in measure 2, however, has a different function: It prepares the *p* legato starting in measure 3 (1-beat).

Conduct example 16.4 in a subdivided 3-beat. The preparation at the end

Ex. 16.2. Exercise; rests in staccato, (a) 4-beat; (b) 2-beat

Ex. 16.3. Beethoven, Symphony No. 3, "Eroica," first movement, mm. 1-6

Ex. 16.4. Haydn, Symphony No. 88, first movement, mm. 1-4

of measure 3 should also include the **sf** on the downbeat of measure 4. In example 16.5 there are two beats to a bar (see also example 12.4). Small gestures suffice to mark the time while the orchestra sustains the **ff**, but use the second beat in measure 277 to prepare the tutti chord, staccato. All rests require no more than unobtrusive beats, except when used for preparation. *Two* in measure 289 is non-staccato beat!

The drumroll in example 16.6 requires no big gesture while the other instruments rest. Beat full-staccato to prepare the chords (see p. 243). In example 16.7 be sure that the time-marking beats in measure 107 are neutral and do not lead the first violins into a false entry—as has happened in prominent orchestras! Beat light-staccato in measure 108.

Example 16.8 is in 1-beat, with the first and second *G.P.*s used for preparation. Mark time in measure 7 and prepare in measure 8 the **pp** in the violins. A time beater, not a conductor, would use the same large downbeats throughout this example.

Ex. 16.5. Beethoven, *Coriolanus* Overture, mm. 276-96

Ex. 16.6. Tchaikovsky, Symphony No. 5, fourth movement, mm. 463-72

Ex. 16.7. Mozart, Symphony No. 39, K. 543, fourth movement, mm. 104-10

Ex. 16.8. Beethoven, Symphony No. 9, second movement, mm. 1-12

The second and third beats in the first bars of example 16.9 must be hardly noticeable. This increases the tension of the music and the attention of the orchestra.

A new section with a change of tempo is shown in example 16.10. To establish the rhythm and character of the *Allegretto vivace,* beat the rests light-staccato. In such cases the neutral beat would not give the conductor the needed control.

Ex. 16.9. Verdi, *Un ballo in maschera,* Act I, Invocazione, at #36

Ex. 16.10. Liszt, Piano Concerto No. 1, second movement, fifteen measures
before F

RESTS AT THE BEGINNING OF A PIECE

There is no rule dictating how to beat when a piece starts with several rests. Since the rests appear in the parts and are counted by all the players, including those who do not come in at the very start, skipping could cause confusion. Whether to beat the rests in a neutral manner or with some kind of expression depends upon the character of the opening. In any event, do not beat the rests in a way that could lead the players into a premature attack. If you decide to skip beats, the change should be entered in the orchestra parts.

While no special treatment is needed in example 16.11, a neutral-legato start in example 16.12 would lack tension; start light-staccato, and beat full-staccato on the fourth count for preparation.

To get a good pizzicato entry in example 16.13, beat *One* and *Two* light-staccato. In example 16.14, a completely neutral first beat would lose the drama of the opening; directly from ATT at the top of the field of beating, give a clear but not too emphatic downbeat, and continue with a

Ex. 16.11. Liszt, Piano Concerto No. 1, thirty-two measures before D

Ex. 16.12. Tchaikovsky, *1812* Overture, mm. 96-98

Ex. 16.13. Liszt, *Les Préludes,* mm. 1-4

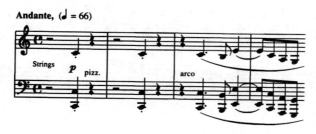

RESTS IN ACCOMPANIMENT

The following two examples show the special care with which rests must be treated in accompaniments.

Use neutral beats in measure 96 of example 16.16. Be sure you are in time, even a little ahead, on the second beat in measure 97, and synchronize the preparatory third beat with the triplet in the solo violin, to be in position for

Ex. 16.16. Tchaikovsky, Violin Concerto, first movement, mm. 96-101

the fourth beat. Give a sharp beat before each of the off-beat chords with neutral beats between. Prepare the last measure (***fp***) by picking up the beat from the violin.

In example 16.17, you must know the words as well as the music and be sure which syllable falls on which beat. The preparatory beats must be flexible, because the singer is allowed a certain liberty in recitative. Your downbeat in the third measure coincides with *cin-*, followed by two *secco* chords in strict tempo. If necessary, wait on Four so as to be sure that the next downbeat comes exactly on *dir-*. Do not drag the neutral beats, and be ready for the next downbeat! The singer traditionally holds the high A flat, wait for him on Two and time your preparatory beat to be with *-to*, precisely on *Three*. Use the accented upbeat on Four to prepare the fanfare in the brass.

Remember this handy rule:

> *When there are several rests in the accompaniment, keep with or a trifle ahead of the tempo, but always use the last rest for a good preparation. If necessary, wait just before giving this preparatory beat.*

Ex. 16.17. Verdi, *Aïda*, Act I, "Se quel guerrier" (No. 2), eleven measures before B

Additional examples for the study of beating rests:

Barber: *Overture to The School for Scandal,* mm. 6 and 7
Beethoven: Symphony No. 8, 1st movement, fifteen measures from the end
Dukas: *L'Apprenti sorcier,* beginning of Vif, **$\frac{3}{8}$**
Haydn: Symphony No. 102, 4th movement, Coda

Kodály: *Háry János* (Suite), 1st movement, mm. 73–76
Mahler: Symphony No. 1, 1st movement, last ten measures
Nielsen: Symphony No. 3, 1st movement, beginning (1-beat)
Rossini: Overture to *Semiramide,* last measures of *Andantino* $\frac{6}{8}$; mm. 63–65 of *Allegro*
Shostakovitch: Symphony No. 1, 1st movement, mm. 8 and 9
Sibelius: Symphony No. 5, last nine measures
Wagner: Prelude to *Parsifal,* passage in $\frac{6}{4}$

Rests at the Beginning of a Piece

Bach: Mass in B Minor, "Et resurrexit"
Bizet: *L'Arlsienne* Suite No. 1, 1st and 2d movements
Dvořák: Symphony No. 8, 2d movement
Haydn: Symphony No. 86, 4th movement
Saint-Saëns: Symphony No. 3, 2d movement
Sibelius: Symphony No. 2, 1st movement
Verdi: *Aïda,* Prelude to Act I

Rests in Accompaniment

Beethoven: Violin Concerto, 1st movement
Bizet: *Carmen,* all recitatives
Grieg: Piano Concerto, 1st and 3d movements
Haydn: *The Creation,* No. 12 (Recitative)
Mozart: *Die Zauberflöte,* Act I, No. 8 (Finale), Recitative
Rachmaninoff: Piano Concerto No. 2, 3d movement

The recitative from Mozart's *Die Zauberflöte* included in the list is a dialogue between tenor and bass extending over 120 measures. It lends itself to practice in class, with two students singing the vocal lines, another student playing the piano (from the full score!), and all students taking turns conducting the accompaniment. For perfect coordination, the conductor must make a clear distinction between neutral and preparatory beats. Consult the score of the NMA (New Mozart Edition), which follows Mozart's autograph. Earlier editions contain inaccurate tempo markings.

CHAPTER 17

The Tenuto Pattern

The tenuto beat is a plane motion with a stop on each count. It resembles the marcato but lacks the aggressive impetus of that beat. The manner in which the beat is sustained depends on the music. The size varies from small to large.

As shown in figure 17.1, the connecting gesture between each count serves as release and preparation. It should not be hurried (as in staccato) or leisurely (as in legato), and it is characterized by a "holding on" to the count, as though you were loath to let go of it. This is still more evident in the pattern of figure 17.2, which gives strong emphasis to single counts, especially when marked $<$ or $<>$. The technique is similar to the ritenuto (see p. 183) but with noticeable intensity—coming from the forearm—on the very slow part of the pattern (heavy line).

The tenuto beat is used for chords that are detached but held and for melodic passages of portamento character. The preliminary beat for tenuto is

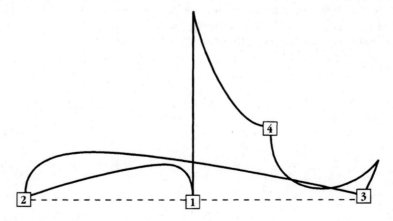

Fig. 17.1. Tenuto, 4-beat

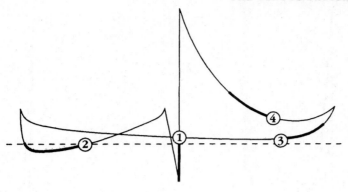

Fig. 17.2. Tenuto, 4-beat (alternate style)

legato. The piano is not the ideal instrument for music of tenuto character. The exercises should therefore be played by a small ensemble.

> *Figure 17.3 is useful for those not too frequent occasions when you want to limit yourself to a very academic time beating. This "dry" tenuto lacks the strong holding quality of the expressive form.*

Since there are no new problems in 3-beat tenuto, apply the principles of figure 17.1. The 2-beat tenuto is shown in figures 17.4 and 17.5. Figure 17.6, the "dry" pattern, is recommended for legato passages in very fast tempo, the stops on *One* and *Two* being very short. For 1-beat, apply figure 15.1. For example 17.1, use figure 17.3; for example 17.2, use figure 17.1. For the 3-beat in example 17.3, use the same procedure as in figure 17.1. Use either figure 17.4 or 17.5 for example 17.4.

Since each half note in example 17.5 is to be held until shortly before the succeeding chord, beat tenuto only on *One* and *Three*. *Two* and *Four* are legato gestures and are easily reduced to connecting links between the tenuto beats. They may even be slightly out of tempo—a little late. In example 17.6,

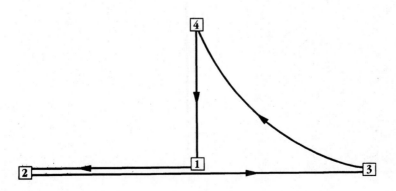

Fig. 17.3. The "dry" tenuto, 4-beat

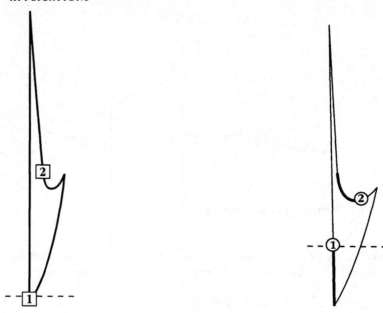

Fig. 17.4. Tenuto, 2-beat   **Fig. 17.5.** Tenuto, 2-beat (alternate style)

the sustained chords require the tenuto beat. Use the tenuto beat in example 17.7 for the **pp** accents in the first bars; for the **ff** chords use the more emphatic pattern of figure 17.5. For the triplets in measures 368 and 369, the tempo is more relaxed; use subdivision (see p. 221).

Fig. 17.6. The "dry" tenuto, 2-beat

Ex. 17.1. Exercise

Ex. 17.2. Exercise

Ex. 17.3. Exercise

Ex. 17.4. Exercise

Ex. 17.5. Exercise

Ex. 17.6.   Puccini, *La Bohéme,* Act III, one measure before #21

Ex. 17.7.   Schubert, Symphony No. 8, "Great," second movement, mm. 364-80

In example 17.8, the brass chords in the fifth and sixth measures need the tenuto for the intense sustained quality. Support with the left hand.

At the *rit.* in the second measure of example 17.9, the accompaniment should be carefully synchronized with the solo. Subdivide the triplet if necessary. If two pianos are available, the practice will be more realistic. The ending in the third and fourth measures is of a type found in many pieces: repetition of the same chord detached. This is best controlled with the tenuto beat (see p. 221).

Ex. 17.8. Hindemith, Symphony *Mathis der Maler,* first movement, four measures after #23

Ex. 17.9. Grieg, Piano Concerto, second movement, twenty-seven measures after B

Ex. 17.10. Bruckner, Symphony No. 7, second movement, mm. 4-9

In example 17.10, the tenuto pattern, which by means of its connecting gestures gives emphasis to the main counts, is more effective here than regular subdivision.

Indicate the crescendo in measure 35 of example 17.11 by increasing the expressiveness in the tenuto beat.

For example 17.12, apply the same technique as in example 17.5.

For the third counts in measures 7 and 8 of example 8.11, use a tenuto beat to sustain these chords within a continuous crescendo. A tenuto beat in example 16.15 will insure the full value of the closing **_ff_** eighth note chords.

Ex. 17.11. Beethoven, Symphony No. 4, first movement, mm. 34-37

Ex. 17.12. Wagner, _Tannhäuser,_ Act III, Scene 1, fifty-seven measures after B

CHAPTER *18*

Different Uses for Basic Patterns

The application of the six basic patterns has so far been limited to musical examples whose very nature corresponded to the distinctive qualities of each of these patterns. In other words, when the example referred to a legato passage, a legato beat was recommended; similarly, for staccato passages, a staccato beat was suggested. There have been a few exceptions. But in actual conducting it occurs frequently that the beat pattern does not conform to the notation. The following discussion will cover typical cases.

NEUTRAL-LEGATO

As explained previously, this beat is used for soft and emotionally neutral passages. It is also used to mark time when nothing rhythmical occurs (sustained notes) and to indicate rests. It is useful in accompaniment to keep the orchestra subdued. While used primarily for legato, the neutral-legato may also be applied to detached passages, as shown in example 18.1. A staccato beat in leading the strings would be pedantic. Neutral-legato lets the music flow in a simple and natural way without preventing the players from articulating: detached eighth notes followed by portato (see fig. 34.1).

Ex. 18.1. Beethoven, Symphony No. 7, second movement, mm. 1-10

Similarly, when you do not want the orchestra to play a sharply detached staccato, you may use neutral-legato instead of staccato. This method can be applied to the beginning of examples 2.6 and 10.8. There, and in the following discussion of choice of beat, the pattern chosen often depends upon the way the orchestra responds to your gesture. Thus, the beat may assume a corrective function: If the orchestra's playing is too detached, the neutral-legato will tell the players to decrease the sharpness of the staccato; if the music is not played sharply enough, an unmistakable staccato beat will bring out the desired articulation.

EXPRESSIVE-LEGATO

This beat has such a definite character that it is applied only when the music is both legato and espressivo.

LIGHT- AND FULL-STACCATO

The appearance of single staccato beats in legato passages has already been discussed; they are used for phrasing, for accents, and as preliminary beats to strengthen a forceful start.

Slurred passages do not necessarily require a legato beat. Often, especially in fast tempo, clear direction needs a staccato gesture. For example 18.2, use light-staccato in measures 48–50. Full-staccato is used in example 18.3 and 18.4, despite the phrase markings. Try to beat legato and you will see how inadequate it is.

A staccato beat may be used in passages where no staccato is marked but where you wish to concentrate the players' attention on the rhythm. In example 18.5, light-staccato beats starting on *Two* in measure 9 help to

Ex. 18.2. Rossini, *William Tell* Overture, mm. 46-50

Ex. 18.3. Beethoven, Symphony No. 6, first movement, mm. 45-50

Ex. 18.4. Brahms, Symphony No. 1, first movement, mm. 38-45

Ex. 18.5. Beethoven, Symphony No. 7, first movement, mm. 8-12

emphasize the rhythm and assure unified playing by the strings on *Four.* Be sure not to slow down in your anxiety to stress rhythm—it would upset the ensemble (see p. 332).

Ex. 18.6. Offenbach, *Les Contes d'Hoffmann,* Act II, No. 9, Olympia's Aria

The use of a gentle staccato, a gesture between neutral-legato and staccato, has already been suggested several times. This beat uses a quick motion before the counts, but there is no stop. Apply it where the detached quality is not felt very strongly but where legato would be inappropriate. A gentle staccato is applied in example 18.6 because of the rather slow tempo. Staccato with full stop on the count would be too jerky, and the legato beat would not express the rhythmic vitality.

MARCATO

The aggressive character of this pattern makes it applicable only to strong and forceful music. Sometimes a marcato beat may be used in legato to emphasize the rhythm strongly, but this procedure causes monotony if repeated too often.

TENUTO

The use of the expressive form of the tenuto beat has already been discussed. The "dry" form used on single counts for purposes of phrasing has also been treated. When employed for whole bars, the "dry" form (figs. 17.3 and 17.6) indicates the rhythm in an academic manner. Use it chiefly as a corrective measure to control the ensemble or when for other reasons the rhythm must be stressed in a completely neutral way. It is helpful in accompaniment to point out the counts clearly and avoid misunderstanding.

In the first few measures of example 15.3, this beat prevents the brasses from dragging; be sure to keep strictly in time and do not delay the beat by waiting for the sixteenth notes.

Strangely, the "dry" tenuto beat is sometimes taught as the standard pattern. The lifeless nature of this beat, however, prevents adequate musical expression and results in mere time beating. This undesirable effect does not occur in rapid tempo, especially in 2-beat; here the "dry" tenuto sometimes serves as a substitute for legato. In this case, the legato rebound on *One* would make the quick gestures confusing. In the first measures of example 19.39, the "dry" tenuto beat, done by the wrist alone, is easily seen to be the most convenient gesture.

LEGATO AND STACCATO
SIMULTANEOUSLY

When legato and staccato are played simultaneously by the orchestra, the beat usually has the character of the leading melody.

Beat legato in example 18.7; the moderate staccato needs no special attention. The staccato beat in example 18.8 changes to legato with the entrance of the main theme in viola and bassoon. You may use an occasional gentle staccato beat to express both melody and counterpoint. In example 18.9 the woodwind passage in measures 13ff. (2-beat) would be conducted legato if it stood alone. The staccato beat is used, however, for two reasons: The brisk viola figure requires more attention, and the winds would naturally play legato. Furthermore, the staccato beat insures a good attack on the triplet figures in the violins and bass instruments.

There are passages where several important but different themes occur and to which the same pattern cannot be applied for any length of time. Sometimes the gentle staccato is useful as a compromise beat. Often it is necessary to change quickly from one pattern to another to get the best results. In example 18.10, use a gentle staccato motion (1-beat). Beat neutral-legato in example 18.11, changing to a slightly expressive gesture in

Ex. 18.7. Beethoven, Symphony No. 3, "Eroica," second movement, mm. 69-73

Ex. 18.8. Tchaikovsky, Symphony No. 4, second movement, mm. 75-80

measure 212. Return to neutral beats in measure 213; in the next bar, add some staccato quality to the beat for the release of the sustained brass chord and to lead the detached notes. Then change back to neutral-legato.

Additional examples for the study of passages in which legato and staccato are played simultaneously:

Berlioz: Overture *Le Carnaval Romain,* passage starting at the
thirty-fifth measure of the *Andante sostenuto* $\frac{3}{4}$
Debussy: *La Mer,* 3d movement
Haydn: Symphony No. 101, 2d movement
Mahler: Symphony No. 4, 1st movement
Mendelssohn: Symphony No. 4, 2d movement

Ex. 18.9. Dvořák, Symphony No. 9, "From the New World," fourth movement, mm. 154–59

Ex. 18.9. *Continued*

Ex. 18.10. Elgar, *Enigma* Variations, Var. 2, mm. 6-9

Prokofiev: Symphony No. 5, 4th movement
Tchaikovsky: Symphony No. 5, 4th movement, m. 414
Verdi: *Otello,* Act III, beginning
Wagner: Prelude to *Die Meistersinger von Nürnberg,* thirty-eight measures before *Sehr gewichtig*

SIMULTANEOUS DIFFERENT DYNAMICS

An orchestral score often has different dynamic markings occurring simultaneously. The timpani or brass may enter softly while the rest of the orchestra is playing a loud passage, or a solo instrument may play *f* while the

Ex. 18.11.   Smetana, "The Moldau", mm. 211-15

rest of the orchestra plays ***p***. In most cases the baton directs the larger group of instruments and the left hand takes care of the others if needed. Thus, the left hand may give the warning ***p*** gesture while the right has a large *espressivo* beat, or a neutral-legato with the baton may be combined with a stimulating gesture of the left hand.

In measures 1 and 3 of example 18.12 the right hand beats ***fp***. The left hand addresses the violins and indicates their sudden ***p*** (see also p. 95).

When crescendo and dimuendo occur at the same time, both hands are needed. The baton again is concerned with the large group, and the left hand leads the others.

In example 18.13, the left hand cues in the ***p*** entrance of first violins and cellos, while the baton indicates ***f***. In the second half of the measure the size of the beats decreases. The left hand takes over the diminuendo of the woodwinds in the following measure, while the right addresses the crescendo in the other instruments. In example 18.14, the left hand leads the instruments on the top staff and the baton leads the others.

Gustav Mahler and Richard Strauss were among the first composers who, in the interest of a well-balanced overall sound, applied contrasting dynamics to various instrumental groups. Their scores provide ample material for study. Since then, careful dynamic markings have become common practice. It must be insisted that they are meticulously observed by all players, although the conductor's gesture may occasionally contradict the dynamic indications in their parts.

Ex. 18.12. Mendelssohn, Symphony No. 3, "Scotch," fourth movement, mm. 1-5

Ex. 18.13. Wagner, *Tristan und Isolde,* Prelude, mm. 54-58

Ex. 18.14. Wagner, *Tristan und Isolde,* Prelude, mm. 65-67

Additional examples for the study of passages with simultaneous different dynamics:

Barber: *Second Essay for Orchestra,* passage starting two measures before #11

Berlioz: *Symphonie fantastique,* 4th movement, thirty-nine measures from the end

Brahms: Symphony No. 2, 4th movement, twelve measures after C (109th measure of the movement)

Debussy: *La Mer,* end of 1st movement

Dvořák: Symphony No. 9, "From the New World," 1st movement, passage starting at #9

Mahler: Symphony No. 5, 3d movement, (Scherzo; in the revised edition of the score the composer changed many dynamic markings)

Mendelssohn: *Fingal's Cave* Overture, several passages

Sibelius: Symphony No. 2, 2d movement, several passages

Strauss, R.: *Tod und Verklärung*

PROBLEMS OF ORCHESTRATION

Generally speaking, the nature of the instrumental groups is such that the winds need an especially clear and precise beat while the strings call for a warmer gesture. The combination of both requires an intelligent mean, the nature of which is an essential part of a conductor's communication with the players. This will be discussed in greater detail in chapter 26.

Similarly, the extent to which the conductor should indicate articulation and dynamics is closely connected with the response of the different instruments and groups. Certain results are obtained rather easily from the strings, but you must work harder to get them from the winds, and vice versa. A crescendo in the woodwinds requires a larger gesture than in the brass. It is an erroneous notion that the massive effects of the brass need a large gesture. On the contrary, a small and very definite beat controls the brass instruments most effectively and prevents them from dragging.

How to beat pizzicato depends entirely on the musical context. Lack of unity in pizzicato is a very common flaw, but young conductors need not assume that they are always to blame. Even a correct beat does not secure a unified attack if the players are not attentive. Generally, string players tend to anticipate pizzicato entrances, and the conductor must be especially careful when such an entrance occurs in combination with other instruments. The preparatory gesture must be distinct and incisive.

When pizzicato occurs alone, it is directed like staccato, as in example 18.15; the last chord requires a sharp full-staccato, but not too large. In example 18.16, as in examples 9.7 and 16.13, the soft pizzicato needs a small staccato beat and may be assisted by the left hand. The left-hand gesture uses the preceding count for preparation and imitates the action of plucking the string. Some conductors use this so effectively that they rely on it alone for the pizzicato.

When some strings play pizzicato while others play arco, or play pizzicato in combination with wind instruments, there are two possibilities. If the rhythm is established and steady, a special gesture would disturb the players

Ex. 18.15. Bizet, *Carmen,* Act I, No. 4, final five measures

Ex. 18.16. Wagner, *Tristan und Isolde,* Prelude, mm. 108-11

rather than help them. But when the rhythmic pulsation is not continuous and often after rests, a staccato preparation helps secure a unified attack.

Beat legato in example 18.17, with no special gesture for the pizzicato. The same applies for examples 5.18 and 10.3.

In measures 292 and 294 of example 16.5, the same instrumental combination is used, but the strings play arco the first time and pizzicato the second. Consequently, the preparation for the second chord has a staccato quality.

Ex. 18.17. Schubert, Symphony No.7, "Unfinished," second movement, mm. 268-75

Additional examples for the study of passages in which pizzicato occurs alone or in combination with various instruments:

Beethoven: Symphony No. 4, 1st movement, introduction
Franck: Symphony in D Minor, 2d movement
Haydn: *The Seasons,* No. 18 (Recitative)
Mendelssohn: Symphony No. 3 (*Scotch*), 3d movement
Prokofiev: *Peter and the Wolf,* several passages
Schuman, William: Symphony for Strings, 3d movement
Strauss, Johann: *Pizzicato* Polka
Tchaikovsky: Piano Concerto No. 1, 2d movement
Tchaikovsky: Symphony No. 4, 3d movement

CHAPTER *19*

Holds

The handling of holds and interruptions is among the more difficult techniques a conducting student must learn to master. No general rule can be
applied to the great variety of situations, but it is helpful to divide holds into
categories, in particular those holds that occur at the end of a piece, those not
followed by a rest (usually necessitating a short break), and those that are
followed by a rest. Various types of interruptions also need to be discussed.

CONCLUDING HOLDS

Many pieces have a fermata on the last played note. Regardless of the note
value, beat only one count and sustain it as long as you feel the music requires.
The manner of execution depends upon the orchestration and the dynamics.

The effectiveness of a *f* is increased by raising the baton for the fermata.
Merely stopping the motion of the baton is not sufficient to sustain a *f* or a *ff*;
only a diminuendo would result. Maintain the volume by indicating intensity
with either the right or the left hand. The left-hand gesture was explained on
p. 24. Some conductors indicate a continued *f* by moving the baton very
slowly, the same way as in the ritenuto beat (see fig. 14.1). In *p*, simply
stopping the baton on the fermata is sufficient. In *pp*, the left hand keeps the
orchestra subdued.

The end of the hold is indicated by a cutoff. The gestures are similar to
those for a general cutoff, described on p. 196. Because of the indefinite
length of the hold, however, the cutoff must be clear and unmistakable in
order to insure the simultaneous stopping of all players. Although the gesture
is sudden and quick, it must avoid any suggestion of an accent at the very end
unless an accent is marked by the composer. In the last bar of example 19.1,
stop beating on *Three*; sustain a moderate *f* with the left hand. In example
17.8, the hold actually starts on the second beat of the seventh measure; it is
not necessary to beat for the last measure. While in example 19.2 the last
pizzicato chord will take care of itself, the first violins in example 19.3 need an

Ex. 19.1. J.S. Bach, Mass in B Minor, "Kyrie eleison" (No. 3), mm. 57-59

Ex. 19.2. Brahms, Symphony No. 3, fourth movement, mm. 307-9

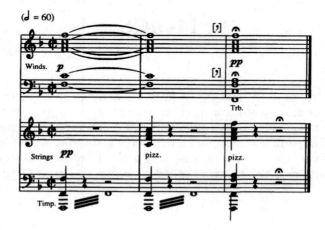

Ex. 19.3. Wagner, *Faust* Overture, mm. 439-41

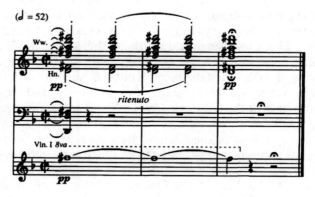

extra gesture of the left hand for a cutoff. This gesture must be unobtrusive and clearly directed toward the violins, so that none of the wind players will mistake it for the concluding cutoff (see p. 273).

Examples 19.4 and 19.5 both illustrate *diminuendo* on the fermata. The first is played by the winds (the last string chord again takes care of itself), the second begins softly and dies away in the strings. Indicate the *diminuendo* in example 19.4 by gradually lowering both hands, if the right hand was in a raised position; if not, use the left hand alone. A wind chord, no matter how soft, always requires a cutoff. The *morendo* in example 19.5 may be expressed by a "dying-away" gesture, which is very effective for strings; both arms slowly fall to the side with no definite cutoff. Two similar endings are shown in examples 17.7 and 17.9, with the $<$ $>$ expressed by raising and lowering both hands together or the left hand alone. The size and intensity of the gesture depend upon the orchestra's response. In example 19.6, the uplifted left hand sustains the *ff* tutti while the right hand directs the kettle drum. The baton waits on *One* and cuts the drumroll on *Three*, then joins the left hand for the tutti cutoff. The gesture directing the kettle drum must be relatively small. Beat the first three counts in the last bar of example 19.7. The fourth beat is superfluous since the pizzicato needs no cutoff. Sustain the violins throughout with the left hand.

Ex. 19.4. Dvořák, Symphony No. 9, "From the New World," fourth movement, final measures

Ex. 19.5. Grieg, *Last Spring,* final measures

Ex. 19.6. Beethoven, *Die Weihe des Hauses* Overture, final measures

Ex. 19.7. Shostakovich, *The Golden Age,* final measures

Since only one section of the orchestra in example 19.8 has a fermata on the last chord, while the other part holds the fourth and fifth counts, you must beat all six counts. The sixth beat is small, so that it cuts off part of the orchestra and does not look like the concluding cutoff.

Ex. 19.8. Reger, *Mozart* Variations, final measures

HOLDS NOT FOLLOWED BY A REST

Such holds may or may not require a cutoff. If they do, there may be only a short break for "breathing," or there may be a longer pause. The length of the pause is often a question of interpretation. Consider how differently the fermata in "The Star-Spangled Banner" is treated by conductors! Only the techniques are discussed here. Their application to the following examples may vary, depending on personal preference.

If there is only a slight interruption after the hold, the cutoff gesture is also the preparation for the next count.

Figure 19.1 shows the technique of making a hold and cutoff on any count in 4-beat. The beat is repeated on each count : $\boxed{1}$ is for the hold, $\textcircled{1}$ is for the cutoff and also serves as a preliminary to $\boxed{2}$. It helps to click on the repeated count for a clear release.

The principle of repeating the beat after the hold is applied to 3-beat, 2-beat, and 1-beat in figures 19.2–19.4. It can easily be applied to all other patterns.

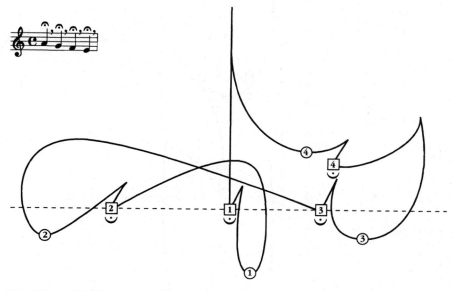

Fig. 19.1. Hold and cutoff on each count (short break), in 4-beat

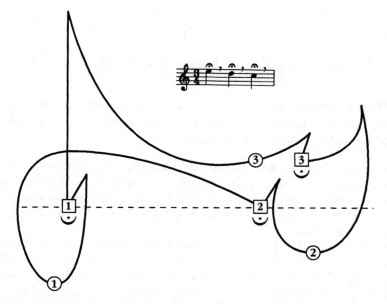

Fig. 19.2. Hold and cutoff on each count (short break), in 3-beat

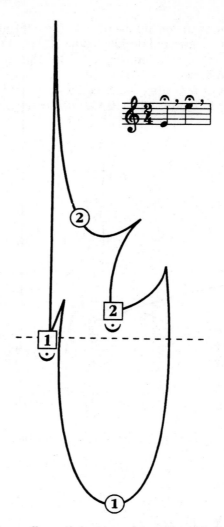

Fig. 19.3. Hold and cutoff on each count (short break), in 2-beat

> *When the note under the fermata is of greater value than one count, it is not necessary to repeat any beats, as will be seen in the following examples.*

In example 19.9, the hold in measure 2 is treated according to figure 19.1. The fermata in the fourth measure, however, includes several counts; stop on ☐1☐ for the hold, then (skipping *Two*) beat ③, which serves the double purpose of cutting off the hold and preparing ④. Thus, only three gestures are used in this measure.

In this context, the chorale settings are used as exercises for the handling of fermatas, although in Bach's time their main purpose was to mark the phrase groups. For the hold in the second measure in example 19.10, stop on ☐1☐ and use ② for cutoff and preparation. In measure 4 of example 19.11, stop on ☐3☐; cut off and prepare with ④.

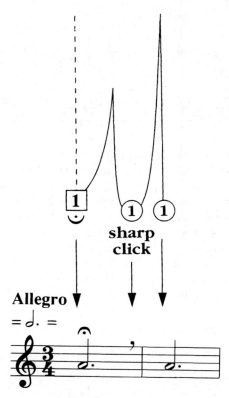

Fig. 19.4 Hold and cutoff on each count (short break), in 1-beat

Ex. 19.9. J.S. Bach, Chorale setting

Ex. 19.10. J.S. Bach, Chorale setting

Ex. 19.11. J.S. Bach, Chorale setting

Since the cutoff in example 19.12 also serves as preparation, it must have all the different expressions of the preliminary beat. In measure 2 it is full-staccato. In the last measure the orchestra has a half-bar rest. After a sharp cutoff of the second fermata, use a neutral downbeat (synchronized with the first chord of the piano), and prepare the staccato chord with *Two*.

In measure 2 of example 19.13, use a full staccato cutoff, which prepares the tutti attack (see below, p. 229). In example 19.14, stop on ⬚1 in the fourth measure. Following the usual procedure—beating the cutoff ③ strictly in tempo—results in a whole beat pause. Considering the very slow tempo, the conductor may prefer to shorten the pause, perhaps by as much as half, using an eighth-note beat.

Ex. 19.12. Liszt, Piano Concerto No. 1, opening five measures

Ex. 19.13. Schumann, Symphony No. 1, first movement, mm. 1-6

Ex. 19.14. Haydn, Symphony No. 101, first movement, mm. 1-5

For examples 19.15–19.17, use figure 19.3. (For more on ex. 19.15, see exx. 20.8 and 20.9.) In example 19.17 change from *f* to *p* with a definite but small cutoff. Apply figure 19.4 to example 19.18. Though the held note comes after the beat, just stop on *One* and wait for the orchestra to finish the bar.

When a fractional value occurs after a fermata, do not change the regular procedure (see p. 93). Thus, in example 19.19 the third fermata is treated just as the first two are.

Ex. 19.15. Schubert, Rosamunde, Ballet Music, No. 9, mm. 56-60

Ex. 19.16. Beethoven, Symphony No. 7, first movement, mm. 87-89

Ex. 19.17. Haydn, *The Creation,* Duet (No. 32), mm. 152-54

Ex. 19.18. Beethoven, Symphony No. 9, second movement, mm. 176-179

Ex. 19.19. Borodin, Symphony No. 2, first movement, mm. 1-7

The two types of combined cutoff and preparation, one with and one without repeated beat, are illustrated in examples 19.20 and 19.21. In the third measure of example 19.20, only two gestures are used: The hold is on *One*, while *Two* cuts off the winds and also prepares the string entrance (staccato gesture!). This way of beating does not follow the notation, for the dotted quarter should be held until after *Two*. However, *it is not unusual for the beat to contradict the notation under a fermata, provided the beat is convenient and will not confuse the players.* In example 19.21, the hold for the first violins is on D, not on E flat as in some older editions. The cutoff gesture (second beat repeated!) should be rather gentle and smooth so as to result in a very slight break.

In example 19.22, all counts are subdivided except the very first. The first eighth beat on *Two* has two functions: It cuts off the fermata and prepares the entrance of oboes and bassoons. For another example with a similar start, see example 9.5.

Ex. 19.20. Beethoven, Symphony No. 3, "Eroica," fourth movement, mm. 29-32

Ex. 19.21. Beethoven, Symphony No. 3, "Eroica," fourth movement, mm. 51-56

Ex. 19.22. Beethoven, Symphony No. 2, first movement, mm. 1-2

The following two examples have rests after the holds. They are dicussed here because the technique involved is the same as in the previous examples, owing to the fact that the rest actually includes only part of the count.

In example 19.23, beat *One* ⬚1⬚ in measure 133 and wait for the lower instruments with their fermata, then beat *Two* for cutoff and preparation. In example 19.24, wait on *Two* ⬚2⬚; a sharp downbeat on *One* in the following measure cuts off the fermata and prepares the next attack (see p. 381).

While the fermata in measure 4 of example 19.13 may be executed without repeating the third beat, some conductors desire a longer break and therefore repeat *Three.* But if this is done, beat the repeated *Three* downward so that the players will not confuse it with *Four.*

Ex. 19.23. Schumann, Symphony No. 4, first movement, mm. 132-35

Ex. 19.24. Schumann, Symphony No. 4, first movement, mm. 143-48

Additional examples for the study of fermatas followed by a short break:

Beethoven: Symphony No. 6, 1st movement, m. 4
Copland: *A Lincoln Portrait,* m. 211
Franck: Symphony in D Minor, 2d movement, m. 100
Haydn: Symphony No. 104, 1st movement, mm. 1 and 2; 2d movement, mm. 25, 115, 117
Rimsky-Korsakov: *Scheherazade,* 4th movement, eleven measures from the end
Schoenberg: *Kammersymphonie,* m. 4

If the interruption after the hold is longer than one count, a different technique is used. There are two separate gestures, one for cutoff and one for the preparation.

The nature of this cutoff is similar to that at the end of a piece. However, the cutoff gesture now carries the baton from one complete stop (⌒) to another (ATT) in the most simple and direct manner. To prepare the attack after the pause, use the position of attention and the regular preparatory beat just as at the start.

There can be no hard and fast rule for the application of these gestures. The procedure depends on the position of the baton at the fermata and on where you want the baton to be at attention. Figure 19.5 shows some of the more useful of several possibilities. Whenever an upward or sideways cutoff could be mistaken for a signal to continue, use a downward cutoff.

Depending on interpretation, the well-known fermatas in example 19.25 can be done in three different ways (see also p. 98).

1. Without pause. The cutoff and preparation are done with the same downbeat. This works best if the baton, while sustaining the fermata, moves up very slowly before sweeping down for the next *One*, all in one continuous gesture.
2. Separate gestures for cutoff and preparation, strictly in time, as indicated after the first fermata in example 19.26 (see fig. 19.4).
3. Separate gestures, but with a freely timed pause between, as indicated after the second fermata in example 19.26. Many conductors treat the first five measures as an introduction to the movement, taking the cutoff and the downbeat after the first fermata in tempo but waiting longer after the second fermata. The cutoff after the second hold must carry the baton to where it can start the second violins in the clearest and most comfortable way.

Ex. 19.25. Beethoven, Symphony No. 5, first movement, mm. 1-7

Ex. 19.26. Beethoven, Symphony No. 5, first movement, mm. 1-7 (notation changed to reflect alternate conducting style)

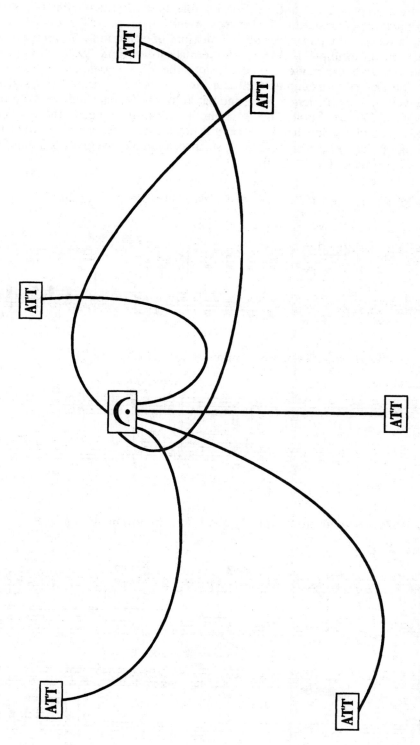

Fig. 19.5. Fermata, cutoff, and pause

In examples 19.27 and 19.28 a definite break is made after the slow introduction before starting the fast movement. You must feel for yourself how long to wait on the pause. For the 1st measure of example 19.27, refer to the comment on example 11.3. After the fermata in example 19.28, the music continues with a start after the count, since the *Vivace* goes *alla breve.*

The first *ff* in example 19.29 is a kind of introduction in itself and is followed by a short silence. Raise the baton for the fermata and use a strong downbeat for the cutoff. The *p* subito in measure 5 needs the sudden appearance of the left hand. Be careful not to have the baton too high in cutting off the fermata in measure 6, so as to be in a convenient position for the *allegro* attack (see p. 279).

Ex. 19.27. Rossini, *Il Barbiere di Siviglia,* Overture, mm. 23-28

Ex. 19.28. Haydn, *The Seasons,* Introduction (No. 1), mm. 1-6

Ex. 19.29. Beethoven, Symphony No. 1, fourth movement, mm. 1-8

In the two following examples, the pauses are indicated by the composers: in example 19.30 by using the sign ∥; in example 19.31 by inserting a fractional rest with a fermata.

Ex. 19.30. Mendelssohn, *A Midsummer Night's Dream,* Nocturne, mm. 25-27

Ex. 19.31. W. Schuman, Symphony No. 3, Part II, mm. 35-39

Additional examples for the study of fermatas followed by a longer pause:

Bartók: *Dance* Suite, Finale, m. 17

Beethoven: Symphony No. 3, 4th movement, m. 348 (before *Poco Andante*)

Brahms: Symphony No. 1, 4th movement, before the beginning of the *Allegro* section

Haydn: Symphony No. 103, 1st movement, before the beginning of the *Allegro* section

Rossini: Overture to *Tancredi,* m. 121 (beginning of the recapitulation)

Sibelius: Symphony No. 3, 1st movement, three measures from the end

Smetana: "Dance of the Comedians" from *The Bartered Bride,* m. 2

Even if there is no interruption after the hold and no cutoff is required, a gesture is needed to resume the progress of the music.

In examples 14.12 and 19.32, since the notes under the fermata have a greater value than one count, wait on the first beat of the held note and use the second—or, in general, the last—for preparation with no cutoff. Since this gesture leads unequivocally into the next count in strict tempo, it must be smooth rather than sharp, so that players cannot mistake it for a cutoff.

Stop the beat in example 19.33 for the fermata on *Two*, releasing the horn with a left-hand gesture. Soon after the flute reaches the fermata, the singer releases her sustained note. Wait for her to take a breath and, with a smooth connecting gesture, coordinate the attack of her next phrase with the flute going into *Three* while the strings continue their pizzicato.

Sometimes the method of skipping beats on a fermata can lead to misunderstanding about the release and the continuation of the music. Whenever this may occur, it is necessary to beat all the counts. In example 19.34, the bass instruments may enter prematurely unless the four counts in the third measure of the example are clearly indicated. Wait on *Two* for the hold; the preparatory third beat should not be too large, while *Four* is done with an incisive motion. In the first measure of the example, do not neglect the correct indication of the rests; *Two* and *Three* are neutral but distinct beats; *Four* is preparatory.

When in example 19.35 some notes are tied over to the same notes on the next count, with no new instruments entering, no additional gesture is required; just continue beating after the hold according to the notation. In measure 236, release the winds with the left hand (see p. 256 and pp. 272–273).

In the concluding measure of example 19.35, the winds end with a quarter note while the strings finish the pizzicato. A literal interpretation would sustain the full value of the wind chord. In Brahms's time, however, it was customary to shorten such a chord slightly to coordinate it with the fading pizzicato sound. (Some modern "literalists" insist on timing such wind chords independent of the strings' pizzicato, betraying thereby their indifference to questions of performance practice.)

Ex. 19.32. Mendelssohn, *A Midsummer Night's Dream,* Overture, mm. 656-60

Allegro di molto, (♩ = 144)

Ex. 19.33. Humperdinck, *Hänsel und Gretel,* Act II, Scene 1, mm. 5-9

Ex. 19.34. Barber, Symphony No. 1, two measures before #15

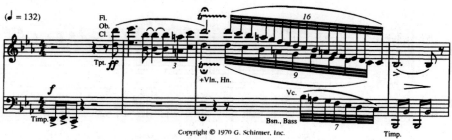

Ex. 19.35. Brahms, Symphony No. 2, third movement, mm. 233-40

In the following ten examples, the beat used for the hold is repeated. However, this is done differently from the cutoff and preparation previously discussed. As shown in figures 19.6–19.10, the baton leaves the hold without any special gesture and merely resumes the motion with which it entered the hold. The smoothness of this motion precludes the possibility of clicking.

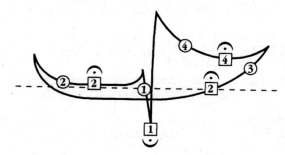

Fig. 19.6. Holds without cutoff; 4-beat

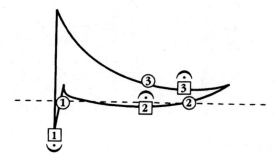

Fig. 19.7. Holds without cutoff; 3-beat

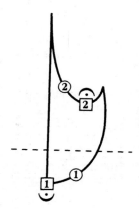

Fig. 19.8. Holds without cutoff; 2-beat

In example 19.36 the beat after the hold can have the value of either a quarter or an eighth. By beating a quarter you will make the sixteenth note a little calmer. In slow passages such as the one in example 19.37, subdivision of the last count gives more control at the fermata. Lead into the next bar with either an eighth or a quarter beat. In the second measure of example 19.38, the repeated *Two* is a small gesture to indicate the change to **p** and to release the accompanying instruments (see p. 364). The first two fermatas in example 19.39 need an especially smooth continuation so that the various entries blend into one another. After the third, however, use a sharp staccato gesture to cut off and then to prepare the sudden **ff**. In example 19.40, hold on *Two* and continue with a preliminary eighth beat.

Ex. 19.36. Offenbach, *Orphée aux Enfers,* Overture, mm. 60-61

Ex. 19.37. Offenbach, *Orphée aux Enfers,* Overture, mm. 73-74

Ex. 19.38. Mozart, *Die Entführung aus dem Serail,* K. 384, Overture, mm. 150-56

Ex. 19.39. Beethoven, Symphony No. 4, fourth movement, mm. 345-52

Ex. 19.40. Mascagni, *Cavalleria Rusticana,* Romanza e Scena, mm. 35-38

Use figure 19.9 for example 19.41, noting the difference between this technique and that used for example 19.18, which follows that of figure 19.4.

Ex. 19.41. Berlioz, *Roméo et Juliette,* "Queen Mab," Scherzo, mm. 1-5

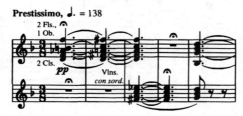

Allow sufficient time in example 19.42 for the G after the hold, without rushing the repeated fifth beat. In example 19.43, the beat after the hold (upbeat quality) must indicate the change of tempo and dynamics; use figure 19.10. While the cellos and basses in example 19.44 hold the B, give a small but well-timed preliminary beat for the *Allegro,* with no break.

Sometimes, especially in accompaniment, there is no time for a regular preparatory beat. A short smooth gesture is needed, one that, without being in tempo, leads convincingly into the next count. The pattern for this is identical with the tenuto of figure 17.1. Use this technique in example 19.45 for connecting the two fermatas; a small beat serves as cutoff (see below, "Holds on Rests", p. 243).

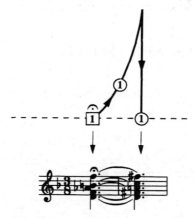

Fig. 19.9. Illustrated pattern for the fermata in example 19.42

Ex. 19.42. Rimsky-Korsakov, *Scheherazade,* third movement, mm. 160-61

Ex. 19.43. J. Strauss, *Vienna Blood,* No. 3, mm. 163-67

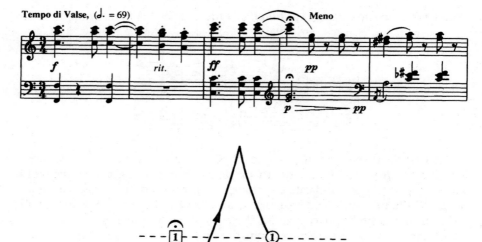

Fig. 19.10. Illustrated pattern for the fermata in example 19.44

Ex. 19.44. Beethoven, *Leonore* Overture No. 3, mm. 36-38

Ex. 19.45. Mozart, *Le Nozze di Figaro,* K. 492, Act IV, Finale (No. 28), mm. 422-25

Additional examples for the study of fermatas without cutoff:

Without Using an Extra Beat

Beethoven: Symphony No. 6, 3d movement, end of the section in $\frac{2}{4}$, m. 203 (the fermata in m. 204 requires a cutoff followed by a preparatory beat)

Borodin: Symphony No. 2, 3d movement, last measure

Gershwin: *Rhapsody in Blue,* mm. 1 and 15

Gershwin: *Porgy and Bess,* Act II, #86

Haydn: Symphony No. 97, 4th movement, twenty-seven measures from the end (a similar passage occurs earlier in this movement)

Mahler, Symphony No. 1, 4th movement, two measures before #40 (in the $\frac{8}{8}$ measure, stop on the last beat and use the release gesture to prepare the rhythm for the following slow $\frac{4}{4}$ while the basses sustain their note)

Mahler: Symphony No. 6, 1st movement, mm. 359–61.

Mussorgsky-Ravel: *Pictures at an Exhibition,* No. 8, "Catacombs"

Rimsky-Korsakov: *Scheherazade,* 2d movement, mm. 415 and 417 (in m. 419, an extra gesture is required: *Two* is repeated!)

Sibelius: Violin Concerto, 1st movement, eleven measures before #4; 6-beat with a fermata on the first count (the connecting gesture leading to the next count must be coordinated with the soloist, while at the same time you bring in basses and timpani; the beat must be flexible to allow for the increase of speed in the solo part, resulting in a 2-beat two measures later)

Using an Extra Beat

Berlioz: *Symphonie fantastique,* 1st movement, forty-sixth measure of the *Allegro* section (*Two* must be repeated to lead the violas and cellos, which play different notes on the downbeat after the fermata!)

Borodin: Symphony No. 2, 3d movement, second and third measures after B (*Three* must be prepared because of the change of harmony)

Delius: *Brigg Fair,* passages after #3 and #6

Franck: Symphony in D Minor, 1st movement, m. 186 (in mm. 188 and 190, no extra beat is required!)

Gershwin: *Rhapsody in Blue,* mm. 9–11 (Stop on the third beat in measure 10; the repeated *Three* will tell the clarinetist to continue with the triplet.)

Sibelius: Symphony No. 2, 1st movement, four measures before P

Strauss, Johann: *Voices of Spring,* eighty-second measure of the Coda

HOLDS FOLLOWED BY RESTS

In examples 19.46 and 19.47, the beat on the rest serves to cut off the hold and prepare the following count. For the measure 390 of example 19.48, apply figure 19.8, but without waiting on *One*. In measure 391, an incisive downbeat secures a clear release and prepares *Two*. For the hold in example 19.49, wait on *One*, skip *Two*, and cut off on *Three*. Then wait for the singer, who traditionally starts after the cutoff. Synchronize your fourth beat (*p* staccato!) with *waste-.*

Ex. 19.46. J.S. Bach, Chorale setting

Ex. 19.47. J.S. Bach, Chorale setting

Ex. 19.48. Schoenberg, *Verklärte Nacht,* mm. 390-91

Ex. 19.49. Haydn, *The Seasons,* Recitative (No. 3), mm. 36-38

Additional examples for the study of fermatas followed by rests:

Borodin: Symphony No. 2, 3d movement, one measure before A
Franck: Symphony in D Minor, 2d movement, m. 96
Kodály: *Háry János (Suite), 4th movement,* third measure after #2
Rimsky-Korsakov: *Scheherazade,* 2d movement, mm. 111 and 121
Rossini: Overture to *Semiramide,* sixty-second measure of the
   Allegro $\frac{4}{4}$

HOLDS ON RESTS

In cases like examples 16.6, 14.6, and 21.16, neglect the rests. Just keep the baton up during the interruption in readiness for the next attack. In measure 4 of example 19.50, the stop for the fermata carries the baton to the left for "attention." *Three* is the gesture for a start after the count. (In a footnote, the composer asks for two different tempi: ♩ = 84–92 is the main tempo, but the passages in the low strings are to be played at ♩ = 144. Therefore, *Four* in mm. 1 and 3 prepares the faster speed, but the main tempo is resumed on *Three* in m. 2.)

The fermata in example 19.51 is on a whole rest. Beat a neutral *One* for cutoff, and wait; *Two* serves as preparation. In example 9.5 the fermatas are directed in a similar manner. The notation in example 19.52 is not followed

Ex. 19.50. Mahler, Symphony No. 2, first movement, mm. 1-5

Ex. 19.51. Franck, Symphony in D Minor, third movement, mm. 210-213

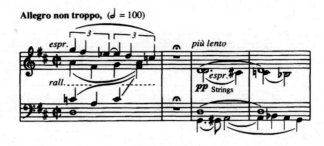

Ex. 19.52. Weber, *Euryanthe,* Overture, mm. 51-54

literally. In measure 52, the stop is on *One,* because the orchestra needs no further beat to play the three chords. After the wait, prepare on *Two.* Although the time signature is **C,** the composer's metronome indication asks for a 2-beat.

There are two ways to conduct the passage in example 19.53. You may cut the first chord with *One* in measure 282 and then wait; a sharp upbeat on *Two* starts the violins. Alternatively, the chord may be cut with the baton in high position (no downbeat!); after the pause, beat *One, Two* in tempo, but remember that *One* must not be too emphatic or it may be mistaken for the attack. (The second method is similar to using an extra beat for the beginning of a piece; see p. 98)

In example 19.54, the players start counting at the double bar; therefore, beat *One, Two* at the beginning of the *Presto,* thus establishing the new tempo. To be ready for this, beat the **sf** in measure 853 with a vigorous rebound and keep the baton high during the pause (see the first movement of Tchaikovsky's Symphony No. 6, in which a similar transition occurs at the end of the introduction).

Ex. 19.53. Weber, *Der Freischütz,* Overture, mm. 281-83

Ex. 19.54. Schumann, Symphony No. 4, fourth movement, mm. 852-55

In measure 105 of example 19.55 beat *Four* to cut off, raising the baton only slightly; pause and repeat *Four* to prepare. The third beat in measure 106 and the fourth in measure 107 are treated similarly. Apply the pattern of figure 19.6.

In example 19.56, stop on *Three* in measure 4, cutting off with the left hand; repeat *Three* after the pause (refer to figure 19.7). Use the left hand again when you stop on *Three* in measure 6, and resume the tempo on *Four* (preparation). Since the notes before the first hold in example 19.57 are pizzicato, just stop on *Four*, which is repeated. In example 19.58, the fourth beat in both bars is repeated, *Three* in the second measure of the example serves as preparation.

Use the pattern of figure 6.4 for example 19.59. In the second measure of the example, stop on *Two* by moving the baton to the left with a short turn of the wrist. The clarinet now plays the cadenza without being directed until it comes to the last B flat (⌒). Beat *Two* again, this time as an upbeat leading into the next measure, using a gesture that prepares *f* legato. The stop on *Two* and repeated beat are done in a similar manner in the fourth measure, but the upbeat is now *p* staccato. (Note that the sideways motion used here on *Two*

Ex. 19.55. Dvořák, Symphony No. 9, "From the New World," second movement, mm. 105-8

Ex. 19.56. Berlioz, *Symphonie fantastique,* first movement, mm. 4-7

for the stop is much more convenient than carrying the second beat to the top of the field.) Subdivide in measures 68–70 of example 19.60 for good rhythmic control. After the pause at the end of measure 69, beat *One* directly in the following bar without preparation.

In measure 26 of example 19.61, sustain *One* with the baton. Release the singers with an unobtrusive left-hand motion, then cut off the orchestra with a

Ex. 19.57.   Berlioz, *Symphonie fantastique,* first movement, mm. 12-15

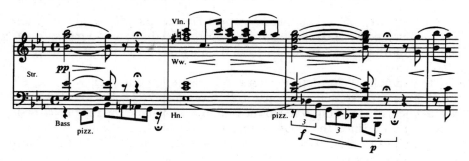

Ex. 19.58.   Berlioz, *King Lear* Overture, one measure after #8

Ex. 19.59.   Liszt, Hungarian Rhapsody No. 2, mm. 23-27

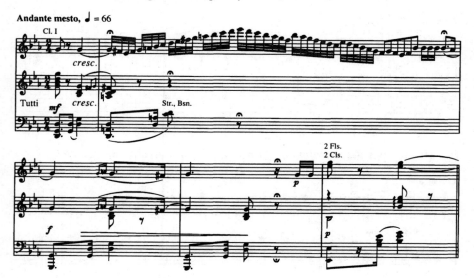

Ex. 19.60. Liszt, Hungarian Rhapsody No. 2, mm. 68-72

Ex. 19.61. Humperdinck, *Hänsel und Gretel,* Act III, "The Witch Waltz," mm. 22-28

decisive gesture. Right after this, bring in the singers with your left hand. They should begin their crescendo without hesitation. The baton, which has remained "in attention," is then used to attack measure 27 with a 1-beat preparation, just like a start after the count.

In example 19.62, *One* in the second measure of the example is repeated. Inexperienced conductors sometimes try to prepare the repeated beat with an extra gesture, instead of following the regular procedure, in the erroneous belief that this increases their control. By beating the **pp** chords light-staccato at about shoulder level, you have plenty of space for the second downbeat after the pause. This downbeat is a vigorous full-staccato.

Ex. 19.62. Puccini, *La Bohème,* Act I, eleven measures after #14

In example 19.63, stop and wait on the downbeat in measure 356, then continue as shown in figure 19.9. Bring in the strings with a gentle but clearly inviting upward movement of the baton. A similar upward movement, but slower (*Meno presto!*), leads the winds after the second fermata.

The same technique is applied to accompaniment in example 19.64. Cut the chord in measure 64 by beating *Three,* and wait for the singer; then repeat *Three* as preparation. In example 19.45, the third beat in measure 424 is repeated.

Ex. 19.63. Schumann, Symphony No. 1, third movement, mm. 353-60

Ex. 19.64. Haydn, *The Creation,* Aria (No. 15), mm. 63-67

Additional examples for the study of fermatas on rests:

Bizet: *Carmen,* Act II, "Torreador Song", m. 24
Copland: Orchestral Variations, Theme
Haydn: Symphony No. 103, 1st movement (development section),
and 4th movement
Hindemith: Symphony *Mathis der Maler,* 3d movement, one measure
before #10
Kodály: *Háry János* (Suite), 5th movement, upbeat
Tchaikovsky: Symphony No. 6, 4th movement, eleventh, fourteenth,
and sixteenth measures after F

DIFFERENT NOTE VALUES UNDER A FERMATA

When some instruments have a different note value under a fermata than others, the conductor must be careful not to omit any necessary beats (see exx. 19.6–19.8). While the left hand sustains the tutti *ff* in example 19.65, the baton waits on *Two,* moves quickly through *Three,* and cuts off the timpani on *Four.* This *Four* is done with a small gesture; a larger one is used for the repeated fourth beat, which cuts off the tutti and prepares the next bar. In measure 202, the first wait is on *One,* and the second wait occurs on the third beat, which also ends the timpani roll.

The third beat in example 19.66 must be given very clearly to start the double tonguing in the trumpets, the tremolo in the strings, and the percussion. Save the left hand for the crescendo. In example 19.67, while the baton sustains the strings (on the sixth beat), cut off the flute quietly with the left hand.

In measure 199 of example 19.68, indicate the entrance of horns, trumpets, and timpani after the count with an extra downbeat (small!) or with a gesture of the left hand. *One* in the next bar cuts the hold.

Ex. 19.65. Beethoven, *Die Weihe des Hauses* Overture, mm. 201-4

Ex. 19.66. Copland, *A Lincoln Portrait,* mm. 270-71

Ex. 19.67. Brahms, Symphony No. 4, fourth movement, mm. 128-31

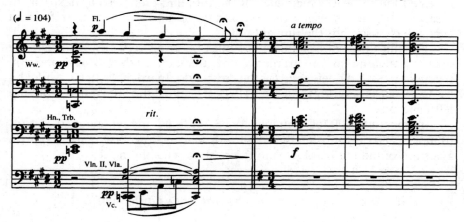

Ex. 19.68. Schumann, Symphony No. 1, third movement, mm. 196-202

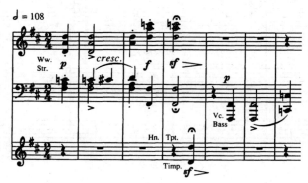

Additional examples for the study of different note values under a fermata:

Beethoven: Symphony No. 8, 1st movement, forty-two measures from the end

Berlioz: "Marche Hongroise" ("Rakóczy March"), *La Damnation de Faust*, last measure

Enesco: Roumanian Rhapsody No. 1, second measure

Haydn: Symphony No. 102, 1st movement, last measure of the introduction

Liszt: *Les Préludes*, before the double bar after D

Schuman, William: Symphony No. 3, Part 2, m. 141 (contrabass!)

INTERRUPTIONS

Most interruptions are executed by stopping the beat, if necessary with cutoff. After the pause, which may be short or long, prepare the next attack. Since the players may overlook an interruption, especially if it is not clearly marked, it is sometimes advisable to use a sudden warning gesture of the left hand.

For examples 19.69–19.71, the regular preparation follows the break. Use no rebound in measure 55 of example 19.70, since you need the upward gesture for preparation. In example 19.71, use the left hand for cutoff; after the interruption, beat the fourth eighth beat as preparation for the next phrase.

The traditional interruption in example 19.72 is very brief. Do not bounce the baton in the third measure of the example, but keep it down as in a tenuto beat. Immediately after the third quarter note, begin the legato preparation,

Ex. 19.69. Elgar, *Enigma* Variations, Var. 12, mm. 1-3

Ex. 19.70. Beethoven, Symphony No. 9, fourth movement, mm. 52-56

Ex. 19.71. Brahms, Symphony No. 4, second movement, mm. 108-11

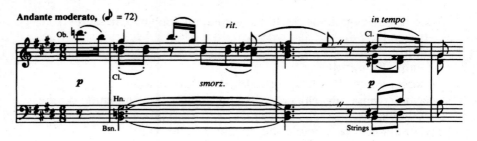

Ex. 19.72. J. Strauss, *Vienna Blood,* No. 4, mm. 201-4

which is somewhat shorter than the regular whole beat; otherwise the interruption would be unduly prolonged.

In example 19.73, the most practical way of indicating the interruption is to use an extra quarter beat at the end of measure 473, which virtually becomes a $\frac{5}{4}$ bar (♩ ♩ ♩). The extra beat serves as cutoff and is followed by the downbeat of measure 474.

To direct a very short interruption *(Luftpause)* between two bars, move the baton downward immediately after a stop at the top of the field of beating. This use of the down-stroke is an only exception to the rule that the baton must change direction in order to lead the orchestra into an attack. This downward gesture is gentle in *p*, forceful in *f*. This procedure for attacking the first count in a bar is applied occasionally to directing other entries (see p. 319).

An extra quarter beat (♩ ♩ ♩ ♩) may be used in example 19.74 to indicate the break and to prepare the next measure. For a very short interruption, however, the following procedure is preferable. Subdivide the third count, the last quarter beat being a somewhat sudden upward gesture which, after a very

Ex. 19.73. R. Strauss, *Don Juan,* mm. 472-74

Ex. 19.74. Vaughan Williams, *A London Symphony,* first movement, mm. 12-14

Reprinted by permission of the copyright owners.
Stainer & Bell. Ltd., London

short stop at the top of the field, is succeeded by a gentle downbeat. The latter starts the next bar without preparation. The motion of the baton may be supported by a smooth gesture of the left hand.

In example 19.75, subdivide the second half of measure 290, using an accented upbeat on the last eighth. Hesitate on this beat and proceed directly into the new tempo. Since this leaves no time for preparation, the first two beats in *molto più mosso* must be sharp and determined. In measure 292, use the accented upbeat again on *Four* and continue with the downbeat after a momentary break.

In example 11.6, cut the tutti fermata, wait, and beat *One* (m. 1382) as preparation; hesitate briefly after a small but snappy *Two.* (In m. 1381, do not forget to cut off the percussion instruments, which is best done with the left hand.)

Ex. 19.75. Mahler, Symphony No. 2, first movement, mm. 290-93

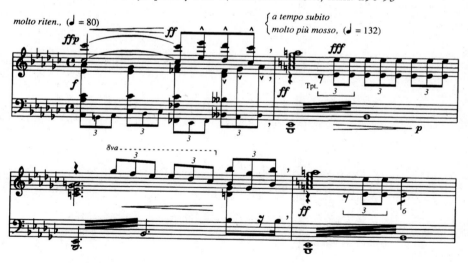

Additional examples for the study of interruptions:

Bartók: Concerto for Orchestra, 5th movement, m. 572

Bartók: *Music for Strings, Percussion, and Celesta,* 4th movement, mm. 25 and 51

Berg: *Lulu* Suite, Variations, last six measures

Brahms: Variations on a Theme by Haydn, after each variation

Britten: *Four Sea Interludes,* No. 4 ("Storm"), between #7 and #8

Gershwin: *Rhapsody in Blue,* seventh measure after #15, three measures before #37, one measure before #39

Hindemith: Symphony *Mathis der Maler,* 1st movement, double bar before #12; 3d movement, double bar after #34

Mahler: Symphony no. 1, 4th movement, between #12 and #14

Mussorgsky: *A Night on Bald Mountain,* four measures after F

Sibelius: Symphony No. 2, 1st movement, double bar after N, and at O.

CHAPTER 20

Accents and Syncopation

ACCENTS

For the indication of an accent, the beat that precedes the accent is always used for preparation, its size and character depending on the degree of the accent to follow. The emphasis that is put on the accented beat can vary widely. Tenuto, marcato, or even staccato may be used for stronger accents. In staccato passages, emphasis is obtained by the increased sharpness of the beat.

An especially strong accent requires a particularly effective preparation. If the accent is on the first count of a measure, the accented upbeat of figure 2.5 is used. To accent the last count of a measure, prepare with a backward thrust of the arm as described for example 4.4. For a strong accent on *Two*, in 4- or 3-beat, the regular patterns do not allow enough space for adequate preparation. Therefore, in 4-beat carry the baton to the right on the rebound of the first beat with a quick curved motion, then sweep to the left for the accented *Two*. In 3-beat this procedure is reversed.

The object of the preparation is to secure a unified attack. Conductors sometimes try to get this result by hesitating just before the accent, a procedure that often fails in its purpose because the players do not coordinate properly. The method given above is an aggressive one in the sense that it actually carries the players into the accented count. In soft music, of course, in order to avoid overemphasis, the aggressiveness should not be made too obvious. This can be accomplished by beating the unaccented counts with a minimum of gesture. In that case, a small preparation will still suffice.

The left hand may also be used to indicate an accent. The gesture includes the preparation on the preceding count and the indication of the accent itself. The preparation is made by an upward motion of the left arm (while the right hand continues its motion undisturbed!). The accent may be indicated in several ways. For example: in *p*, a sharp motion toward the players, the tip of the thumb and index finger together; in *f*, a strong downward movement with the hand or the fist.

In examples 20.1 and 20.2, the composer's time signature is ¢, but many editions print C, an error that may have led conductors to take the introduc-

Ex. 20.1. Schubert, Symphony No. 8, "The Great," first movement, mm. 9-11

Ex. 20.2. Schubert, Symphony No. 8, "The Great," first movement, mm. 29-31

tion to this symphony more slowly than intended by Schubert (see p. 404). Lift the baton slightly higher on *Four* in measures 9 and 10 to prepare the accents in *p*. The accent in *ff* (ex. 20.2) can be prepared with an accented upbeat.

In the third measure of example 16.11, a staccato gesture cuts off on *Three* and also provides the preparation for the accented cello attack; beat *Four* legato and somewhat larger than the following *One*. For the accents in example 20.3, use very incisive gestures.

For the accented fourth counts in examples 20.4 and 20.5, use a curved preparation on *Three*. *Four* is done with a sharp staccato gesture. Observe that in example 20.4 the accent is followed by a neutral beat. In example 20.5, in the third measure of the example, beat *One* with a snappy rebound and *Two* in a down-left direction and stop, skipping *Three*; prepare the new tempo on *Four*. This means that here the preparatory beat starts from down left.

For a sudden tutti staccato chord, as in examples 9.7 (m. 28) and 16.14 (mm. 2 and 3), use the same technique as for an accent.

Various accents in 3-beat are shown in examples 19.35, 20.6, and 20.7. In fast tempo, the gesture indicating accents must be made with very little arm

Ex. 20.3. Sibelius, *Finlandia*, four measures before F

Ex. 20.4. Verdi, *Aïda,* Act II, Introduzione, two measures before A

Ex. 20.5. Verdi, *Aïda,* Act II, Ballabile (No. 6), three measures before I

Ex. 20.6. Tchaikovsky, Symphony No. 5, third movement, mm. 260-66

Ex. 20.7. Barber, *The School for Scandal* Overture, mm. 138-42

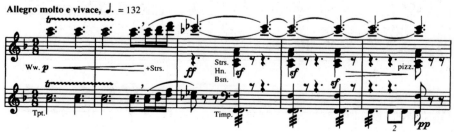

motion; the necessary quick turns of the baton should be made with a flexible wrist (for more on ex. 20.7, see p. 273). So as to use a minimum of gesture for the accents in example 20.8, only a very slight beat is needed on *One* in measures 4–6.

In example 20.9, raise the baton only slightly to prepare the accents on *One*. In example 20.10 use larger beats on *Two* to prepare the accents; use small gestures elsewhere so that the accents are more prominent. The suggested metronome speed follows the advice of a member of Sousa's band.

Conduct 1-beat in example 20.11. The beat in the second measure of the example is a preliminary beat, just as if the piece started in the next bar. Beat staccato for the *sf*. In example 9.21, the accent in *ff* can be expressed by marcato, the one in *p* by tenuto.

Ex. 20.8. Schubert, *Rosamunde—Ballet Music,* No. 9, mm. 3-6

Ex. 20.9. Schubert, *Rosamunde—Ballet Music,* No. 9, mm. 19-27

Ex. 20.10. Sousa, "The Stars and Stripes Forever," mm. 79-86

Ex. 20.11. Bizet, *Carmen,* Act IV, Entr'acte, mm. 73-81

Allegro vivo, ♩. = 80

Additional examples for the study of accents:

Beethoven: Piano Concerto No. 5, 1st movement
Beethoven: Symphony No. 4, 2d movement
Borodin: "Polovtsian Dances" from *Prince Igor*
Brahms: Academic Festival Overture
Gershwin: *Rhapsody in Blue*
Haydn: Symphony No. 92, 1st movement (development section)
Haydn: Symphony No. 97, 1st movement *(Vivace)*
Mahler: Symphony No. 6, 1st and 2d movements
Tchaikovsky: *The Nutcracker* Suite, "Ouverture miniature"; "Danse
  russe (Trepak)"
Verdi: *Messa da Requiem,* Dies Irae (the time signature is ¢, but
  subdivide for *sf*)
Wagner: Overture to *Tannhäuser*

SYNCOPATION

Syncopated passages without accents require no special beat. The gestures must be incisive and the rhythm steady. You must beat, so to speak,
between the notes, not on them. Discipline yourself to keep strictly in tempo,
neither rushing nor dragging. Occasionally, it is better to beat tenuto or
staccato, even in legato phrases, to give the orchestra a solid feeling for the
rhythm.

Examples 20.12–20.15, as well as example 15.5, show syncopations in
various rhythms. Example 20.15 requires special concentration and a beat that
is very precise without becoming stiff. If two pianos are available, practice this
entire section of the concerto; have the solo part played on one piano and the
orchestra part on the other. Conducting this accompaniment is a challenging
exercise for a conducting student.

Syncopated notes with accents are indicated on the preceding beat, which
is staccato. The sharpness of the beat increases with the degree of the accent.
In contrast with an ordinary accent, which is *on* the count, this staccato beat is
not prepared. The beat itself is the preparation for the syncopated note that
comes after the count. Again, never beat the syncopation, beat the rhythm!

Ex. 20.12. Sibelius, *Finlandia,* five measures after G

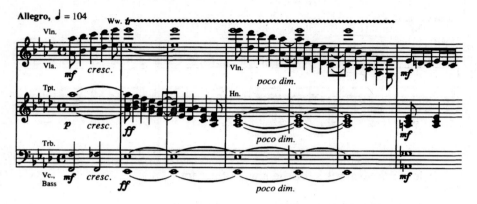

Ex. 20.13. Tchaikovsky, Symphony No. 5, third movement, mm. 68-72

Ex. 20.14. R. Strauss, *Till Eulenspiegel,* mm. 6-12

Ex. 20.15. Schumann, Piano Concerto, third movement, mm. 188-97

Examples 20.16, 20.17, and 20.18 are all in 3-beat. In measures 4 and 6 of example 20.18, do not accent the second beat or you will weaken the strong accent on the third. Syncopated passages in 2-beat are shown in examples 9.17 and 20.19.

Although example 20.20 can be done in free style (see p. 302), practice with the syncopation beat, a vigorous staccato.

Ex. 20.16. Brahms, Symphony No. 2, first movement, mm. 63-67

Ex. 20.17. Brahms, Symphony No. 2, first movement, mm. 118-20

Ex. 20.18. Stravinsky, *L'Oiseau de feu,* "Danse Infernale," mm. 3-6

Ex. 20.19. Beethoven, *The Creatures of Prometheus* Overture, mm. 119-22

Ex. 20.20. Smetana, *The Bartered Bride,* Act II, No. 1, Furiant, mm. 205-12

Additional examples for the study of syncopations:

WITHOUT ACCENTS

Beethoven: Symphony No. 4, 1st movement, (*Allegro vivace*; also with accents)

Debussy: *Nuages,* five measures from the end; also strings pizzicato in the next measure

Mascagni: *Cavalleria Rusticana,* arrival of Alfio (*Allegretto* $\frac{2}{4}$)

Mozart: *Die Zauberflöte,* Act II, No. 17 (Aria), three measures from the end

Sibelius: Symphony No. 4, 1st movement

Verdi: *La Traviata,* Act I, No. 2 (Allegro vivo **C**), passage beginning in m. 38

WITH ACCENTS

Bartók: *Music for Strings, Percussion, and Celesta,* 4th movement, m. 235

Brahms: Symphony #2, 4th movement, at F

Dvořák: Symphony #7, 3d movement

Gershwin: *Rhapsody in Blue*

Prokofiev: "Classical" Symphony, 1st movement, at #17

Puccini: *Tosca,* Act I, m. 4

Respighi: *Feste Romane,* 2d movement, after #12

Rimsky-Korsakov: *Capriccio Espagnol,* at M

Weber: Overture to *Der Freischütz,* m. 53

ACCENTS ON OFF-BEATS

Accents on off-beats are indicated in the same way as syncopated notes with accents—that is, by a sharp staccato on the preceding beat.

Example 16.2b, directed in 2-beat, is instructive for accents both on and off the beat. Remember that the rests not used for preparation are neutral. While the indication of the accented off-beats in example 16.12 offers no problems, the staccato chords in example 20.21 require much concentration on the part of the conductor. The beat should be primarily concerned with the chords and not the string passage. In measure 143, *One* is *f* staccato, *Two,* light-staccato, and *Three* is the preparation for *Four.* In measure 144, *One* is a sharp downbeat for the off-beat chord, *Two* again is light-staccato, and so on. Use rather small gestures and keep strict time. Example 20.22 is conducted in 2-beat; the *f* chords that end the phrases are treated like syncopations with accents (see also ex. 12.4).

Ex. 20.21. Tchaikovsky, *Romeo and Juliet,* mm. 143-45

Ex. 20.22. Beethoven, *Coriolanus* Overture, mm. 19-29

For the beats that are followed by accents in examples 20.23, 20.24, and 20.25, use a clear staccato with a quick rebound on *Two.* Example 7.7 is the same for 1-beat. In example 20.26, the off-beat accent is combined with sustained notes, but the technique remains the same. This is also true for the syncopated entry on *One* in the second measure.

The serenade from the Act II of *Die Meistersinger von Nürnberg,* example

Ex. 20.23. Smetana, "The Moldau," mm. 1-2

Ex. 20.24. Smetana, "The Moldau," mm. 28-30

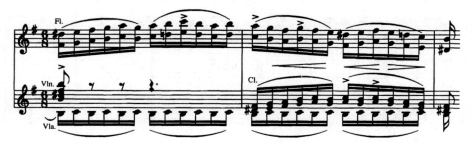

Ex. 20.25. Ravel, *Daphnis et Chloé*—Suite No. 1, two measures before #93

Copyright 1911 Durand & Cie.
Used by permission of the publisher,
Theodore Presser Company, Sole Representative U.S.A.

Ex. 20.26. Barber, Symphony No. 1, mm. 1-2

Copyright © 1970 G. Schirmer, Inc.

20.27, is a tricky challenge because of the continually changing fermatas (with and without repeated beat) and accents (both on and off the beat). Repeat the beat on the fermata in measures 36 and 38, but not in measure 37, in which *Three* (preparatory!) follows the hold directly. The accents in measure 37 are

Ex. 20.27. Wagner, *Die Meistersinger von Nürnberg,* Act II, No. 6, "Den Tag seh ich erscheinen," mm. 36-38

on the beat, those in measures 36 and 38 are after *Three* and *Four* respectively. It is strongly suggested that this entire serenade be studied and practiced.

Additional examples for the study of accented off-beats:

Barber: Symphony #1, 2d and 3d bars after #50.
Beethoven: Symphony No. 4, 3d movement
Beethoven: Symphony No. 6, 4th movement
Brahms: Variations on a Theme by Haydn, Variation 5
Brahms: Violin Concerto, 3d movement
Dvořák: String Serenade Op. 22, Finale
Mozart: Overture to *Die Zauberflöte, Allegro*
Schuman, William: Symphony for Strings, 3d movement, passage starting at m. 58
Tchaikovsky: *Romeo and Juliet* (Overture-Fantasia), three measures from the end
Verdi: *Messa da Requiem,* No. 3, at #61, "Quam olim Abrahae" (although marked **C**, this passage is directed with a 2-beat by most conductors)
Wagner: Overture to *Tannhäuser, Allegro*

fp

A *fp* is executed in much the same manner as an accent. It requires a staccato or marcato beat, and the left hand is used often to secure a unified and sudden drop in dynamics. This warning gesture (palm facing the players) comes almost together with the *fp* beat.

In example 20.28, *fpp* in strings, tremolo, requires a very definite and unhesitating preparation. You get the best results with a clear sweep of the point of the baton. In measure 22, the beats on *One* and *Two* indicate both the tutti chords and the timpani *ffz* on the off-beats; *Three* is neutral-legato, giving the timpani enough time to fade away; *Four* is the precise preparation for the sharp downbeat (not too large) indicating the *ffp*.

As demonstrated by example 20.29, control of the *fp* is especially important for the operatic conductor because of the frequent occurrence of a soft accompaniment immediately after a sharply attacked chord. In examples 20.30 and 20.31, the same technique is used for a change from *f* to *p* (or *pp*) within one beat. Since the baton cannot indicate both *f* and *p* with one gesture, the left hand is needed.

It sometimes happens that there is a change from *p* to *f* within a single beat. This is not, strictly speaking, an accent, but it is convenient to discuss in this chapter the technique for directing such a change. The gesture used must

Ex. 20.28. Dvořák, Symphony No. 9, "From the New World," first movement, mm. 22-27

Ex. 20.29. Bizet, *Carmen,* Act IV, No. 27, mm. 147-50

Ex. 20.30. Shostakovich, Symphony No. 5, second movement, three measures before #55

Ex. 20.31. Sibelius, Symphony No. 2, third movement, mm. 1-4

bring out the element of surprise inherent in the music. Hence, in contrast to an accent, no preparation should be felt on the preceding beat. The effect is achieved by suddenly enlarging the beat on which the *f* enters.

Start to beat measure 138 of example 20.32 as though the *p* would continue uninterrupted, but extend the downbeat quickly with the baton tipped downward. Use the left hand for the *p* subito in measure 139.

In example 20.33, the second beat in measures 90 and 94 is larger, but the first beat must not give away the change prematurely. Use the left hand in measure 95.

Ex. 20.32. Beethoven, Symphony No. 6, first movement, mm. 135-40

Ex. 20.33. Tchaikovsky, Symphony No. 4, third movement, mm. 88-95

Additional examples for the study of *fp*:

Barber: *Essay for Orchestra,* fourth measure after #19
Beethoven: *Fidelio,* No. 7 (*Arie mit Chor*)
Beethoven: Symphony No. 2, 1st movement, introduction
Franck: Symphony in D minor, 3d movement, m. 5; also m. 53
Mahler: Symphony No. 1, 4th movement, passage between #36 and #37 (regardless of the sustained *f* in the horns, the beat must reflect the *fp*)
Prokofiev: "Classical" Symphony, 1st movement, one measure before #9
Rossini: Overture to *William Tell, Allegro Vivace* $\frac{2}{4}$
Smetana: "The Moldau," m. 126
Wagner: *Lohengrin,* Act I, Scene 1

CHAPTER *21*

Phrasing

To indicate phrasing, several different techniques are used. They will be explained in connection with the examples. Although methods of phrasing differ, they have this in common: a decreased intensity at the end of a phrase and by contrast a fresh motion at the beginning of a new one. A slight break results but with no delay in the rhythm, which remains steady. Thus, the players shorten slightly the last note before the break.

In the first measure of example 21.1, beat tenuto (the "dry" tenuto) on *Two*, not leaving it until just before *Three*, so that the third beat is somewhat hurried. In the second measure, go only halfway to the right for *Three*, and immediately start *Four* with an animated gesture. In the third measure, beat tenuto on *Three* in the manner described for example 17.5. Study figure 21.1 for details of gestures.

The following six examples show different phrase endings after the first beat; the method of directing them varies. Notice the difference between the techniques used here and those used for interruptions. In the latter case, the rhythmic structure of certain bars had to be altered; in phrasing, however rhythmic continuity is not affected.

In example 21.2, beat *One* in measure 214 with a vigorous staccato and large rebound, just as if the piece started on *Two*. The first beat in the fifth measure of example 21.3 is staccato with a quick rebound, which provides breathing space and introduces the new phrase on *Two*.

In measure 190 of example 21.4, the composer indicates the phrasing. Beat tenuto on *One*, then swiftly prepare the accented *Two* (see fig. 21.2).

Ex. 21.1. Exercise

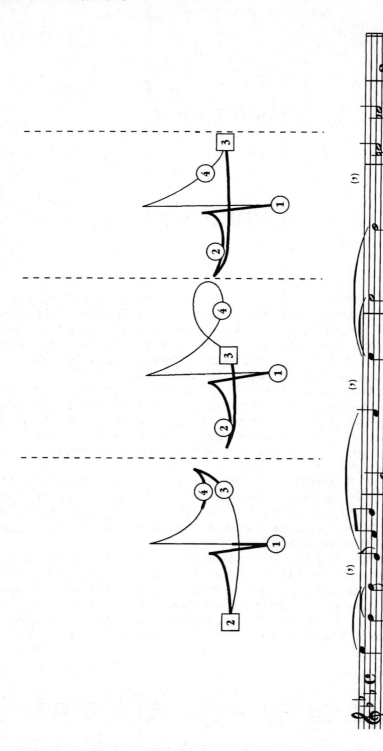

Fig. 21.1. Phrasing for example 21.1

Ex. 21.2. Wagner, *Die Meistersinger von Nürnberg*, Prelude, mm. 211-15

Ex. 21.3. Sibelius, *Finlandia,* at I

Ex. 21.4. Schoenberg, *Verklärte Nacht,* mm. 188-92

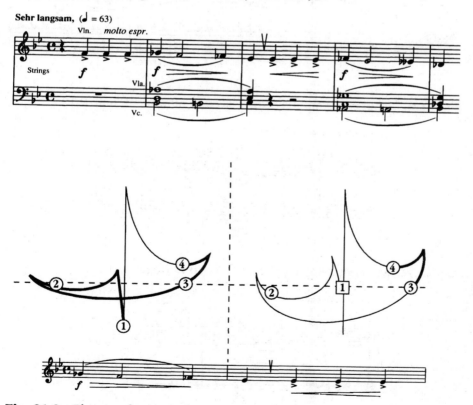

Fig. 21.2. Phrasing for example 21.4

The second beat in measure 178 of example 21.5 is very small. Continue the downbeat in the next bar with an espressivo gesture, thus gaining an animated start for the new phrase. Use the same technique for the next phrase, which begins after a rest. In example 6.7, stop on *One* in the fourth measure, and prepare a new start on *Two* with a very soft and gentle gesture. In measure 237 of example 19.35 there is a break because of the rest, and a calm legato beat would be sufficient. If a pronounced break is desired, beat tenuto on *One*. In example 9.3, beat tenuto on *Three* in measure 2 and resume the staccato on *Four*. A straight gesture is used to reach *Three*. After the staccato beats in measures 1 and 2, the holding quality of the tenuto brings out the structure of the musical phrase. For measure 10 of example 21.6, apply a technique similar to that used in example 21.1, measure 2. In example 21.7, beat tenuto on *Four*, prepare with *Five* (fig. 21.3).

There are other instances of phrasing in which the objective is not to build the melody but to achieve clear separation between successive chords or to secure a sharp release after a sustained note. These are illustrated in the remaining examples of this section.

Ex. 21.5. Mendelssohn, *A Midsummer Night's Dream,* Overture, mm. 176-82

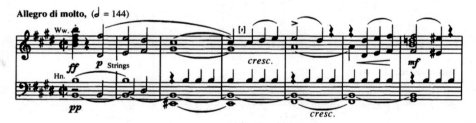

Ex. 21.6. Schubert, Symphony No. 5, second movement, mm. 9-11

Ex. 21.7. Schubert, Symphony No. 5, second movement, mm. 17-18

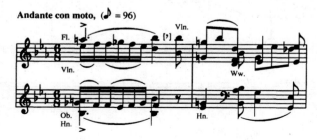

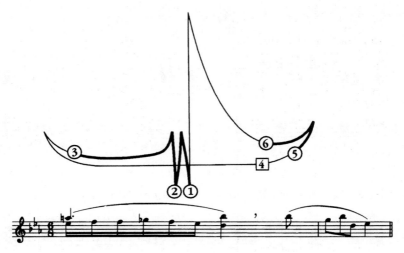

Fig. 21.3. Phrasing for example 21.7

In the second and third measures of example 21.8, beat tenuto on *One* and *Three*, using *Two* and *Four* for preparation (staccato).

In the typical symphonic ending shown in example 19.2, a separation must be made before the last chord is attacked. Stop on *One* in measure 308 and use a delayed *Two* to prepare the final chord. To separate the chords in measures 239 and 240 of example 19.35, beat *One* with a gentle staccato beat, followed immediately by a small preparatory gesture that leads into the chord on *Two*.

A rhythmic figure following a sustained note gains clarity if an energetic beat is used to cut the long note. Thus, *Three* in measures 50 and 51 of example 21.9 is a sharp staccato. Similarly, in measure 201 of example 21.10, both *Two* (accent) and *Three* (cut) are given sharply.

While *Three* in measure 167 of example 21.11 is neutral, *Three* in the next bar is preparation, as is *Two* in measure 169. Cut the phrase with a sharp downbeat in measure 170. In example 21.12, give a sharp beat on *Four* in measure 38. (A short break after the quarter note assures a clean attack of the staccato passage; for this the violin players must lift the bow for a split second.)

In example 20.7, a sharp staccato beat on *Three* in measure 139 secures a unified ending of the trill in the woodwinds and trumpets, and indicates a

Ex. 21.8. Verdi, *Aïda,* Act I, Scena (No. 3), nineteen measures before O

Ex. 21.9. Weber, *Oberon,* Overture, mm. 50-53

Ex. 21.10. Weber, *Oberon,* Overture, mm. 200-202

Ex. 21.11. Tchaikovsky, Symphony No. 6, first movement, mm. 167-70

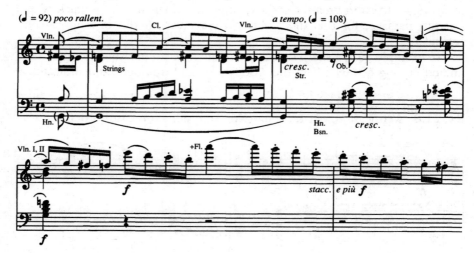

Ex. 21.12. Wagner, *Die Meistersinger von Nürnberg,* Prelude, mm. 35-39

slight pause. The same technique in 1-beat is shown in example 7.10, measure 95 and example 14.12, measure 21.

Additional examples for the study of phrasing:

Brahms: Symphony No. 3, 3d movement, at I
Copland: *The Tender Land* Suite, 1st movement, the last seven measures
Gluck: Overture to *Iphigénie en Aulide,* m. 20
Liszt: Hungarian Rhapsody No. 2, *Andante mesto*
Mahler: Symphony No. 5, 4th movement (*Adagietto*)
Prokofiev: "Classical" Symphony, 2d movement
Tchaikovsky: Symphony No. 5, 1st movement, introduction
Wagner: *Siegfried Idyll*

SUSTAINED NOTES

After a sustained note has been attacked, the remaining counts are very often treated as neutral beats. To beat during soft held notes with anything more than a small neutral beat is meaningless. In f, sustained notes are held most effectively with the left hand.

Example 21.13 is a combination of sustained notes and accents, and its adequate direction requires a well-controlled baton technique. The left hand maintains the intensity, while the function of the baton is limited to an unmistakable indication of the accents on and off the beats; neutral beats are used for the unaccented counts. Use four strokes (subdivision) for the accents in measure 90 (see p. 147).

Crescendo and diminuendo on a sustained note are not usually directed in the same way as in a melodic line. The change is expressed chiefly by the left hand while the intensity of the beat increases or decreases. In other words, the size of the beat is not as important as the change in intensity revealed by the general attitude of the conductor.

If the forearm has sufficient intensity and the facial expression is convincing, you can indicate the crescendo in example 21.14 with small baton gestures even without using the left hand. (The tempo must not drag by "milking" the crescendo; even though the strings divide the bow, beginning with an up-bow, there is a limit to the increase in volume.)

The diminuendos in example 19.28 may be expressed with the left hand while the baton, on the second and third counts, simply marks time and stops on the fermata. Subdivide *Four* in each of the first three bars and use the last eighth for preparation in order to avoid interfering with the diminuendo.

Direct the diminuendo in example 21.15 with the left hand, and use fairly small beats with the baton. Subdivide the quarter notes to lead the descending octaves securely.

In example 21.16 there are eight beats to a measure, with a staccato eighth note preparation and staccato downbeat (fp!). The following two eighth beats are neutral, the next leads into the new chord. The second of these, the fourth eighth beat, also prepares a unified pizzicato attack. Hence, it is

Ex. 21.13. W. Schuman, Symphony for Strings, first movement, mm. 77-92

Ex. 21.14. Weber, *Der Freischütz,* Overture, mm. 1-4

Ex. 21.15. Beethoven, *Leonore* Overture No. 3, mm. 1-3

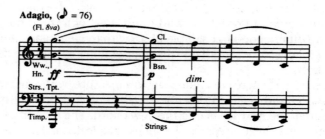

Ex. 21.16. Beethoven, Symphony No. 1, first movement, mm. 1-5

Ex. 21.17. Weber, *Oberon,* Overture, mm. 19-23

somewhat larger than the neutral eighth beats and is very precise. The left hand, which had been raised with the ***fp***, helps to lead the change of harmony and the pizzicato. The sixth eighth is used for an unobtrusive cutoff (winds). It is not necessary to beat the seventh eighth, but keep in time so that the preparation on the last eighth is strictly in tempo. The second measure is done like the first, except that the preparatory last eighth indicates ***p*** and legato (the tempo is well established and the pizzicato will work without staccato beat). Because of the crescendo in measure 3, the beats are no longer neutral. You may use tenuto on the fifth and seventh eighths to build the crescendo. In measure 4, the left hand sustains the first violins, the right cuts off the rest of the orchestra by clicking on the third eighth. On the fourth eighth the baton picks up the legato, while the palm of the left hand turns quickly toward the violins, indicating the sudden *p*.

In example 21.17, cut off the violins, cellos, and basses on the second eighth in measure 21, then count to yourself, but do not beat until the last eighth, which prepares the tutti chord. Beating out this measure would weaken the suspense. The brilliance and dramatic impact of the sudden *ff* are increased by beating the preparation a trifle late. Do not forget that the bounce after the downbeat carries the baton into the position of attention for the violin attack (*Allegro*).

Additional examples for the study of sustained notes:

Beethoven: Symphony No. 3, 2d movement, mm. 158 and 159
Beethoven: Symphony No. 5, 2d movement, mm. 149–153
Brahms: Symphony No. 4, 3d movement, at I
Gounod: *Faust,* Act I, introduction
Prokofiev: Symphony No. 5, 1st movement, passage beginning at #24
Sibelius: *Finlandia, Andante sostenuto*
Strauss: *Till Eulenspiegel,* the fermata measures after #38
Wagner: Prelude to *Lohengrin,* passage starting at the entrance of the trumpets
Wagner: *Götterdämmerung,* Act I, Prelude

SHAPING THE MELODIC LINE

The manner of interpreting a melody is one of the most individual characteristics of a musician. Just as a melody played by different soloists may produce varying impressions, so a melody played by an orchestra under different conductors may not affect the listener in the same way. The gestures by which conductors convey intentions to the players are at least as important as verbal explanations during rehearsal. In fact, at the first rehearsal with an unfamiliar orchestra, skillful conductors can lead a melody according to their intentions by means of their gestures alone.

In short, the shaping of a melodic line is achieved by means of a purposeful combination of the basic techniques that have been discussed. The use of legato, staccato, and tenuto beat for indicating articulation has been explained. It has been shown that changes in the size of the beat affect not only the dynamics but also the phrasing. In addition, such subtle variations in the size of the beat, even from count to count, can express the inflections of the melody that are not indicated by interpretation marks but are "behind the notes." The value of variations in the intensity of the beat, from very intense to completely neutral, has also been treated.

Only by a vital and natural combination of all these elements can the conductor's gestures present a musical conception to the players. The manner of doing this cannot be put into any formula. Yet, the conductor's feeling for the music will be reflected in the size, intensity, and shape of the beat. Now it will be helpful to review some of the melodic passages in previous examples.

Beating the music in example 3.5 *espressivo* with the same size and intensity on all counts would not get much personal reaction from the players. Personal reaction means that each player, in this case in the string section, has the feeling of being a solo performer. To inspire the musicians, the beat needs variety of size and intensity, corresponding to the music's flow.

The following way is suggested, but it is not the only possible way, nor the "right" one. Use a fairly large, incisive beat in measure 119, decreasing size and intensity in measure 120, but with an expressive preparatory gesture on *Four.* A smaller beat on *Four* in measure 121 and more relaxed beats on *One* and *Two* in measure 122 make for a good contrast before the crescendo, which is rendered more effective by the sudden increase in intensity. The first two beats in measure 123 are large, *Three* is very incisive. The second beat in measure 124 is small, the third an expressive preparation. In measure 126, the beat becomes smaller and more relaxed.

You cannot express the whimsical charm of example 19.29 by academic time beating. Every aspect of the conductor's appearance is important—for instance, facial expression, variety in the beat. Here again, every player must be inspired to feel like a soloist and to be completely in the music.

One way of using contrasting beats to bring the whole passage to life is here suggested. Remain motionless after the cutoff of the first fermata. With the small staccato preparation (*Three* in m. 1), relax your manner and facial expression. In measures 2–4, use a legato downbeat and a small "dry" tenuto on *Two* for cutoff; then staccato on *Three* and *Four,* the preparation becoming a little more animated each time. The downbeat in measure 5 is hardly noticeable because of the sudden appearance of the left hand (*p* subito), which remains lifted during the rests and is used for the cutoff on the second fermata. The right hand gives a delicate staccato beat on *Three* (m. 5), changing into legato on *Four.*

In 1-beat, the continued up-and-down motion of the baton may easily become monotonous, with a fatal effect on a melodic passage. This can be avoided in two ways—either by using a graceful curved motion of the baton rather than a straight up-and-down motion, or by changing the size of the beat. A typical passage on which to try these methods is the second theme of the first movement of Beethoven's Fifth Symphony, shown in example 21.18.

Ex. 21.18. Beethoven, Symphony No. 5, first movement, mm. 52-70

Direct measures 52–55 with small forceful gestures, indicating the *secco* character of measures 56–58 with an incisive downward gesture of both arms (m. 57 is preparatory). The gesture in measure 59, to lead the entry of the French horns, should have an upbeat character. The three **sf** notes are marcato. Immediately after the third, the gesture changes to prepare the entry of the **p** legato melody. The rise and fall of the melody is brought out by the size of the beat; in the unstressed measures the beat is very small. An alternative method is to use small gestures throughout and lead the melody with the left hand. If the cellos and basses tend to enter late in measures 65 and 70, let the beat in these bars have a staccato quality.

CHAPTER 22

Changes of Meter and Tempo

Changes of meter and tempo within an ongoing movement occur infrequently in Classical music. They are found mostly at the beginning of a new section, as at the transition from a slow introduction to the lively main section in a symphony or overture, or in the course of an operatic finale where shifting stage action must be integrated with the music. In modern scores, however, such changes may occur at any point as part of the musical fabric from phrase to phrase, even from one bar to another. From the conductor they require careful study and an unmistakable beat.

CHANGE OF TIME SIGNATURE WITHOUT CHANGE OF TEMPO

Examples 22.1–22.4 offer useful exercises. They contain typical changes of meter such as occur in modern music. We can distinguish between two types: (1) Most often, the rhythmic unit remains constant, although the time signature changes. In this case the conductor must be certain that, for instance, ♩ equals ♩ exactly. Exceptions to this rule are usually specifically indicated by the composer. (2) Sometimes, although the meter (time signature) changes, the tempo (pulse) is maintained by keeping the bar length constant. This is usually indicated in the score.

Ex. 22.1. Exercise

In example 22.1, use l-beat in measure 5, 3-beat in measure 10. Resist the temptation in example 22.2 to slow down in the seventh and fifteenth measures! Apply 1-beat in measures 9, 10, and 16, 2-beat in measure 17.

In example 22.3 keep the rhythmic value of the beat constant in measure 4. The change in the 7th measure makes one old bar equal to half of a new bar. *In measure 10, the 2-beat remains constant.* According to tradition the special indication o = o· is omitted; in fast tempo, when 2-beat is used throughout, it is customary that at the change to 6-time, bar equals bar. On the other hand, it is taken for granted that at the change from ₵ to ¾ (m. 14), ♩ equals ♩. As a result of these traditions, which contradict strict logic, measures 10 and 14 are of different length.

Direct example 22.4 in 1-beat in measures 3–7. Use figure 13.5 for

Ex. 22.2. Exercise

Ex. 22.3. Exercise

Ex. 22.4. Exercise

measure 15. Be sure that the sixteenth note values remain constant in measures 3 and 10–13, and beat accordingly with unmistakable downstrokes.

Examples 22.5 and 22.6 clearly show the difference in applying 6-beat for the time signature $\frac{6}{4}$ (ex. 22.5) and subdivided 3-beat for the time signature $\frac{3}{2}$ (ex. 22.6). (Unfortunately, composers do not always indicate this correctly; they may mark double time, $\frac{6}{4}$, in passages that actually are in triple time, $\frac{3}{2}$; in such cases the conductor must use personal judgment.) Note that in the two succeeding passages the value of the quarter note remains constant.

Review the following examples in which the pulse (in conjunction with the beat) remains the same, although the *pattern* of the beat changes with the time signature: examples 17.8, 19.48, 25.1, 12.14, 12.16, 13.3, 13.5 (m. 2), and 13.13.

The $\frac{3}{4}$ measure in example 22.7 offers no particular problem, because the quarter beat was present in the subdivision of the previous measures. In example 22.8 the composer indicates that the bar length is unchanged at the *alla breve*.

Ex. 22.5. Shostakovich, Symphony No. 5, third movement, two measures before #81

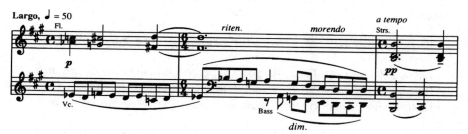

Ex. 22.6. Shostakovich, Symphony No. 5, third movement, at #85

Ex. 22.7. Copland, *A Lincoln Portrait*, mm. 20-24

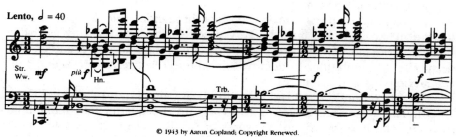

Ex. 22.8. Beethoven, Symphony No. 3, "Eroica," third movement, mm. 377-87

Additional examples for the study of passages in which the time signature changes while the beat remains constant:

> Barber: Symphony No. 1, from the beginning until #4 (study score pp. 1–10)
>
> Berlioz: *Roméo et Juliette,* 4th part (Scherzo), transition to *Allegretto* $\frac{3}{4}$
>
> Brahms: *Tragic* Overture, double bar at K, *Molto più moderato* $\frac{4}{4}$
>
> Liszt: Piano Concerto No. 2, *L'istesso tempo* $\frac{6}{8}$ (twelve measures after K)
>
> Mahler: Symphony No. 6, 2d movement, passage between #88 to #95
>
> Puccini: *La Bohème,* Act I, passage between #9 and #10
>
> Rimsky-Korsakov: *Scheherazade,* 2d movement, transitions at H and N
>
> Sibelius: Symphony No. 2, 2d movement
>
> Tchaikovsky: Symphony No. 4, 4th movement, *Andante* $\frac{3}{4}$
>
> Wagner: *Siegfried,* Act I, Scene 1

In the above examples, the beat was constant regardless of the change of time signature. In the examples that follow the beat changes with the time signature. Hence, the conductor must "think" the rhythmic unit, just as in the handling of asymmetrical time patterns. The slightest uncertainty in the beat may jeopardize the ensemble.

In example 22.9 the ♪ remains constant throughout; therefore, the 1-beat starting in measure 386 must be very precise and sure, securing a steady sixteenth note movement. Be especially careful of the return to $\frac{2}{4}$, and do not delay *Two!* (An ambitious student will do well to practice Act III, Scene 3 of *Die Meistersinger* in its entirety.)

The $\frac{3}{4}$ in example 22.10 is done with 1-beat (straight, or subdivided *One, Three*). The $\frac{4}{4}$ bars are beaten *alla breve* with the quarter unit remaining constant. The first seventy-six measures of Act III, Scene 2 of *Tristan und Isolde,* from which this example is taken, are notable for being the first

Ex. 22.9. Wagner, *Die Meistersinger von Nürnberg,* Act II, Scene 3, mm. 383-91

Ex. 22.10. Wagner, *Tristan und Isolde,* Act III, Scene 2, mm. 47-58

instance of frequent rhythmic changes of this type. The full score should be studied and used for practice (see ex. 13.4).

The use of two different time signatures within one measure, as shown in example 22.11, is rare. In effect, the second measure of the example is a $\frac{9}{16}$ measure to be directed with a lopsided 4-beat, 2 + 3 + 2 + 2 (see p. 165), as indicated by the composer's "battre à 4." The metronome marking points to subdivision in the first measure. Even if the conductor does not subdivide each count, the continuity of the sixteenth-unit must be preserved.

In example 13.6, be sure to keep the tempo steady when returning to 2-beat in the last measure; do not rush!

When conducting the passage shown in example 13.7 as a whole, set the metronome at 144, which gives the quarter beat and thereby establishes the eighth unit. Double tempo in the sixth measure results in ♩ = 144 (composer's mark: ♪ = ♩).

The passage in example 13.9 begins at a speed of ♩. ♩ = 46, which

Ex. 22.11. Stravinsky, *Dumbarton Oaks* Concerto, two measures after #3

actually means ♩ = 160. With the stringendo, the tempo increases to about ♩ = 178 in the eighth measure. A definite feeling for the eighth unit is best maintained by counting to yourself and using sharp downbeats in the first through the twelfth measures. (Counting the small units to yourself is useful in conducting passages of this kind!)

Review example 13.10 by conducting the entire passage in continuity. Consult the full score for this example as well as for example 13.14, to which the same techniques described above should be applied.

Additional examples for the study of passages in which the rhythmic unit remains constant while the beat changes:

Bartók: Concerto for Orchestra, 1st movement, mm. 488–509 (see Appendix A, No. 9)

Copland: *El Salón México*

Dvořák: Scherzo Capriccioso, passage in $\frac{2}{4}$ (m. 561)

Strauss, Richard: *Don Juan,* m. 30

Strauss, Richard: *Don Quixote,* transition to Variation 8

Stravinsky: *Le Sacre du Printemps,* 1st part, ("Jeu du Rapt"), passage between #43 and #48

Stravinsky: *Les Noces,* Parts 1 and 2

Wagner: *Götterdämmerung,* Interlude between the Prelude and Act I ("Siegfried's Rhine Journey"), transition from Schnell $\frac{6}{8}$ to Rasch $\frac{3}{4}$

If a string group is available, the first movement of Stravinsky's Concerto for String Orchestra is highly recommended for class study. The same composer's Symphonies of Wind Instruments also offers an excellent opportunity to apply the techniques discussed here.

CHANGE OF TEMPO WITH RHYTHMIC RELATIONSHIP MAINTAINED

Sometimes the note values of the new tempo are related to the previous ones, which may be indicated by the composer by means of markings such as *doppio movimento, mezzo tempo,* ♩ = ♩ and others. Concerning this last indication, composers are not in agreement as to which note value represents the old tempo and which the new. In Classical music the musical context gives the clue, while modern composers generally use the relation: $\quarternote$ (old) = $\halfnote$ (new).

Example 22.12 illustrates a number of typical changes of tempo and beat. Use 2-beat in the sixth measure, 1-beat in the thirteenth. Observe that the relation between measures 16 and 17 is based on the equality of the two bars. The marking *Tempo stretto come avanti* in example 22.13 indicates that $\eighthnote\eighthnote\eighthnote$ (old) equals $\eighthnote\eighthnote\eighthnote$ (new); therefore, the quarter beat equals the previous half beat (note that, at this point, the tempo is taken more slowly than at the beginning of the movement).

In the *Presto* (1-beat) of example 22.14, the whole measure equals the quarter beat of the previous tempo.

Ex. 22.12. Exercise

Ex. 22.13. Franck, Symphony in D Minor, third movement, mm. 121-26

Ex. 22.14. Brahms, Symphony No. 2, third movement, mm. 31-37

In example 22.15, for an unmistakable indication of the tempo change ($\flat = \flat$), it may be helpful to subdivide the last quarter beat in the second measure. In any case, "think" the eighth note values in the old tempo just before starting the *Doppio mosso*.

The quarter beat of the Allegro in example 22.16 is twice as fast as the quarter value in the *Lento*.

For the second measure in example 22.17, apply figure 13.2; the eighth beats are twice as fast as the quarter beats in the preceding measure. The second beat in each bar should be sufficiently sharp to bring out the syncopations.

In example 22.18, subdivide the third quarter beat in the second measure; the second eighth of the subdivided beat serves as preparation for *Four* in the new tempo, which is twice as fast as the old tempo. If the metronome markings in example 22.19 are strictly observed, each of the slow beats in measure 18 equals four fast beats of the preceding tempo. Good control is needed to indicate the sudden change with calm, small gestures.

Ex. 22.15. Barber, Symphony No. 1, at #4

Ex. 22.16. Copland, *A Lincoln Portrait*, mm. 54-58

Ex. 22.17. Hanson, Symphony No. 3, first movement, one measure before
#13

Ex. 22.18. Strauss R., *Tod und Verklärung,* fourteen measures after D

Ex. 22.19. Dukas, *L'Apprenti Sorcier,* mm. 14-20

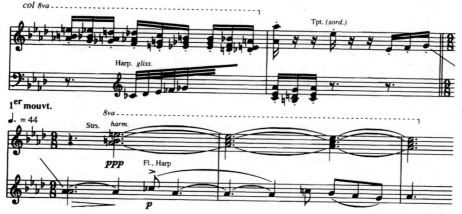

The tempo change in example 18.2 is, in effect, ♪ = ♩. In example 12.9, change from slow to fast (♩ = ♪).

Additional examples for the study of tempo changes with rhythmic relation maintained:

Britten: *War Requiem,* "Dies Irae," at #49 (five eighth notes equal a quintuplet in the new tempo)

Carter: *The Minotaur,* Suite, passage beginning at #66

Delius: *Brigg Fair,* passage between #38 and #39

Kodály: *Psalmus Hungaricus,* transition at #9

Mahler: Symphony No. 1, 1st movement, at #4

Rimsky-Korsakov: *Scheherazade,* 2d movement (*Moderato assai*) 4/4 at F

Schoenberg: *Kammersymphonie,* passage beginning with m. 249

Sibelius: Symphony No. 3, 2d movement, 13th measure after #6, *Tranquillo*

Strauss, R.: *Till Eulenspiegel, Gemächlich* 2/4, nineteenth measure, *doppelt so schnell;* twenty-fifth measure, *wieder noch einmal so langsam*

Stravinsky: L'Oiseau de feu (Suite), Finale, *Doppio Valore Maestoso* at #19

CHANGE OF TEMPO WITHOUT RHYTHMIC RELATIONSHIP

Some tempo changes occur without relationship between the last beat in the old tempo and the first beat in the new. If there is an opportunity in the music for a preparatory beat, the new tempo is established just as at the beginning of a piece. This is the case in examples 9.5, 19.44, and 19.67 (after a fermata), example 19.70 (after an interruption), examples 20.5 and 20.29 (after a rest), example 20.28 (after a sustained note), example 19.65 (after the last beat in the bar, but feasible only because of the slow tempo which allows subdivision on the last count), and example 14.13 (at the end of a ritardando).

However, a sudden transition may leave no opportunity for a preparatory beat. This requires a clear and determined gesture, especially for the first few beats in the new tempo. The conductor must be absolutely sure of the tempo, and lead the players with unmistakable beats. Still, some sudden changes are so difficult that they can be played satisfactorily only as a result of rehearsing.

In example 22.20, the first three beats in measure 32 must be given without any hesitation, yet without rushing, with small staccato beats.

No interruption is intended in measure 20 of example 22.21; simply start the new tempo on *Three.* In example 22.22, use a simple and very clear wrist motion for the downbeat at *Presto,* addressing the first violins. (The first note in m. 514 has been changed to D by conductors who believe that the start of the violin run ought to be identical with that in the *Leonore* Overture No. 2. Beginning the run with the C, they feel, anticipates the tonic chord and

Ex. 22.20. Nicolai, *The Merry Wives of Windsor,* Overture, mm. 31-33

Ex. 22.21. Enesco, Roumanian Rhapsody No. 1, mm. 18-21

Ex. 22.22. Beethoven, *Leonore* Overture No. 3, mm. 509-15

weakens the effect of the tutti entrance twenty-one measures later. The autograph is lost, and there exist no textual sources that deserve to be called authentic, unless the D found in one of Beethoven's sketches for *Leonore* Overture No. 3 is considered sufficient evidence.)

Some conductors subdivide in example 22.23 for the sudden *poco meno,* but it is better just to slow down the 1-beat. Allow the players time for the second and third quarter notes in your calm and graceful upbeat.

In example 22.24, the transition into a quicker tempo in measure 353 must be indicated with particular certainty because of the syncopation; use a precise staccato.

Ex. 22.23. J. Strauss, *Voices of Spring,* mm. 194-202

Ex. 22.24. Beethoven, Symphony No. 4, third movement, mm. 349-57

The following six examples show change of tempo in combination with change of rhythmic pattern.

In example 22.25, the gesture on *Two* in measure 194 uses the accented upbeat and is timed as a preliminary beat in the slower tempo. In the fourth measure of example 22.26, an incisive *Two* is needed to establish the new tempo firmly.

In example 13.15, within no more than four bars, the quarter beat changes abruptly from ♩ = 116 to ♩ = 80 and again to ♩ = 138.

Ex. 22.25. Harris, "When Johnny Comes Marching Home," mm. 192-96

Copyright © 1939 (Renewed) G. Schirmer, Inc. (ASCAP)

Ex. 22.26. W. Schuman, Symphony No. 3, Part II, mm. 300-304

Copyright © 1941 (Renewed) G. Schirmer, Inc.

An energetic full-staccato beat is needed for the Vivo in example 22.27. In example 22.28, the composer indicates not only a change of pattern (1-beat) but also a suddenly faster tempo. Therefore, lead the first two measures of the *Più mosso* with especially clear downbeats. The gradual increase of the tempo leads to a brief stop after the hurried ending of the pizzicato passage (m. 14). Although the break is not printed in the score, the composer demanded it.

Ex. 22.27. Rimsky-Korsakov, *Capriccio Espagnol,* fifth movement, five measures after X

Ex. 22.28. Barber, *The School for Scandal* Overture, mm. 298-317

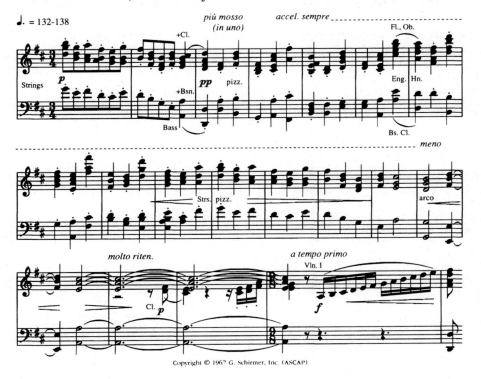

After the interruption, direct the *meno* with 3-beat, *poco espressivo.* Measure 314 (*molto riten.*) is done neutral-legato, but in measure 315 beat *Two* and *Three* staccato to prepare for the detached notes, played hesitantly by the clarinets. For a *tempo primo* (♩. = 132), use staccato gestures, not too large but very determined.

Example 13.9 illustrates a change to slower tempo and to the 3-beat pattern.

Additional examples for the study of sudden tempo changes without rhythmic relationship:

Bartók: *Music for Strings, Percussion, and Celesta,* 3d movement, m. 54 (5/4) ♩ = 80, m. 55 ♩ = 104

Beethoven: Symphony No. 5, 2d movement, mm. 205 (*Più mosso*) and 218 (*Tempo I*)

Beethoven: Symphony No. 6, 3d movement, m. 234 (Presto)

Berlioz: *La Damnation de Faust,* "Menuet des Feux-Follets,' several changes from *Moderato* to *Presto*

Debussy: *La Mer,* 2d movement, at #25

Dvořák: Symphony No. 9. 3d movement, *a tempo* at #2

Janáček: Sinfonietta, 4th movement, at #7

Mahler: Symphony No. 1, 4th movement, at #22

Roussel: Suite in F, 3d movement, six measures after #26 (*Allegro giocoso*)

Stravinsky: *Pulcinella* Suite, at #27 and #30

Tchaikovsky: Symphony No. 5, 2d movement, *Moderato con anima* (m. 66)

Verdi: *Aïda,* Act II, Scene 2 (Gran Finale), start of the ballet music (*Più mosso*) at E

CHAPTER 23

Application of Baton Technique

APPLYING BATON TECHNIQUE TO THE SCORE

The discussions in the Appendix show how to apply baton technique to a complete score. Some of these detailed suggestions may be considered too personal; in fact, certain passages can be directed in several different ways. The further you advance, the more you will develop your own technique and will use the gestures that suit your artistic personality. Some musicians maintain that a detailed planning of gestures has little value and that if the conductor knows the score thoroughly, gestures will follow automatically. Since the gestures of even experienced conductors are not always adequate at first rehearsals, a novice will profit from such planning. Especially in difficult passages, the student may have to conduct his imaginary orchestra again and again before the sequence of motions is well-balanced and fits the music.

Two basic requirements should be kept in mind: (1) a strong feeling for the rhythm of each individual part as well as for the whole, which combines different rhythms, is needed to direct the players with authority; (2) only if all the dynamic gradations are firmly fixed in your mind can your gestures be combined in a simple and natural way. Even highly talented young musicians, especially if their experience has been limited to the piano, need self-discipline to reach perfection with regard to rhythm and dynamics.

In order to direct the theme in example 23.1 with conviction, the conductor must study its rhythmic structure, especially the frequent change from $\frac{6}{4}$ to $\frac{12}{8}$.

A polyrhythmic passage of the type shown in example 23.2 needs careful study. You must know the various rhythmic figures and the way they are combined or your gestures will lack firmness. You will do well to direct each rhythmic pattern separately before you conduct the whole.

Furthermore, the importance of knowing the orchestration thoroughly cannot be overstated, not only for cuing but for the conductor's planning as well. As the baton moves, the conductor's mind is focused on a line that contains all the important musical elements and interpretation marks in terms

Ex. 23.1. W. Schuman, Symphony for Strings, first movement, mm. 1-12

Molto agitato ed energico, ♩. = 76

of the instruments. Which musical elements are important? The conductor must decide when to direct the melody, how much attention to give to the inner parts, and which details need special attention. The choice of "what to conduct" lends individuality to the interpretation. For example: when two groups play the melody, the larger one is usually led more directly, but if a particular orchestral color is desired (as strings with solo woodwinds, the woodwind color predominating), the smaller group is addressed. The effect of a passage may be greatly enhanced by directing countervoices more strongly than the main melodic line. Generally speaking, however, it is unwise to pay too much attention to inner parts and to use elaborate gestures for a great number of small details, for this disturbs the logic of the overall musical picture and may easily become a mannerism.

Advance planning of gestures can create a serious danger: preconceived ideas might become so firmly fixed in your mind that when facing the orchestra you forget that you are leading human beings and no longer an imaginary group of musicians. Most essential for a conductor is to stick to a

Ex. 23.2. Schoenberg, *Five Pieces for Orchestra,* No. 4, mm. 292-293

Molto allegro ♩ = 132

clear concept of how to bring the score to life, but at the same time you must never lose contact with reality and you must adapt your gestures to the responses and needs of the players.

Factors such as the quality of the players are important, because with less-experienced musicians the conductor's concern is with elementary needs, while with well-trained players a conductor's indications are directed more toward interpretative ends. In experienced orchestras, the players themselves supply a good deal of precision and expression upon which the conductor can rely. Still, details of tempo, dynamics, and articulation that are not marked in the orchestral parts need stronger gestures than those that are. The results of rehearsal must also be considered: well-rehearsed details require less indication during the performance than those that have not been prepared.

THE DANGER OF OVERCONDUCTING

The fact that a great variety of techniques has been discussed does not mean that they are to be constantly applied. Not every interpretational mark requires a gesture. Not every accent or every detail of phrasing must be indicated. An overloading of gestures would indeed interfere with the spontaneity of the performance.

Above all, you should keep in mind that you do not "play the music!" The musicians play, while you simply give directions. Stopping conducting altogether and leaving the orchestra to its own devices is a proven method for the student to develop an understanding for the proper use of gestures.

ADJUSTMENTS WHILE IN ACTION

No one can foresee at all times how the players will respond; hence, the conductor's ear must be keen enough to realize what the orchestra is doing and, if the results are not as desired, gestures must be adjusted accordingly.

The importance of the ability to maintain a definite tempo has already been stressed. If the players hurry or drag the music, a firm beat must counteract this. It may even become necessary to use staccato or tenuto (especially the "dry" tenuto), even if the music is legato. If the tempo threatens to become uneven in staccato passages, the sharpness of the beat should increase. Such corrective measures, however, must not take the form of jerky gestures. Caution must be exercised particularly in accelerating the tempo when the players are dragging, because the acceleration may become too great. On the other hand, the common error of using an enlarged, spasmodic beat can cause the tempo to drag still more. The best way of maintaining control is with relatively small but firm beats. This also applies to cases when you may have to correct your own tempo. In general, it is easier to speed up after having started too slowly than to curb an overly fast pace. In slow tempo, a subdivided beat may effectively prevent hurrying.

But the beat is secondary; it is most important that the conductor's feeling for the tempo be so strong that it cannot be affected by any irregularities on the part of the orchestra. Even though the beat may have to yield to the players for one or two counts for the sake of ensemble, the conductor must be able to restore the correct tempo. As an invaluable exercise, you should practice with a pianist who can follow the beat as an orchestra would but who deliberately slows down or hurries, forcing you to find the corrective gestures with which to lead back to the original tempo. You should practice this exercise with different rhythms, legato and staccato, and at different speeds.

Such flexibility is particularly useful in accompaniment because of unexpected delays, stops, and other emergencies. It is usually easier to wait than to catch up. If the latter is necessary, small beats are much more effective than large ones. Nervousness may lead to frantic motions that aggravate rather than remedy the situation. Conductors must remain calm in an emergency and should learn to anticipate difficulties before they arise. The same is true for adjusting entrances that are either missed or played prematurely. A useful technique to smooth out an early entrance is to hold the offender with a left-hand gesture while leading the rest of the group with the baton, being sure to bring the former into unity with the others. An angry wave of the hand would only confuse the issue. The conductor's job is to help the performance and not to discipline the players.

The conductor's awareness for the musicians' needs should include even such mechanical problems as putting on and taking off mutes or turning pages between movements. More important, the way you lead the players cannot be separated from their musicianship. You should allow an individual player considerable freedom in the performance of a solo passage by simply conducting the accompaniment.

To what extent the players watch the baton depends partly on the individual musician's technical ability and alertness. Yet, except for the rare occasions when attention is completely absorbed by a very difficult passage, the average player makes a considerable effort to watch the baton. If this were not so, it would be hard to explain the remarkable influence exercised by an able conductor at a first reading of unfamiliar music. Still, the conductor should cooperate with the players by assisting them with very clear and, if necessary, larger gestures, either in passages of great technical difficulty or when something goes wrong and decisive leadership is demanded.

The conductor's function, however, goes far beyond the mere exercise of control. Technique must be a means through which a conductor vitalizes the orchestra, and lets the music sing; then, gestures will not become mechanical. When conducting combines technical mastery with musical inspiration, the players feel that the conductor is working with them. By acting as an artistic leader rather than a disciplinarian you will affect the players positively. Only a direct and positive approach inspires the players for a vital performance.

CHAPTER *24*

Free Style

FREE STYLE OF CONDUCTING

It often happens that a student attends a concert that is led by an accomplished conductor and finds that the leader's gestures do not correspond with the patterns and methods studied so arduously. You wonder if you have been wasting your time and whether what you have learned can be applied to actual conducting.

Typically, the author of the present text was challenged at one time by a young man preparing for a conducting career, who came to see him after a concert: "Maestro, I have been watching you all evening, but I could not help noticing that you do not conduct the way you teach in your book!" "Well," was the reply, "haven't you read the chapter on Free Style?" It was, of course, a tongue-in-cheek answer, but it still pointed to the difference between an academic use of learned gestures and spontaneous music making in a live performance.

What in this book might be called good usage in conducting conforms to the traditional patterns, but it is not always easy to recognize the patterns, since there is room for considerable variation. Furthermore, the rapidity with which the gestures follow each other makes it difficult to discern them. The student's plight may be compared to that of a person with a good theoretical knowledge of a foreign language who, entering the country where the language is spoken, has difficulty with the swiftness of everyday speech. In both cases increasing experience will clear up the confusion.

Nevertheless, the student is correct in concluding that the conductor uses some gestures that do not conform to any of the patterns. Some of these gestures are discussed below.

The direction of any beat may be changed to secure a particular result. For intense lyricism in 4-beat, it is effective to carry ② higher than usual and to reach ③ with a diagonal movement, especially when the third beat is emphasized. In very strong passages, downbeats may be used on each count to stress the attack. (This should not tempt a young conductor to adopt an all-downbeat technique!)

The chords in measures 21–23 of example 24.1 are led by some conductors with successive downbeats. The bars shown in example 24.2 conclude an entire movement. Since it would be awkward to end with an upward gesture, use a downbeat for *Two* in the last measure. This downbeat is a sharp motion to direct the accented off-beat.

In fast 2-beat, the gesture easily becomes monotonous and does not lend itself to the directing of expressive passages. Therefore, conductors sometimes use curved motions, carrying the baton to the right on *One* and to the left on *Two*. This method avoids the continual stress on the first beat, which in certain lyric passages, as in example 24.3, can become quite disturbing.

Also in 2-beat, it is possible to emphasize *Two* by using a not-too-large but energetic sideways stroke, preferably to the left, when an upward *Two* would be inconvenient; this means that the first beat is very small.

The beginning of the movement shown in example 24.4 (mm. 1 and 3) can be done by beating *Two* to the left with a strong but short gesture. In measures 2 and 4, beat only *Two* (upward) as preparation.

It has already been pointed out that certain beats may be weakened in order to emphasize others by contrast. In free style the weakening may be

Ex. 24.1. Beethoven, Symphony No. 9, first movement, mm. 16-24

Ex. 24.2. Walton, Symphony No. 1, first movement, final measures

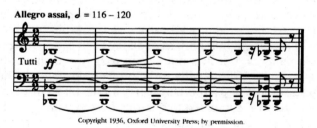

Ex. 24.3. W. Schuman, Symphony for Strings, third movement, mm. 177-183

Ex. 24.4. Beethoven, Symphony No. 7, fourth movement, mm. 1-6

carried to the point where such beats disappear altogether. In all cases, however, the first beat should be omitted only when there is no likelihood of a misunderstanding. Many players follow the music by counting bars and need the downbeat. The same applies to skipping rests, which is done fairly often because the conductor does not want to waste gestures. For instance, in example 11.12, the fourth and fifth eighth beats may be omitted in measures 2 and 4, though the rhythm must be maintained strictly. Generally, a conductor with limited experience will do well to indicate all the rests if there is the slightest possibility of a misunderstanding.

In orchestral accompaniments, a careful handling of rests is required when the orchestra pauses for several successive measures. In each of these measures (general pauses) the first count should be indicated by a clear downstroke, omitting the other counts. In many cases, this free-style procedure is more secure than the indication of all the counts. Not to beat at all during passages of this kind is advisable only if the players have been informed at which bar the conductor will resume the regular beat. A good example of such a case occurs at the end of the violin cadenza in the first movement of Mendelssohn's Violin Concerto; from the beginning of the cadenza do not beat thirty-five bars, but resume the regular 2-beat one measure before the entrance of first violins, first flute, and first oboe.)

Whether to beat or omit rests is particularly important in accompanying recitatives. Many Italian opera conductors traditionally use a downbeat for all chords regardless of the count on which they fall. This is practicable only when orchestra parts include the words of the recitative; otherwise beats must be very clear and the first counts must be unmistakable, even while the orchestra is waiting during several rests.

Not beating at all for a number of bars while the orchestra continues playing must also be classified as a free-style characteristic. When not indulged in for the sake of showmanship this can have a genuine musical purpose. Passages in chamber music style may need little or no indication from the conductor. The fact that no beat is given may challenge the players' initiative and result in an especially well-balanced and delicate performance. Besides, it may be helpful for young conductors to realize that the musicians can to a certain extent play without direction, and not control every single count, or every detail. But if the beat is stopped, it must be resumed smoothly at the proper moment, or the performance will become shaky.

It may sometimes be effective to beat with the left hand instead of the right. In example 16.8 you may direct the timpani solo (m. 5) with the left hand, saving the right for the tutti in the next measure.

In certain syncopated passages in which the syncopation is in effect a change of time signature, you may beat the accents instead of the rhythm. Do this only when all the instruments have the same rhythmic pattern and no misunderstanding is possible. The conductor must be sure that clear-cut control allows a return to the regular rhythm with absolute certainty.

As was mentioned earlier, example 20.20 may be conducted in free style. Use three beats for measures 205–6, beating on each **sf** and returning to 1-beat in measure 207, as though the music were written in the notation shown in example 24.5.

The use of free style for preparatory gestures will be discussed in chapter 26. While free style adds variety to the beat and sometimes brings out effects that the regular pattern cannot achieve, it loses its meaning if used too frequently. It can be dangerous if it weakens the players' feeling of security, especially in unfamiliar music. Also, it may confuse an orchestra that is not highly experienced.

Ex. 24.5. Illustration of free-style notation for example 20.20

THE ART OF ACCOMPANIMENT

In conducting an orchestral accompaniment you face essentially the same problems as in accompanying a soloist at the piano, but the particular kind of alertness and flexibility that are the mark of a good piano accompanist are required to an even greater degree by the conductor: Your gesture must both follow the soloist and lead the orchestra. For, even though the players adjust to the soloist to a certain extent, they must rely on the leader for most of the coordination.

Perfect ensemble between the soloist and the orchestra is obtained more easily when the conductor and the soloist work out their interpretation beforehand. Even then the conductor must be ready for unexpected tempo modifications. However, considerable skill and attention are demanded of the leader in order to maintain a good ensemble when there has been limited rehearsal time.

Agreement on the starting tempo is essential when an introduction precedes the first solo entrance. The conductor must set the pace in a way that conforms to the soloist's playing. Lack of consistency in tempo could cause discomfort, if not embarrassment. Sometimes a brief orchestral introduction consists merely of broken chords, as at the beginning of Sibelius's Violin Concerto. To be sure of the tempo, the conductor might hum the solo theme inaudibly before giving the upbeat.

A few technical hints follow. In slow tempo, resist the temptation to subdivide the beat unless subdivision is absolutely necessary. It is much better to use slightly larger and very calm gestures that, so to speak, contain the smaller values and make musicians listen to the soloist. If they listen carefully, they follow even rubato passages without the conductor's help. A desire to stay together with the soloist must not result in stiff gestures with overly large beats, or the accompaniment will drag. Do not hesitate unnecessarily on the counts, but keep the gesture moving with a light forearm. Be prepared to delay or hasten toward the next count. A special warning is given against waiting on the last count in the bar with uplifted arm; if a delay is necessary, move slowly upward, then come down quickly. Generally, such adjustments must not cause the rhythm to become uneven. Despite rhythmic nuances, the conductor cannot afford to lose sight of the basic rhythm. Both the soloist and the orchestra expect a certain firmness from the conductor.

This brings up the question of when you should lead and when you should follow. To decide this, you must understand the nature of the instrument or voice that you are accompanying. There are cases in which it is evident that the soloist must follow the conductor's beat in order to achieve coordination.

In example 24.6, a new tempo begins, after the fermata, with a start after the count. The conductor must take the lead to assure coordination of the low strings with the piano part. The syncopated rhythm requires a firm beat, based on complete understanding between soloist and conductor.

Most violin soloists prefer to follow the conductor's beat in example 1.7 for the "exit" of the second trill.

On the other hand, the conductor should know where to wait for a singer to breathe, or for a difficult shift of position in the violin, or where to speed up with a quick run on the piano—to mention only a few such adjustments. It goes without saying that you should listen carefully to the solo part. Above all, you must know it thoroughly. In rapid passages with many notes on each count, you must know the groupings of the notes within the measure so as to synchronize your beat with the soloist. It is sometimes easier to follow the left hand of a piano part when this is rhythmically simpler than the right. Also, it may help to have a look at the soloist when the ear alone does not suffice. For

Ex. 24.6. Prokofiev, Piano Concerto No. 3, second movement, one measure before #63

good dynamic balance, however, you must rely on the ear alone. The dynamic marks, as printed in the parts, are more or less relative and must be corrected by your indications whenever necessary. If you cannot hear the soloist with reasonable ease, you may be sure that the audience cannot either.

You should get practical experience in accompanying instrumentalists and singers, even though you may have at your disposal only a piano or a small ensemble. Numbers 10–12 in Appendix A include typical examples of orchestral accompaniment. In this practice the soloist should occasionally avoid watching you and may even take various liberties, thus increasing the difficulty of your task.

ALEATORY MUSIC

Aleatory music (*aleatorius*: "where the dice may fall") has gained new significance in contemporary music. Within a general trend toward improvisation in music, some composers do not restrict the performer to predetermined notes, rhythms, and dynamics. Instead, they welcome participation in the creative process by letting the performer make choices within alternatives. This method of composing has brought about novel systems of notation in the form of charts, diagrams, and various geometrical figures. Although most of the time the traditional staves are used, the performer must learn how to read such scores and, in addition, observe the instructions that usually accompany aleatory works.

Characteristic of this style is the utilization of a great variety of sounds. Some effects are produced by handling traditional instruments in an unorthodox manner, others by including in the score unusual instruments and all sorts of mechanical devices. Consequently, the conductor, aside from studying the score, may have to undertake some investigation and experimentation as part of advance planning. This includes assembling the needed properties and, in some cases, securing the services of expert players.

The conductor will not find it difficult to apply the beat patterns that have been discussed in this book to the direction of aleatory works. Improvisation may require a very flexible beat for timings that are done on the spur of the moment. Also, the conductor will have to pay special attention to the giving of signals to individual performers or groups of players whose entries "happen by chance." As the timing is likely to differ from one performance to another, it is important to establish a clear understanding of the type and meaning of each signal. Usually, the players perform from full scores, or at least from cross-cued parts—a time-saver in rehearsal which facilitates the rapport.

PART THREE

EXECUTION AND PERFORMANCE

CHAPTER 25

Achieving Complete Physical Control

GENERAL APPEARANCE

Control of physical gestures, posture, and movements, necessary to everyone who appears on a public platform, is especially important for the artist, because his poise and ease of movement not only impress the public but—and this is far more significant—also affect the artist's own performance. On the podium you need freedom of motion more than other musicians, because conducting consists of musical expression directly by gestures. Like other performers, a conductor must find a happy medium between tension and relaxation; you will show this in the way you mount the podium and face the players—and indeed in every gesture you make.

Authority over the players, knowing what you want musically, and confidence in your technique enable you gradually to overcome idiosyncrasies such as stamping the feet, wandering about the podium, moving the body unnecessarily, and making grimaces. The two extremes to be avoided are shyness and exhibitionism. Every gesture you make should be meaningful for the players. You should concentrate upon meeting the demands of the music and of the orchestra and waste no time or energy for superficial gestures having only audience appeal.

The conductor must not be carried away by emotions, especially in rehearsal. Despite intense involvement in the music, some part of your mind must act as a control mechanism and prevent you from losing yourself in the music to the extent that your ears no longer bring an objective perception of what the musicians are doing. In this way, you will be able to think ahead and be alert for any emergency, and the players feel that they can rely on you in any situation.

FIELD OF BEATING

It is important to remember that the field of beating is described by the *point of the baton,* and it is here that the attention of the orchestra must be focused. This object cannot be achieved if the center of motion is the hand, with the baton carried along as a lifeless appendage. With the point of the baton as the center of motion, it is easy to coordinate the playing of groups seated relatively far apart. Then the conductor does not feel the necessity of "going to the orchestra with his gestures" but rather draws the players toward the podium, strengthening the feeling of security and authority.

The center of the field of beating in the standard form (as used for the figures) is directly in front of the conductor, about midway between the shoulder and the waist levels. Therefore, it is important that the conductor's desk, just high enough for the score to be read easily, should not interfere with the beat.

Moving the field of beating slightly up or down may bring variety into the beat, but the student is cautioned against the continual use of an abnormally high or low field. Moving the center of the field sideways, either by carrying the arm over or by turning the body, should be done only when it accomplishes a definite purpose, such as addressing one particular group strongly. The players on the opposite side of the orchestra must never be allowed to lose sight of the baton. Too frequent change of the field of beating disrupts the continuity of gesture and confuses the players. This is also true for moving the field toward or away from the body.

Much has been said in previous chapters about the relation of the size of the beat to the dynamics. It has also been pointed out that the intensity of the gesture is at least as important as the size. Loud music does not always require a large beat, and a conductor can use small but intense motions most effectively. Several prominent conductors, in fact, have achieved magnificent results by keeping their field of beating always quite limited in size. Yet, this technique is effective only when serving a particular type of personality.

There are situations in which, for reasons other than dynamics, the size of the field must not be too large. In fast tempo, large gestures are easily blurred and lose their effectiveness. In leading a chamber group, the gestures can be smaller than those used in leading a large orchestra. Also, an operatic conductor, directing in a darkened orchestra pit, must be certain that his gestures are within the lighted area of the desk.

USE OF THE EYES

The eyes are an invaluable means of maintaining personal contact between the conductor and the players and should be used as much as possible, while a minimum amount of time is spent in looking at the score. If you cannot entirely memorize the music, you must still be able to keep your attention on your group most of the time, referring to the score only at intervals of several bars. This ability can be built up by training. Learn to see a number of measures at once, so that by glancing down at the score you know what is coming. Of course, you must know the score so well that you will have no fear of losing the place while you are looking away. Without this knowledge, you are apt to turn your eyes toward the players too late, with a resulting feeling of discomfort. Not only the preparatory gesture but the way you look at a player can communicate in advance what kind of expression you expect. However, don't stare at a musician before a tricky solo passage. It might make the player nervous.

INDEPENDENCE AND USE OF THE LEFT HAND

That the left arm must be independent of the right is generally taken for granted. The conductor must be able to beat steadily with the right arm and feel no muscular tension in the left. The achievement of this independence, however, is a problem for the student, who will often automatically make some kind of movement that mirrors the right arm. There are exercises that are useful for training the arms to perform different gestures simultaneously. Some of the best follow.

Describe a circle with one arm while moving the other up and down. Practice first with the forearm, then with the entire arm. Alternate arms suddenly.

Beat time steadily with the right hand while the left independently makes typical conductor's gestures, such as indications for dynamics, accents, and warnings. Use various rhythms in the right hand, and be sure to include twelve beats in a measure.

Practice beating different rhythms in both hands. Start tapping the edge of a table, since hearing the rhythm makes it easier to coordinate. Tap 3 against 2, and 3 against 4. It helps to think of the fractional values within the bar, as shown in figure 25.1.

It is a good rule to avoid doubling the baton gestures with the left arm because it is a wasted motion. Nevertheless, even the best conductors do it

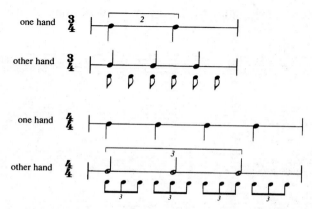

Fig. 25.1. Fractional values for practice beating exercises

occasionally, but only at moments of great climax. To double continually is a sign of lack of control.

In general, the function of the left hand is to indicate details of interpretation, while the baton focuses attention on rhythm. The ability of the left hand to express the most subtle nuances as well as the most dramatic accents is one of the characteristics of fine conducting. When and how to use the left hand are matters of individual taste, but it should always tell the orchestra something essential. If the conductor uses the left hand continually, the players will ignore it.

In earlier chapters the use of the left hand has been discussed in connection with dynamics, articulation, cuing, accents, and so on. These gestures may reinforce the indications of the baton or express details that the baton cannot bring out adequately, even, in some cases, express the opposite of the baton gesture. The rest of this chapter will deal with other typical functions of the left hand.

The left hand is used often to bring out a particular group of instruments (see the instruments on the top staff in example 18.14). When you want to cue in a group without disturbing the general line of the baton, use the left hand. In example 18.4 it can indicate the entry of the strings in measure 40, or the trumpets and timpani in measure 41. In example 20.22, use the left hand for emphasizing the off-beat chords in measures 20 and 27. Apply a sharp downward gesture with the fist. This must not interfere with the smooth progress of the baton to the following neutral beat. (Note that in m. 27 the left hand is lifted simultaneously with the downbeat of the baton!) The left-hand gesture may differ from that of the right in regard to phrasing, dynamics, and articulation. In examples 18.13 and 18. 14, for instance, each hand indicates a different degree of dynamics.

In measures 49 and 50 in example 25.1, the baton indicates neutral-legato while the left hand builds the expressive ◁▷. In example 25.2, the right hand beats staccato throughout, while the left may indicate tenuto for the first violins in measure 3 and the cellos and basses in measure 4.

Another helpful gesture of the left hand is the raised finger for attention— for example, when an instrument is about to enter after a long rest. Also, a number of fingers may be raised to warn the orchestra that you will change the

Ex. 25.1. Brahms, Symphony No. 3, first movement, mm. 47-50

Ex. 25.2. Beethoven, Symphony No. 8, second movement, mm. 1-4

number of beats in a measure. For instance, if you are beating all the counts in 4-time and at a *più mosso* want to beat *alla breve,* raise two fingers one bar before the change. This is an emergency gesture, not necessary when the change is marked in the parts or has been sufficiently rehearsed.

When not in use, the left hand should be in a neutral position. It is best to hold it on or near the lapel, whence it can move easily for the various gestures. Occasionally, you may keep the hand at the side, though this sometimes looks stiff or gives a conductor an appearance of indifference if used too long. Resting the hand on the desk, on the hip, or in the pocket is not recommended.

Turning a page must not interrupt a left-hand gesture; it is better not to begin a motion than to stop it in the middle. Better still, know the score so well that turning a page can wait a few measures. The most rigid way to test brachial independence is the ability to perform all conducting patterns with the left arm, not in reverse motion, but in strict conformance to the movements that are normally assigned to the right arm. Aside from the possibility that an accident may put a conductor's right arm out of action, the skill derived from such exercise will make the effort worthwhile.

A conductor who chooses to dispense with the baton frees the right hand for a variety of gestures described as being typical for left-hand motions. Still, for clear direction, especially in rhythmically tricky passages, the players need an unmistakable point of orientation leaving no doubt "where the beat is." The fingertips of an outstretched hand may serve this purpose, but generally baton-less conductors develop techniques that suit their physique and artistic personality.

CHAPTER *26*

On Preparation in General

TECHNIQUES IN STARTING

The first thing to do after reaching the conductor's stand is to make sure, with a quick glance, that all the players are present. Why such precaution? It actually once happened that the leader of a prominent orchestra had to stop the proceedings at a public concert when he noticed, too late, that a musician, needed for a solo entrance, was not on stage!

Gone are the times when the orchestra's director supervised the tuning. Now the concertmaster takes care prior to the conductor's arrival. Once at the podium, the conductor must not linger, must not indulge in unnecessary talk, must not look at the score before the playing begins, but assume the position of attention. In doing so the conductor can set the mood for the opening, at the same time addressing the group of instruments that plays first. Spreading out both arms as a signal for getting ready is a very bad habit. In fact, the left arm need not be used for every start. In other words, the conductor's preparatory steps must not be perfunctory but display the authority that the players rightly expect.

A little story involving the noted conductor Fritz Busch might serve to underline the importance of the conductor's authoritative position of attention. A guest conductor invited by the opera in Stuttgart to lead a trial performance had not yet given the first upbeat when Busch, the music director of the company, whispered in the ear of the opera manager: "We won't hire him." After an unsuccessful performance the manager wondered: "How did you know before the first note was played?" "Quite simple," was the reply, "the fellow picked up the stick nervously, put it down again, dawdled, finally grabbed the stick again. . . . A competent conductor doesn't act this way."

Securing a good opening attack can be a problem that is not always solved successfully. The first requirement is that all the players be ready and alert; do not give the preliminary beat until all eyes are on you. It is also indispensable that conductor and players be in agreement on the number of beats in a measure. In a large majority of cases the regular preliminary beat will secure a unified attack. However, certain instrumental combinations present difficulties that require special consideration. Soft entrances, for instance, involving wind groups, harp, celesta, high violins, all entering simultaneously, can cause a coordination problem. It is caused by the purely physical difference in the way each instrument "speaks." For instance, the oboe player reacts differently at the attack than the trumpet player, and various other instruments respond differently in very high or very low registers. Despite these differences, a good ensemble must be achieved, or the entrance will be "arpeggiated." This difficulty occurs not only at the beginning but also in the course of a piece, especially after rests.

The solution of such problems depends to a certain extent upon the understanding between the conductor and the players. As far as the beat is concerned, two extremes are possible—a dry or a flexible one. Some conductors use an anticipatory beat. The played attack does not coincide with the baton movement but follows it by as much as half a second or longer. For this, the conductor uses a rather "dry" beat (tenuto, or for *f* attacks, marcato), on the opening count and *waits* for the orchestra, then proceeds as usual. Thus, the first beat (but not the count!) takes a little longer than the subsequent beats. Some orchestras are accustomed to the use of this technique, and conductors visiting these orchestras will do well to adapt their beat to this firmly established habit, for it would take a big effort to replace it. In the face of the players' "late action," a guest conductor will overcome initial discomfort and prevent the music from dragging by maintaining a steady beat.

The reason that such an anticipatory beat works is that players are accustomed to adjusting their attacks so that they follow immediately after the beat. Many conductors, however, adhere to the principle of having the orchestra always playing strictly "on the beat." A flexible and more rounded beat is helpful to secure a good ensemble at some difficult attacks. With this beat, you "breathe" with players and almost "put the notes in their mouths." After preparation, the beat curves down and up with a very plastic gesture, while the attitude and facial expression say to the players: Now—start! Every conductor must find the method that is most effective for him.

Ex. 26.1. Verdi, *Il Trovatore,* Part IV, No. 14, mm. 1-4

The difficulty in example 26.1 is caused by the oboe, second bassoon, trumpets in the low register, and trombones, all of whom start ***ppp*** and must be synchronized with the rest of the orchestra. The anticipatory beat may be used here; a small, clear downbeat anticipates the played attack. If the flexible gesture is used, the left hand can help express the inviting quality with a smooth, gentle motion toward the orchestra.

When the music in example 1.8 is played by a well-trained orchestra, the strings will listen to the solo English horn and adjust their playing in case of a slight delay in the attack. No special beat is needed.

For a perfect start in example 18.1, no amount of rehearsal will do the trick unless the beat is clear and helps the players to concentrate on a unified attack.

CUING

It is not mandatory to indicate every cue; in fact, there are cases where cuing could be harmful. When the players know the music very well and you give an unnecessary cue, it may be interpreted as an invitation to play loudly. In fast tempo, it is often impossible to give many cues within a few bars; do not let your gestures become too involved or confusion will result. Still, the conductor should not give cues sparingly, as they constitute one of the chief means by which personal contact is maintained with the players, giving them a feeling of security, and cooperation.

Whether you give a cue or not, you should be aware of the entries. This means that you must know the score so well that you know what each instrument is doing all the time. There are three ways of giving a cue: with the eyes, with the baton, and with the left hand.

Some conductors like to show their superior knowledge of the score by throwing the left hand in the direction of the entering instruments as the first note of the entry is played. The players dislike it, and quite justifiably. Cuing is helpful only if done a little in advance of the entry and, while a spectacular gesture may impress the public, it is apt to make the players nervous. Do not get into the habit of giving all cues by pointing. The left hand should be used primarily to indicate a special kind of attack or the expression with which the particular entry is to be played.

Most of the time, the best way of cuing in your players is to look at them. Turn your eyes toward the players one count in advance in moderate tempo, and about two counts in fast tempo. Using your eyes is best for two reasons: First, you should not use more motion than you need in conducting; second, the expression of your eyes and your general facial expression can tell the players more about your intentions than fancy hand waving.

A review of some of the earlier examples provides an opportunity for practical suggestions.

For example 1.5, shortly after assuming the position of attention, look at the harp, then start. Not too soon, but no later than the fourth beat in measure 2, turn your eyes toward the flute. Since the orchestra pauses in measure 329 in example 1.7, your beats are small but distinct in order to keep the rhythm clear. In the fourth beat, include an unobtrusive preparation for the horns by turning your eyes toward them. The G-Minor chord in the next measure is played by the strings without the first violins; turn your head toward the other sections. At the same time think about the grace notes (G, B flat, A) in the solo violin while beating the last count in measure 330, so as to start measure 331 exactly with the soloist (see p. 303).

To start example 1.9, address the string section in a general way without pointing out any special group. You may have to prevent the double basses from starting too loudly, as they sometimes do: Put your left hand unobtrusively in *p* position. Watch the entries of clarinets, oboes, and second bassoon.

For the opening of example 2.4, after attention, turn the body and baton *halfway* to the left. This establishes closer contact with the first violins, which is desirable when they have a passage of solo-like quality. Be sure that the rest of the orchestra can see the beat.

In example 2.6, do not turn your baton to the left, since it would be awkward to move the field of beating a few seconds later to address the other string groups.

In the fast tempi of examples 5.8 and 5.11, turn your eye toward the flutes (ex. 5.8) and to the first violins (ex. 5.11) at least two beats before the entries.

Address the violins and then the violas (plus bassoons) in example 8.17 for the small crescendos. In measure 134, there are simultaneous entries of the oboes, horns, and trombones. During the preceding bar, look at the oboes and horns, then concentrate on the accented trombone entry. Your beats on the accented counts, played alternately by trombones and clarinets, should be especially incisive. Cue in the flutes; four measures later the kettle drum; and, on the *ff*, the trumpets.

Generally speaking, cues are given for three purposes: First, you may simply remind the players to enter after a number of rests. This depends partly on the reliability of the individual players, but certain entrances are so difficult for the musicians that cues must be given in any case. Besides, there are cues that are expected as a matter of habit, and their omission may cause uncertainty.

There is nothing particularly difficult about the oboe entrance in example 26.2 since it occurs after a rest of only a few measures. The player, however, may be surprised if the cue is not given and may not enter in time.

Second, a cue may be given to insure precision of attack. In example 26.3, the eye is sufficient for the woodwind entrance in measure 17, and a gesture would be superfluous. However, the strings in the next bar do need some gesture, not because they would get lost after only one measure rest but to insure a clean and precise attack. A staccato motion on *Two* strengthens the rhythmic feeling of the players; it should be small and delicate. At the same time, the left hand takes care of the *p* in the winds.

Ex. 26.2. Beethoven, Symphony No. 6, third movement, mm. 85-93

Ex. 26.3. Beethoven, Symphony No. 1, first movement, mm. 13-20

In example 26.4, a gentle staccato gesture on the second quarter in measure 65 helps the violins to enter precisely—an assistance especially needed here because the fast passage starts after the count. Most conductors subdivide this count. It should be done unobtrusively, resuming the legato line by the third quarter.

When there is danger of a delayed entrance, for instance, in tutti entrances after rests in fast tempo, one might beat the preceding count slightly ahead of time. Thus, in example 8.32, *Two* in the next to the last bar may be somewhat hurried. While this is a matter of experimentation, a conductor with good control may execute such an entry without an anticipatory beat, especially with the help of the left hand. There are certain passages in accompaniment, however, that can hardly be done without this type of beat.

Beat the preparation for the tutti entrance in example 26.5 a little ahead of time to avoid a delayed attack. Just how much in advance to beat depends partly upon the soloist's playing and partly upon the conductor's experience with the orchestra. If the soloist hurries the passage, it may be necessary to apply subdivision in measure 55 in order to reestablish a firm rhythm (subdivided 2-beat).

Third, often the conductor wants to lead an entry in a particular way: loud or soft, expressive or emphatic, lyric or dramatic. The purpose for this is not just to give a cue but to convey to the players the conductor's intentions concerning the interpretation of the music. This use of preparatory gestures to lead an attack in which the cuing per se is unimportant is so fundamental that it is treated under a separate heading.

Ex. 26.4. Haydn, Symphony No. 88, second movement, mm. 63-66

Ex. 26.5. Mendelssohn, Violin Concerto, op. 64, third movement, mm. 53-56

PREPARATION IN ITS BROADER ASPECTS

It is erroneous to think that preparatory gestures are used only to start a piece. On the contrary, they are used continually and constitute one of the most effective tools by means of which the conductor brings life and variety into the performance. In a sense, all conducting is preparation—indicating in advance what is to happen. With preparatory gestures, the conductor not only brings in the instruments with a particular shading and expression but also emphasizes the salient points of the melody and underlines the phrase groups.

Mere time beating would never be enough to accomplish musically significant results. If you did not use preliminary gestures in example 11.12, the players would still play the notes correctly. But to bring out the tenderness of the string entry on *Three* in the first measure and the strong, noble staccato chord in the second, preparatory gestures are needed; in fact, they are more important than the beats themselves. The more the conductor can express in these gestures, the more the players will respond in the way of shading, articulation, and expression.

In example 26.6, the purpose of a stimulating second beat in measure 133 is not so much cuing as expression; an incisive gesture secures a brilliant entry in the violins. Use the same kind of preparation on the fourth beat for the cellos and basses. Lead the energetic cello passage in measure 132 with small gestures so as not to confuse the violas, who are playing **p**.

Often it is necessary to use one or more smaller and less intense beats before the preparation so that the larger stronger preparatory gesture may be

Ex. 26.6. Weber, *Oberon,* Overture, mm. 132-34

more effective. If you were to use large beats for the crescendo in example 11.6, it would be difficult to find a more powerful motion for the preparatory downbeat in the second measure of the example, a downbeat that is needed for a rhythmic *ff* attack of the motive ♪♪♩ . Therefore, indicate the crescendo with the left hand and save the larger baton gestures for this preparation.

Despite the feeling of *One* that dominates the first movement of the Eroica (see ex. 16.3), the musical context in example 26.7 calls for three beats per measure. Use forceful beats for the tutti chords and the preparations on *Three*, but lead the violin passages (played *mf*) with rather small yet incisive gestures. This treatment is not only helpful technically but also conforms to the music's structure.

In example 26.8, the beats in measures 437 and 439 should be clear

Ex. 26.7. Beethoven, Symphony No.3, first movement, mm. 65-69

Ex. 26.8. Brahms, Symphony No.1, first movement, mm. 436-42

without too much intensity so that the downbeat preparation and accented *Two* in measures 438 and 440 will be more effective. In measure 441, however, *Two* is used to prepare the important entrance in the bass instruments.

FREE PREPARATORY GESTURES

The rule that preliminary beats must be given in strict time cannot always be observed. Some exceptions have been discussed in the chapter on holds and interruptions. There are other cases in which the rule may be neglected. Sometimes it is not possible to give a strict preparation in an emergency, especially when following a soloist. It may be necessary to cut the preparation short, so that the orchestra will not enter late. A typical example is the beginning of Beethoven's Piano Concerto No. 5. In the first movement, measures 3 and 5, the coordination of the tutti attacks with the end of the piano cadenzas can present a problem, but skillfully timed free preparations will bring about the desired effect. Even in the absence of an emergency, it may be more convenient to dispense with a strict preparation, namely, when a correctly timed gesture may be either too long or too short.

The tempo marking in example 26.9 is disregarded in the preparations for the fermatas. The preliminary beats are free and take into consideration the quiet feeling of the opening. In fact, the first beat that needs strict timing is the preparation for the violin entrance.

Freely timed preparatory gestures are justified only if the results are satisfactory. The student should first master the strict technique; it will then be an interesting experiment to try other methods. It is quite possible that very dramatic or very delicate attacks may be executed in an extremely effective way by ignoring the pulse of the music in the preparation.

Ex. 26.9. Mendelssohn, *A Midsummer Night's Dream,* Overture, mm. 1-9

PREPARATION WITH SUBDIVISION

In slow tempo, a full beat preparation may be too long, and it might be necessary to subdivide the count preceding the entry. This will result in a clearer gesture and establish closer contact with the musicians.

While quarter beats are adequate in measure 88 of example 26.10, an

Ex. 26.10. Beethoven, Violin Concerto, second movement, mm. 87-92

attack on the *f* in measure 89 requires a vigorous eighth note preparation both in the interest of clarity and to express the drastic change in the music. Therefore, subdivide on the third count (see p. 150)

In example 26.11, the fourth count in measures 1 and 2 can be subdivided to obtain a precise sixteenth note (see the comments in connection with ex. 9.5). The same subdivision is helpful in the third bar, because without a clear indication of *Four, and,* the violins would not feel secure in their triplet.

Even at the very start of a piece, as in examples 9.5 and 11.3, subdivision may be useful to facilitate the playing of a short anacrusis. Beating *Four, and,* at the beginning leaves no doubt about the tempo. For the first eighth beat, use a small sidewise motion; the upbeat on the second eighth is the actual preparation and requires a larger gesture. This type of subdivision is a special case of the use of an extra beat for a start after the count (see p. 98).

Ex. 26.11. Mozart, *Die Zauberflöte*, K. 620, Overture, mm. 1-4

CHAPTER *27*

Score Study and Preparation of Orchestra Materials

PURPOSE OF SCORE STUDY

Studying a score serves a double purpose: to learn the music in terms of notes and markings and to establish a conception of the composition in the broadest sense. Except for the fact that reading an orchestral score is more demanding than the study of a solo part, the conductor's task as an interpreter is not unlike that of other musical performers. The working process, however, is different. The conductor's interpretive ideas must be developed before they can be applied to actual playing. In contrast, the solo performer, who may have started out by reading the music, enjoys the leisure of work in the studio for practical application. In other words, an instrumentalist's or vocalist's home-work leads directly to a performance in public, while a conductor, prior to rehearsing the orchestra, must create an imaginary performance. This image must reflect all the aspects of music making, from minute details to the broad flow of the music from the first to the last measure.

Some of the conductor's ideas may change in the course of rehearsals. Still, beginning with the first rehearsal, you must face the orchestra with a clear conception of the score and be prepared to answer questions regarding each musician's part. Unless the players are instructed quickly and efficiently, a conductor's authority will suffer.

Circumstances beyond the conductor's control can interfere with proper preparation, such as late arrival of music furnished by a soloist, or stepping in for an ill colleague. The ability to sight read a score, sometimes used as a test in conductor competitions, may disclose presence of mind, technical skill, and a flair for quickly grasping the essentials of a certain musical style. It does not, however, tell about a conductor's potential as an interpreter. Interpreting music is a decision-making process that requires time to make choices concerning tempo, phrasing, articulation, sound balances, and other details in all their complexity.

As with any performer, a conductor's interpretive ideas concerning the music of former times depend to a considerable extent on attitudes toward questions of musical style. Such questions will be discussed in later chapters in an attempt to shed light on methods of how to "read behind the notes." Here we are concerned with the initial study of a score and ask, first of all, on what kind of score to base our study. This question is of particular importance in regard to music written before 1900.

SELECTING THE SCORE

Strange as it may seem, interest in the reliability of orchestra materials is a rather recent trend among conductors. Speaking of the Viennese classics, for instance, it was long taken for granted that the *Gesamtausgaben,* published during the second half of the nineteenth century, were beyond reproach. Although they were superior to earlier editions, the editors had often assumed a "father knows best" attitude and all too frequently had not adhered to the original text. One need only compare the old Mozart Edition's version of the ("Haffner") Symphony (K. 385) with the photocopy of the manuscript to discover alterations of notes, rhythms, phrasings, even of tempo signatures. It is not surprising, therefore, that recordings of the work, even when conducted by outstanding musicians, are not true to Mozart's text.

No matter how essential the reference to autographs, they are not always the most authentic sources. Beethoven, for example, used to enter corrections, not only in fair copies written by copyists for the publisher but also in printed proofs. Moreover, composers have made significant changes long after publication but failed to inform the publisher. The far-reaching corrections Mahler made in his symphonies are now included in revised editions, as are important alterations made by Debussy in his *Nocturnes.* Nevertheless, these works are still sometimes performed without the composers' corrections by conductors who remain unaware of authentic sources.

One more word about the selection of editions within the Classical repertory: Although, as a rule, a conductor must rely on the research done by musicologists, he should learn about editorial methods and keep informed about available publications. Since the Second World War, great strides have been made in republishing the orchestral works of many of the great masters. The new volumes are relatively expensive but available at music libraries where they can be consulted by conducting students. Some of these revised editions are now being offered in the form of less costly study scores. They are superior to older publications which, though still on the market, do not always live up to the claim of being *Urtexts.*

METHODS OF SCORE STUDY

Not all schools of music offer special courses in score reading and score playing. A conducting student whose education has been deficient in this respect must fill the gap with self-training. First, the student should play, on the keyboard, Bach chorales printed with the original clefs on four staves, then string quartets, chamber music with transposing wind instruments, and finally, orchestral music. In class work, several students should get together and take turns in playing and checking on each other's performances. Some musicians, thanks to talent or hard work or both, excel in playing from full scores, but more modest efforts are no less valuable. Those who do not play the piano at all and must forgo this self-testing exercise use methods that they have found most useful, relying on their inner ear and making sure that no detail in the score has slipped their attention.

This brings up the question whether playing the piano is indispensable for a conductor. The answer is: not indispensable but highly desirable. Very few orchestra leaders of prominence have been totally devoid of keyboard facility. If Arturo Toscanini, whose instrument was the cello, went to the trouble of practicing the piano to the point that he could coach singers without the help of an accompanist, a young musician ought to make a similar effort.

The study of unfamiliar scores proceeds in steps, although the order of steps may vary. Agreement exists regarding the first step: perusing the score on a getting-acquainted basis. Many conductors then undertake a form analysis in terms of phrase groups and larger segments. This may go hand in hand with, or be followed by, an investigation of the harmonic and contrapuntal structure. In the case of serial compositions, the tone row, or smaller units, must be determined and pursued throughout all permutations. When studying the orchestration, the conductor must make it a habit to clarify what each player is doing at any given moment, not merely which notes are being played but, equally important, how they are to be performed in regard to rhythm, dynamics, and other markings. Painstaking attention to these elements during score study will bear fruit when orchestra rehearsals begin, and the conductor, thanks to solid preparation, is able to "be with the players."

ON LISTENING TO RECORDINGS

No matter how impressive a recording played by a great orchestra under the direction of a prominent conductor may be, listening to it can never be a substitute for serious score study. It holds the risk of imprinting in one's mind the interpretive ideas of another musician, possibly even getting confused when consulting several different renditions. A young conductor who wishes to become a master of the craft must learn to study a score without leaning on outside help. Symphonic recordings appeared on the market no more than about seventy years ago, and the great conductors of former times, who had to do without them, were none the worse for it.

Surprisingly, some teachers of conducting have been using recordings to teach baton technique in their classes, a rather unprofessional method that produces clones instead of helping students to develop their individuality.

Nevertheless, an outstanding recording can be quite stimulating. It supplements the musical imagination by giving a vivid picture of the orchestra's sound. Using it for your exercises, however, would give you only a passive experience. The best method while practicing your conducting technique is to hum or sing the music.

From a student's point of view, the most useful employment of mechanical reproduction is to record, preferably in the form of a videotape, one's work with an orchestra, as it ought to be part of a conducting student's curriculum.

MEMORIZING A SCORE

Some musicians absorb music so quickly that they know it from memory after thorough score study. Those who find memorizing more difficult should not force themselves to an effort that can be nerve-racking in performance without being appreciated by the orchestra. Players dislike to sense a strain in their leader's mind, especially a strain that can be attributed to a conductor's insistence on working without score. Although, in the eyes of the public, dispensing with the conductor's stand has become a status symbol, you must not forget that, unless you can do without score in rehearsal, you may not know the music as well as you pretend. You should also remember that the quality of the orchestra's performance does not improve by the absence of the conductor's stand but has at times been jeopardized by a sudden loss of memory on the leader's part.

Some prominent conductors prefer to have the score available in performance, no matter how sporadically they make use of it. Knowing the music from memory is not an end in itself but a means to maintain eye communication with the players. In fact, certain passages can be directed effectively only if the conductor's eyes "are not in the score." Here are a few examples: (1) the beginning of a piece (giving the first beat while looking down to the music would not be conducive to an inspired start!); (2) a sudden tempo change (looking at the players calls for better attention); (3) incisive short chords (lack of precision is quickly remedied by eye communication); (4) chorus attacks (chorus singers do not react well to the beat unless addressed directly by the conductor).

Generally speaking, the conductor's attitude toward memorizing the music should be dictated by common sense. In performance, use the score as little as possible, but to spend many hours on memorizing for the purpose of public display could be a waste of time that might be put to better use by probing more deeply into the background of a composition.

MARKING A SCORE

A widespread, though not commendable, habit among conductors is to start entering pencil marks the moment they open a score for study, including signs that merely duplicate printed ones. It is not uncommon, for instance, for a change to *alla breve* to result in a page being disfigured by three large ¢ signs marked in red or blue on the top, center, and bottom of the page. There is no taboo against an occasional mark to facilitate score reading, but a conductor must not proceed indiscriminately and make marking a compulsive routine. People who defend the messing up of scores should be very sure that they are not deficient in score reading—not to mention the nuisance they cause others who have to use the same copy and will suffer from the idiosyncrasies of colleagues.

Unless the legibility of a score is poor, it should not be necessary to pencil in signs for cuing. You should at least wait to enter signs that duplicate printed notation until, in the course of rehearsals, you find that you need warning signals to feel secure.

Marking phrase groups can be useful when the metrical structure of a composition changes frequently. Being reminded of irregular bar grouping, a conductor concentrates with greater ease on the many other details that require attention.

The primary function of score marking is to enter all the information that the conductor wishes to be added to the printed orchestra parts for the sake of clarification and of reducing the need for verbal comments in rehearsal.

PREPARATION OF ORCHESTRA MATERIALS

Careful preparation of orchestra parts requires many hours of work, but time and effort are well spent. Rehearsal hours, often restricted and costly, must be put to the best possible use. Moreover, verbal explanations to clear up textual questions not only waste the orchestra's time but disrupt the momentum that is essential for effective rehearsing. The conductor must, therefore, see to it that parts, in good condition and properly marked, be ready for distribution to the players prior to the first rehearsal.

EXAMINATION OF MATERIALS

A distinction must be made between merely transferring into the orchestra parts those marks that the conductor had entered into the full score and the more time-consuming collating of score and parts in regard to every textual detail. Only thorough examination of all the parts makes them conform to the correct text and assures the discovery of misprints. Musicians cannot do their best when playing from poorly printed, torn, or messy parts. To be told "the material is so bad that we can hardly read the notes" is frustrating for a conductor who is about to bring out fine points of interpretation. Awkward page turns can also be annoying. They can upset coordination in the strings or ruin the effect of a forceful tutti attack. To arrange for page turning during a pause, a portion of a page may have to be rewritten and used as an insert. Other deficiencies to be watched include missing *arco* signs after a pizzicato, discrepancies regarding *con sordino* and *senza sordino* (strings and brass), and errors in the notation of clefs or key signatures.

Quick identification of any place in the score is of vital importance in rehearsal. The old system of rehearsal letters or numbers is less practical than the successive measure numbering found in newer editions. If bar numbers are missing, they should be added to the parts.

MARKING PARTS

Although conductors' views on the need and nature of supplementary markings vary, their usefulness is beyond question. Orchestra musicians prefer playing from well-marked parts to using erasers and pencils continually during rehearsal. They remember conductors who, while rehearsing a relatively simple and short work, had bowings and dynamics changed in every measure, with the result that the rest of the program remained underrehearsed. Whenever needed, partial indication of articulation must be completed. Frequently, the context leaves no doubt, as at the start of the third movement of Beethoven's Sixth Symphony where only the first four notes bear staccato dots. Similarly, in example 22.14, it is clear that staccato playing goes on when the marking stops after four measures. Still, each case is to be judged on its merits, and analogy must not be made a rule in the absence of articulation signs.

Example 27.1 is typical of "streamlining," an editor's impulse to substitute analogy for the variety intended by the composer. After having played tongued notes for four bars, the clarinets change to slurring with the **pp**. To prevent a misunderstanding, Dvořák, in addition to marking the slurs, marked the measure 19 *legato*. Nevertheless, the older editions printed slurs for each of the six measures. (The new Dvořák edition, published in Prague, must be consulted for all the works of the composer.)

The sixteenth notes in measure 9 of example 18.5 are not marked staccato. Beethoven wanted the **pp** in the measure 10 to coincide with a change of bowing style. The staccato must not be "given away" while the winds still play legato.

In older editions of the music shown in example 10.7, several legato signs were added to Haydn's text, another instance of analogy replacing the intended variety.

Aside from articulation and phrasing (along with breathing signs for the winds), useful information to be entered into orchestra parts includes: the number of beats per measure that the conductor intends to use; skipping of repeats, holds, and breaks; and ritards that exceed minor tempo modifications.

Signs for dynamics are entered to replace the printed ones or to provide additional information. Usually, they serve to improve orchestral balance, be it to prevent one group of instruments from overpowering another or to help a

Ex. 27.1. Dvořák, Symphony No. 9, "From the New World," fourth movement, mm. 15-20

solo player to be heard without forcing the tone. Sometimes signs are added for a special effect the conductor wishes to achieve, such as the expressive molding of a phrase or a cogent dramatic contrast.

What Felix Weingartner wished to achieve by adding markings to the eighteen measures from Mozart's Symphony No. 41, shown in example 27.2, was *Belebung* (animation). No fewer than fifteen added dynamic signs serve this purpose, whereas according to Mozart's autograph the entire passage is to be played *piano*. Weingartner did not hesitate to impose on Mozart's theme an entirely unMozartean *piano subito* after a crescendo, added to the second measure, typical of a highly questionable, and gratuitous, manipulation of a masterpiece.

A sudden piano followed by a big crescendo is sometimes inserted for a strong buildup toward the end of a piece. In the case of the overture to *Don Pasquale,* this effect had the sanction of Arturo Toscanini. As shown in example 27.3, Italian conductors follow an old tradition by inserting dynamics in measures 3–7.

Whatever the merits of added or changed dynamics, it must be kept in mind that the effect exercised on the players by written signs is quite different from the directions they receive by means of gestures. Unless planned with caution, written signs can lead to unwanted exaggerations. In general, a conductor should avoid overloading orchestra parts with pencil marks and trust in the ability to communicate expression without the help of written signs. In example 27.2, for instance, expressive playing in the strings can be obtained just as effectively, and with more delicacy, by the conductor's gesture alone. Still, there are cases when practical reasons demand a change of printed signs. Two examples follow, the first from Brahms's Symphony No. 1, the other from Mozart's Overture to *Le Nozze di Figaro.*

It is advisable to replace the f in measure 42 of example 18.4 by *meno forte*. String players rarely react properly to a single f that immediately follows a ff. Any gesture to subdue the players for the sudden change of dynamics would have to be overly dramatic.

Unless the strings in example 34.8 are marked **pp** in measures 65 and 66, staccato notes of oboes and flutes (edited orchestra parts erroneously print legato) are not heard sufficiently. Indicating the **pp** to the strings by a gesture would be too fussy. Counting on a pit orchestra with no more than fourteen string players, Mozart could not have foreseen this problem. (For similar reasons, strings and brass must be marked **fp** in mm. 262–263, 276–277, and 280–281 of the same overture.)

BOW MARKING

Printed bowing signs began to appear sporadically in orchestral scores about 100 years ago. Russian and French composers made the start, while German musicians were slow in adopting the habit. In fact, Richard Strauss advocated individual bowing to allow each player to find the solution best suited to his technique. Yet, when acting as a conductor, Strauss would ask for a special bowing style, as for the beginning of Mozart's Symphony in G Minor, (K. 550). Here he preferred to have the violins start with down-bow.

Most present-day composers include bowing signs in the scores. By now

Ex. 27.2. Mozart, Symphony No. 41, K. 551, first movement, mm. 62-79 with dynamic markings suggested by Weingartner

Ex. 27.3. Donizetti, *Don Pasquale,* Overture, mm. 199-204

unified bowing is taken for granted to such an extent that string players feel uncomfortable when asked to proceed on their own instead of emulating the concertmaster's bowing. Nevertheless, some string passages in the works of Wagner, Brahms, Bruckner, and Strauss profit from individual bowing.

Bowing signs have been added, anonymously, to string parts within the Classical repertory. They are often pedantic, unimaginative, and distort the original phrasing. Whenever necessary, they must be corrected. Sound, expression, and rhythmic incisiveness depend to a considerable extent on bow action. A young conductor who has never played a string instrument can learn about bowing technique by playing chamber music with fine string players and by discussing all pertinent questions with the section leaders of the orchestra. Moreover, a novice conductor should study the authoritative analysis of "Bowing Patterns" and "Tone Production" in Ivan Galamian's text *Principles of Violin Playing and Teaching.* Such an effort, together with some experimentation, will help a "non-string" conductor to develop sufficient know-how to mark string parts in line with interpretive ideas. In this sense, bow marking might be called the most essential part of a conductor's prerehearsal preparations. It would be unwise, however, not to change bowing signs if during rehearsals other solutions turn out to be more effective. Also, preferences may differ from one string group to another.

As an example for marking a string part, Appendix D reproduces the first violin part of Mozart's Symphony No. 35.

CHAPTER *28*

Rehearsal Techniques

It has been said that the conductor acts as a "time saver." There is truth in this statement: Conductorless orchestras spend more time on rehearsing. One understands, therefore, why orchestra players, when evaluating a conductor's ability, often put efficient rehearsing on top of a questionnaire. Thus, being important for a young conductor's success, it could be expected that rehearsal techniques are taught in music schools as part of their conductor training program. Yet, there are few schools where this training is offered.

Similar to the conductor's baton technique, which may be defined as a highly individualized craft to evoke specific responses on the part of the players with the most effective gestures, verbal communication in rehearsal must be equally specific, easily understandable, and congruous with the conductor's musical intentions.

The following comments are made with professional orchestras in mind, although not all communities in the United States can afford an orchestra that need not be augmented by students or amateur players. The conductor's handling of rehearsals would then have to take into account the different levels of musical skill and the divergencies in the players' general attitudes, which cannot possibly be the same for those pursuing their training or avocation and professionals who come to earn their livelihood. Even when working with fully trained and experienced players, the conductor adjusts rehearsal methods to the quality of the group and the kind of program that is to be prepared within a certain number of rehearsal hours.

REHEARSAL PLANNING

In planning a schedule, the conductor makes certain that, within the available time, each composition receives its fair share of preparation. Technically intricate works and difficult contemporary music, whose reading is sometimes aggravated by poorly printed parts, require extra rehearsal time. Therefore, in devising programs, the conductor will do well not to overload them with such scores. Also, the conductor will attempt to commence readings of unfamiliar works several weeks prior to performance, possibly in sectional sessions that allow string and wind players to rehearse at different times. Although such an arrangement seems plausible enough, it is, unfortunately, frequently blocked by union restrictions.

When the conductor decides exactly what to practice at each meeting, conditions too diversified to be enumerated will exert an influence, but, knowing the capacity of the players, it is possible to foretell almost to the minute how much work will be accomplished. Obviously, a guest conductor enters a situation unlike that of the permanent leader and may have to arrange schedules from day to day. But even the regular head of an orchestra must be flexible to meet situations such as a musician's sudden illness or the late arrival of solo artists. The threat of emergencies has caused some organizations to insist that all musicians be present for the duration of every rehearsal. However, keeping musicians sitting around in idleness for long periods is hardly desirable. A well-planned schedule permits excusing those players who are not needed during the initial or concluding portions of a session.

It would be unwise for a guest conductor to change the orchestra's seating arrangement, unless the present seating is detrimental to the performance. To make a change merely for personal convenience would defeat its purpose. Musicians need time to adjust to a different placement because their sense of ensemble depends largely on the way they hear themselves and their colleagues onstage. The merits of seating systems are not discussed here because their evaluation is linked to conditions of enormous variety. A conductor must "know" an orchestra and the hall before it is possible to arrive at the most satisfactory solution. Leopold Stokowski, an expert in these matters, never stopped experimenting with seating arrangements during a long career. One requirement, however, never changes: The conductor must be seen by all the players.

One aspect of orchestral seating deserves special mention: the often-discussed question whether the historically justified separation of first and second violins, on the left and right of the conductor's stand, should be preserved for the performance of music of the Classical era. The antiphonal effect produced by such an arrangement seems to speak in its favor. Yet, only a good deal of experimentation will tell a conductor whether alternating string seating according to a particular program is advisable.

EFFICIENT REHEARSING

Before starting a rehearsal, the conductor greets the orchestra briefly, makes certain that all the musicians for whom the score calls are present (see p. 312), and ascertains that the tuning of the instruments has been completed. Generally, conductors should be cautioned against making speeches, giving detailed instructions prior to actual playing, or attempting to enlighten the orchestra by musical analyses. Professional musicians tend to be critical and suspicious of words until convinced in terms of music.

Careful tuning must not only precede a rehearsal but be repeated during its course whenever the intonation is out of line. Problems of intonation, partly due to the nature of the instruments and different for strings, winds, and percussion, arise from various sources and cannot all be solved by tuning. Instruments must be in perfect shape, each player's technical ability must be matched by a keen ear and, last but not least, all musicians must make a constant effort to maintain a unified pitch by listening to their colleagues' playing. Keyboard instruments and harps add special complications because, in spite of the best efforts, the orchestra's pitch is apt to rise in the course of several hours' playing. Still, initial tuning is the first step toward achieving true pitch. The concertmaster usually supervises tuning, which should be completed before the rehearsal begins and must never be permitted to degenerate to a perfunctory routine.

Whether to use an electrical device to sound the A or adhere to the time-honored custom of letting the solo oboe give the pitch remains a matter of opinion. The manner in which the tuning is handled is most important. Sounding the A for two or three seconds and letting the entire orchestra plunge immediately into the all too familiar chaos of "tuning up" cannot produce good results. Stringed instruments, woodwinds, and brasses must check the A separately while the others maintain silence. String players are to spend sufficient time on careful tuning of all their strings so that there would not be an unpleasant surprise should all violins and violas be asked to sound, for example, their open G strings in unison.

With the rehearsal under way, it is for the conductor to decide when to interrupt for corrections. Experience alone teaches at what point a conductor's gestures and facial expressions will suffice to communicate musical intentions to the players and which details make verbal clarification imperative. In the first instance, a conductor will rely on skill with the baton and will refrain from repeating a passage if imperfections can be straightened out without comment when the same music is played later on. However, time would be wasted by repeating a page over and over if problems at a particular place call for discussion. Some conductors first go through an extended portion of a piece without interrupting. There may be virtue in this procedure if a composition is new to both conductor and orchestra; some kind of perspective can then be gained as a guide for further rehearsal work. Otherwise its value is doubtful, and letting errors pass just for the purpose of "playing through" is usually a waste of time. This is not to advocate stopping the music for every mishap. A musician frequently notices his error, at least as quickly as the conductor, and would rightly resent it if fuss were made over every wrong note, an oversight of change of key or clef, or a misunderstanding perhaps caused by blurred print. In such cases an exchange of glances settles the matter. But the conductor must not hesitate to act when technical or stylistic details render explication necessary or when the general quality of playing is not satisfactory. It is the conductor's responsibility to establish the highest possible level of performance from the very beginning of a rehearsal. Indeed, the first five minutes are often decisive for the results of a working session.

Four principal objectives must be kept in mind in preparing an orchestra for performance: (1) familiarity with the music for flawless reading; (2) apprehension of the tempi and their modifications; (3) coordination of dynamics, rhythm, articulation, and phrasing; and (4) a conception of style and spirit germane to the composition. It should be added that the success of a rehearsal depends greatly on the orchestra's general training in ensemble playing. A well-trained, attentive orchestra need not be verbally instructed about tempo, about slowing down or speeding up, about holds, breaks, and other elementary details, because skilled musicians are able and willing to follow a clear beat and to be guided by telling gestures. They also expect authority and efficiency from their leader when it becomes necessary to discuss passages whose rendition needs verbal explanation. The ability to express oneself plainly and concisely is an important part of the conductor's craft. It is the conductor's responsibility to keep up the momentum of the rehearsal while the playing is interrupted. Here are some practical suggestions.

1. Before interrupting, be sure of what you are going to say.
2. Educate your orchestra so that everyone stops right at your signal and then observes silence.
3. Speak loudly enough to be heard by the entire orchestra. Begin your comments without hesitation and whenever possible formulate them in terms of clearly defined technical advice. If you ask for a certain kind of expression, sing the phrase no matter how unattractive your voice, rather than indulge in poetical language. (Paul Hindemith, when a young concertmaster, once reported in exasperation: "Now we have rehearsed Brahms's First under three conductors within a few weeks and each time we arrived at the horn solo in the finale, the conductor started talking about the sunrise!")
4. Never say "Once more" after interrupting without giving a good reason, unless things have so obviously gone wrong that the necessity for repeating is clear.
5. When remarks are addressed not to all musicians but to sections or individual players, first identify the instruments concerned, then the passage in question, then explain why you are not satisfied. Discussions of extended solo passages ought to take place in private, which is preferable to a lengthy discourse in front of the orchestra.
6. Do not discuss musical details without being sure that the players have turned to the right page and know exactly what you are talking about.
7. Once you have begun working on a passage you must persist until improvement is noticeable, unless a player is not capable of coping with a particular problem because of technical limitations. (Even a taskmaster such as Toscanini, in rehearsing Debussy's *Fêtes* with a renowned European orchestra, went on without fussing when he noticed that some measures were beyond the capacity of a certain player.)
8. Announce distinctly and unmistakably the place where the music is to be resumed. When playing from parts without bar numbers, some musicians, in order to find the place, may have to count many measures of rest. Allow them sufficient time, and perhaps repeat the announcement. When singers participate, do not forget to give them word cue and pitch.
9. After proper announcement, resume the music as soon as practicable and without lingering.
10. Spoken comments while the musicians are playing should be used sparingly by the conductor.

11. Do not spend so much time on the first movement of a work, or the first act of an opera, that the remaining portions will be underrehearsed.

12. Do not rehearse every piece each time in its entirety. To play in rehearsal, other than the final one, long stretches of music without problems is a waste of time. Use rehearsals for passages that need work.

This list of suggestions, by no means complete, can be augmented by helpful advice found in books written by various conductors, including the amusing set of rules that Richard Strauss once proposed to young conductors.

TECHNICAL ADVICE AND ITS APPLICATION IN REHEARSAL

Some supplementary words seem to be in order to affirm the superiority of precise technical advice as compared to general criticism. With regard to dynamics, we know that indicating disapproval by exclaiming "too loud" or "too soft" rarely remedies the fault if the material is not marked properly. As previously suggested, parts should be marked beforehand by the conductor. However, no matter how experienced, a conductor may have to revise markings in rehearsal. Acoustics is a frequent cause for modification; peculiarities of the performing musicians another. After all, and fortunately so, music is not made by machines but by human beings, notwithstanding the present trend of electronic music.

Methods other than markings can improve dynamics. String players may have to be instructed to include more notes in one bow for greater softness or to change the bow frequently to develop more strength. Pressing the bow on the strings, or moving it slightly, obviously affects the dynamics, as well as the bow's traveling speed. Again, the best sonority may be achieved by playing a passage in another position, that is, on a different string. Conductors knowing the nature of each instrument are familiar with these and many other tricks of the trade and obtain quick results. *Probieren ist selbstverständlich, aufs Ausprobieren kommt es an,* is a phrase of Otto Klemperer—rehearsing is taken for granted; what matters is experimenting.

To appraise the sound balance, the conductor may have to listen from the rear of the hall, letting an assistant lead the orchestra. As a rule, though, familiarity with stage and auditorium enables one to judge the overall effect from the podium in spite of the greatly distorted sound picture which, unavoidably, the conductor must endure. In most halls the sound level of trumpets and trombones is just right if the conductor barely hears them. The same is true for horns in *piano* passages, while they often must be encouraged to bring out a *forte marcato*. Woodwind solo lines should hit the conductor's ears quite strongly to make sure that their sound carries into the auditorium. This, of course, must not be accomplished by forcing the tone, which would hurt the solo instrument's sound quality and intonation. The solution lies in having the accompanying instruments play more softly, but no amount of entreaty will help unless the musicians listen to the solo passage, so that they themselves can hear it clearly. Whenever essential details of the orchestral texture are covered by heavy accompaniment, it is useful to let players demonstrate an obscured passage by performing it alone.

For articulation in wind instruments, the conductor may have to discuss different ways of tonguing. Unified articulation in strings requires a clear understanding of the various bowing styles, both for "off-string" and "on-string" playing, while for molding of phrases the players must know when to lift the bow for a moment or which portion of the bow to use for a group of notes. Nor must one forget the rule that every note is to be held for its correct value, not longer and not shorter; and furthermore, that one is not to drop the end of a phrase by making a uncalled-for diminuendo. All too frequently, the last note of an appoggiatura-like phrase is dropped too much and rendered inaudible in the hall. The discussion of such basic elements of good music making points vividly to the twofold function of rehearsing. Rehearsals, while serving to prepare a program, must also be aimed toward the long-range purpose of training a team of musicians by creating understanding between the orchestra and its leader as well as cooperation between the players themselves.

Good playing habits must become second nature. This includes questions of style such as embellishments, whose execution often calls for comment. Once aware of such problems, players will not begin every trill (to mention only one of the most frequently occurring ornaments) on the main note as a matter of routine but be anxious to have the question discussed in rehearsal.

In many ways the success of a rehearsal is contingent on the cooperation of the orchestra members. This includes studying the music prior to the first rehearsal. As a general observation, percussionists are likely to outdo their colleagues in this regard. Especially when a score requires quick alternation of numerous instruments, percussion players often memorize their parts. Most wind players and string section leaders prepare themselves thoroughly for the first reading. It is indicative of an orchestra's team spirit to what extent all its members make a similar effort. Special attention must be given to contemporary compositions that utilize instruments and sound devices outside an orchestra's standard equipment. In the discussion of aleatoric music (see p. 304), it was pointed out that preparations are to begin long before rehearsing.

Versatility is indicative of a professional orchestra. To do justice to music from many periods and of diverse national backgrounds, the conductor must establish a conception of musical styles so that the musicians are ready to change their approach from one composition to another. After having rehearsed a Tchaikovsky symphony for an hour, the orchestra may sound heavy in a Mozart work that follows next, but, when asked to recall the proper orchestral texture, skilled players will adjust their performance without hesitation.

A conductor's methods vary according to the character and technical aspects of music. Selecting a sequence of measures typical of a composition's style and using it for extended practice can set a valuable pattern for the entire rehearsal. Tricky passages often call for special attention. For a correct reading of certain rapid runs or for securing good intonation in spite of troublesome intervals each string section or small wind group may have to play alone to "clean up" their lines before the tutti is put together. This method of "dissecting" is very helpful in rehearsing polyrhythmic patterns in contemporary music, because it serves to throw light on episodes whose musical context might otherwise remain obscured. In so-called pointilistic music, there is an added problem for the players who, unlike the conductor, are not aided by the full score and find themselves in need of orientation. To learn in rehearsal how their entries relate to other instruments can be a tedious and time-consuming process, unless one includes in each player's part a condensed score of complementary voices, showing how brief cues, frequently only one or two notes falling on an off-beat, fit into the whole.

THE PSYCHOLOGY OF THE CONDUCTOR-ORCHESTRA RELATIONSHIP

So far, the technical aspect of rehearsing has received preference, although, directly or by innuendo, questions of psychology have come into view. It has been pointed out that the conductor must try to formulate ideas so that whatever is to be communicated to the players finds attentive and willing ears. In rehearsing a professional orchestra, the director's position cannot be explained simply in conventional terms referring to leader-group relation but, for a number of reasons, deserves special consideration in terms of group psychology.

First of all, the director deals with a heterogeneous group of individualists, a circumstance that is not only unavoidable but desirable. It is not skill alone that makes a first-rate orchestra player; such a musician must be an artist, with the temperament and qualities characteristic of a performer. Second, by virtue of their talent, ability, and experience, musicians are likely to be critical, sometimes even resentful, of their leader. Many of them consider themselves, not always without reason, at least a conductor's equal when it comes to interpreting and rehearsing music. Third, excellence in performance cannot be expected from musicians merely obeying orders but only if they are motivated by an impulse derived directly from the music to which they devote their skills, hearts, and minds. If education is the art of opening people's minds, then the conductor's function in rehearsal must be called educational, not in the sense of formal teaching but of bringing to the fore all the best qualities latent in the musicians. To accomplish this the conductor must be regarded by the group as *primus inter pares.*

Exercising authority in rehearsal is a challenge not easily met by a young conductor who has to give directions to older and more experienced musicians. A conductor is not supported by a set of incontestable regulations like a young lieutenant commanding a platoon. In fact, he may feel that he must almost "fake" an authority, which is made difficult by the many critical eyes focused on him. However, a conductor's thorough knowledge of the score, clear beat, and enthusiasm for the music help to overcome an orchestra's mental resistance to a conductor's limited experience. Such problems do not exist for a conductor who knows how to maintain discipline without forgetting a sense of humor, who combines firmness with diplomacy, and, still more important, who keeps interest alive throughout the rehearsal by impressing on each player that cooperation is essential. When the conductor notices lack of attention, the question to ask is whether the problem is not a lack of leadership from the podium.

It should be added, though, that it is difficult for a young conductor to judge who is to blame for unsatisfactory results, the conductor or the orchestra. Nowadays it seems almost superfluous to warn against falling victim to what could be called an occupational disease among conductors a generation ago, namely, the loss of a sense of proportion caused by an egocentric "power complex" that made them act unfairly and rudely toward the orchestra. Conductors are liable to err as much as players, and it would be unwise to try to hide an error. As Pierre Monteux once told his students: "When you make a mistake you must admit it, but of course"—he added with a twinkle, "you must not make mistakes too often!"

Much has been written to unveil for the general public the secret world of orchestra rehearsals. The stories and anecdotes found in books and other publications are legion. They tell, not always accurately, about the legendary abilities or eccentricities of famous musicians. Tales of this sort are a boon to hero worshipers but of limited interest to professionals. They rarely hit a musically significant point and sometimes even support mediocrity, as in the often-repeated story of the orchestra player who, after having listened impatiently to the famous maestro's explanations, retorted brusquely: "Just tell us whether you want this passage played *forte* or *piano*." If the story is true, this man was either a disagreeable person or a semi-educated musician unable to realize that the sweat and toil the creators of great music put into their work obliges us to make every possible effort in bringing their compositions to life. It cannot be done in terms of mechanical measurements alone. There are many gradations of *piano* and *forte*, numerous ways of playing staccato, and other means of musical expression that evade academic definition. Likewise, there are limits to the conductor's efforts to translate intentions into technical language. The intrinsic meaning of music, the subtleness of a phrase, or the dramatic impact of an emotional outburst may not be felt by all the players unless the conductor possesses the suggestive power of revealing what is "behind the notes." How to do this cannot be taught. Each conductor must find a particular way to project feelings, by virtue of personality, by singing a phrase with the appropriate expression, or by hitting on the illuminating word.

A flair for what to say, and what not to say, is part of a conductor's psychological perception and calls for presence of mind. To know how to word criticisms, to feel when to give encouragement, to sense when a tense moment is best relieved by a joking remark, all this affects the relationship between the leader and the group. Still, the reason that one conductor wins the cooperation of an orchestra while another fails is difficult to give. It would be wrong to assume that there is a certain type of personality or a particular trend in musicianship that appeals to players, but it is safe to state that there is one attitude that they resent, the "chummy" approach of pseudo-camaraderie. Basically it is not a question of liking or disliking their leader but of feeling respect. Unless musicians respect the conductor, they will not "play for him," as the saying goes.

THE CONDUCTOR-SOLOIST RELATIONSHIP

Rehearsals with guest soloists can be irksome due to limited time and differences in musical taste. The first circumstance usually proves to be less serious, because with the help of an expeditious rehearsal an attentive orchestra led by a conductor who has mastered the art of accompaniment has little if any trouble as far as coordination is concerned. It is the general style and details of interpretation that can cause embarrassment. It is therefore essential that conductor and soloist meet prior to the rehearsal to discuss important points and try to establish a general understanding. It is comforting to know, though, that most artists of real stature are eager to cooperate with the orchestra. In any event, the conductor need not fear loss of prestige by trying to suit the soloist, as long as this can be done without jeopardizing the orchestra's playing. A conductor's main concern is to achieve the best possible performance, and it would be unreasonable to expect the soloist to alter substantially, within the span of a brief rehearsal, a rendition that has become part of himself.

It is the duty of the conductor, after having consented to the choice of a solo artist, to show courtesy to a guest in spite of disagreement or disappointment; it would be ill-advised for the conductor to demonstrate any such feelings to the orchestra or, worse, to the public. Unfortunately, a few soloists believe that they have discovered the one and only way to do justice to a composer and to a work. Even in these extreme cases, a conductor who is not equally foolish should remain master of the situation. Again, some diplomacy and the right word said at the proper moment will help.

CONCLUDING REMARKS

This survey of psychological factors that make their influence felt in the conductor's work would be incomplete without giving some thought to a problem conductors share with performers in general. It stems from the dualistic nature of artistic activities and must be solved by balancing emotional impulses with rational control, a complicated process and not necessarily the same in rehearsal and actual performance. Bruno Walter once remarked that, in rehearsal, while working with full mental intensity, he was careful not to be carried away emotionally, not just for the sake of saving physical strength but in the interest of undivided concentration on the orchestra's delivery of the music. Other performers have spoken about the "control mechanism" whose functioning they consider to be of fundamental importance, and they have warned against being "a hundred per cent absorbed." Without listening with an alert mind and adjusting gestures to whatever the moment demands, the conductor would cease functioning as a leader. Conducting students, due to nervousness and involvement in their preconceived ideas, often do not hear what is actually going on in the orchestra and must first learn the art of unbiased listening. The simplest and most effective method for self-education is to stop beating and let the orchestra play by itself (see the section

"Overconducting" in chapter 23). Students will be surprised to notice how much momentum is provided by the players without any effort from the podium and that they had been wasting gestures on details that needed no direction. They will also notice that they perceive the sound of the orchestra with greater clarity and objectivity, to the benefit of their overall judgment (see p. 301).

Another point that sometimes escapes attention is closely related, namely, the invaluable opportunity for the conductor to utilize rehearsals for testing a rendition of a work, particularly a composition he leads for the first time. Musicians called to go over a familiar piece have been heard to remark that they could have played as well without rehearsal, which was needed only by the conductor. While such a statement should be taken with a grain of salt, it is certainly true that the conductor "needs" rehearsals; they are no less essential for a conductor than for the players. The primary consideration is not *who needs* a rehearsal but *what use* is being made of it. Indeed, the fact that the conductor, while working with the orchestra, still has to decide on details of interpretation should contribute to making a rehearsal an exciting experience. It is the happy combination of objectivity and initiative, rationalization and feeling, discernment and intuition that, in addition to technical skill, is the decisive factor in leading a successful rehearsal.

CHAPTER 29

Conducting Opera

The opera pit has been called a training ground for young conductors because of the special skill that is needed to control stage and orchestra within a musical style that is marked by frequent changes of tempo and meter. Clear yet flexible gestures are essential for the coordination of rubato passages, fermatas, and other peculiarities of operatic singing. All this, together with problems caused by last-minute emergencies, as they are bound to occur in a theater, requires musical leadership that combines authority with presence of mind.

In terms of baton technique, conducting an opera is not different from leading symphonic music. Special attention must be given to the visibility of the beat. The choice of gesture may depend on the orchestra's seating in the pit and on the distance from the performers on stage. Also, problems of lighting are quite common. The conductor must make sure that the beat is always visible to all performers.

Dissimilarities between symphonic and operatic conducting can be traced partly to the difference in art form, partly to the working conditions that prevail in opera companies. A discussion of the opera conductor's work must therefore be divided between questions of interpretation and those that deal with practical matters.

STUDYING AN OPERA SCORE

Inspired by the story and its leading characters, an opera composer attempts to integrate music, words, and stage action. Therefore, an opera conductor's first concern should be to review the libretto and its background. When studying the score, the conductor's attention must be equally divided between orchestra and voices. Singing the vocal lines will help to fix them firmly in mind. Their meaning and expression are inseparable from the musical interpretation of an opera.

This leads to the question of language. In the case of an opera written in an unfamiliar language, the conductor must nonetheless know the meaning and inflection of every word. Neither dictionaries nor printed translations provide the information needed to appreciate the subtle relationship between words and music. A conductor will, therefore, benefit from being advised by a musical assistant who masters the language and can clear up questions of diction.

Presenting operas in their original languages is a recent trend, the reversal of a tradition that had prevailed during the nineteenth century, when opera composers believed that their works would fare best if sung in a language readily understood by an audience. Verdi, when producing his operas in Paris, wanted them to be sung in French. Wagner enthusiastically reported on a performance of *Lohengrin* in Venice with Italian artists singing in Italian.

Advocates of "opera in the original language" maintain that the sound of words with their specific color and inflection is no less a part of the composer's concept than the sound of the music itself. Unfortunately, by extending this principle to a lengthy half-spoken Italian recitative in a Mozart opera, the average listener is rendered unable to perceive the meaning of words, not to mention their subtle implications. One is reminded of Lord Chesterfield's famous definition of opera as "a magic scene contrived to please the eyes and ears at the expense of the understanding."

Performing opera in translation brings about problems of a different kind. Whatever the merits of an English version of a foreign-language opera, it may interfere with the conductor's interpretation of the music. This can be caused by words that hinder good singing, unwarranted changes of notes and rhythms, or the choice of a phrase that implies a meaning so different from the original that it no longer corresponds to the musical expression. By substituting words and meanings, operatic translators often become arbiters of style, both musically and dramatically. It is interesting to note that opera composers usually do not mind omitting or adding notes within a musical phrase, as long as its delivery is made more effective by the change, another proof of a composer's desire to "reach" the public.

PERFORMANCE PRACTICE IN OPERA

In connection with "Selecting the Score" (see chapter 27), it could be stated that great strides have been made in republishing the scores of masterworks. Fortunately, thanks to the joint efforts of editors and publishers, similar progress has been made in the operatic field. All of Mozart's stage works are now available in the researched volumes of the NMA. More recently, two important projects have been initiated: new complete editions of Rossini's and Verdi's operas. Within the French repertoire, Berlioz's dramatic works have been reissued. The scores of Bizet's *Carmen* and Offenbach's *Les Contes d'Hoffmann* have been made available in versions that reflect the composers' original intentions.

Notwithstanding the value of these publications, they do not always solve the knotty question of which version deserves to be called the "final" one. We shall never know Mozart's preference regarding the Prague and Vienna versions of *Don Giovanni*. Italian composers of the nineteenth century have, in the course of various productions, made changes in their scores without disclosing which alterations were meant to be permanent. When Verdi rewrote sections of *Il Trovatore* for the Paris Opera, he omitted some passages, adjusted cadenzas to suit the local cast, but he also introduced new ideas of considerable interest. Yet, this version has found little attention.

Making cuts in operas, a time-honored procedure, has been subject to much controversy. Some omissions have the sanction of the composers, but most cuts must be ascribed to conductors who, for various reasons, considered it desirable to shorten the music, sometimes only by a few measures, then again by leaving out entire sections. Cuts, no matter how obscure their origin, tend to become habit-forming. A typical example is the omission of ten measures in the Duettino, No. 14, in *Le Nozze di Figaro*. Although their authenticity is assured, and restoring them would lengthen the duet merely by a few seconds, the truncated version remains common practice.

To decide on deletions in an opera is not an easy matter. Even if not handicapped by financial limitations or casting problems, a conductor must not decide about accepting a traditional cut, or restoring a previously omitted section, until there has been time for careful study. Not every printed score deserves to be called authentic. Few composers acted like Puccini who, having made drastic cuts in *Madama Butterfly* after an unsuccessful premiere, demanded that the original vocal score be withdrawn (still, some copies had been sold and became collector's items). In fact, to insist on uncut performances indiscriminately might lead to being holier than the pope! Leonora's Cabaletta in Act IV of *Il Trovatore* is an example. This section has recently been restored (although with a cut!) by musicians who believe it to possess musical and dramatic significance. Their opinion was not shared by Verdi who, four years after the work's premiere, cut the Cabaletta when he produced the opera in Paris.

Cuts are merely one aspect of "traditions" in opera that a conductor must neither accept nor reject summarily. Gustav Mahler saw in tradition nothing but "the most recent bad performance," although he did not tell by what yardstick the quality of a performance was to be judged. Seen in proper perspective, tradition has its place in opera. Pierre Monteux's reading of *Pelléas et Mélisande,* for instance, followed instructions received from Debussy. Similarly, thanks to lifelong collaboration with the composer, Arturo Toscanini's interpretation of Puccini's operas could claim a high degree of authenticity. Seen in this light, contemporary interpretations that are now being preserved by recordings will provide documentary evidence beyond the merely written information concerning past performance practices.

An operatic tradition that has rightly been challenged is the unrestrained addition of high notes for no other purpose than to show off a vocalist's top range. It developed in the nineteenth century among singers of the Italian school and must not be confused with the eighteenth-century practice of displaying vocal virtuosity through improvised ornaments and variations. In fact in Mozart's time it would have been considered bad taste to interrupt the flow of the music by inserting, or even sustaining, a high note.

Generally speaking, a line must be drawn between operas in which taking liberties with the vocal writing is stylistically justified and those that were meant to be sung strictly according to notation. The first opera composer to reject changes was Gluck who, in the preface to one of his works, stated:

> *The more one strives for perfection and truth, the more important become correctness and accuracy. One example is the aria "Che farò senza Euridice" from the opera* Orfeo. *The slightest change, be it its pace or expression, would turn it into a comic song for a marionette theater. In an opera of this kind, any note sustained too long or too briefly, any change of tempo, any grace note, trill, or figuration, would completely ruin the effect of a scene.*

Mozart did not subscribe to Gluck's austere principles. Relying on singers with solid musical training, he expected them to adorn solo parts with grace notes and variations. If necessary, he assisted them. One of Mozart's embellished versions of an aria has been preserved. He wrote it for the slow section in the concert aria "Non so, d'onde viene" (K. 294), which shows that variations were not limited to the repeat of a melody but could be applied right from the beginning (see NMA II/7/2).

According to Tosi's treatise on ornamental song (see Recommended Reading, p. 472), an eighteenth-century classic, improvised embellishments were "the most laudable part" of a singer's ability and "the greatest delight for connoisseurs." His enthusiastic statement was tempered by a warning: Perfection in this art required "understanding, imagination, adherence to strict tempo, profound knowledge of harmony, and exquisite taste." Mozart's contemporary, Johann Hiller, expressing similar thoughts in a book on vocal ornamentation, suggested that performers without thorough schooling in composition should leave the composer's text unchanged, words to be taken to heart by conductors and singers who attempt to restore former performance practices.

It is not surprising that Mozart wanted secco recitatives to be treated with complete freedom, almost like spoken dialogue, using the singing voice only occasionally. For the supper scene in the Act II of *Don Giovanni,* he encouraged the artists to improvise their lines even while the orchestra was playing, and he did not mind that every performance turned out to be different. Mozart's operatic scores reveal his intense involvement with the stage, but they cannot be set apart from his orchestral works. Whether designed for the theater or the concert hall, music created in the same workshop possesses common traits within the totality of a composer's style. Questions of Mozart interpretation, as discussed in previous chapters, therefore apply as well to his operas. One might go one step further by stating that his dramatic works, like those of other German composers, do not conceal a close link to instrumental conception.

Verdi seems to have had this in mind when he claimed that, beginning with Rossini, Italian composers were "melodists," in contrast to the German school, which remained focused on "harmonization and orchestration." (He named Haydn, Mozart, Beethoven, Mendelssohn, Schumann, and Wagner as non-melodists.) Although Verdi's judgment is to be taken with a grain of salt, it helps to understand the nature of Italian opera during the first half of the nineteenth century. The fact that many of these works were scored with accompaniments as stereotypical as their metric structure, harmonic setting, and orchestration had at one time led to a condescending attitude toward Rossini, Bellini, Donizetti, and the early Verdi. Now brought back to the repertory, many of these works retain their effectiveness thanks to the emotional impact of vocal lyricism.

It is fashionable to refer to these works as *bel canto* operas, although considerable disagreement exists about the meaning of *bel canto*. "Beautiful song" might be understood simply as an evenly produced attractive voice, but most musicians associate it with perfect vocal control, especially in florid passages. This last point, however, was hotly disputed by none other than Rossini, who once remarked: "*bel canto* generally is confused with *fioriture*. That is a mistake." He went on to define the elements out of which *bel canto* is made. We owe this information to a friend of Rossini's, the Belgian writer Edmond Michotte. His detailed report on Rossini's views is part of an essay published one hundred years ago and available in translation ("An Evening at Rossini's in Beau-Séjour (Passy) 1858" by Edmond Michotte translated by Herbert Weinstock, Chicago: University of Chicago Press, 1968.)

For the conductor, operas of this period carry problems caused by the lack of reliable information on performance practices. Digging out early recordings of arias sung by artists who enjoyed popularity in those days is an unscholarly method of investigation, unsuited to arrive at valid conclusions. "Traditions" not traceable to the composer do not deserve our serious attention. If there ever existed legitimate performance practices, we no longer have access to them, which is also borne out by the lack of unanimity among Italian conductors. It seems symptomatic that, even in the case of Verdi's operas, the authority of a Toscanini, who still performed under the composer's direction and on several occasions discussed with him the interpretations of his works, did not find general recognition among his younger colleagues.

Toscanini, despite his reputation as a strict taskmaster who always insisted on complying with the composer's text, was not as puritan as some of the present Italian conductors. An artist who at the rehearsal of a Verdi opera had interpolated a high note was upbraided by the conductor: "Toscanini would not allow you to sing this note." The singer kept quiet but took it upon himself to write to Toscanini, who replied by return mail: "This *puntatura* (a note higher than the written one) is, I believe, as old as the opera itself. I have always allowed it and, permit me a heresy, prefer it to the original."

Deviation from written notes was taken for granted in the days of Rossini and Donizetti, but how and to what extent notes were changed can no longer be ascertained. Source material is limited to variations and cadenzas compiled by song masters whose musical competence was disputable. Mathilde Marchesi's collection, still used by coloratura sopranos, includes nine different cadenzas to "Ah! fors'è lui" in *La Traviata,* all written in Rossini fashion, which would hardly have pleased Verdi, who had his own way of writing cadenzas. Tracing the gradual change in Verdi's use of cadenzas is of considerable interest. Before abandoning them altogether for his last three operas, he had, beginning with *Un Ballo in maschera,* decided to integrate cadenzas with the concluding bars of an aria in order to preclude any change.

This was in line with Verdi's increasing reluctance to make concessions to singers and conductors. His letters testify to his displeasure when he learned about infringements on his sovereignty as composer. When a conductor had changed *mf* to *ff* in the overture to *La Forza del destino* (m. 168), Verdi exploded: "The principle that conductors create music leads to the abyss . . . a path to bad taste and falsification."

Verdi prepared metronome indications with care, but like many other composers he could not avoid occasional misjudgments, probably because he tried to determine speed while playing his music at the keyboard prior to an opera's first performance. Signs such as *col canto, a piacere,* and fermatas allowed for rhythmic flexibility. The custom of increasing the speed during the concluding sections of pieces with strong dramatic momentum can be called idiomatic, but, aside from such occasional liberties, Verdi's music was meant to be performed with a firm feeling for the rhythm and a steady pace.

No information exists as to how Verdi reacted to the insertion of high notes. It can be assumed that he permitted some changes, at least through the middle period of his career. It would be difficult to imagine, for instance, that he expected a tenor to adhere to the written G at the end of "Di quella pira" in *Il Trovatore.*

Top notes have always been an obsession with opera singers as a stimulant for applause and an expedient on the road to fame. At one time, the general manager of the Metropolitan Opera, overruling the conductor, requested a soprano to end Micala's aria in *Carmen* with a high B flat. The conductor, a prominent French musician, left the company.

It is not unusual for composers to write optional top notes, letting a singer choose between the higher and lower version. Even then, vocalists sometimes prefer to perform an aria in a lower key rather than to forgo the effect of a high note. Under the right circumstances, transposing the music has a legitimate place in opera, namely, as a means to adjust the vocal range to individual needs.

When Mozart transposed the aria "Mi tradì" in *Don Giovanni* from E flat to D major, he was not concerned about single notes but was thinking of the soprano's *tessitura.* In contrast, the two transpositions frequently heard in the Act I of Puccini's *La Bohème* (Rodolfo's aria and the final duet) serve no other purpose than to allow the tenor to reach out for more comfortable top notes (although the higher versions are optional!). In this instance, the printed orchestra parts provide alternate versions. Most of the time, orchestra parts must be written in the desired key, because string players are not accustomed to transpose music at sight.

Puccini's scores are notable for meticulous marking. He indicated minute tempo changes, dynamics, expression, articulation, even some bowings. Yet his operas are usually performed with additional modifications, some of them authorized by the composer, if we are to believe the comments published by one of his coworkers (Luigi Ricci, *Puccini: Interprete di se stesso*, Milan: Ricordi, 1954). Puccini, like many opera composers, did not always consider questions of orchestral balance. A large band in the pit, playing accompaniments marked *f* or *ff*, drowns out even the biggest voices. Aside from changing the printed dynamics, conductors will do well to keep the beat small and resist the temptation to indulge in demonstrative gestures for an emotional outpour.

Performance practices with relation to Wagner, Strauss, and their contemporaries in France are discussed in chapter 34.

THE SINGING VOICE

Just as the director of an orchestra is expected to possess a working knowledge of musical instruments in regard to range, tone projection, and playing technique, an opera conductor must learn to gain insight into the art of singing. The opera conductor will appreciate the fundamental difference between handling an instrument that is manufactured, and can be purchased, and the voice of a professional singer, which in most cases is developed gradually by training the voluntary muscles (lips, tongue, uvula, diaphragm) that a singer must learn to control.

Upon entering the operatic society, a young conductor is likely to be surprised, if not befuddled, when listening to the shoptalk of singers exchanging their views on voice placement, breath control, and other intricacies of vocal production. Some strange, fanciful concepts are firmly fixed in a singer's mind and lend security in a life that, after all, rests on two small vocal cords. The ideas of vocal artists are as divergent as the views proposed in a myriad of books on vocal technique, some of which claim to teach the only "right" method of singing. A sensible and concise presentation of the subject matter is offered in a paperback, *On Studying Singing*, by Sergius Kagen, whose approach is mixed with a healthy dose of skepticism.

Many singers are "sold" on their "voice teachers"—a misnomer, because voice cannot be taught: Babies are born with it! What *can* be taught is how best to use a voice for professional work. Among the thousands of "teachers of singing" in Europe and the Americas, relatively few have been lucky to produce more than one single outstanding singer, whereas teachers of instruments can often boast of a "stable" of successful former students.

All too many teachers neglect to care for their students' correct speaking. Ezio Pinza, famous for his *Don Giovanni* and rightly praised for his flawless singing, used to explain why he was not in need of vocalizing in the dressing room as were most colleagues before a performance: "I make it my business to speak correctly all the time and can easily proceed from speaking to singing." Pinza also recalled that, after having trained his voice for two years without doing any performing, he learned how to use his voice thanks to his association with great conductors.

Singers feel comfortable with conductors who understand their work, and their problems, and are able to help them to do their best on stage. A singer is in top form when free of muscular tension and, so to speak, feels like "walking on air." With the help of a sympathetic leader in the pit, an opera singer's delivery of a tricky passage, or a delicate high note, can be greatly facilitated.

It is important to realize that singers do not hear their own voices the way others hear them—in fact, if they did, there might be something wrong with their technique. Only by physical sensation can a singer be satisfied that the voice is properly projected. In other words, if it *feels* right, then it will *sound* right! Sensations, however, are highly individual and defy analysis.

All this a newcomer to opera will have to ponder while increasing experience will provide insight into the mysterious world of professional singing. The best way to learn is being actively involved by coaching singers and listening attentively to an accomplished artist's performance.

REHEARSING OPERA

A symphonic program, consisting of about eighty minutes of music, is usually prepared in four rehearsals. One might expect that full-length operas of 120 to 200 minutes (not counting intermissions) would require a proportionate number of rehearsal hours, divided into reading sessions and stage rehearsals. An opera such as Strauss's *Der Rosenkavalier,* no less exacting than, say, his *Till Eulenspiegel,* would then call for at least eight rehearsals, not taking into account time-consuming scene changes and other problems on stage. Yet the facts of operatic life tell otherwise: rehearsal conditions that are taken for granted in the concert hall would in opera be regarded a luxury that financially hard-pressed managers can ill afford.

To make the best use of rehearsal time, more than musical competence is demanded from an opera conductor. With the ever-present specter of overtime for orchestra, chorus, and stage hands, the conductor is often forced to pinch minutes. Under these circumstances, even the most accomplished musician would be at a disadvantage without knowledge of the theater and meticulous advance planning. Advice on how to prevent trouble is offered here in the form of suggestions that supplement an earlier list (see p. 333).

1. As a first step, meet with the stage director to establish an understanding in regard to the general conception of the work and its realization in performance. Discuss cuts and, if an opera is sung in translation, clear up textual questions.

2. Arrange that all vocal artists receive early information pertinent to the performance. If there could be doubt about the correct version, well-marked vocal scores must be sent to them. This includes the person in charge of training the chorus.

3. Operatic orchestra materials are often messy and of poor legibility. Advance checking and marking of orchestra parts is therefore of the essence.

4. Participate as extensively as possible in the coaching of the singers. Instruct the assistant in charge, about tempi and other points of interpretation.

5. Once the entire company is assembled for rehearsals, intelligent day-to-day planning is needed to obtain the best results. During ensemble sessions with piano avoid having singers sit around idly for long periods. Their time is put to better use by working individually with the stage director.

6. Once the soloists have memorized their roles and sung the entire opera in ensemble, room rehearsals for staging should start. To believe that musical preparation ends when staging begins would be unrealistic.

7. Be present at all staging sessions. This way you are involved in working out details of acting to be integrated with the music. Also you retain musical control. Tempi get easily out of hand when singers concentrate on stage business.

8. Make sure that the pacing during piano rehearsals conforms to performance tempi. It is disconcerting to singers to hear a conductor change tempi when orchestra rehearsals commence.

9. Attend several chorus room rehearsals to secure a good understanding. Once the pacing is set for a choral group, noticeable tempo changes are risky and often result in shaky performances. Similarly, if an opera involves dancing, tempi must be discussed with the choreographer. It is helpful to tape record a piano version of the ballet music to be used for rehearsals.

10. The coordination of backstage music is facilitated by the use of video monitors. Still, music played or sung behind the scene is often a source of trouble. In order not to waste rehearsal time, discuss with the assistant not only tempi but questions of location.

Rehearsal planning is linked to the availability of solo artists. Late arrivals restrict ensemble study. Competence and experience on the part of individual performers are no substitute for the team work that results from daily rehearsals by the entire cast for several weeks.

Much also depends on the conductor's ability to work with singers. Rehearsing vocalists is quite different from directing instrumentalists. Extensive experience in vocal coaching is needed to identify with the performers on stage. Their job is not always appreciated by musicians who have never tried to step into an opera singer's shoes. Aside from being concerned with music, words, acting, and vocal technique, singers must maintain communication with the leader in the pit and fellow performers on stage. (An occasional attempt to take a singer's place is a valuable lesson for opera conductors!)

It would be unreasonable to expect artists to sing with full voice in all rehearsals. In fact, a conductor should insist that the members of his cast save their vocal strength for those occasions when balancing the ensemble, with or without orchestra, makes it imperative for all to sing the way they would in performance.

It is customary to arrange for at least one orchestra session together with the singing cast prior to the first stage rehearsal with orchestra. In fact, singers should attend most orchestra readings. Having the orchestra perform lengthy simple accompaniments without hearing the singing voice would be almost meaningless. Orchestra readings should, therefore, not coincide with staging sessions.

Except for the final dress rehearsal, scenes need not be taken in order but should be scheduled to allow for a maximum working time. An aria can sometimes be done in front of the curtain during a long scenery change. Spoken dialogue or secco recitatives can be omitted for the first stage session with orchestra. Immediately preceding the final rehearsal, a complete run-through with the piano in the pit provides ample time for corrections.

CONDUCTING IN THE PIT

An opera conductor assumes the dual role of leader and accompanist. When to lead and when to "go with the stage" cannot be formulated. Such decisions, often made on the spur of moment, depend on unpredictable circumstances. Still, it is conductor's responsibility never to lose sight of the musical and dramatic fusion throughout the performance, with a duty to coordinate the ensemble and to guide the singers with sympathetic understanding. A tug-of-war would be out of place in the presence of an audience. Disagreements are to be straightened out in rehearsal prior to the next performance.

Eye communication, whose importance has come up repeatedly, is of special significance in opera conducting. In order to "be with the performers," a conductor must keep sight of the stage most of the time. True, if a work has been thoroughly prepared, singers should not look down to the pit except in crucial moments, but the conductor ought to be ready to meet their eyes whenever need be. This does not imply that the orchestra takes second place. Conductorial skill requires constant awareness of all happenings on stage and in the pit. Quick glances directed to the musicians, together with efficient stick technique, assure orchestral control.

How to seat orchestra players in an opera pit has never been determined to everyone's satisfaction. Placing an orchestra in a lengthy rectangle creates problems of coordination and sound balance that must be solved according to existing conditions. Aside from visual inconvenience, the distance in seating makes it difficult, if not impossible, for musicians to hear the other players. As one example, a timpanist playing in unison with a double bass pizzicato (usually at the opposite end of the pit) must rely on the conductor's beat for a unified attack.

Even the conductor faces the dilemma of receiving a grossly distorted sound, both from stage and pit. Unless he examines the acoustics by listening to a performance from different locations in the hall, he is bound to misjudge balances. Often it is the brass or percussion that overwhelms the ensemble, but sometimes the blame must go to the high overtones of a piccolo or a triangle. Then again it happens that violin passages played on the E string upset the balance, whereas a switch to the A or D strings can make these instruments almost inaudible.

In many houses the orchestral sound is not sufficiently projected to the stage, so singers may not hear a soft accompaniment, such as at the beginning of the "Habanera" in *Carmen.* Here, conductors have on occasion asked the orchestra to perform the first measures *forte,* but the problem is better solved by the use of amplification with backstage speakers that are heard by the singers, though not by the audience.

CHAPTER *30*

Conducting Choral Works with Orchestra

Instruction on how to train and direct choruses is found in textbooks dealing exclusively with the art of ensemble singing. The following comments are limited to the question of whether directing choral works in combination with instruments requires an approach that differs from leading an a cappella group.

The direction of any musical performance is conditioned on the relation between gesture and response, a relation that is subject to the individuality of the leader and the reaction of the performers. Thus, vocalists may react differently to a gesture than string or wind players do. Within the framework of generally accepted beating patterns, a conductor must therefore apply techniques that are effective in relation to a chorus and are also easily understood by instrumentalists.

It would be unrealistic to claim that the baton technique usually applied to directing a professional symphony orchestra is identical with practices commonly employed in conducting an unaccompanied group of voices. First of all, a choral director can dispense with the use of a baton. The singers, placed close to the stand and, as a rule, performing from memory, are in a position to follow the most subtle hand motions. Moreover, thanks to ample rehearsal time, which allows frequent repeats of the same passages, the group is familiar with all the details of the conductor's interpretation. Consequently, a conductor will be understood by singers even when using "free style" gestures to a greater extent than customary in orchestral conducting. Such gestures, if used skillfully for the sake of spontaneous expression, are sometimes more effective than conservative leadership.

Choral directors with limited orchestral experience may find that the players' reactions to their beat does not correspond to their expectations. The lack of understanding is usually more noticeable during purely instrumental sections. Once the voices join in, professional musicians are likely to adjust to the rhythm of the chorus. Such problems, relatively minor in the performance of Classical music, increase in connection with intricate twentieth-century scores.

To what extent a choral expert succeeds in acquiring the skill needed to control orchestral playing is a matter of ambition and opportunity. A choral conductor cannot hope to achieve desired results in the course of a few rehearsals without having learned to anticipate how an orchestra reacts to gestures and verbal instructions. Such knowledge is also useful in preparing a chorus for singing with the orchestra. Technically speaking, a last-minute switch from a more or less improvised manner of directing to "professional" conducting should be avoided. If a conductor wishes to employ a baton in performance, it should first be used during the last chorus sessions.

When performing oratorio, be it in a concert hall or in church, questions of acoustics and seating arrangements must be part of advance planning to assure a satisfactory balance of vocal and instrumental sound. Equally important is the careful preparation of orchestra materials (see p. 325). It should be of interest to choral directors that Brahms, when leading performances of his *Ein deutsches Requiem,* made changes not included in printed scores, partly for expression, partly to improve balances (see p. 408; for a detailed report by the author, see *Bach,* Vol. 7, No. 4, published by the Riemenschneider Bach Institute, Berea, Ohio).

In view of the large number of eighteenth-century works in the standard oratorio repertory, the study of performance practices should be part of a choral director's training. For the performance of Bach's choral works, it should be kept in mind that they were intended to be sung by children and young adults to the accompaniment of small orchestras. Vocal opulence is therefore less important than simplicity of expression and a convincing delivery of the religious content of the text.

Finally, a word of advice to orchestral conductors without extensive choral experience. As in opera, the leader must identify with the singers at all times, not merely by giving cues but by aiming for musical integration and clear projection of words. "Speaking with the chorus" helps the enunciation, while "breathing with the chorus" serves coordination. After the short breaks needed to take a breath, preparatory gestures secure unified attacks. Independence of the arms is essential to controlling the orchestra with the right hand, reserving left-hand motions to mold the phrasing of the vocal line.

Working with singers will be more successful when a conductor is familiar with the rudiments of vocal production, including pitch problems, projection of vowels, and enunciation of consonants. (For works performed in Latin, learn the meaning of the words and how they are pronounced!) Also, the conductor should arrange that, prior to the arrival of the orchestra at rehearsal, time is allowed for the chorus to warm up. This is due not only for vocal reasons but to refresh the feeling of ensemble. Rhythmically difficult passages will be sung with more precision if, during the warm-up period, the chorus is asked to speak words in strict time.

PART FOUR

INTERPRETATION AND STYLE

CHAPTER *31*

Aspects of Interpretation

INTERPRETATION OF A SCORE

When we speak of interpreting music, we think of an essential factor in musical performance that, transcending the sound of notes, communicates the music's meaning, its spirit and emotional content. Igor Stravinsky, in his "Poetics of Music," gave much thought to the dual role of the performer which he divided into executant and interpreter: "One can only require from the executant the translation into sound of the musical part . . . whereas one has the right to seek from the interpreter, in addition to the perfection of his translation into sound, a loving care—which does not mean . . . a recomposition." By requesting "loving care" and warning against "recomposition" (to be understood as tampering with the score) Stravinsky eloquently expressed a composer's hopes and fears.

If we accept Stravinsky's term "translation" for the process of transforming abstract signs into concrete sound, which he called a performer's primary task, we still would have to determine where translation ends and interpretation begins. This might turn out to be almost impossible, because musicians are not robots. A performer, trying to bring to life the inanimate symbols with which music is written, cannot help producing sounds that in some measure reflect the performer's perception, experience, and feelings—in short, a unique personality.

It is generally assumed that solid musicianship combined with performing experience qualifies a musician to act as an interpreter. Consequently, concertgoers expect that within the framework of a musical score and proven traditions the preservation of a composer's intentions is assured. Professionals are more skeptical. They know that traditions are tenuous, that the score does not tell everything, and above all that performers claim the right to serve the composer in line with their own artistic views and musical tastes.

355

Thus, it is no surprise that music schools do not offer special courses in interpretation. They trust their faculty members, no matter whether they teach instruments, voice, or conducting, to be perfectly able to convey to their students all they need to learn about the rendition of music from all periods and all styles.

Not all music scholars share such an optimistic view. Heinrich Schenker, for one, was critical of conductors when he commented on the interpretation of Beethoven's *Eroica* Symphony. In a sixty-page essay, which he proudly called "the first presentation" of the work's "true content," Schenker devoted one section to analysis, another to a report on a significant textual source (a score containing Beethoven's own corrections), and a final section with detailed suggestions for the symphony's interpretation.

Conductors, like most performers, are not easily persuaded to accept advice from scholars (Otto Klemperer's snide remark, "musicologists know a lot about 'ology' but nothing about 'music,'" comes to mind). Instead, they are inclined to justify their more or less idiosyncratic ideas by a "natural feeling for music," a notion no less vague than calling a performance "convincing" or insisting on each performer's privilege to follow his "rationale."

As early as in the eighteenth century musicians argued the question whether a performer was to express his own feelings or those of the composer. Invariably the verdict favored the composer. If we believe Hector Berlioz, this trend did not change during the Romantic era. Berlioz clearly stated that interpretation should not be subjected to a conductor's "individual feelings" but should reflect the composer's feelings.

How to draw the line between an arbitrary interpretation and a conscientious treatment of a composer's score is too complex a matter to be determined by rules. Perhaps Stravinsky's alluring "loving care" formula can show the way out of a labyrinth of intangibles, which certainly must not exclude the expression of feelings. The ability to express and project emotions is part and parcel of a performer's equipment, although young conductors must not take refuge in the categorical statement "this is the way I feel the music" in order to avoid argument. Music can be "felt" in several different ways, proven by eminent conductors who changed their interpretation of a work in the course of continued study and increasing knowledge.

While studying a score a conductor's initial steps toward a meaningful interpretation might be conditioned by circumstantial factors. Recalling, for instance, a very impressive reading by a respected colleague, one may be inclined to emulate such a performance. Even negative memories can influence a conductor's approach. A special situation arises when conductors face an unfamiliar score written in a style totally outside their experience. They might then consult a recording led by a conductor who specializes in this type of music. Listening to recordings can also be helpful when a work is being directed by its composer, although in the case of multiple recordings it has happened that a composer's ideas about his own music had changed through the years (see also p. 323).

The following comments, being addressed to young conductors with flexible minds, are intended to present an open view of choices on the way from initial score study to final preparation for orchestra rehearsals.

DIFFERENT ATTITUDES TO INTERPRETATION

Attitudes toward musical interpretation oscillate between two extremes. One extreme would be marked by taking unrestricted liberties with the score, the other by literal adherence to it. In the first instance, a performer "re-creates" the music by molding the score according to personal judgment. This can include changing notes, markings, tempo instructions, and orchestration. Not long ago we could hear romanticized and reorchestrated versions of Handel's *Messiah*. Conductors who preferred an arrangement to the *Urtext* obviously believed that vesting *Messiah* with modern devices was a legitimate means of conveying its spiritual message to our audiences.

Due to the now-prevailing approach to Baroque music, arrangements of this type have almost become a relic from the past. In the field of post-Baroque classics, however, the new trend toward preserving the proper style is still running parallel to performances that place individual tastes before stylistic considerations. Some conductors still adhere to a philosophy, once the consensus among musicians, that masterworks, in order to stay alive, must be reshaped in line with the artistic climate of each generation. It has even been suggested that composers, had they lived in our time, would have given their approval.

Musicians who advocate adherence to the composer's ideas challenge this theory. If the public's receptivity, they ask, is indeed conditioned by shifting psychological trends, how can it be explained that historically oriented performances are enjoyed by present audiences no less than modernized versions. If it is true that in our "fast-moving" society some music of the past cannot be appreciated unless played at a quicker pace, how can it be justified that some other, equally old, music is now often performed more slowly than marked by the composer? If conductors are praised as masters of the "Mozart style," how does one account for a surprising lack of unanimity in their readings of Mozart's works? How do we then define style? Perhaps we should, in this context, speak rather of shifting performance fashions and limit the use of the word "style" to demonstrable musical realities based on historical sources.

THE QUEST FOR AUTHENTICITY

A young conductor, reluctant to accept questionable concepts of style and distrustful of traditions that cannot be traced to the composer, will have to learn how to make choices. While a truly authentic performance is out of our reach, the quest for authenticity, despite its utopian nature, remains a worthwhile challenge. Admitting that ultimate truth is unobtainable is one thing; another is trying to eliminate avoidable stylistic errors. Besides, utilizing information about a composer's intentions need not lead to impersonal music making, as little as identifying with another person need deprive us of human warmth and understanding.

The quest for authenticity must not be mistaken for a puritan approach in the sense of the everything-is-in-the-score maxim, which, earlier in our century, led some musicians to apply modern usage to eighteenth-century works. They went so far as to object to rhythmic alterations in Baroque music, to any added appogiaturas and other embellishments in Mozart operas, and to any unwritten tempo modifications. They failed to recognize that literal rendition can distort a composer's ideas as much as the taking of unwarranted liberties.

Aside from using a reliable score and learning about performance practices, a conductor should look into a work's general background. Seeing a single work in the perspective of the composer's entire output will widen and intensify the conductor's understanding. Mozart's instrumental works, for instance, cannot be appreciated without knowledge of his operas. Insight into Schubert's and Schumann's symphonies requires familiarity with their songs and piano compositions. Extended to other composers, the imperative to become familiar with a composer's body of works opens up a wide field of study. If remaining "student for life" has been called the mark of a true artist, this certainly applies to conductors who are expected to master a repertory larger and more varied than that of any other musical performer.

CHAPTER *32*

Choice of Tempo

GENERAL CONSIDERATIONS

Orchestra players, when asked about the conductor's primary function, are likely to single out the setting of the pace. Similarly, a composer's first concern, when entrusting a score to a conductor, is the grasp of the proper tempo. Conductors themselves, when studying an unfamiliar score, try right from the start to feel the music's pulse, knowing that a well-chosen tempo will make a variety of musical details fall into place, which otherwise might turn out awkward and unconvincing. They also know that the choice of tempo can be marked by pitfalls. Tempo markings are vague, be they worded in Italian or the vernacular. Metronome indications do not always hit the mark, as admitted by composers when their markings are put to a test in performance. No wonder that Mozart called the choice of tempo not only the most essential but the trickiest thing in music.

Any attempt to determine, once and for all, the "right" tempo for a piece of music would be simplistic and mechanical. There is consensus, however, that a performance would suffer without the benefit of a "basic" tempo, which in spite of occasional modifications can be generally maintained. How to determine a basic tempo cannot be put into rules, but it has long been recognized that only by viewing a movement in its entirety can we hope to capture its pulse. Thus, Leopold Mozart suggested in his *Violinschule* (1756) that before deciding on the tempo of a movement one should look for a characteristic passage, often occurring later in the piece, that might be more enlightening than its beginning.

In general terms, the choice of tempo is based on tempo markings, the rhythmical and formal structure of a composition, its style, and orchestration. Moreover, the pacing should be reasonable in the sense of being playable (or singable) and effective by allowing the unfolding of phrases; at the same time, the pacing should make an orchestra sound its best. With musical performance not being a science but an individualistic craft, all these elements pass through the medium of the performer's personality. To make the pulse of the music one's own is of particular significance for the conductor, whose effectiveness depends on a secure feeling for the beat, something that does not develop overnight. A conductor must have "lived with the music" in order to project its pulse with conviction and spontaneity.

APPLICATION OF A CHOSEN TEMPO

The conductor's preparatory study does not always lead to a valid concept of the tempo, mainly because working in the studio lacks certain features that mark orchestral teamwork in the concert hall. Acoustics could be the reason, but aside from this a conductor may discover in rehearsal that a chosen tempo does not "work" with the orchestra. Misjudgment of this kind need not be explained by lack of experience. Conductors of proven ability have sometimes made tempo adjustments during rehearsals or in the course of performances. A notable instance occurred at a Bayreuth Festival in the 1930s when Toscanini modified his pacing of *Parsifal* to such an extent that, from the first to the fourth performance, the total playing time decreased by twenty minutes. It is of interest that witnessing musicians were inclined to attribute the maestro's change of mind to psychological factors.

That the conductor's beat, set in motion by a mental impulse, can be conditioned by one's state of mind is not astonishing. Nervousness, fatigue, overenthusiasm, and other psychological factors can lead to directions that are at variance with the original scheme; as a result the conductor is not always aware of the shift of tempo.

Special precaution against straying from the basic pace is needed in rehearsal. Playing a passage many times over can cause the beat to slow down, particularly when the repeats serve to clarify the musical texture. Having completed corrections, the conductor should let the orchestra repeat a longer section for the sake of continuity and to make sure that the correct speed is resumed. Some conductors (Toscanini is said to have been among them) have found it useful occasionally to consult a pocket metronome in rehearsal to check tempo fluctuations.

A psychological influence on the choice of tempo of a different sort has been noticed in recording sessions. Listening to a playback between "takes" can make a conductor alter a tempo that does not seem to produce the desired effect. The impression on a listener who hears mechanically reproduced music in a room can be different from that in a concert hall or in an opera house. One could argue against such a double standard in tempo choice. But it is undeniable that in live performance a conductor's pacing of a given work is not always identical with the one found on the same conductor's recording of the same work—perhaps one of the reasons that conductors are rarely satisfied with their recordings and dislike listening to them. It also serves as a warning to students not to rely on recordings in matters of tempo.

TEMPO MODIFICATIONS

The nature of certain compositions suggests a strictly maintained pulse. Many dances, perpetual-motion-like pieces, or movements built primarily on rhythmic propulsion require a persistent beat from the first to the final measure. Beethoven's *Allegretto scherzando* in his Eighth Symphony would suffer unless performed in this fashion (ex. 25.2). These instances, however, are rare when seen in the perspective of all the music written by Classical and Romantic composers. In the light of most of their works, relentless adherence to a fixed tempo would put a straitjacket on the performer. It would prevent a conductor from letting the music breathe and from giving meaning to the rise and fall of a melodic line. The need for subtle flexibility in the pacing of music has led some composers to use metronome markings that suggest a tempo span rather than a fixed speed. In place of $\quarternote = 80$, for example, they might prefer to write $\quarternote = 76–84$.

Thinking in terms of a tempo span, which implies minor modifications without losing sight of the basic pulse, is a useful means to preserve the essential character of the music as reflected in its rhythm. As an example, consider the Prelude to Wagner's *Die Meistersinger von Nürnberg* and assume as its basic tempo $\quarternote = 108$ (see ex. 21.2). Increasing the speed to $\quarternote = 120$, or slowing it down to $\quarternote = 96$, would change the music's character noticeably, while it is maintained by keeping the tempo within a span of $\quarternote = 104–112$.

When, or when not, to deviate from the regular beat is closely linked to a conductor's sensitivity and empathy for the music, but also to learning and insight. Subtle tempo modifications, often hardly noticed by the listener, serve different purposes. Relaxing the pulse may assure clarity in intricate passages, render significance to a phrase, or underline an unexpected modulation. Picking up the speed may put a lively theme into sharper relief or allow freer rein to the musical momentum. Still, a conductor should test the validity of such modifications by letting the music, at least once, pass through the mind in strict tempo. It will then be possible to judge where the music fares better by being played at straight speed or where sticking to a regular beat would be pedantic and hinder the music from conveying its meaning to the listener.

TEMPO RELATIONS

The examples for tempo relations quoted in chapter 22 referred to cases where composers had entered specific indications in the scores. Such relations, however, had existed long before composers began to express them by mathematical formulas. They can be divided into two categories: manifest and latent relations.

We speak of a manifest tempo relation when a musical episode returns, or is anticipated, in the form of a quotation, be it in identical or altered notation.

The theme of the slow introduction, shown in example 32.1, returns in example 32.2 in shortened form, in the fast section to precede the recapitulation. The tempo relation is $\eighthnote = \halfnote$.

In example 32.3, "Senta's Ballad," from Act II of *Der Fliegende Holländer,* contains a melody that is quoted in the overture, shown in example 32.4. Note that Wagner indicated the metronome for the Ballad; the overture has no metronome markings (see p. 108).

Quotations of this kind are frequently found in operatic overtures. Since the musical ideas were conceived to serve a dramatic function, familiarity with the opera provides a better insight into the expression and tempo of the

Ex. 32.1. Mozart, Serenade No. 9, "Posthorn," first movement, mm. 1-4

Ex. 32.2. Mozart, Serenade No. 9, "Posthorn," first movement, mm. 152-58

Ex. 32.3. Wagner, *Der fliegende Holländer,* Act, II, No. 4, mm. 39-42

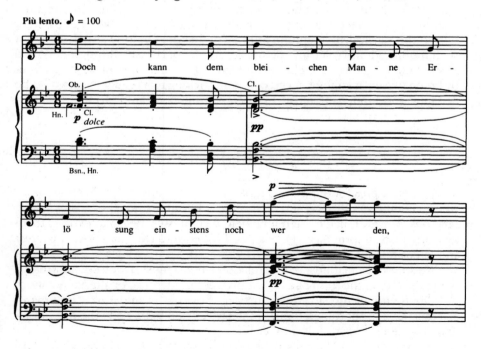

quoted passage than the study of the overture alone. The same is true for orchestral excerpts from operas, such as selections from Wagner's *Ring* cycle. Knowledge of the entire work is needed to grasp the style of the music and its dramatic connotation (see Appendix C).

An interesting manifest tempo relation, shown in examples 32.5 and 32.6,

Ex. 32.4. Wagner, *Der fliegende Holländer,* Overture, mm. 65-68

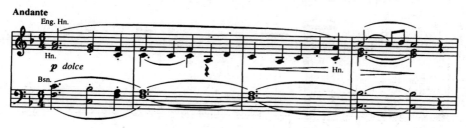

Ex. 32.5. Mozart, *Don Giovanni,* K. 527, Act I, No. 13, mm. 139-43

Ex. 32.6. Mozart, *Don Giovanni,* K. 527, Act I, No. 13, mm. 171-73

also occurs in the Ball Scene in the first finale of *Don Giovanni.* Although Mozart's intentions are unmistakable, they are not always observed in performance.

Prior to the Ball Scene, an invisible stage band plays the Contredanse shown in example 32.5, marked *Allegretto.* Consistent with the usage of the time, a tempo of ♩ = 100–104 can be assumed. This is to continue, after the entrance of the pit orchestra, for the remaining section in ²⁄₄, including the passage in D minor quoted in example 32.6. Like the Contredanse, a Minuet was played backstage earlier in the opera. Now, in the Ball Scene (ex. 32.7), it is not only repeated, but put in conjunction with the Contredanse and a German Dance not heard previously. To make the combination possible, Mozart chose a fast German Dance in ³⁄₈ and a moderately fast Minuet (the "slow Italian type"—see p. 392). Thus, within a tempo span of ♩ = 96–104, Mozart made it possible for the three dances to be played to the same beat.

A latent tempo relation, although not always provable, exists when the musical context at a tempo change suggests a continuation of the music's pulse. Three examples, taken from overtures of Mozart and Beethoven, serve as illustrations.

In example 32.8, the transition from the introduction, *Andante* ¢, to the

Ex. 32.7. Mozart, *Don Giovanni,* K. 527, Act I, No. 13, mm. 454-57

Ex. 32.8. Mozart, *Don Giovanni,* K. 527, Overture, mm. 29-33

Allegro ¢ is marked by rapidly repeated measured notes, thirty-second notes in the Andante (second violins and violas) and eighth notes in the Allegro (violas and cellos), calling for an uninterrupted flow with the relation ♩ = o. (For a smooth transition it is useful to apply 1-beat to the first few allegro bars before changing to 2-beat.)

In the overture to *Die Entführung aus dem Serail,* a tempo relation can be established between the fast and slow sections by the formula o = ♪ (one measure of the *Presto* equals the eighth beat of the *Andante*). The *Andante* is quoted from the opera's opening aria and offers a manifest tempo relation. Example 19.38 shows the return to the *Presto.*

Example 32.9 shows another instance where latent and manifest tempo relations are combined. A rhythmic figure, first heard in the horns, then in timpani, establishes the relation ♩ = ♪ for the transition from *Un poco sostenuto* ¢ to Adagio ¾. The theme of the *Adagio* is taken from the tenor aria in the opera, previously quoted in the introduction of the overture.

Manifest tempo relations are rarely subject to controversy, but there can

Ex. 32.9. Beethoven, *Leonore* Overture No. 2, mm. 423-28

be disagreement in regard to latent relations. Some conductors, for example, maintain that, in symphonies of the Classical Viennese school, introductions are invariably linked to the main sections by a precise rhythmic relation. Even though in some instances a good case can be made for assuming such relation, it would seem wrong to exclude the element of surprise as created by contrasting tempi. In the case of the four Beethoven symphonies that begin with an introduction, the composer's metronome markings leave no doubt that the fast sections are to start with a new rhythmic impulse.

METRONOME INDICATIONS

Mälzel's metronome, now mostly replaced by electric or watch-like devices, was first hailed as the salvation from forcing music into *tempi ordinari,* to quote Beethoven. Unhappy with the traditional Italian tempo markings, he praised the invention as a means to give full expression to the "free genius." Later on, Beethoven was less sure and expressed doubts—the same doubts that have been shared by musicians until the present time. Still, in spite of being maligned for being unreliable and misleading, the metronome has survived. Beginning with Berlioz, metronome markings are found in most French scores, and many nineteenth-century composers in other countries followed suit. Today, virtually all composers make use of metronome indications.

Beethoven's use of the metronome is of special interest, not merely because he was the first outstanding musician to experiment with it but in view of considerable controversy regarding his metronome markings. The fact is that he continued using it, even after he had come to recognize its limitations. Shortly before his death, he urged his publisher to delay printing the score of the *Missa solemnis* until the metronome list would be ready—a plan that he did not live to carry out. Not only from letters to his publishers, but from conversation books, we know how Beethoven labored before deciding on metronome figures. He seems to have experienced the frustration that is all too familiar to every musician who has tried to determine tempi metronomically. A certain speed may now appear convincing but is objectionable when tested the next morning, or a metronome figure that fits the beginning of a piece may become questionable when applied to other sections of the same movement.

In short, the pulse of living music cannot be captured by a mechanical device, which explains why composer-conductors have not always observed their own markings. Stravinsky, for one, who had long insisted on strict adherence to his metronome figures, came to admit that, with increasing experience in conducting his works, he sometimes revised his original ideas about tempo (without, unfortunately, having these changes entered into the printed scores).

In spite of these odds, even the most skeptical conductor would welcome metronome markings by Bach, Mozart, and other masters, had they been able to avail themselves of the device. In Beethoven's case, the critics of his metronome figures have failed to explain why, sometimes within the same work or movement, some of his markings are readily accepted, others flatly rejected. Perhaps they forget that the metronome was never intended to pinpoint the speed of music. It was meant to provide information regarding the character of the music and to prevent the performer from straying too far from the composer's intention. For the conductor, metronome indications are invaluable as guides to define tempo spans that preserve the true character of the music.

The third movement of Beethoven's Seventh Symphony (see Appendix A, No. 4) may serve as an example. It bears two markings: *Presto* $\frac{3}{4}$, $\textit{d.}$ = 132, for the main section; *Assai meno presto,* $\textit{d.}$ = 84 for the Trio. The *Presto* is usually performed at a speed identical with, or at least close to, Beethoven's metronome. It is not uncommon, however, for the Trio to be played as slowly as $\textit{d.}$ = 60, to the effect that it assumes a character quite different from the one reflected in the composer's marking. A less excessive slowing down, say a speed of $\textit{d.}$ = 72, would still conform to *assai meno presto* and remain within a reasonable tempo span of $\textit{d.}$ = 72–84.

Beethoven's metronome did not allow the definition of very slow or very rapid beats. Its calibration started with 50 beats per second and ended with 160 beats per second. This ought to be kept in mind when we consider, for instance, the marking $\textit{♪}$ = 84 for the second movement of Beethoven's Fourth Symphony. Did he really wish the music to be "felt" in eighth notes throughout the movement, or would he have preferred the marking $\textit{♩}$ = 42, had his metronome permitted such an indication? *Cantabile* for the first violins, then for the flute, seems to call for a melodic flow within three calm beats. This will not prevent a conductor from using subtle subdivision for the sake of secure coordination (see ex. 16.15).

CHOICE OF TEMPO IN HISTORICAL CONTEXT

Performers are inclined to believe that their views on interpretation grew out of their personal experience and reflect their individual judgment. Actually, we cannot help being "children of our time" and would be hard pressed to prove to what degree our views are in fact our own without being subjected to performance fashions that shift from one generation to another. This would include our feeling for musical speed. Seen in historical perspective, there have been "fast" and "slow" times. For instance, there are clear indications that after 1850, under the influence of the so-called Wagnerian school, a tendency existed toward slowing down the music of the Classical era. In the present century it could be observed that a majority of conductors who had roots in the nineteenth century showed a similar trend, whereas a new generation of musicians now generally prefers livelier tempi.

This new tendency arose from a growing interest in former practices and makes itself especially felt in the interpretation of slow movements in Classical works. They are now sometimes performed at a pace that musicians who are unwilling to accept these new ideas would find overly fast. A striking example is the second movement of Mozart's Symphony No. 34 (K. 338). It is written in $\frac{2}{4}$ and marked *Andante con moto* to which Mozart later added *quasi Allegretto*. Depending on a conductor's taste this music can now be heard at a metronomic speed of ♩ = 60, but at other times at ♪ = 60, which is twice as slow! Discrepancies of this magnitude did not exist in the early part of our era. As compared to their colleagues in former generations, musicians nowadays obviously find it more difficult to reconcile their differences of opinion.

Similar differences manifest themselves in the evaluation of the metronome's usefulness. Felix Weingartner, in his time a respected interpreter of Beethoven's symphonies and author of a widely acclaimed guidebook advising conductors on the performance of those symphonies (1906), had disapproved of most of Beethoven's metronome markings as misleading or impractical. He was not alone. By mid-century, George Szell, admired for his Beethoven recordings, declared that he had come to disregard those metronome figures altogether. When Leonard Bernstein's reading of Beethoven's Ninth Symphony was televised in 1989 from near the Berlin Wall, listeners could notice that his choice of tempi disclosed a similar disregard.

Yet, in the course of our century's final quarter, a new and radically different trend arose among a sizable group of conductors who believe in taking Beethoven's, and other nineteenth-century composers', metronome markings at face value. In fact, the pendulum did swing all the way: For some performers it has become an article of faith that all those indications are to be followed literally. An attempt to clarify some pertinent questions and further discussion of Beethoven's metronome markings will be found in chapter 34.

All radical views should be viewed with suspicion. Young conductors will do well not to fall for shifting performance fashions but to preserve an open mind when making decisions in the light of each individual case.

CHAPTER 33

Aspects of Performance Practice

THE STUDY OF PERFORMANCE PRACTICE AND THE QUESTION OF TRADITIONS

Ours is the first century that has seen an increasing interest in performing practices of former times. Initially it was limited to a reorientation toward the music of the late Baroque, but in recent years more and more scholars and performers have begun to review questions of style within the post-Baroque, Classical, and nineteenth-century repertoire. Seen in this context, the study of performance practice ought not to be confined to any special period, or periods, and might include our own century. For the purpose of the present text, comments offered in this and other chapters will focus on music created since about 1750.

Originally, the term "performance practice" referred to rules and habits that in the eighteenth century served to bridge the gap between notation and execution. Students were then guided by textbooks filled with musical examples to illustrate "this way it is written" and "this way it is played." Some suggestions differed from one text to another, as could be expected in a time when taking liberties with notes and rhythms was based partly on rules, partly on the taste of each performer.

No clear line can be drawn to mark the end of ambiguity in music notation. Liberties continued, especially in opera, far into the nineteenth century. Even Schubert was obliged to accept changes in his songs made by a famous baritone friend. Generally speaking, however, and particularly in orchestral and other ensemble music, the written text has ceased to be subject to the performer's discretion since the days of Beethoven.

In 1832 Ludwig Spohr published his *Violinschule*. There he expressed the view of the time by distinguishing between *richtiger Vortrag* and *schöner Vortrag*. "Correct" execution included true pitch, exact rhythm, steady tempo, and observation of the composer's markings. "Beautiful" execution required a refined treatment of dynamics, accents, and phrasing. Moreover, it called for tempo modifications. Passion was to be expressed by increasing the speed; tenderness and sadness by slowing it down. Students were advised to develop taste and feeling and to emulate the outstanding performers of the time. A footnote informed the reader, merely as a matter of historical interest, that former customs could be looked up in Leopold Mozart's book.

Spohr's patronizing reference to Leopold Mozart and his contention that current habits superseded former performance styles must be seen in the light of a prevailing faith in "progress." In fact, he upheld a tradition of long standing. Mozart had not hesitated to rewrite the scores of Handel oratorios according to the ideas of his generation. Likewise, when Wagner edited Palestrina's Stabat Mater, he transformed Renaissance music into a romantic piece charged with explosive passion. (From Wagner's essay "Über das Dirigieren" we learn much about his thoughts on interpretation. He had no qualms about making changes in Classical scores but chided conductors who took liberties with his own works.)

The foregoing discussion included references to rules, practices, customs, habits, and traditions, a medley of terms that characterize the manner in which performance problems have been, and still are, approached. Such variety could be confusing, unless we keep in mind that whatever the source of information, be it old treatises, instruction books, contemporary reports, and so on, it must be understood in context. Some rules, particularly those formulated by prominent authors of the past, retained validity for considerable time, while other performance habits were short-lived. Questions of this kind require intensive study, and the select bibliography found in Recommended Reading should prove useful.

A word needs to be said about traditions, because young conductors might be exposed to categorical statements by their elders referring to traditions. At the beginning of his career, the author of this book was scolded by his superior for having conducted an *Andante* in $\frac{6}{8}$ meter in a Mozart opera using a 2-beat. "All reputable conductors do this in six" was the stern advice. Apparently, by resting his case on tradition, this musician saw no value in investigating matters of style.

Another instance of a widespread and rarely contested tradition is connected with the handling of a *da capo* in Classical minuets (see also p. 392). There is incontrovertible proof that it was expected that the inner repeats were always to be observed, meaning in fact that the main section was to be played in exactly the same manner when repeated in the *da capo*. Surprisingly, this item of performance practice has slipped the attention of scholars. Thus, the *New Grove Dictionary* informs its readers: "It was traditional to omit internal repetitions when recapitulating the first section." Traditional in what sense? Obviously, the writer failed to investigate the time table! This tradition was initiated—by whom?—around the middle of the nineteenth century, long after the Classical era.

Traditions must be traceable to the composer to deserve serious attention, whereas those merely originated and proliferated by performers should arouse suspicion. Unfortunately, the latter category includes a fairly large number of questionable tempi that have found entrance into present performance customs, since some performers seem to find it difficult to free themselves of traditions.

Not all conducting students participate in musicological studies. Within existing curricula, questions of interpretation are discussed in classes that primarily serve the training of performing skills. Some instructors take interest in the history of musical performance; others are content with handing down to their pupils the more or less valid traditions inherited from their teachers.

A conductor, while working out interpretative ideas, must be prepared to make choices. The conductor's education, therefore, should cover the broadest possible basis and encourage curiosity in every field of music, including historical studies. Awareness of style, far from being a hindrance to personal involvement, enables a conductor to decide with better understanding how to apply former customs to present realities, such as the instruments now in use, the training of the players, the size of the concert halls, and other facts that are part of our musical daily life.

The following examples illustrate interpretive questions that come up in the daily work of present-day conductors and could be categorized as twentieth-century performance practice.

CHANGING THE COMPOSER'S TEXT

For a long time, conductors have taken it upon themselves to change notes, rhythms, orchestration, and the order of movements. If we add cuts, dynamics, and phrasing, a list of all the tamperings with scores might easily fill as many volumes as the music itself. Although arguments about the rationality of those more-or-less arbitrary changes are likely to continue as long as music is performed by human beings, it can be stated that, in the course of the last few decades, musicians have turned to respect the composer's text to a much higher degree than former generations. Many musical performers now believe that the aim of score study is not merely to learn *what* is written but *why* the music was written in a certain way. Before questioning the validity of a particular scoring, conductors are now inclined to give the composer, as it were, the benefit of the doubt!

Compare the return of the triplet motive in example 33.2 against the first time it appears in the symphony, as shown in example 33.1. For the second time, the composer added violas and horns for fuller chords and a different tone color. In this new context, he lengthened the concluding notes to quarter notes.

The trills (second violins) are longer the first time in example 33.3 than in

Ex. 33.1. Beethoven, Symphony No. 6, first movement, mm. 53-54

Ex. 33.2. Beethoven, Symphony No. 6, first movement, mm. 328-30

Ex. 33.3. Beethoven, Symphony No. 6, second movement, m. 33

the repeat, example 33.4. This could be explained by the switch to the E string, which produces a sound different from that on the A string, or simply by a composer's wish for variety. (Why shouldn't there be variety in music as in nature, which inspired the music?)

In neither case would it make good sense to establish an analogy that Beethoven had not intended.

In Haydn's and Mozart's scores it happens not infrequently that the concluding note at the end of a phrase group is of different length for one or several instruments as compared to the notation for the rest of the orchestra.

Ex. 33.4. Beethoven, Symphony No. 6, second movement, m. 105

Discrepancies of this kind do not always favor a unified ensemble. Still, the notation should not be altered without a study of the musical context.

For three measures in example 33.5, the winds play dotted quarter notes, the violins and violas eighth notes, while the low strings are coordinated with the quarter notes of the singers. The two last measures present a problem: To have the low strings continue with quarter notes would not serve any apparent purpose but might upset the ensemble. A change to eighth notes is therefore suggested.

Ex. 33.5. Mozart, *Le Nozze di Figaro,* Act II, No. 15, mm. 392-97

The flute solo in measure 164 of example 33.6 would be covered by the violins, unless their quarter note is shortened to conform to the release of the winds. No such change would be in order in measure 8 of example 33.7, where the appogiatura on the downbeat justifies a slightly longer chord in the string accompaniment.

In example 33.8, in measures 2 and 4, the half notes in the low strings and bassoons must not be shortened, although they are sustained beyond the tutti chords. The three ponderous half notes are an important musical statement, quoted from the opera's second finale, where they echo the ghostly knocking at the door. In Mozart's catalog, however, the third bass note appears as a quarter note, as shown in facsimile in figure 33.1. This case is one of several instances that make us wonder whether Mozart had changed his mind or

Ex. 33.6. Mozart, Symphony No. 38, fourth movement, mm. 162-65

Ex. 33.7. Mozart, Symphony No. 38, fourth movement, mm. 6-8

simply showed little concern for such details. (Mozart's handwritten catalog is an invaluable reference for tempo information on the performance of his works. A complete discussion of this important source can be found in Jean-Pierre Marty's *The Tempo Indications of Mozart;* see Recommended Reading).

Ex. 33.8. Mozart, *Don Giovanni,* K. 527, Overture, mm. 1-4

Fig. 33.1. Entry for *Don Giovanni* in Mozart's catalogue

CHANGING THE ORCHESTRATION

Conductors alter the composer's orchestration to clarify the thematic structure for the benefit of the listener or to obtain an orchestral sound that is more to their liking. These changes include shifting notes from one instrument to another, adding instruments for a fuller orchestral texture, or lightening it by letting some instruments pause. Furthermore, in view of technical imperfections that curtailed the composers' choices in former times, orchestra parts are adjusted to take advantage of our superior instruments.

In example 33.9, the horn passage that introduces the second theme of the movement (see ex. 21.18) is given here to the bassoons, obviously because in Beethoven's time the notes A and B could not be produced on horns in E flat. Many conductors find the bassoon sound inadequate in this context and have horns play the first three measures, either alone or in combination with the bassoons (sometimes the bassoons are supported by one horn only).

In example 33.10, to expect a bassoonist to play these low notes *pppppp*, as suggested by the overly anxious composer, would be unrealistic. A bass clarinet usually substitutes. (Thanks to electronic sound control, the substitution is not needed in recorded performances.)

Ex. 33.9. Beethoven, Symphony No. 5, first movement, mm. 303-10

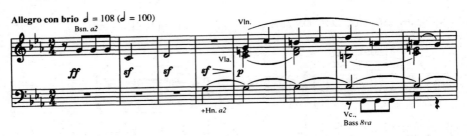

Ex. 33.10. Tchaikovsky, Symphony No. 6, first movement, mm. 159-60

Even with doubled woodwinds, the inner voices in example 33.11 do not stand out sufficiently unless horn and trumpet parts are changed. Three trumpets are needed for the arrangement shown in example 33.12. The violas, scored in unison with the celli, are more helpful when they participate in the melodic line (Schubert could not count on more than two or three celli as part of a small string group!). Arrangements of this type are suggested only for orchestras with large string groups performing in big halls.

The change in example 33.12 follows a recommendation of Felix Weingartner. Best known among his writings are the comments on the interpretation of Beethoven's symphonies (see Recommended Reading). In spite of its controversial nature, Weingartner's study is a valuable introduction into the problems of orchestral balance in Beethoven's scores. Warned of these problems, a conductor is better prepared to find personal solutions.

Wagner was the first to revise the orchestration of Beethoven's symphonies and to publish his recommendations. In the second movement of the

Ex. 33.11. Schubert, Symphony No. 8, "The Great," first movement, mm. 679-81 (original)

Ex. 33.12. Schubert, Symphony No. 8, "The Great," first movement, mm. 679-81 (with alternate scoring)

Symphony No. 7, for instance, he had the trumpets double the clarinets in measures 75–90 (the opening of this passage is shown in example 33.13). This change meant leading the first trumpet to a high B in measure 84. The coordination of trumpets and timpani, typical of the Classical style, was disregarded by Wagner (see also above, p. 369). Having performed the work in this manner, he proudly reported: "The effect was so excellent that no one among the listeners felt to lose, but rather to gain, which on the other hand did not impress anyone as a novelty or a change." (Wagner's German prose is as confusing as this literal translation!)

Ex. 33.13. Beethoven, Symphony No. 7, second movement, mm. 75-82 (with Wagner's changes for the trumpets)

Weingartner, who does not subscribe to Wagner's arrangement, suggests letting the second trumpet play the E an octave lower in the interest of better balance, a reasonable change in this particular case. Not all the alterations, however, that Weingartner recommends for second horn and second trumpet should be accepted without examining the musical context.

Example 33.14 presents the original text, while Weingartner's changes have been added in example 33.15. The changes concern mostly dynamics. Also, in measures 128–130, the second horn is lowered by one octave. At first sight, analogy seems to speak in favor of this alteration. Yet, if the lower F would have seemed essential to the composer, he could have given it to the second bassoon, just as he scored this instrument independently in the symphony's second movement. In this case, there is no compelling reason to alter Beethoven's text. Should the *a due* for the horns disturb the balance, the second horn pauses. Doubling the flute for the crescendo, as Weingartner suggests, can be useful, but his arbitrary markings for dynamics are questionable.

The authenticity of the *p* in measure 136 is uncertain, except for the first violins. The autograph, as for Beethoven's Symphonies Nos. 2 and 3, has disappeared. Still, it is to be hoped that conductors will be less dependent on guessing once the nine symphonies can be studied from a thoroughly researched edition.

Problems such as the orchestration of the second theme in the *Scherzo* of the Ninth Symphony (mm. 93ff.) will remain. Doubling the woodwinds by four horns, as it has become customary since Wagner's time, introduces an orchestral color quite alien to the Beethoven sound. Yet playing the theme as scored is even more unsatisfactory, with or without doubling, while marking the strings *p* (as it has been tried) quenches the rhythmic impact. Weingartner, who devotes no fewer than seventy pages to the interpretation of the Ninth, used to add a pair of trumpets to carry the melody at the repeat. One wonders whether he would not have had second thoughts, had he lived longer, just as he abandoned some other all too radical changes in later years.

In his revision of Schumann's symphonies, Weingartner reorchestrated entire passages. Other conductors limit changes to dynamics and avoid some of the doubling but add woodwind doubling to *f* passages. Even purists admit that Schumann's symphonies, when played exactly as scored, suffer from lack of thematic clarity and insufficient contrast which obscure the structural build-up.

In the first and last movements of Schumann's Fourth Symphony, some timpani notes clash with the harmonic setting. "Wrong notes" in the timpani also occur in works of other composers of the same period. Unlike the Classical masters, they accepted dissonances for the sake of an important timpani effect. Taking advantage of the modern device that permits a quick change of pitch, conductors now substitute notes that fit the harmony. Filling in timpani notes, however, where a composer wrote a pause is quite another matter. The intermittent use of kettle drums was a characteristic feature of the Classical orchestra. Tempting as it may be to add timpani notes to the "Tempest" section in Beethoven's Sixth Symphony (beginning with m. 78), it would introduce an element foreign to the composer's style. In fact, the "delayed" timpani entrance in measure 106, after a pause of twenty-two bars, heightens its effect.

Similar caution should be observed in regard to shifting double bass

Ex. 33.14. Beethoven, Symphony No. 1, first movement, mm. 124-37

Ex. 33.15. Beethoven, Symphony No. 1, first movement, mm. 124-37 (with Weingartner's suggested changes)

passages to the lower octave, a procedure that will be discussed in reference to Brahms's scoring. Players and conductors should view questions of orchestral setting within the broad aspect of an entire work and not from the narrow angle of a single passage in an individual part. The double bass line in the fourth and fifth movements of Beethoven's Sixth Symphony proves this point. After having made repeated use of the C string for the "Tempest" music, the composer refrained from using it for the first section of the finale yet returned to taking advantage of the low bass notes for the movement's climax (mm. 175ff.). Alterations of the bass part in the first section are therefore not justifiable.

DOUBLING

"To double woodwinds is indispensable in *forte,* and whenever they are playing an important theme" is a quote from the notes added by Richard Strauss to Berlioz's text on orchestration. Strauss was then thinking of older works, because, in his own scores, based on a string group of 16-16-12-10-8, he balanced winds against strings without the need of doubling.

Wind doubling dates from the eighteenth century. When Haydn made use of it during his last visit to London, his string players probably numbered 12-12-6-4-5, a far cry from his resources in Esterháza, (5-5-2-2-2). Mozart, at least on one occasion, enjoyed the luxury of a large string group and doubled winds. Rules for doubling did not exist. Similar to modern custom, arrangements were made according to changing conditions and available forces, always with the purpose to achieve a better sound balance. (When Beethoven negotiated the terms for the first performance of his Ninth Symphony, he requested a string group of 12-12-10-6-6 and double woodwinds.)

Within our standard repertory, wind doubling is used in Handel oratorios (when presented in large halls), rarely in a Haydn or Mozart symphony, but frequently for works of Beethoven (Symphonies Nos. 3, 5, 6, 7, and 9), Schubert (Symphonies Nos. 7 and 8), Schumann, Brahms, Bruckner, and Tchaikovsky. This list is not complete. It remains within the discretion of the conductor to augment any section or to double a single instrument when need be.

Doubling must be marked clearly in individual parts to indicate which measures are to be performed by the assistant players. In the case of orchestras with only one extra player in a section, the conductor determines whether doubling applies to the first or second voice. Sometimes it will be necessary to have a special part written for the assistant musician. Yet doubling remains subject to change. Only while rehearsing in the concert hall can a conductor judge with certainty where doubling is required keeping in mind that stylistic considerations are of equal significance.

On the other hand, doubling indicated in the score by the composer may upset the equilibrium. Particularly in works of Classical composers, notes that are scored for two wind players in unison may sound too heavy. In these cases, most of which concern horns and trumpets in the higher ranges, it might be helpful to let one of the players pause (see above, p. 376).

Lightening the string sound by a temporary reduction of the number of players is common practice, either for passages that require the refined sound of a chamber orchestra or to assure discrete accompaniment. It is believed that in Mozart's concertos the indications *tutti* and *solo* did not simply mark the entrances for soloists (they usually played with the orchestra tutti), but in the sense of the former *con ripieno* and *senza ripieno* (see p. 385). In all these cases, conductors would do best to wait for the rehearsal to determine how many string stands are to participate or whether they prefer to have the inside players pause. The same method applies when a score calls for only half a string section. Once the decision is made, the number of stands or players must be marked in the string parts clearly indicating where the reduction begins and where the tutti is resumed.

RETOUCHING VERSUS ARRANGING

Borrowing a term from painting and photography, the technique of making minor changes in an orchestral score to clarify the musical texture has been called retouching. It leaves the music's structure and expression intact, and it does not interfere with the composer's conception. Conductors who subject a score to more drastic alterations are overstepping the boundary of interpretation by entering the field of arrangements. The line between retouching and arranging may not always be easily definable, but little doubt exists that the rewriting of entire passages, as it was discussed in connection with Schumann's symphonies, exceeds retouching.

Composers have frequently made use of these techniques when revising their works. Mahler's revised scores have been mentioned. Wagner rewrote the score of *Der fliegende Holländer*. The changes made by Mozart in the second version of the first movement of the "Paris" Symphony (K. 297) did not go beyond retouching. The second version of Schumann's Symphony No. 4, however, is for the most part an arrangement of the original one.

A conductor's function is to interpret music. The masters of the past wished their works to be interpreted the way they were conceived. There are no guidelines, however, for conductors to determine which textual changes are compatible with the "quest for authenticity." Unqualified answers cannot be expected in a field where many questions are argumentative. Several questions have been discussed in connection with previous examples. The following ones offer additional material to appraise the pros and cons in regard to textual changes.

Some conductors have made the strings continue their pizzicato through the end of the movement, although the parts used in 1813 under the composer's supervision contain the *arco* signs, as shown in Example 33.16. Example 33.17 shows another change, favored by the conductor Leopold Stokowski, who lengthened the last note of the first violins, for no other reason than that he liked it better this way.

In example 33.18, according to Weingartner's report, Hans von Bülow made the strings play pizzicato in measure 132, presumably to soften the contrast between the *dolce* of the flute and the string chord marked *f*. Yet Beethoven could have prescribed pizzicato had he wished to create this effect. For a large orchestra, as compared to Beethoven's smaller group, the *f* might be reduced to *mf*.

Ex. 33.16. Beethoven, Symphony No. 7, second movement, final measures

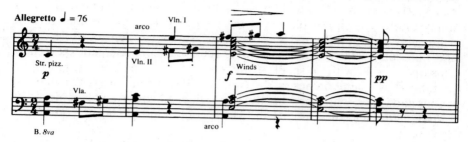

Ex. 33.17. Beethoven, Symphony No. 7, second movement, final measures (with Stokowski's change for the violins)

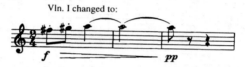

Ex. 33.18. Beethoven, Symphony No. 5, second movement, mm. 129-132

In measure 95 of Ex 7.10, shortening the first note of the violins to a sixteenth note, and following this with a sixteenth rest, assures incisive and coordinated playing. Such a change in notation may not be necessary for a well-trained orchestra, but it often helps to make the violins lift the bow before attacking the next note; in other words, it is a precautionary device that in no way interferes with the musical context.

A similar and equally legitimate change in notation is useful in measure 38 of example 21.12. Crossing out the first of the four sixteenth notes on the fourth count (flutes and violins) makes for better ensemble playing. Besides, it may save rehearsal time.

In example 19.24, the conductor must decide whether the first violins should make a short break after the fermata in measure 146, or to go, without interruption, into the repeated note C, now played softly. The notation in the symphony's original version shows that Schumann did not intend a break, because he connected the two notes by a tie. When performed this way, the up-bow in measure 147 must be unnoticeable in order not to interrupt the line.

An effective method to give a legato line in the strings the definition derived from detached playing is a *divisi* in unison, as used by Mahler in example 33.19. To apply this device without the sanction of a composer would clearly fall into the category of "arranging."

What might be called a borderline case is presented by examples 33.20 and 33.21. Only the melodic lines are quoted. In the original version, which utilizes only strings, the playing is legato throughout. In the final version, Schumann added a flute and an oboe to measure 49 for legato, while violins and violas play detached double notes to achieve a more energetic crescendo. This may work with a small string ensemble. When the symphony is performed by a large orchestra, the two wind instruments are outweighed by violins and violas, which obscure the legato line. A better result is achieved by a *divisi,* with half of the violins and violas continuing the legato pattern.

Ex. 33.19. Mahler, Symphony No. 6, two measures before #15

Ex. 33.20. Schumann, Symphony No. 4, first movement, (original version)

Ex. 33.21. Schumann, Symphony No. 4, first movement, mm. 47-49 (final version)

CHAPTER 34

Aspects of Musical Style

Very few men investigate. Hence, most men are led by authority; and the errors of learned men are received as truth and incorporated into public opinion.
Noah Webster (1816)

CONCEPTS OF MUSICAL STYLE AND TASTE

Musical style can be defined as the sum total of elements that are inherent in a composition. In historical perspective, the term may be applied to a group of composers, usually within a limited time period, or to a single composer's output. Speaking, for instance, of Baroque music, we may be thinking of all the music written from Monteverdi's time until the "late" Baroque (not merely Bach and Handel but a countless number of now-forgotten composers), or else we may confine ourselves to explore what is commonly called the "Bach style."

How does musical style relate to performance practice? Although it would be difficult to determine which comes first, every musical style inevitably presupposes specific practices. Still, from a conductor's point of view, mere application of some often-quoted practices, such as the use of "period instruments," must not take the place of serious study aimed at investigating all the elements that constitute musical style; articulation, phrasing, ornamentation, and a multitude of other details.

Strangely, one of those elements is no longer mentioned when the interpretation of "early music" is under discussion, although eighteenth-century musicians believed it to be the most essential attribute of an accomplished performer. It was then known by the elusive name of "good taste." Wherever we look, in the most authoritative treatises of the time, even in Mozart's letters, we are constantly reminded that good taste was considered more important than skill and musical talent per se.

Perhaps the neglect on the part of scholars to include taste in their research can be explained by the paucity of concrete information. From Mozart's letters it can be concluded that, aside from defining it as grasping the music's proper pace, he identified good taste with a sensitive and flexible presentation of a melody. Father Leopold, in his *Violinschule,* went a step further by calling the application of "unequal notes" a means to develop a student's taste.

The lesson we learn from this is to realize that when the two Mozarts spoke of good taste, their frame of reference was quite unlike ours. This should caution us not to be too quick in hoping that our efforts, no matter how sincere, would have been met with the approval of the great masters of the past. Nevertheless, such skepticism must not discourage a young conductor who is trying to gather as much stylistic information as possible. The discussions in this chapter are meant to lead the way.

BAROQUE MUSIC

The following comments refer to the late Baroque of the eighteenth century and are limited to an outline of basic questions. To gain deeper insight into the Baroque style and its application in performance, a conductor must consult reference books and acquire knowledge of Baroque instruments. Texts do not always furnish ready answers, because the intermixture of rules and liberties, which is peculiar to this style, often calls for the performer's judgment, no less now than in the old days.

Depending on their national background, the authors of the time differed in matters of tempo. Within each school, however, the speed of music was defined according to tempo categories, often with reference to mathematical formulas. This included the pacing of the dances that have come down to us in the form of suites. Some authors even utilized mechanical devices that predated Mälzel's metronome. All this information has been compiled by scholars such as Dolmetsch, Donington, Neumann, and Sachs (see Recommended Reading).

Quantz, in his text on flute playing, measured tempi by relating them to the human pulse. His figures were later translated into metronome speeds. For example, a *Siciliano* $\frac{12}{8}$ required four beats per measure at about $\quarternote = 52$. The same pulse should be generally applied to movements in $\frac{12}{8}$, as to the *Largo ma non tanto* in Bach's Concerto for Two Violins (see ex. 12.5).

A question related to tempo concerns the slowing down of cadences that conclude a section. If not exaggerated, such ritards are stylistically justified. They must, however, not be applied as a matter of routine. C. P. E. Bach pointed out that a "concluding trill" should be slowed down only at the very end of a piece and that music of "fiery or sad" nature was to be played in strict tempo to its conclusion—in the first instance in order not to stop the momentum, in the second not to carry the sad expression too far.

Turning to dynamics, the so-called terrace dynamics, an alternation of soft and loud sections without intermediate shadings, relate only to music written for organ or harpsichord. Its general application would not conform to Baroque practice, as little as would romanticized performances with excessive dynamic markings. The dynamic range was by far not as extensive as ours.

Dramatic crescendos and diminuendos were still a thing of the future. Yet performers knew of subtle dynamic gradations within a melodic line. Music created in the "era of sensitivity" did not lack expressiveness. It was for good reason that C. P. E. Bach praised the clavichord, which had also been his father's favored clavier, as an instrument that permitted dynamic shadings.

In the eighteenth century, the art of phrasing, which included imperceptible short breaks to separate the segments of a phrase, was an important part of music education. It was often left to the performer's taste, which explains the scarcity of phrasing marks in many Baroque scores. In the case of Bach, the vacuum is filled by fairly frequent indications as, for instance, in the carefully phrased violin part of the "Christe eleison" in the B-Minor Mass. Other sections of the Mass offer further examples, as do the scores of the *St. Matthew Passion,* a number of cantatas, the "Brandenburg" Concertos, and sonatas for various solo instruments. These phrasings, which are distinguished by much variety, are a guideline for marking those Bach scores that lack phrasing. It should be noted that Baroque phrasing cannot be separated from articulation, ornamentation, and the "inequality of notes." Obviously, this presents problems in ensemble playing, which existed already in the old days. Quantz instructed "good leaders" to practice unmarked passages with the tutti players because, as he put it, the "greatest beauty in performing required that all play the same way."

Bach's scoring of the second, fourth, and fifth "Brandenburg" Concertos indicates that each of the accompanying string parts was to be played by several players (*di ripieno*). For performances in large halls, the number of strings may also have to be augmented for the other three concertos, yet always preserving the character of a chamber orchestra. In regard to both wind and string instruments, the practice of letting the number of players depend on a given situation can be traced back to Handel. Throughout the *Messiah* score he marked *con ripieno* (all strings) or *senza ripieno* (small string group) but altered the signs when he produced the work at different places and with different orchestras. Sometimes Handel's orchestral introductions, though marked *forte,* bear the sign *senza ripieno,* but, when the same passage is repeated, we find the sign *con ripieno.* This would not make sense, unless we assume that Handel, seated at the keyboard while attacking a new tempo, felt more secure by having the beginning played only by the musicians placed near him. Once the pace was established, everyone could join in. This precaution now being superfluous, we may confidently start those numbers with full orchestra.

Conductors should examine the printed continuo parts needed for the Baroque continuo. Some modern arrangements are too elaborate, others too monotonous. A continuo setting in Bach's hand can be studied in the Harpsichord Concerto No. 6 in F-Major (BWV 1057), a transcription of the fourth "Brandenburg" Concerto. When replacing the solo violin by the harpsichord, the composer combined the solo playing with continuo accompaniment.

For *secco* recitatives in oratorio and opera, the keyboard was joined by cello and double bass (earlier by viola da gamba and violone). Chords, even when written in long notes in the score, could be shortened in performance. When Bach wrote out the low string parts for the *St. Matthew Passion,* he used quarter notes for those chords, with rests in between.

About one-half of the twenty-seven instruments (not counting keyboard instruments) that Bach utilized have no equivalent in a modern orchestra. The tone color of those that still exist has changed due to differences in construction. To what degree the Baroque style is approximated in a performance by a modern orchestra depends on the conductor's ideas and the musicians' ability to adjust their playing habits.

OLD VERSUS MODERN INSTRUMENTS

Just as it seems unlikely that the Classical masters would have listened to our orchestras with undiluted pleasure, we would probably not have been satisfied with the orchestral sound of their time. Improved intonation, evenness of tone, technical precision, increase in the number of string players—all this speaks in favor of modern orchestras. Yet our forefathers would hardly have appreciated the overly brilliant sound, the raise of pitch, and the sheer loudness often accompanied by muddiness in the lower ranges—all part of the overall sound produced by our wind and string instruments. Thinking in terms of sound levels, the present *mezzoforte* would, at Mozart's time, have equaled a *forte,* if not a *fortissimo.* It has become customary, therefore, to adjust present playing habits in line with stylistic considerations when we perform pre-Romantic music.

Reducing the number of string players for better balance is only part of the adjustments. The conductor must attempt to achieve the mellowness combined with crispness of sound that marked eighteenth-century music making. A decision must also be made about how obsolete instruments are best replaced. The *flute à bec* can no longer be called obsolete thanks to the revival of recorders. Still, whether recorders, limited in sound volume, can be used for the Fourth "Brandenburg" Concerto and other works of Bach has to be determined according to a hall's acoustics. The *cornetto* (no relation to the cornet!), a woodwind instrument of the once widely used family of *Zinken,* is found in scores of Bach, Handel, and Gluck. A trumpet usually serves as replacement, although the two instruments have little in common. Within the oboe family, an English horn must substitute for the *oboe da caccia* and the *oboe d'amore,* unless players trained to perform on the old instruments are available.

The piano has no place in the Baroque orchestra. A harpsichord must be chosen, even if the acoustics make amplification necessary. When an organ is needed, a good electric organ may be preferable to a large pipe organ, which does not lend itself to the Baroque style.

Chamber music groups that perform on eighteenth-century instruments have found that application of the required techniques often furnishes the answer to questions of interpretation. The nature of the old instruments helps to determine speed, phrasing, and other details of performance. For the conductor, these findings are of more than theoretical interest, because conclusions can be drawn for the performance on modern instruments.

An invaluable source for the study of string playing during the second half of the eighteenth century is Leopold Mozart's *Violinschule.* It is available in an English translation and should be required reading for conductors. Aside from being a text on violin playing, it contains a wealth of information on the performing habits of the time. No fewer than 75 out of a total of 268 pages are devoted to bowing and phrasing. The great variety of bowing will surprise those who believe that, in Mozart's time, bowing was handled in a rather square and unsophisticated fashion.

Successive up-bow passages are suggested in example 34.1 as a "successful" technique. For each up-bow, more strength is to be applied to the first note (or the first two notes) than is used for the subsequent notes, which are to be slurred "quietly and gently." As an alternative, one may "also try" to play the exercise with up-bow for the first half of the measure, down-bow for the second. In example 34.2, successive up-bows are recommended for detached playing. Putting a "short stress" on each note makes the music "bolder and gives it more spirit."

Ex. 34.1. From L. Mozart, *Violinschule*

Ex. 34.2. From L. Mozart, *Violinschule*

It must not be forgotten that, in Mozart's time, the bow, shorter than a Tourte bow and of different shape, produced a lighter tone. Moreover, string sonority has since been affected by a number of mechanical alterations (bridge, sound post, bass-bar, neck, chin rest) and by replacing catgut with other materials for the strings. Although we now use modernized instruments and a different bow, Leopold Mozart's teachings remain significant, if for no other reason than that they played an important role in the education of his famous son.

A word needs to be said about the use of "period instruments" in modern times. The value of their employment by chamber groups has been pointed out, provided it is understood that instruments do not make music—people do! In other words, the fundamental question does not relate to the choice of instruments but to the manner in which these instruments are being played. Since we cannot revive musicians of bygone days, we cannot ascertain exactly in what way they performed. Their performing habits were in line with their training and experience and reflected their general outlook on the art of music. Most essentially, we cannot hope to match their "gut feeling" while making music. Physically and mentally, we are made of different stuff than our colleagues hundreds of years ago.

It is, therefore, no more than wishful thinking to expect that the use of period instruments allows the modern listener to "hear the music as it was heard by composers of the past." Actually, it might be of greater interest to know whether these composers liked what they heard. Some of them expressed their dissatisfaction with instruments and performers.

Unfortunately, the revival of period instruments has been misused in the wake of a commercially supported "authenticity" vogue. Its apostles have failed to re-create the conditions under which performers used to work within a given society. This would entail "period audiences" and the return to halls that remain brightly lit during concerts, letting the public applaud after each movement of a symphony, even claiming the immediate repeat of an especially appealing movement, and other conventions of the time.

Conductors should beware of "gimmicks" and concentrate their efforts on a wide range of studies, always searching for pertinent information on stylistically justified solutions. Looking into a composer's world and workshop is the surest way to bring music to life with the means at our disposal. Ultimately, how to proceed remains the conductor's sole responsibility.

HAYDN

After the completion of the new edition of Haydn's symphonies, the formerly used, often greatly distorted, printed parts are now being replaced in orchestra libraries. A set of study scores includes textual notes that relate to source materials and allow conductors to select alternate versions. Conductors should also consult H. C. Robbins Landon's book *The Symphonies of Joseph Haydn,* an important source of information in regard to all aspects of performance practice (see Recommended Reading).

Under the auspices of the Joseph Haydn Institute (Cologne), a new edition of Haydn's collected works is near completion. It is edited by prominent Haydn scholars and will eventually include all of Haydn's works for orchestra. A fairly large number of symphony scores are already available, and study scores and performance materials are in preparation.

Haydn's habit of marking phrasing only partially did not present a problem to his musicians, who were familiar with their director's preferences. When supplementing unmarked passages with slurs, we cannot do better than emulate the composer's phrasing patterns. In the case of triplets, it is sometimes difficult to determine from an autograph whether a small slur calls for legato or is merely a triplet sign on top of detached notes. It might happen, therefore, that a conductor disagrees with an editor's choice.

Early Haydn and Mozart symphonies, scored for strings and a small wind group, were performed with harpsichord. The direction was divided between the concertmaster and the maestro at the keyboard, who supported the orchestra by improvising his part in thoroughbass fashion. When the orchestral setting became more compact, the need for complementing it on the keyboard decreased. Yet, when Haydn directed his symphonies in London during the early 1790s, he was seated at the keyboard (a harpsichord during his first visit, later a pianoforte) and would occasionally play a passage not indicated in the score. Generally speaking, a harpsichord should be added, at least to Haydn's first forty symphonies.

Although the continuo keyboard in Haydn's late oratorios is scored for cembalo, a *hammerklavier* modeled after the early pianofortes seems to be more appropriate (see below, p. 397). Into the nineteenth century, the terms cembalo and *clavicembalo* remained in use but also applied to instruments with hammers.

Tricky string passages in Haydn's symphonies let us conclude that the members of his relatively small band at Esterhaza possessed considerable technical skill. Haydn would not have marked the finale in Symphony No. 57 *Prestissimo* had he not counted on his string players' dexterity.

Haydn's minuets are usually of the *Allegretto* type, similar to Mozart's custom (see below, p. 392). Sometimes he marked a minuet *Allegro*, which then must be conducted with a lively 1-beat. The minuet in Symphony No. 97 is of special interest, since all repeats are written out, and, consequently, the da capo does not skip repeats (see below, p. 392).

Haydn's use of the trombones in *The Creation* and *The Seasons* can serve as a lesson in performance practice. The altos, tenors, and basses of a choir were at that time often supported by trombones (formerly, so were the sopranos, but the use of soprano trombones or *cornettos* had been discontinued). The participation of trombones was marked in the scores by *colla parte,* though details were usually worked out in rehearsal. Haydn, by writing out the trombone parts, left no doubt which choral passages needed brass support.

MOZART

With all the volumes of the new Mozart edition (NMA stands for *Neue Mozart-Ausgabe*) being available in hardcover and paperback, most other editions of Mozart's works must now be considered obsolete. In addition to the full scores, orchestra parts for a number of symphonies and concertos are also for sale. The editors have taken pains to indicate in the scores whether the notation can unquestionably be traced to Mozart or has been augmented by editorial additions. However, the same caution has not been extended to the orchestra parts, which do not distinguish between Mozart's text and an editor's sometimes unconvincing decisions. Consequently, conductors may have to scrutinize each orchestra part.

Another caveat ought to be mentioned. It concerns the availability of authentic sources. In some cases, Mozart autographs, although known to be extant, were not accessible to the editors, which may necessitate future revisions. Still, the NMA deserves to be called the most reliable source of reference for the performance of Mozart's music.

While the music in example 34.3 was marked ¢ by Mozart, the willful change to **C** has been perpetuated in all editions prior to the NMA. The music is felt in four pulses per measure, but the conductor may subdivide certain counts for clearer definition, as for the thirty-second notes in the timpani, keeping the subdivided beats very small and maintaining the flow of the music. (This introduction has been performed as slowly as ♪ = 63. Aside from ignoring the signature ¢, such an interpretation disregards the relationship between the descending scales in m. 2 and their recurrence in mm. 72ff. of the *Allegro*. See p. 393.)

Ex. 34.3. Mozart, Symphony No. 39, K. 543, first movement, mm. 1-3

As a general rule, our conducting patterns (which did not even exist in Mozart's days) must never interfere with the music's pulse. Primary concern is the feeling for the meter, while the number of beats is merely a practical consideration. The *Andante* ¢ in *Eine kleine Nachtmusik* (ex. 4.9) is to be felt in two quiet units regardless of the conducting pattern. The same applies to movements in $\frac{2}{4}$ or $\frac{6}{8}$ time, when the tempo marking is *Andante* or faster.

The angular pattern of a regular 4-beat would not allow a tender flow of the melodic line in the *Andante con moto* in example 34.4. A gracefully subdivided 2-beat is recommended (see p. 122). Richard Strauss suggested that this movement, as well as the movements quoted in examples 11.12 and 34.5, must be felt and "possibly conducted" without subdivision. A regular 6-beat in example 34.5 would put undue emphasis on each eighth count and fail to give life to the swaying repeated notes. Subdivision with a feeling of two pulses should be applied to the beginning and similar sections of the movement.

Ex. 34.4. Mozart, Symphony No. 39, K. 543, second movement, mm. 1-4

Ex. 34.5. Mozart, Symphony No. 40, K. 550, second movement, mm. 1-4

Mozart was meticulous in the choice of tempo and could be critical of performers whom he believed to be guilty of rushing or dragging. He favored fluency but objected to pushing the speed to a point where the notes could no longer be heard distinctly. His tempo indications were carefully chosen within an established order of tempo categories, as demonstrated by the corrections he made in his manuscripts. As a typical example, the first movement of the G-Minor Symphony (K. 550) was originally marked *Allegro assai,* but this indication was crossed out by Mozart and replaced by the slower *Molto Allegro. Allegro assai,* however, remained for the much livelier finale of the symphony. For the slow movement in the String Quartet (K. 465), he changed *Adagio* to *Andante cantabile* to indicate a more fluent pace. Conductors should, therefore, not fall for the temptation to slow down the *Andante cantabile* in the "Jupiter" Symphony (ex. 11.12) to an Adagio!

The following list of tempo categories conforms to the order found in textbooks from Mozart's days. They were divided into four groups: slow, moderately slow, moderately fast, and fast.

Grave	Moderato
Largo	Allegretto
Adagio	Allegro
Larghetto	Allegro molto
Andantino	Allegro assai
Andante	Presto
	Prestissimo

Larghetto did not indicate a really slow pace but belonged to the *Andante* group. *Andantino* ranked as a tempo slightly slower than *Andante.* Within the group of rapid tempo markings, an *Allegro assai* called for a speed almost as quick as a *Presto.*

Assai (to be understood as "very") was one of the many qualifying words used by Mozart for the sake of differentiation. Using *Andante* as an example, Mozart added words such as *cantabile, sostenuto, moderato,* or *maestoso* to ask for a somewhat slower pace, while a more flowing *Andante* was marked by *con moto* or *molto. Più andante* ("more going") was an equivalent to *più mosso.*

An analysis of Mozart's application of all such qualifying terms is part of Jean-Pierre Marty's *The Tempo Indications of Mozart* (see Recommended Reading). Marty's survey of all of Mozart's tempo markings, as explicit as it is enlightening, is a musicianly study that ought to be required reading for interpreters of Mozart's music.

The alla breve sign ₵ can be counted among modifying tempo indications. From a Mozart letter we know that he used it to secure a quicker pace than expected in movements marked **C**. It seems unlikely, however, that *alla breve* exactly and invariably indicated double tempo, as taught by contemporary theorists.

Much confusion regarding *alla breve* signs in Mozart's scores has been caused by faulty editions. We must turn to the NMA for reliable information. Moreover, we ought to trust Mozart's judgment, as, for instance, in the case of the overture to *Le Nozze di Figaro* which he marked **C**, not ₵, to the disbelief of some musicians. True, the music calls for being directed "in two," but despite the designation *Presto* (in his handwritten work catalog Mozart notated *Allegro assai* **C**) the speed must not be unduly accelerated, lest the turns (before the quarter notes!) in the first violins (mm. 14–15) and the staccato runs in the winds (mm. 65–66, see example 34.7) become unplayable.

On the other hand, whenever Mozart indicates *alla breve,* even in "slow" movements, it must be reflected in the choice of tempo. A typical example is the *Larghetto* **¢** in the Piano Concerto K. 595. It requires two calm beats per measure, and its flowing melodic line would suffer if "felt in four." This *Larghetto* also demonstrates how an *alla breve* sign determines the music's feeling for the rhythm. For instance, in an *Adagio* marked **C** the eighth notes are the counting units, whereas the *alla breve* sign would suggest that quarter notes are so used.

The minuet tempo deserves a special word. Mozart distinguished between the regular minuet, mostly marked *Allegretto,* and the slow minuet which he called "Italian" (see p. 363). The regular minuet had one pulse to the measure, at a speed of ♩. = 56–66. The slower type, often marked *Tempo di Menuetto* as in the *Rondeau* of the Violin Concerto in A Major (K. 219), called for a more deliberate pace, ♩ = ca. 96. When the fourteen year-old Mozart first encountered the slow minuet in Bologna, he was surprised that it had "so many notes" and, therefore, required a slower tempo.

The proper handling of the repeats in the *da capo* of a minuet was explained on p. 369. Mozart took great care to add *senza replica* to the **D.C.** whenever he wished to curtail the *da capo*. In the absence of such a signal, the repeats in a Mozart minuet must be observed ("exactly as the first time") when the Menuet is played again after the Trio.

Like Mozart's tempo indications, his markings for dynamics show care and musical logic. They must, of course, be understood within the practice of his time.

In example 34.6, the woodwinds end softly, although the last note of their phrase coincides with a *forte* in the other instruments. Musical logic prevailed over considerations of balance, whereby it must be remembered that the relatively moderate *forte* sound of Mozart's orchestra made the contrast less noticeable (see ex. 34.3 for the beat pattern).

The two different uses to which Mozart put the *fp* sign are explained in

Ex. 34.6. Mozart, Symphony No. 39, K. 543, first movement, mm. 13-14

his father's *Violinschule:* It could indicate a strong and sudden accent or a moderately emphatic attack immediately followed by a decrescendo. The first type, creating a dramatic effect, appears frequently in Mozart's operas, as in the second finale of *Don Giovanni* during the Commendatore scene. Examples for the second type are found in the overture to *Le Nozze di Figaro.*

Musical and technical reasons speak against a literal *fp* in example 34.7. As to the low strings, the bow action makes it virtually impossible to play four equally strong notes in quick succession before a sudden *p*, nor can the violins sustain a full *f* until lifting the bow for the retake needed to begin the subsequent passage in *p*. Accordingly, the first half measures 35 and 37 must be played *f*>*p* by the entire orchestra.

The playful nature of the theme in example 34.8 calls for a quick diminuendo after the downbeats in measures 59–64, rather than for drastic accents (see p. 327).

In measure 2 of example 34.3, literal observance of the notation would make the strings sustain the *forte* for the entire half note in contradiction to the piano in the winds. It can be assumed that Mozart expected the strings to make a decrescendo leading to *piano.*

Mozart indicated staccato by dots or vertical strokes (wedges) above

Ex. 34.7. Mozart, *Le Nozze di Figaro,* K. 492, Overture, mm. 35-38

Ex. 34.8. Mozart, *Le Nozze di Figaro,* K. 492, Overture, mm. 59-67

notes. A study of his autographs reveals a lack of consistency in the use of the two signs, and the inconsistency can be confusing, leading some editors of Mozart's music to replace all of his strokes with dots, a procedure that obscures Mozart's intentions. It must be understood that in his scores strokes serve a double purpose: They may indicate the shortening of a note, but every so often they ask for an accent, whether the note is short or long. Fortunately, the NMA reproduces Mozart's notation faithfully. A good example is the autograph of the finale of the "Jupiter" Symphony, reprinted in figure 34.1, showing clearly how meticulous Mozart could be in distinguishing between dots and strokes. It should be noted that, when indicating a *portato* . . . . , Mozart consistently marked dots with a slur.

The first three notes of the melody in example 34.9 have wedges, but only the first two are short. The third wedge calls for an accent (like leaning on a note) on the sustained A, which is tied to the next note. Measure 35 shows Mozart's inconsistency: Dots are mixed with wedges, as seen also in figure 34.2. The *fp* signs in the accompaniment must be understood as $f\!\!>\!\!p$.

Ex. 34.9. Mozart, Symphony No. 35, K. 385, second movement, mm. 33-35

The proper application of "strength" and "weakness" within a melodic phrase was discussed in all textbooks of the time. Mannerisms resulting in faulty accents were criticized, often with reference to the reciting of poetry. Just as a spoken line could be spoiled by undue stress on a word, music would suffer from wrong accentuation. A valuable source of information is D. G. Türk's *Klavierschule* (1789), which contains a detailed discussion of accentuation, embellishments, and other questions of interpretation.

Three chapters in his Leopold Mozart's *Violinschule* deal with ornamentation but do not furnish answers to all questions. The most comprehensive scholarly presentation of all questions concerning Mozart's use of ornaments is found in Frederick Neumann's *Ornamentation and Improvisation in Mozart*, in which a wealth of information is compiled in no fewer than 300 pages.

Taking textual liberties with solo parts in the form of improvised embellishments and variations was not only legitimate practice in Mozart's days but an essential part of instrumental and vocal training. At present, attempts are being made to revive what for a long time had been a lost art. It should be remembered, however, that only those musicians who mastered the craft of composition were considered competent to change the written text. The problem does not come up in orchestral music because in ensemble playing performers were not supposed to go beyond the written ornamentation.

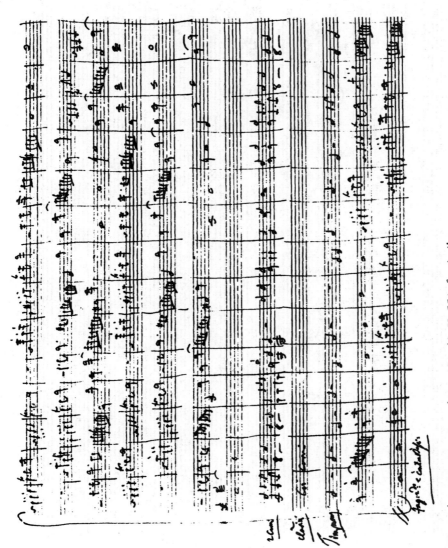

Fig. 34.1. Mozart, Symphony No. 41, K. 551, facsimile

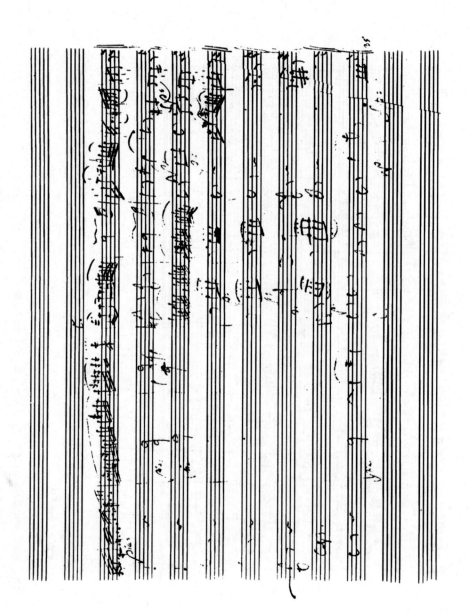

Fig. 34.2. Mozart, Symphony No. 35, K. 385, facsimile

As a performer on the keyboard, Mozart excelled in the art of improvising variations, which played a special role in the *da capo* sections of slow movements. He was also among the first composers to discard the harpsichord. Since about 1777 he gave preference to the *hammerklavier,* then called fortepiano. The instrument that he purchased around 1782 is still in existence. When in Vienna, he used it for all solo appearances and also for accompanying in the opera pit. Its sound, different from that of a harpsichord or a modern piano, fits perfectly into the texture of Mozart's orchestra.

An instrument used by Mozart for its distinctive color is the basset horn. It must not be replaced by a bass clarinet. Conductors should see to it that a pair of basset horns are part of the orchestra's equipment and that clarinet players are encouraged to practice the instrument (which is also needed for a number of Richard Strauss's works).

BEETHOVEN

Little is known about Beethoven as conductor of his works, but reports tell about the way he performed his piano music. He insisted on a perfect legato to produce a singing tone. Calling himself a "tone poet," he regarded music as a means to project his most personal emotions and visions. Thus, his playing was highly expressive, even rhetorical, and marked by tempo modifications that could be combined with drastic dynamic effects, such as broadening the pace for a big crescendo. Still, he was intent on rhythmic precision and on setting the right basic tempo. Much can be learned about Beethoven's performance style from Carl Czerny's comments on the composer's piano works, including his chamber music and concertos (Czerny's work is available in English translation; see Recommended Reading.). Czerny had first-hand knowledge of Beethoven's intentions, probably more so than any other pupil, which makes his detailed notes and metronome suggestions a valuable source of information.

Beethoven's symphonies include a total of sixty metronome indications. More than twenty seem to fit the music perfectly. Some of the remaining markings appear to be "on the fast side"; a few even suggest misjudgment, as can be expected whenever a composer determines the metronome without testing the speed repeatedly in performance.

If we keep in mind that the metronome's function does not go beyond determining the basic character of a composition, accepting all of Beethoven's markings at face value would be as wrong as dismissing them altogether. The metronome marking ♪ = 92 for the *Larghetto* in the Second Symphony (ex. 8.16) is among those markings that have met with disbelief. Yet, it may have made sense to the composer. First, the time signature $\frac{3}{8}$ calls for a light flow of the melody; second, in his arrangement for piano trio Beethoven amended the marking to *Larghetto quasi Andante* (in line with eighteenth-century tradition; see above, p. 391). Most important, there is reason to assume that ♪ = 92 was meant to indicate the upper speed limit for the entire movement, which, according to testimony, was to be played with tempo modifications. Aside from speeding, or slowing, a number of passages, the secondary theme (beginning at mm. 75 and 239) was to have the character of an *Allegretto.*

Starting the movement at $\flat$ = 84, which appears to be appropriate for the main theme, would remain within a reasonable tempo span.

Significant conclusions can be drawn from the way Beethoven used metronome indications within the same work, no matter how inconclusive his tempo markings may have been. The first movement of the "Pastoral" Symphony is marked *Allegro ma non tanto* $\frac{2}{4}$, $\downarrow$ = 66. The metronome for the *Allegro* $\frac{2}{4}$ in the third movement is $\downarrow$ = 132, which clearly indicates that, in the composer's mind, the two tempi were to be identical. The soundness of his judgment, however, has been questioned. Although most conductors accept Beethoven's metronome in the third movement, they contend that the speed for the beginning of the symphony is excessive and that the music calls for a 2-beat. Perhaps they forget that Beethoven, not concerned with beating patterns, wished to make sure that the first movement was felt in one leisurely pulse per measure. In fact, the *ma non tanto* would not have made sense if combined with the marking $\downarrow$ = 132. In practical terms, if we again assume that Beethoven's metronome marking refers to the upper speed limit for the entire movement within a span of $\downarrow$ = 56–66, a 2-beat at $\downarrow$ = 112 would not rush the beginning and would allow for a flexible pacing of the movement, which contains numerous passages that lend themselves convincingly to a 1-beat without jeopardizing the conductor's control. In the third movement, however, the impetuous rustic dance was conceived in two forceful beats; hence the metronome marking $\downarrow$ = 132.

Beethoven carefully checked and rechecked the metronome chart for the Ninth Symphony at various times. Even if his metronome may not have been entirely accurate, he would certainly have noticed any significant deviation from one beat per second once he had put the movable weight of the pendulum on 60. When Beethoven's metronome developed irregularities, he called it "sick" and gave it "to the watchmaker to regain its steady pulse." It seems unlikely, therefore, that he was far off the mark when he indicated $\downarrow$ = 60 for the *Adagio molto e cantabile* $\frac{4}{4}$. It has been said, with some justification, that Beethoven, when determining the speeds for his first six symphonies, saw these earlier works in a light different from that in which they were conceived. This argument, however, would not be valid in the case of the Ninth Symphony. Interestingly, its autograph shows that *e cantabile* was added in large letters as a modifying afterthought to the original, much smaller, *Adagio molto. Cantabile* held a special meaning for Beethoven, who once said, "Good singing was my guide; I strove to write as flowingly as possible." When played at $\downarrow$ = 40, as the *Adagio* has often been performed, the melody is no longer singable in terms of human song. Moreover, the second subject of the movement, *Andante moderato* $\frac{3}{4}$, is marked $\downarrow$ = 63, leaving no doubt that Beethoven felt little difference in the pacing of the two themes.

Another disputed metronome marking in the Ninth Symphony concerns the Trio of the second movement, *Presto* ₵, $\downarrow$ = 116 (o = 116, found in some editions, was a printer's error). The preceding *Molto vivace* $\frac{3}{4}$, $\downarrow\cdot$ = 116, leads directly into the Trio with a stringendo of eight bars. What the composer's intentions were can only be guessed. The implicit tempo relation is as puzzling as the sudden throwback to a measured and seemingly slow 2-beat after an exciting increase in speed. Erasures and instructions to the copyist in the autograph show that the Trio had been planned as a *Presto* $\frac{2}{4}$ but was changed by turning two $\frac{2}{4}$ measures into one *alla breve* measure throughout the Trio (note that the marking *Presto,* $\downarrow$ = 116, makes good sense when applied to a $\frac{2}{4}$ meter!). As one of several solutions, none of which can claim authenticity, one might reduce the tempo somewhat after the fermata in measure 395. This allows for an acceleration but still permits the tempo relation ♩. = ♩ from the last $\frac{3}{4}$ measure to the first *alla breve* measure. Conductors' preferences vary widely in regard to the speed of the *Presto*. Some stay close to Beethoven's metronome marking by playing the Trio at ♩ = 126, others take it as fast as ♩ = 152. The *poco ritard.* at the end of the Trio speaks against exaggerated speed because slowing down just for the concluding bar would be meaningless if the tempo is rushed. (For a complete discussion by the author on this topic, see also *The Metronome Indications in Beethoven's Symphonies,* listed in Recommended Reading.)

The meanings of traditional signs are often subject to a composer's habits. In Beethoven's scores, a single *f* frequently replaces a *sf*, both in *forte* and *fortissimo* passages. In soft passages, the word *dolce* is used, not merely to ask for soft playing but to indicate a gentle *espressivo*.

In a letter written in 1825, Beethoven complained about a copyist who had failed to pay attention to details in copying the score of the String Quartet Op. 132. Everything, he wrote, was to be copied exactly according to the manuscript, in particular slurs and dynamics. For staccato, he pointed out that "it is not indifferent" whether to put wedges or dots.

A set of handwritten parts for the Seventh Symphony, still extant, had been corrected by the composer for its first performance. From these corrections, shown in example 34.10, we can conclude that, after a fully sustained quarter note (*ten.*), the two eighth notes, played up-bow and down-bow, are to be detached sharply before the on-the-string portato in the measure 52 (see mm. 3–4 ex. 18.1).

Eighteenth-century practice did not require sustaining each note to its full value. Consequently, the *tenuto* sign served to preclude, in the absence of a slur, a break before the following note. *Ten.* appears in Mozart scores, as in the first movement of the Symphony in E-flat Major (K. 543). Beethoven, continuing the tradition, applied it importantly to the main themes in the finale of his Violin Concerto and in the *Coriolanus* Overture (see ex. 12.4).

It is often assumed that all trills in Beethoven's music are to begin on the main note. Actually, he never abandoned entirely the eighteenth-century custom of starting trills on the auxiliary, as can be seen from measured trills, such as in the Sixth Symphony (second movement, solo flute, m. 131) or in the Ninth (third movement, first violins, measure 129). Moreover, Beethoven's fingerings in his piano music show alternate use of the two styles.

In example 34.11, the melodic line in the second violins calls for a trill

Ex. 34.10. Beethoven, Symphony No. 7, second movement, mm. 51-58

Ex. 34.11. Beethoven, Symphony No. 3, "Eroica," second movement, mm. 114-17

starting on the main note, while in violas and bassoons it must begin on the auxiliary. Repeating the E in the lower voice would weaken the impact.

The absence of grace notes at the end of a trill does not necessarily mean that the composer would have objected to an "afterbeat."

For the *Larghetto* theme in the Second Symphony (ex. 8.16), the afterbeat is not marked in the score but is found in Beethoven's arrangement of the work for piano trio. The trill itself should begin on the upper note. Repeating the C sharp would interfere with cantabile playing.

In example 34.12, the trill has a written exit. Opinions differ on whether to start it on the main or the upper note. Repeating the C sharp gives stronger impact to the **sf**; also, it brings out more effectively the broken chord of the dominant seventh.

The treatment of grace notes, especially when appearing in groups of two or three notes, varied in Beethoven's days. No rule determined whether such ornaments were to be played on the beat or to be anticipated. Sometimes, grace notes slurred to a downbeat note demand anticipation, although they are written after the barline.

In example 34.13, it is inconceivable that Beethoven would have expected the winds to play the *gruppetti* on the downbeat. Although tied to the following notes, the grace notes in examples 34.14 and 34.15: must be anticipated.

In example 34.16, two grace notes in the form of an ascending third were usually played on the beat, very quickly.

The grace notes in example 34.17 have been interpreted in three different

Ex. 34.12. Beethoven, Symphony No. 2, fourth movement, mm. 1-2

Ex. 34.13. Beethoven, Symphony No. 7, third movement, mm. 181-88

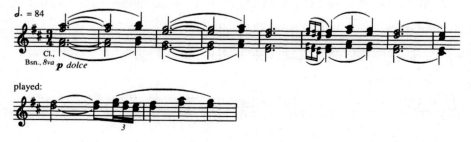

played:

Ex. 34.14. Beethoven, Symphony No. 6, second movement, mm. 4-5

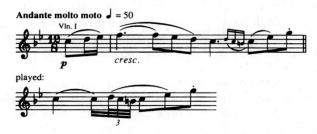

Ex. 34.15. Beethoven, Symphony No. 6, fifth movement, mm. 62-63

Ex. 34.16. Beethoven, *Leonore* Overture No. 1, mm. 58-63

Ex. 34.17. Beethoven, Symphony No. 7, second movement, mm. 27-34

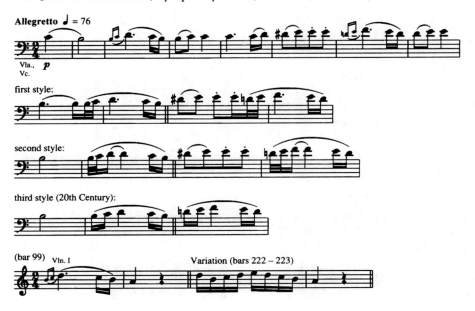

ways. The first and second styles conform to optional practice in Beethoven's time. The third, now adopted by many conductors, came into use around 1920. The first style deserves preference, because repeating the same note on three successive downbeats seems alien to the composer's manner of shaping a melody. Moreover, for a later-occurring variation, Beethoven let the note D, not the B, fall on the downbeat.

The interpretation of the grace notes in the *Marcia funebre* of the Third Symphony remains controversial. Some conductors insist on playing the grace notes in the double basses on the beat. Others, who believe that they should be anticipated, refer to the repeat in the *Minore*. There the notation is changed, in one instance from grace notes to a triplet before the barline. The autograph has long disappeared and the sources are not always conclusive, which explains why some details in the present editions of the *Eroica* are based on editors' guesswork. The following example speaks in favor of anticipated triplet figures.

A comparison between an entry in one of Beethoven's sketchbooks and the final version is of interest. Originally, the composer had the strings play the triplet in measure 10 on the downbeat, as seen in example 34.18. For the final version, shown in example 34.19, he changed his mind, putting the triplets in measure 9 before the barline.

Conductors also differ in their handling of repeats. F. A. Habeneck (1781–1849), the French conductor whom Wagner respected as an outstanding interpreter of Beethoven's symphonies, used to skip all repeats. Weingartner a century later recommended not repeating the first movement expositions in Beethoven's third, fourth, sixth, and seventh symphonies. In our time, many conductors are inclined to observe all these repeats.

With the exception of the Ninth Symphony, Beethoven wanted all first movement expositions to be played twice. To have the Eroica's exposition repeated had been an afterthought. The manuscript sent to the publisher did not include it, but Beethoven, after a first hearing at a private concert, mailed a

Ex. 34.18.   Beethoven, Symphony No. 3, "Eroica," second movement, mm. 9-11 (sketch)

Ex. 34.19.   Beethoven, Symphony No. 3, "Eroica," second movement, mm. 9-11 (final version)

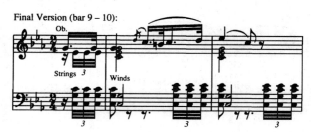

letter, together with a manuscript page indicating a first and second ending, requesting the publisher to include a repeat. Beethoven's change of mind is the more noteworthy, as the work was then criticized for being too long. His decision was probably motivated by his regard for structural balance: An exposition of merely 155 measures, followed by a long development section (246 measures), and a recapitulation (including the coda) of no less than 294 measures would have merely served as an introduction of ideas without carrying the weight that Beethoven wished to impart to the exposition within the movement's total form.

The only repeat in a "slow" movement occurs in the First Symphony. Actually, to call its second movement "slow" would be a misnomer. When paced in line with Beethoven's metronome instruction, this *Andante cantabile con moto* won't appear to be too long, even if the repeat is made.

None of the *da capo* signs in "minuets" and scherzos (Symphonies No. 1, No. 2, and No. 8) indicates a curtailing of the main section when played the second time. Therefore, the inner repeats ought to be observed both times (see above, p. 369).

All repeats in the Seventh Symphony's third movement are essential for the overall structure. Conductors who fail to observe them are likely to drag the tempo of the Trio (see p. 366 and Appendix A, No. 4).

MUSIC IN THE ROMANTIC ERA

The heading is taken from the title chosen by Alfred Einstein for his informative and highly readable book on romanticism in music. In regard to performance practice, it must be kept in mind that early Romantic composers, including Schubert, Mendelssohn, Schumann, and Berlioz, did not expect their music to be treated in a willful manner. Schubert, for one, insisted that his markings were to be observed meticulously, that nothing was to be added, and a steady tempo maintained at all times. It was Liszt and Wagner who turned to individualism in music interpretation. Liszt's numerous pupils, and conductors under Wagner's influence, included some of the most prominent performers of their time. They promoted the new trend, which was to cast its shadow well into our century.

This raises the question of whether the liberties taken by the proponents of the Liszt-Wagner school were essentially different from those suggested, for instance, in Spohr's teachings (see above, p. 368). One need only read the instructions that Hans von Bülow gave his students regarding the interpretation of Beethoven's Fifth Piano Concerto to recognize that what had formerly been minor modifications had now become drastic alterations. What had been a desire to bring music to life through subtle shadings and inflections had now turned into demonstrative manipulation. As a typical and fairly recent example, a conductor grown up in this tradition would start the *Allegro vivace* in Schubert's overture to *Die Zauberharfe* (D. 644) at a speed of $\d = 92$ but make an abrupt accelerando in the twenty-fourth measure, leading to $\d = 126$ for the tutti entrance.

Letters, memoirs, and other contemporary writings tell about nineteenth-century performance practice and provide a wide field of study for curious conductors. Some of the source material has been presented by scholars in musical periodicals and other publications. The following brief comments, limited to a small number of composers, bring up points of particular interest to conducting students and are meant to encourage further investigation.

SCHUBERT

Of Schubert's orchestral works the first three symphonies are available in the new Schubert Edition. Symphony No. 7 can be studied in its authentic form thanks to the facsimile print of the autograph and two study score editions, both with textual notes. Current orchestra materials contain numerous errors. (According to the new Deutsch Catalog [1978], Schubert wrote only eight symphonies; the spurious No. 7 is no longer counted. Consequently, in the new numbering, the "Unfinished" is No. 7, and the "Great" C major is No. 8. Although it will no doubt take several years for the new numbering to become generally accepted, these two symphonies are listed in this book according to new numbering.)

The correct time signature for the introduction of Symphony No. 8 is *alla breve*. The marking **C**, which appears in all editions, is misleading. If "felt in four," the opening theme loses the character of a merry *Wanderlied* and deprives the downbeat accents of their natural impact (see exx. 20.1 and 20.2). Consequently, they are often "underplayed" in performance. Moreover, the repeat of the theme at the end of the movement (mm. 672ff.) must relate to the introduction.

Schubert's habit of writing overly large accent signs can be confusing. Editors have sometimes mistaken them for diminuendo, as in the final measure of Symphony No. 8. Here, the huge accent sign is combined with a *sf*, a combination not unusual in Schubert's manuscripts. Also, he frequently used this sign to accentuate a phrase. (Diminuendo signs that indicate a phrase accent appear occasionally in Beethoven's scores, as in the *Leonore Overture No. 1*, m. 112.)

The diminuendo sign in example 34.20 is a phrase accent. It does not lead from *pp* to a still softer sound but calls for a slight increase in volume in measure 6 and leading back to *pp*.

For example 8.17, the autograph leaves no doubt about Schubert's

Ex. 34.20. Schubert, Symphony No. 7, "Unfinished," second movement, mm. 3-7

Andante con moto (♪ = 88)

intention. The signs in measures 146 and 148 are accents. Therefore, the p in measure 150 is to be understood as a *piano subito*.

Of Schubert's eighty-seven metronome indications, sixty-five belong to the opera *Alfonso und Estrella,* the others to songs. Although limited in number, they tell a story: All the songs, and most of the vocal pieces in the opera, are marked to perfection, but for several orchestral sections the metronome seems to exceed a reasonable speed. In other words, when guided by the sung word, the composer was on safe grounds, but disregard for orchestral limitations made him misjudge some of the quick tempi. There is more to learn: *Andante molto,* for Mozart still a lively *andante,* now signified a slow andante. *Andantino* was now considered to be faster than *andante. Larghetto,* however, still in the tradition of Mozart and Beethoven, was only slightly slower than *andante.*

Furthermore, Schubert's metronome markings prove the significance of the *alla breve* sign. Even for a song as slow as "Der Wanderer" (*Sehr langsam* ¢, ♩ = 63), he did not choose $\frac{4}{4}$ as time signature but marked it *alla breve*—too slow for the metronome's calibration (♩ = 31). In contrast, "Der Tod und das Mädchen," with the indication Mässig (Moderate) ¢, ♩ = 54, was to be felt in two sustained, but not overly slow, beats.

MENDELSSOHN

Mendelssohn's and Schumann's rather frequent use of the metronome is more revealing than their Italian or German tempo markings. In general, overly fast or slow speeds were avoided. *Larghetto, andante, andantino,* and *alla breve* were applied as in Schubert's scores. Mendelssohn, for many years a busy conductor, was known for elegance, precision, and a gentle expressiveness. It is no wonder that he was attacked by Wagner, who criticized his readings of the Classical masters for being superficial. As a teacher, Mendelssohn categorically forbade any unmarked ritardando and wanted written tempo modifications to be kept to a minimum. He disliked sentimentality, recommended a flowing pace, but objected to nervous rushing. In 1880, a pupil of the composer stated that conductors performed Mendelssohn's works "much too slowly."

Mendelssohn's letters make for interesting reading. From his correspondence with Ferdinand David, who premiered the Violin Concerto Op. 64, we learn details about the performance of this work. We also learn that, in spite of admiration for Liszt's genius, Mendelssohn was critical of his exaggerations in the performance of Classical composers and of his lack of respect for the printed text.

SCHUMANN

To quote from Schumann's writings: "It is equally bad to drag as to rush." "Don't strive for bravura; try to produce the impression the composer had in mind; anything else would be distortion." "If you want to grow, associate with scores, not with virtuosos."

Unfortunately, Schumann's choice of German words for tempo markings does not help us to read his mind. *Ziemlich langsam,* for instance, for the introduction of his Fourth Symphony, was meant to be the equivalent of *andante con moto,* as can be seen from the first version of the work. Conductors can be misled by the German words, unless they trust the composer's metronome.

It has been said that Schumann's metronome was faulty, a statement that is neither provable nor likely. The thirteen piano pieces in his cycle *Kinderscenen* lack tempo indications but are marked with metronome. Some of these markings are readily accepted by pianists; others are firmly rejected. The pace for the famous "Träumerei," ♩ = 100, seems overly fast and was adjusted to ♩ = 80 by the composer's foremost interpreter, his wife Clara. Pianists who choose a slower tempo forget that the music was meant to reflect the dream of a child, not of a sentimental teenager. Generally speaking, early Romantic composers did not want their slow movements performed with excessive languor.

BERLIOZ

Unhappy experiences with conductors who failed to grasp the spirit of his music made Berlioz take up conducting. His writings tell about his ideas regarding interpretation. Present music writers would classify him as a "literal" conductor. He expected from the performers strict observance of every marking, insisted on firm rhythm, and expressed displeasure with what he called the "sempre tempo rubato" style of the Wagnerites. Berlioz's remarks on a conductor's individual feeling, already mentioned on p. 356, are very clear on the subject: "The question here does not concern the conductor's but the composer's feeling. Therefore, composers must not neglect marking their works with metronome indications and it is the conductor's duty to study them well. For conductors to neglect this study is committing an act of improbity."

Ideas about performance are part of Berlioz's *Traité d'instrumentation* and are also reflected in his very personal way of scoring. The doubling of bassoons, the combination of two trumpets with two cornets, divided strings, and other new devices—all this shows an intense involvement both in the potential of each instrument and the exploration of the total orchestral sound. Berlioz was essentially a dramatic composer, and his orchestral writing must be seen in the light of his operas and choral works.

A researched edition of Berlioz's works has been initiated, and old orchestra parts, often heavily edited, must be checked for accuracy. A reliable score of the Symphonie fantastique has been available for some time (Norton Critical Score, 1971). The Largo, which opens the work, bears the indication ♩ = 56 and presents another case where the metronome marking is more enlightening than the Italian term *largo.* Moreover, for a meaningful interpretation of the melody, played by the first violins, we should be aware of its background. Berlioz recalled here a love song, composed when he was a teenager. The song itself no longer exists, but in his memoirs Berlioz quoted the words of the emotional poem that inspired him.

WAGNER

No other composer has given instructions to conductors as specific as those published by Wagner for the performance of the overture to *Tannhäuser* and the Act I prelude to *Die Meistersinger von Nürnberg*. Not included in the scores, his comments must be looked up in the composer's collected writings—which may explain why they are rarely observed. True, Wagner's turgid prose can be confusing, and available English translations are unsatisfactory, but the wishes of a great composer-conductor ought not to be neglected. In Appendix B, the instructions are presented in a translation that, it is hoped, will be helpful.

Confusion has also been caused by Wagner's unrealistic metronome markings. If performed according to metronome, the playing time of the *Tannhäuser* Overture would be at least fifteen minutes. However, Wagner stated that, under his direction, it lasted only twelve minutes. In contrast to the metronome marking for the beginning, ♩ = 50, he wanted this music to be played "not dragging, in walking motion," so a speed of about ♩ = 60 would be more in line with his intention. It is no wonder that Wagner despaired of using the metronome and discarded it after *Tannhäuser*.

Authentic modifications of the printed text in Wagner's operas were preserved by Felix Mottl. Included in the full scores and vocal scores, published by C. F. Peters, they are an indispensable source of information.

Wagner believed that music must be brought to life by a freely shaped melodic line, for which he used the Greek word *melos*. Within this line, however, he insisted on strict rhythm, such as dotted notes and unhurried triplets. In the interest of the music's broad flow, he wanted an *allegro* in $\frac{4}{4}$ time to be directed with a 2-beat whenever possible. He once faulted Hans Richter, his favorite disciple, for directing a passage "in four" when it was meant to be felt and conducted "in two." Modern conductors who, for the sake of a precise rendition of rapid notes beat every count in $\frac{4}{4}$ time, misunderstand Wagner's style (see ex. 12.9).

Wagner liked a full orchestral sound with a minimum of thirty-two violins, twelve violas, twelve celli, and eight basses. The brass had to have power and brilliance; the solo woodwind players had to perform with intensity and expression. Yet, for his operas, he expected every word to be projected clearly from the stage and established the rule that, for all sung passages, the dynamic signs in the orchestra were to be lowered by one degree: a ***p*** became a ***pp***, ***mf*** was changed to ***p***, and so on.

In the Overture to *Rienzi,* and occasionally in other scores, Wagner used turns to begin on the lower note. Most of the time, however, turns in his operas start on the upper note, always in accordance to notation.

Wagner's sometimes overly long slurs in string passages leave the bowing up to the players. Also, he was not an expert at writing for the harp; the harp part in *Tannhäuser* must be arranged to be playable. In the "Liebestod" from *Tristan und Isolde* rewriting the part from B Major to C flat Major is welcomed by harpists.

BRAHMS

Some textual changes made by Brahms after the publication of his scores are missing in the edition of his collected works. A copy of *Ein deutsches Requiem,* used by the composer for conducting, contains black and red marks to modify tempo, phrasing, dynamics, and orchestration. Particularly with regard to the music's pacing, Brahms avoided being too specific in printed editions. Metronome indications were included in the original score of the *Requiem* but later omitted. Among Brahms's orchestral works, only the Second Piano Concerto has printed metronome markings, all of which seem well chosen. Regarding the performance of his Fourth Symphony the composer remarked:

> I have entered some tempo modifications in the score with pencil. For a first performance they may be useful, even necessary. Unfortunately, they often appear then in print (in my works and those of others)—where in most cases they do not belong. Such exaggerations are needed only as long as orchestras (or soloists) are not familiar with a work. Then I often find myself that I cannot do enough pushing or holding back to come near the desired expression, passionate or quiet. Once a work has been completely absorbed, such markings should, in my opinion, be discarded. The more one deviates from this rule, the less artistic, I believe, the performance becomes. I experience frequently with my older compositions how everything just falls into place and how superfluous some of those markings are! However, nowadays people like to make a big impression with what they call a free artistic interpretation.

These words of wisdom, with their somewhat sardonic conclusion, were part of a letter to Joseph Joachim. In another letter to the same friend Brahms discussed questions of phrasing, in particular the execution of two eighth notes connected by a slur. He called the slur over two notes a special case, because the second note is shortened, losing some of its value. Then he adds: "To apply this to larger note groups would mean an execution marked by liberty and delicacy, which nevertheless is appropriate most of the time." For clarification Brahms inserted an illustration for both cases, as shown in example 34.21. Interestingly, this kind of phrasing calls to mind eighteenth-century performance practices.

Two symbols for dynamics, then no longer in use, were revived by Brahms: the diminuendo pin $\diagup\!\!\diagdown$, indicating a phrase accent (see above, p. 404, in reference to Schubert's use of the diminuendo sign), and the ambiguous *pf*. Phrase accents occur frequently in Brahms's scores. For typical examples compare Symphony No. 2 (third movement, mm. 4 and 6, and

Ex. 34.21. Brahms, quotation from a letter to Joseph Joachim, May 1879

fourth movement, m. 7), Symphony No. 3, (third movement, mm. 53ff.), and Symphony No. 4, (first movement, mm. 4 and 6).

As for *pf*, originally standing for *piano* followed by a quick crescendo to forte, Brahms adopted its later meaning, *poco forte,* which calls for a sound level between *mf* and *f*.

When Brahms started composing for orchestra, most double bass players had abandoned the old system of tuning the four strings in fifths, with C as the lowest pitch. Except for the *Requiem* where, for the concluding section of No. 3, some players must lower the E string to D, Brahms refrained from writing notes below E. The same is true for Wagner beginning with *Tannhäuser* (in *Tristan und Isolde* he required lowering the E string to C sharp, but not until *Parsifal* did he expect to find players with five-string instruments). Opinions differ as to what extent double bass players should take advantage of the C string when performing Brahms. Similar changes have never been suggested for Wagner's works, perhaps because he skillfully avoided awkward shifting of octaves. In the case of Brahms, one might point to his piano adaptations of orchestral works, in which arrangements he sometimes utilized the lower range on the keyboard. Nevertheless, conductors must not sanction alterations without careful study of the musical context.

If we are to believe reports by musicians who performed Brahms's symphonies under his direction, he would not have approved of the rushed tempi we now sometimes hear. His music making was relaxed. The kind of excitement that is kindled by a hard-driven pace was not germane to Brahms's nature. Nor would he have been happy with the changes that have been inflicted on the timpani part in the Coda that concludes his First Symphony. He might have wondered whether adding a roll, or altering the rhythm, would give a deeper meaning to his musical message.

BRUCKNER

Bruckner's symphonies have been published in several different versions. In some cases it is questionable whether an "original" version presents the composer's final thought. Deryk Cooke's résumé, "The Bruckner Problem Simplified" (Revised edition for *The Musical Newsletter,* 1975, originally published by Novello & Co.) can serve as a knowledgeable guide.

The tempo markings in the first editions, heavily edited by the composer's assistants, do not always conform to the original ones. Partial metronome indications were added by the editors who, we can assume, knew about their master's intentions.

Three of Bruckner's symphonies require a quartet of Wagner tubas. These instruments, rarely used in the repertory, must be kept in good shape to produce a satisfactory sound. To allow ample time for practice, instruments and parts must be available to the players several weeks prior to rehearsals. Even then, intonation problems should be worked out in sectional rehearsals, preferably in combination with the other brass players.

In interpreting Bruckner's music, the conductor's foremost task is to put all the segments of a broadly conceived symphonic form into proper proportion. The very genesis of Bruckner's music points to structural problems. With the composer's consent, segments of his symphonies were cut, then restored, then altered again. Even Wilhelm Furtwängler, a prominent interpreter of this music, omitted certain passages in the printed score during the early years of his conducting career (at that time he also shortened the second movement of Schubert's Eighth Symphony). In our days, Bruckner enthusiasts frown on any tampering with the text, although a look into the background of the Third Symphony reveals the impossibility of determining what the correct text is. These comments do not imply a critique of Bruckner's music but are intended to impress on young conductors that the interpretation of these monumental works is a challenging undertaking that goes far beyond learning the score.

LATE ROMANTIC MUSIC

Almost one-half of this chapter has been devoted to questions related to the performance of Beethoven's works, questions more numerous than those to be solved in the interpretation of the masters who followed him. In particular, when performing music written during the past 100 years, conductors can rely on a method of scoring that includes instructions more complete and more precise than those in older music. Looking at Mahler's scores, for instance, the new method is evident from the first to the last page. The composer's subsequent revisions have been mentioned. As compared to the first editions, the final versions of Mahler's symphonies contain significant changes in regard to orchestration and dynamics, which goes to show that, although an experienced conductor, Mahler was not immune to misjudgment.

Richard Strauss's ability as an orchestrator is as remarkable in his early scores as in later works. His indications of dynamics, carefully calculated for each instrument, are a built-in protection against imbalances, planned to let every leading voice, both in the orchestra and from the opera stage, stand out distinctly. Strauss was unhappy when his signs were not observed. Why was it, he asked, that balance was achieved when he conducted but all too often neglected under other conductors' direction? "Tempi! Metronome!" was another of his demands. On the other hand, Strauss was a practical man. Talking about the metronome, for instance, he remarked: "My indications must be regarded as ideal tempi allowing any modification that appears necessary to let a singer pronounce the text clearly and comfortably." As to keeping an opera orchestra from drowning out the voices, we must not forget Strauss's effective stick technique (see p. 5). He lived up to his teaching, hardly ever using the left arm and restricting the size of the beat to a minimum. Still, his control of the players was complete, thanks to his eye communication and the impact of his personality.

Most French scores, from Bizet and Saint-Saëns to Debussy and Ravel, leave few doubts about the composers' intentions. The French leaning toward practical reasoning, together with expertise in orchestration, produced a technique of scoring that rarely brings up questions other than those whose solutions require familiarity with the music's style, based on broad knowledge of French music in general. Pierre Monteux's and Charles Münch's interpretations proved that variances in detail are compatible with preserving an idiomatic reading. As for adhering to the composer's text, French musicians of that period, following in the steps of Berlioz, rejected unjustified liberties. We recall Debussy making mockery of the "universal nightmare" caused by the "transcendental interpretation" of masterworks and Ravel chiding a famous conductor for the "ridiculous" treatment of one of his compositions.

Russian composers of the late nineteenth century felt no differently regarding the interpretation of their works. Rimsky-Korsakov's memoirs tell about conductors taking unwarranted liberties and misjudging tempi. Craftsmanship in orchestral scoring was of a high order among Russian composers of that generation, including explicit marking and well-chosen metronome indications. Nicolai Malko, a conductor whose musical education was rooted in the best tradition of his country, remarked that Tchaikovsky wanted his symphonies played "like Beethoven." This would speak against a present trend of exploiting Tchaikovsky's music for a conductor's ego-trip, much in contrast to the admirable self-discipline that distinguished this composer's lifework.

CHAPTER 35

Recollections and Reflections: On Education, Conducting, and A Conductor's Life in Our Time

Education is not to make anything of anybody but simply to open the minds—to go from cocksure ignorance to thoughtful uncertainty.

I have always cherished this motto and used to display it prominently in my studio at The Curtis Institute of Music in Philadelphia as a daily reminder to my students and myself. Those simple words not only explain the purpose and the limits of teaching, but by recommending "thoughtful uncertainty" as a desirable mental attitude, they clearly point to the need of never-ending study.

It is indeed the mark of a true educator to instill in students a thirst for knowledge that will make them seek for a wide range of information beyond what they have learned in school. In other words, the most essential aim of education must be to teach students *how* to study on their own. These are timeless principles that I have always tried to apply to my teaching. Yet, as I look back over more than seventy years of professional work, I cannot help noticing how completely different the world looked to me when I was beginning my musical education.

It was the autumn of 1914 when I, a musically gifted youngster, went to my first symphony concert. Chance would have it that the conductor was Richard Strauss. Watching him at close distance from a box seat right next to the stage, I saw a distinguished looking gentleman standing erect, arms relaxed, handling a stick with small gestures. I also noticed that every so often he would turn his head from one group of players to another. This first experience firmly fixed in my mind how a conductor was to look and act.

During my early years of concert-going the symphony concerts in my hometown, Frankfurt-am-Main, were led by Willem Mengelberg, the famous director of the Concertgebouw Orchestra in Amsterdam, who then commuted between the two cities. The Frankfurt orchestra was seated on a slightly elevated stage that formed an integral part of the boxlike old-fashioned hall. The hall itself remained brightly lit throughout the concert (reading a score while listening to the music was no problem for us!). Even before all the musicians had arrived, Mengelberg would enter the stage from a small side door hardly noticed by the public. Walking leisurely toward the podium, behind the row of first violins, he liked to chat with some of the players, then stop at the concertmaster's desk for an extended chat. When Mengelberg had mounted the podium, the audience applauded a little. It was all very unceremonious. Mengelberg then supervised the tuning, a procedure that took quite a while. Tuning was even repeated in the course of the concert, sometimes after each movement of a symphony.

Today, a young person attending a symphony concert is likely to be left with a conductor's image quite unlike the one I just described. In fact, if it would be feasible to put together a time-lapse demonstrating how the physical aspect of conducting has changed in the course of our century, we would view a startling evolution from relatively simple signals to an increasing use of histrionics. To what extent this change is attributable to the growing power of the "media" may be arguable, but in a world where minds and senses are constantly battered by television and other means of image promotion it would be unrealistic to expect the arts to remain immune.

Some years ago I had occasion to witness a perplexing metamorphosis in a conductor's podium behavior. Attending the final rehearsal for a concert by a prominent music director, I watched him rehearse his orchestra in masterful fashion, very efficiently and with "no-nonsense" gestures. The following day I attended the concert—same program, same orchestra playing exactly the same way. The conductor, however, seemed to be a changed person, displaying the most elaborate sort of "choreography." I felt unable to explain such a Jekyll-and-Hyde phenomenon, and while such an extreme case may not be today's accepted standard, I can assure my readers that it could not have happened in "the old days."

This is not to imply that the "old days" were necessarily *better.* Yet, that they were *different* can be easily substantiated. At present, for instance, concerts are presented with all the trimmings of a "show." The stage, just like in a theater, clearly separates performers and audience. Once the orchestra is assembled, the house lights are dimmed to prepare for the maestro's entrance. Then a slight wait creates an atmosphere of expectation. When the conductor finally appears his every movement is watched as he strides to the podium to assume his role as commander-in-chief. It does not surprise, therefore, that Serge Koussevitzky, famous for guiding the career of young conductors, used to impress on them the vital importance of proper stage appearance.

The far-reaching changes that the world of music has undergone in our century have significantly affected the conducting profession, including conductors' education. At the outset of this text I attempted to enumerate the skills that I consider to be indispensable to the proper training of a conductor. Yet training alone does not open the door to success. Cultural problems as they exist today make it even harder to pinpoint what is most important for learning and exercising the craft of conducting.

To start with academic training, courses in conducting offered by music schools and by the music departments at universities usually involve the use of a textbook to serve as a guiding manual. Such printed instructions for the benefit of musical performers to supplement actual teaching have long been in existence. Many of them were authored by musicians who excelled as performers and pedagogues, leaving no doubt about their books' usefulness. Moreover, it was taken for granted that the acquisition of technical skill warranted verbal explanation. However, educational texts in the conducting field have been late in coming. In fact, the first attempt to present a comprehensive survey of our craft was Hermann Scherchen's *Lehrbuch des Dirigierens,* published in 1929, long after I had entered the profession.

Recalling my student years, I have no doubt that I would have profited from studying an authoritative guidebook such as Scherchen's text, but since I had to do without it, I was forced to find other resources, primarily by observing each conductor's individual gestures and watching how an orchestra would respond to them. Curious as I was, I would also consult orchestra members whose judgment I trusted. Thus, I learned how highly they valued a clear beat that left no doubt "where the conductor was." Once I asked a first-chair player why the orchestra sounded so different under various conductors and was told "it all depends on what is expected from us," an explanation as simple as illuminating.

What I learned this way about orchestral psychology has in fact not changed since "the old days." Similar comments by orchestra musicians might be heard in our time. I also believe that the prerequisites for a successful career in our profession have remained quite the same: In order to succeed one needs talent, hard work, and good luck, the latter also known as "being at the right place at the right time."

In my own case, part of my good luck from a very early age was to have been growing up in a community where musical culture had flourished for many generations. Mendelssohn already had been a frequent visitor to Frankfurt as a pianist and conductor, enjoying his affiliation with an excellent oratorio society. Frankfurt was Clara Schumann's residence from 1878 until she died, a few years before I was born. She taught piano at the same conservatory from which I would graduate, and the musical tradition she founded was very much alive during my early years. Clara Schumann's friend, Brahms, visited the city regularly to play his piano concertos and conduct his symphonies. Musicians who had played under his direction told me in what manner Brahms had performed his music.

I have already mentioned Willem Mengelberg, who was "the" conductor for us music students. He was a portly man of short stature, seemingly suffering from a "Napoleon complex," as some short men do. He could be haughty and arrogant. Although his musical authority was undisputed, he did not enjoy great popularity with the Frankfurt public. Some people even resented him for being a foreigner. His readings of the Viennese classics were criticized for being uninspired, if not superficial. On the other hand, his brilliant performances of the symphonies of Tchaikovsky, and even more so of Mahler, were rightly admired. Yet, generally speaking, Mengelberg was not the kind of artist who would let us walk home after a concert with the feeling of having experienced an extraordinary musical event.

This changed with the arrival of Wilhelm Furtwängler, who took over as music director immediately after the First World War. Tall and youngish looking, he "came and conquered," winning our enthusiastic approval by leading performances of the great German symphonies with inspiring spontaneity. Technically, his gestures were not consistently precise, to the point of being confusing to the players. He compensated for this shortcoming by exercising a hypnotic influence on his musicians, to whom his conception of the music was powerfully conveyed through his strong personality. For the listeners, Furtwängler infused the music with meaning from the first to the last measure—there were no "empty moments."

By that time I had observed numerous guest conductors, coming and going, some average, others prominent. Among the latter I vividly remember Arthur Nikisch, who came to conduct *Die Walküre* the first time that I heard a Wagner opera. I can also recall Mahler's First Symphony, conducted by Bruno Walter, as well as a concert by Fritz Busch, who lead a Brahms program with his brother Adolf playing the Violin Concerto.

My affiliation with an oratorio society, the same that had performed under Mendelssohn, turned out to be a valuable experience. I acted as a rehearsal pianist, took charge of rehearsals when the director was not in town (this way I knew Bach's B-Minor Mass virtually from memory), and, in concerts, was singing with the basses. On one occasion I found myself onstage facing Furtwängler, who was rehearsing Beethoven's Ninth Symphony. As I followed with the score, it seemed to me that he sometimes went too far taking liberties. Another time under Furtwängler I "sang" Brahms's *Ein deutsches Requiem,* which he had preceded by the Fourth Symphony. To this day I believe that as an interpreter of Brahms, and I would add Bruckner as well, Furtwängler was unsurpassed.

Meanwhile, I had graduated from high school (Gymnasium) and had entered the Hoch Conservatory of Music as a composition major. My teacher was Bernhard Sekles, a respected composer and pedagogue, who had tutored me since my twelfth year and now accepted me into the top grade. My hope for a composer's career was encouraged by Paul Hindemith, a fellow Frankfurter, former student of Sekles, and now the concertmaster in both the symphony and opera orchestra. Incidentally, it was Hindemith who introduced me to Béla Bartók, after the premiere of Bartók's opera *Bluebeard's Castle,* and invited me to join a small party at a local restaurant.

In addition to studying composition for more than seven years, playing several instruments, and taking voice lessons, I played chamber music, a practice that I still consider to be of primary importance for a conductor. I also regularly played four-hand piano arrangements of symphonies, overtures, and string quartets—an excellent introduction to a wide range of repertoire—and read a great variety of books on composers and music history. Thanks to being born into a well-to-do family, I owned many full scores of symphonies and operas, which allowed me to train myself in score playing.

In retrospect I believe that my educational background had prepared me well for a conductor's career at a time when my main interest had turned from composing to conducting. Yet, considering the circumstances, one may wonder why I had not enrolled in the conservatory's conducting class. There were two reasons: The course was taught by a violinist without merits as a conductor, and Sekles, my chief adviser, had assured me that conducting could be learned only by experience.

So it came that when, soon after my twentieth birthday, I was hired as an operatic assistant by a provincial German theater, no questions were asked as to my conducting ability. It was taken for granted that a young fellow fresh out of music school could manage to direct the backstage band as part of an assistant's duties, in addition to playing the piano and coaching singers. My first assignment was to conduct selections from Mendelssohn's incidental music to *A Midsummer Night's Dream,* performing backstage and beginning with the *Scherzo.* It was a "sink or swim" situation. Naturally, it felt great to wield the stick, and I didn't hesitate to ask one of the musicians whether he thought I was good enough to lead an entire opera. I am not sure why I chose a rather mediocre second oboe player; perhaps I saw in him a father figure. Whatever the case, looking me over with unconcealed disapproval, the old man brusquely said, "You?? But you are a *Bremser!"* (the German word for "brakeman," the one who applies the brakes to slow down a train).

No doubt, the old grouch was unaware of the fact that he had given me my first conducting lesson. Not wishing to be a *Bremser,* I forthwith rid myself of that heavy forearm feeling and automatically adopted a technique that made the tip of the baton the point of orientation for the players. Moreover, relaxing my muscles, a novel experience, made me develop a flexible wrist.

Conducting, however, was not yet part of my daily work. During a ten-month season I had to assist in forty-two different operas, including the four Ring operas, playing the piano and doing backstage duties. When the chorus director fell ill, I was entrusted with preparing the choruses in *Parsifal.* Besides, long hours spent teaching solo artists their new parts helped me to learn the mechanics of effective coaching and to gain insight into the problems faced by vocal artists.

While acquiring valuable experience in a situation that could be classified as an operatic internship, I continued to be left to my own devices in matters of conducting technique. Within the rare opportunities given to me I had to rely on a trial-and-error method. Aside from the *Midsummer Night's Dream* music, of which I was finally allowed to conduct the overture in the pit, there was a single performance of *Egmont* with Beethoven's incidental music and, late in the season, two performances of *Die Fledermaus,* which I took over without any kind of rehearsal—I just walked into the pit and tried my best. My "best" was sufficient to have the head conductor state in an official report: "a first-rate conducting talent."

While my first year in opera could have been called an "internship," bridging the educational gap between academic training and professional know-how, my second engagement offered me a "residency." In the course of three years at the Darmstadt Opera I conducted more than a hundred performances, while at the same time I assisted the two leading conductors, whose advice in the form of shoptalks, was invaluable. Being promoted to "head coach," I assumed responsibilities that brought some unique experiences. For instance, I was appointed assistant to Siegfried Wagner when he came to direct one of his operas and lead a concert featuring his own and his father's music. I therefore had the chance to hear *Siegfried Idyll* conducted by the son for whom it was composed.

There were other memorable guests: Carl Muck revisited his birthplace, Darmstadt, to rehearse and conduct Beethoven's Missa Solemnis. Again, I was assigned to assist him. Muck, a great musical mind, personified discipline. He exercised complete control with a minimum of physical effort, standing on the podium like a military commander. Muck had been a Bayreuth conductor, just as our *Generalmusikdirektor,* Michael Balling, who took pleasure in indoctrinating me in the Bayreuth traditions when I played for his Ring rehearsals.

Despite the increased speed and prevalence of travel, it is not as customary nowadays as it used to be to journey in search of worthwhile musical experiences. Of course, orchestras, instrumentalists, conductors—even entire companies—tour more frequently and more quickly than in the past. Yet now, as before, it is the major orchestras that attract more musical activity than do the provinces. As a young conductor I felt it essential to seek out important musical events to which I would not have been exposed at home. Thus, in the spring of 1925 I went to Milan to hear Toscanini lead *Falstaff* and, twice, *Il Trovatore*. I knew these operas by heart; yet, sitting in the La Scala opera house, I listened spellbound, feeling like a novice who had everything to learn. It was not merely the carefully rehearsed impeccable rendition but the intense and eloquent molding of each phrase that made the music sound "new." In subsequent years I could observe Toscanini frequently, in rehearsals as well as performances. Today, he is a legend, to me and to countless musicians of former days. He opened for me a new perspective, being the model of a self-effacing performer solely devoted to the letter and spirit of the music.

To be sure, there have been attempts, and not only in Toscanini's case, to "cut down to size" the image of a great man. It would not be difficult as well to name conductors claiming that their work has been marked by a similar devotion to "letter and spirit." Yet, even if we admit that Toscanini was not the only conductor to combine unusual ability with unflinching devotion to his art, it cannot be denied that throughout music history some performers have been surrounded by a mystique beyond rational explanation.

George Szell was another seminal influence in my early years as a practicing conductor, a musician whose superb craftsmanship was as well known as his respect for a composer's intentions. He became a lifelong friend to whom I owe much gratitude. Szell selected me as his associate when, in 1929, he was named chief of the German Opera in Prague. For six years we shared in the conducting of a varied repertoire. From watching Szell at work, I learned the importance of translating interpretive ideas into technical instruction that was quickly and readily understood by the players; he also impressed upon me the great benefit of carefully marking orchestra parts. Besides, Szell and I enjoyed "talking shop" and, on free Sundays, playing the entire Classical literature of four-hand piano music. Being accepted as a partner by such a fastidious musician was, of course, a boon for my ego. After my arrival in the United States, it was Szell who brought me to the attention of the Metropolitan Opera. Trusting his word, the Met's management offered me a position on its musical staff, which was the beginning of my career in America.

Signing my first Met contract coincided with finding a publisher for my conducting text, on which I had been working while looking for employment. The first four years after my arrival in America had not been encouraging. Not being a famous artist, my European background was of little help. My handicaps were twofold: I had never earned a degree—a commodity that, no matter how questionable, is highly valued in America—and, more important, I had not learned how to promote myself. In addition to doing good work, American musicians must know how to deliver a "sales talk."

Problems of this kind did not exist when I entered the Met, at that time located on Broadway at 39th Street. In fact, it almost felt like a homecoming, mainly because the conductors I had to assist had all come from Europe, among them Busch, Szell, and Walter, with whom I had been personally acquainted. An entirely new experience, however, was being associated with a galaxy of outstanding vocal artists. Working with them and discussing questions of voice production added substantially to my understanding of good singing.

There were additional benefits, especially after my promotion to a regular conductor together with administrative duties that involved rehearsal planning and casting. Moreover, I was put in charge of auditions. Listening to and counseling hundreds of young singers earned me the reputation of being a mentor of American singers. In later years, being named artistic administrator by the new manager, Rudolf Bing, I found myself in the midst of New York's music business, well known to artists' agents, public relations people, even to the high echelon of the musician's union, the last being essential, since I had the final say in questions of orchestra personnel.

Preparing the schedules for the Met's annual spring tours brought me into close contact with the musical life in America's "hinterland." Representatives of the local opera committees used to visit my office to disclose their wishes, their likes and dislikes, thus revealing views on repertoire and choice of artists at variance with the taste of our New York public.

All this—administrative experience and exposure to human relations— was put to good use when, after thirteen years, I left the Met to assume the leadership of the Cincinnati Symphony Orchestra. Looking back, I ascribe my success in Cincinnati mainly to three factors: I made the orchestra feel proud of its work, I pleased the ticket-buying public by careful programming without sacrificing my artistic standards, and I maintained good relations with the members of the orchestra's board, whose highest praise was that they could talk to me as to a businessman.

In recounting some of my own experiences, I have tried not to be immodest, yet I believe that in some combination my recipe of talent, hard work, and good luck served me in good stead. In this day and age, however, I find it necessary to qualify the determination of talent for conducting. As I have already indicated, the physical gesturing that audiences are accustomed to seeing by modern maestros is very different from the style of conducting to which I was exposed as a young man. As regards physical aptitude, however, we know that some musicians are gifted with a flair for conducting in the sense of manual dexterity and uninhibited communication with the players. I remember the late actor and comedian, Danny Kaye, who possessed these gifts without the wide range of knowledge that is the mark of professional conductors—in fact, he never learned to read music!

How then to measure conducting talent, or to judge the chances for a successful career? In my teaching I have found that skill in handling the stick can be learned, whereas a keen ear, an easy perception of melody and harmony—easily tested in music dictation—and facility in playing instruments can only be developed. This holds true as well for a performer's emotional involvement and other tokens of an artistic personality. Nonmusical talents, however, such as leadership qualities and the ability to "influence people" are not considered part of conductors' training, although we know that they are invaluable assets for conductors in leading positions.

Furthermore, we must not forget what kinds of people decide on a conductor's career chances, in particular in the case of young American conductors who believe they qualify for a vacancy announced by a symphony orchestra. Their applications are evaluated by nonmusicians, usually by a search committee appointed by the board of directors and by the orchestra's manager. Their judgment is not supported by musical criteria that are meaningful only to professionals but rather by an applicant's assumed market value. The same applies for agents whose business it is to further a conductor's career. Board members, managers, agents, and, needless to say, the public are not interested in stick technique, choice of tempo, phrasing, and all the other intricacies that a young musician was eager to master.

If not musicianship and technical know-how, what then are the credentials that make a conductor eligible for managerial promotion and, therefore, a desirable candidate for a leading post? Nonmusicians are impressed primarily by a conductor's podium appearance as viewed by concert-goers and by the image that, for whatever reasons, a conductor has been able to create, including his potential as a box office attraction.

Facing these "facts of life," conductors derive little solace from the realization that music is not the only field where appointments are often ruled by people who lack competence. Despite these odds conductors must continue to "work hard," hoping for "good luck," and are encouraged by the increasing influence of orchestra committees whose advice is sought for the selection of conductors.

Experienced orchestra players cannot be fooled. They want to be directed by a musician who conveys musical intentions clearly and with authority, uses rehearsal time efficiently, and deserves to be respected as a person and as a leader. I have found, however, that orchestra musicians rarely take issue with a conductor's interpretive preferences. Unless hampered in producing the prescribed notes, a player normally will avoid protesting too much, accepting as a fact of orchestral life each conductor's unassailable, and occasionally unfathomable, ideas!

This does not imply that a conductor's interpretive ideas remain immune from criticisms: Colleagues who for legitimate reasons have different ideas may disagree, while record-buying music lovers and music critics feel entitled to judge the performance of a work merely by comparing one reading with another.

My reference to music critics must not be read as a derogatory remark. Journalists do their job the best they can; so do conductors. They operate without a license; yet again, so do conductors. "Sweep in front of your own door!" I have known colleagues, famed names among them, who had mistaken ideas about the nature of a *cornetto* (scored in Gluck operas) or a *tambour de basque* (Bizet's *Carmen*). There were others who had not learned that an *Allegro assai* in a Mozart score indicates a tempo faster than *Allegro molto,* or those who continue to be confused about the meaning of an *alla breve* sign. These occurrences all boil down to an astonishing lack of curiosity, since pertinent information is readily available.

The common belief that every gifted musician and skilled performer is *eo ipso* a competent interpreter of music is no more than an illusion. The training needed to excel in the former capacity is quite different from the course of study that yields pertinent information on questions of interpretation. I put forth similar thoughts in chapter 31, "Aspects of Interpretation." Yet I would like to add that practicing musicians are not alone in claiming the right to act as interpreters. Musicologists, even those with limited practical experience, not only make a similar claim but are often critical of what performers are doing. Years ago, I suggested to the late Peter Mennin, then the director of the Juilliard School of Music, that he institute a special course on musical interpretation. At first he liked my suggestion, but he developed doubts when I predicted that he might run into trouble with members of his faculty. Highly respected teachers might not react kindly to the idea of divided jurisdiction. Musicians worth their salt are, and always will be, rugged individualists, and arguments on how music is best performed will never end. Much could be accomplished, though, if all would agree on one point: that we must never stop learning.

To conclude this rambling account of recollections and reflections, I now ask for my readers' indulgence when I attempt to put into words, as a kind of personal "credo," my firm belief in three cardinal virtues: Curiosity, Doubt, Tolerance. Curiosity—to remain insatiable in seeking information on the great masters and their music; doubt—to question one's thoughts and those of others, never taking anything for granted; tolerance—to keep an open mind, admitting that we might be wrong and realizing that there are no property rights on ideas. I ought to add the virtue of humility, which expresses itself in being grateful to the great masters of the past. Do we not make a living primarily with performing their music? None of us is able to write even half a page of music that can match what these geniuses produced day after day. Our role is to serve them with loving care.

Discussion of Complete Works
or Movements

The first three selections have been chosen to provide the student with material to practice basic beating patterns—$\frac{3}{4}$, $\frac{4}{4}$, and $\frac{8}{8}$—on music written for string orchestra.

1

George Frederic Handel
Concerto Grosso in G Minor Op. 6,
No. 6—Third Movement (Musette)

Use a score printed in *Urtext*. The piece employs two solo violins, one solo cello, and a small string group (*ripieno*). The figured bass is to be realized on a keyboard instrument, preferably a harpsichord. It is essential that the double basses always play the low E-flat instead of substituting the higher octave; if necessary, their fourth string must be retuned.

According to eighteenth-century authors, a *Musette* was a dance of gentle nature, to be played at a fairly slow pace, smoothly and with a caressing expression. Characteristic for a *Musette* is a drone bass or an extended organ point. In this movement, an organ point of a few bars marks each beginning of the main theme.

In Baroque music, *Larghetto* indicates a tempo within the *andante* group. For a *Musette,* Quantz suggested "one pulse for each beat" (see Recommended Reading). We assume a speed of ♩ = ca.76.

According to the usage of the time, the absence of a sign for dynamics at the outset signified *forte* (translated into modern dynamics, ***mf***). Use a decisive preparatory gesture to coordinate the low strings and the keyboard for a unified start, then apply a *poco espressivo* pattern that reflects the songlike nature of the music. *Two* in measures 3 and 4 is a neutral beat (neutral-legato), but *Three* prepares the next downbeat. In line with Baroque practice, the sixteenth notes can be slightly hurried, although the beat remains steady. Similarly, sixteenth notes such as in measure 5 can be shortened. In the fifth measure, the first violins may play on the G string. Note that in measure 14 the solo violins sustain their notes longer than the *ripieno* players. Do not "overconduct" the passages played by the three soloists alone. Prepare the tutti entrances on *Three* (mm. 18, 22, and so forth). Bring out the celli in measure 30.

The first *piano* section begins in measure 35. This change in dynamics is to be reflected in your gesture. Whenever two eighth notes are slurred, as in measure 35, they ought to be clearly phrased by a slight separation from the following notes. In all likelihood, the "inequality of notes" applies here. Direct the music with tender expression and do not increase the sonority prematurely. Begin in measure 43 with a gentle downbeat, but before moving the baton to the right, prepare the *f* on *Two* (this works best by beating *One* diagonally to the left).

The phrasing for the sharply syncopated rhythm in measure 58 is obviously meant to continue throughout this passage; add slurs in bars where they are not notated. The soft chord in measure 77 is to be played tenuto and, like the following three bars, with beauty of tone.

The cadence in measure 125 marks the end of a section. Baroque custom allows a slight ritard for the return to the main theme. Resume the original tempo in measure 126.

The *Urtext,* faithful to the source, does not add slurs in measures 134, 136, and so forth. It can be assumed that the composer expected the phrasing to continue (see m. 132). A comparison of measures 78 and 161 shows another discrepancy in phrasing—which seems to prove that *Urtext* editions do not always absolve conductors from making their own decisions.

For the concluding measure, beat only *One*. You may extend the length of the chord slightly before releasing it.

2

Antonín Dvořák
Serenade for Strings Op. 22—
First Movement

Use the score of the critical edition (Prague, 1955).

You may pause for a moment to prepare the quiet atmosphere. Then give the preliminary beat, ♩ = ca.88, and direct the first four measures legato, *poco espressivo*. The celli are marked to play with more sonority than the second violins. After bringing in the first violins and the bass pizzicato, increase the intensity of your gesture slightly for the crescendo. A left-hand motion may indicate *espressivo* for the melody. Adjust the beat to the diminuendo in measures 7 and 8 and to further changes in dynamics. For the detached notes beginning in measure 7 (first violins), use gentle staccato beats. *Two* in measure 8 prepares the accent on *Three*.

Stay in tempo for the $\frac{2}{4}$ measure. Use the left hand to assure very soft playing in measure 13, then from measure 16 on build a gradual but expressive crescendo. The *f* in measure 20 is followed by a quick decrescendo: reduce the size of the beat markedly on *Three* and *Four*.

The two accented half notes in the celli (mm. 25–26) are prepared on *One*. Indicate the diminuendo that leads to *pp*, but do not reduce the speed in bars 28–30. Orchestra players tend to drag in soft passages of this kind unless directed with a steady beat.

Soft playing continues with the shift to major key, though with a change of articulation. Use light-staccato. In measure 33, the $\ll \gg$ requires a subtle adjustment of the gesture, but keep *Four* small. Bring in the bass pizzicato at the end of measure 35 and lead the two crescendos, beginning *p* again in measure 37. The beat is more forceful for the accents in measures 38 and 39 but must reflect the return to *pp*. *Espress.* for the celli (m. 43) calls for increased tone; address this section, still keeping the beat small to maintain the *pp* for the rest of the orchestra. Do not exaggerate crescendo or decrescendo.

For the fermata in measure 48, stop on *Three* and continue in tempo on *Four*. In the following measure, emphasize each of the four counts to bring out the phrasing. *Three* in measure 50 requires a sudden switch to a fairly large gesture for the crescendo and to prepare the *fz* (*fp*) on *Four*. For the sixteenth notes in the violins, the beat must remain absolutely steady. Beat light-staccato, even when the articulation changes to legato (see p. 208).

Return to beating legato in measure 54. The orchestration is altered for the recapitulation, but the beating patterns are much the same as discussed for measures 1–24. The continuous use of sixteenth notes in the second violins (measures 54–59) makes a steady beat imperative. Also, the coordination of the leading voices, which drift from one section to another, demands clear leadership. For the *poco rit.* in measure 83, slow down the beat very gradually. In the final measure, stop on *Two*, sustain the chord, then cut.

3

Johann Sebastian Bach
Air from Suite No. 3 in D Major, BWV 1068

(For an authentic edition of Bach's Third Suite, consult volume VII/1 of the New Bach Edition [Bärenreiter].)

Use a subdivided 4-beat, $\flat = 69$–74. The entire piece is done with a legato beat. The main function of the baton is to keep the rhythm moving steadily but unobtrusively and to bring out the various melodic impulses. The continuous flow of the melody must be maintained without undue emphasis of the first beat in each bar.

Use a gentle eighth note preparation for the start and beat the first measure neutral-legato, though with clear definition to lead celli and basses. The *espressivo* begins on the second eighth in measure 2. Here, turn your eyes to the first violins, always beating in the center for all to see. Turn the palm of the left hand toward the 1st violins just before the measure 3, to insure a soft attack. At the same time, address the second violins and lead their melody. Turn back to the first violins on the fifth eighth.

In a similar manner, bring out the various melodic ideas in the inner parts throughout the piece. To do this well, you must know the polyphonic structure and think with the four different parts as they move along. In places such as the first half of measure 5 and the last half of measure 10, there is no melodic movement, and consequently no *espressivo* is needed. When measure 6 is played the first time, lead the bass instruments in their sixteenth note movement. For the second ending, use small neutral-legato beats while the orchestra is sustaining the half note.

Most passages written in sixteenth notes are given more importance than sustained notes, as, for instance, at the end of the 14th measure. Here the violas begin a melodic line that is taken up in the following measure by second and first violins. The fermata in the last bar applies only to the repeat; to conclude the piece stop on the fifth eighth note and keep the baton up as long as you want to sustain the chord, then cut.

Since no dynamics are marked in the original score, each conductor must decide for himself how to shade the music. In any event, the rise and fall of the melody requires changes in the size of the beat, depending on the individual interpretation. The subdivided beat, however, must be clear enough so that the players are never in doubt as to where you are.

Suggestions for embellishments:

> The grace notes on *Two* in m. 2, and on *One* in m. 12, are played on the beat as thirty-second notes.
> The appogiaturas on *Four* in m. 2, on *Three* in m. 8 (F sharp), on *Three* in m. 10, on *Four* in m. 12, and on *Three* in m. 16 are played somewhat shorter than an eighth.
> The three trills begin on the upper note, whereby the starting note can be tied to the preceding (identical) note. In m. 14, the trill has the length of an eighth and is followed by two sixteenth notes (C sharp and B). The trills on the final measure are played as double trills (four sixty-fourth notes).

4

Ludwig van Beethoven
Symphony No. 7 in A Major, Op. 92—
Third Movement

Scherzo

Study how the phrase groups are built. The first section up to the double bar is divided into phrases of two, four, four, six, four, and four bars. The second section starts with a four-bar phrase in the strings followed by an eight-bar phrase in the flutes and clarinets and a four-bar phrase in the violins and violas. The next phrase ends with a sudden *ff*. The succeeding sixteen bars are metrically similar. The following five bars (starting with m. 61) have the oboe and bassoon entrance one measure before the end of the four-bar phrase in the strings; this overlapping entrance starts a two-bar phrase all within measures 61–65. Now there are four phrases of four bars each, then a four-bar phrase and a three-bar phrase, leading back to the repetition. Measures 89–98 are similar to the beginning but with different orchestration; the eight-bar inversion following this is new, as is the next four-bar phrase divided between the strings and the winds. After the six-bar phrase (starting with m. 111) the section ends with eight regular four-bar phrases.

Familiarize yourself with the orchestration (especially in connection with the phrase groups) and the dynamics.

Use 1-beat, staccato throughout. Start with an energetic full-staccato; the preliminary beat has upbeat character (see ex. 9.18). Be sure that the sudden *p* in the third bar is well expressed by the baton and the left hand. While the orchestra is playing the entire second measure *f*, you must think of the *p subito* that is coming. This means that the right hand changes suddenly from a fairly large and vigorous beat to a small and light one. Increase the size for the crescendo and use sharper beats for *sf*.

Do not think it necessary to wave dramatically at each group of strings starting with measure 25. Beat straight ahead and look at the various groups, scarcely turning your head. Save the left hand for the *pp* in measure 33. For the sudden *ff*, avoid any emphasis on the downbeat in measure 43, but immediately snap the baton up to prepare the tutti chords. Return at once to the light *p* beat. Cue in the oboe and bassoon in measure 63. To get an effective climax, lead in the string entrances just before the repetition.

In this fast 1-beat the *ff* must be expressed by the intensity of the beat, not the size; too large a beat would be awkward. Be careful of the sudden *p* in measures 99 and 117. The groups of wind chords starting in measure 118 must be light and delicate.

The rhythmic notation in measures 140ff. often remains unnoticed. Beethoven clearly distinguished between eighth notes followed by eighth rests, on the one hand, and quarter notes on the other.

The left hand sustains the *ff* of the last four bars (first ending) before the double bar; the right hand beats *ff* in only the first of these measures, then marks time with neutral beats for two bars and uses the fourth for preparation. At the second ending, use the left hand for the diminuendo. Some conductors make a ritardando in these four bars, or beat the last one in the tempo of the Trio to prepare the change to the slower tempo. This is not indicated by the composer, and the change of tempo can be executed just by starting off in the new tempo at *Assai meno presto*; the beat in the two first bars of the Trio must be very definite to establish the tempo.

Trio

The first measure in the new tempo bears the number 149 (some editions have different bar numbering). Many conductors take the Trio at a considerably slower pace than that indicated by the composer (see p. 366). Stylistic reasons and the length of the movement (double repetition!) speak against dragging. The phrase groups in the Trio are quite regular and easy to analyze; the orchestration presents no particular problem.

Most of the Trio requires the legato beat. There should be some espressivo quality for the $<\!\!>$ and to lead the melodic line, as in measure

154. This is more effective if you use neutral beats in measures 150 and 152, as well as in 155 and 156.

Starting with measure 199, there is an eight-measure syncopated passage with gradual crescendo. The beat must be very precise (staccato). The downbeat in bar 205 should be emphasized to stimulate the entering instruments. It is more important here to watch the strings than the flutes and first horn. A very energetic marcato is used for the *ff*.

In the *ff* passage you may subdivide, beating *One, Three*, particularly in measures 213 and 214, to keep a firm hold on the rhythmic figure in the trumpets and timpani. For the *fp* in the horns, use a staccato beat changing immediately to neutral-legato. Subdivision in measure 235 leads the eighth note in the low strings securely. To change back to *Presto,* beat as if the passage were written as shown in example A.1.

Starting with measure 260, the first section of the Scherzo is repeated, but *p*. The gestures are small and precise to insure a clear and delicate staccato from the orchestra. The left hand is especially needed in measure 285 where the second section begins, also *p* . The tutti chords (m. 303) are now *pp*; the snappy preparation is extremely small.

Coda

While the change to *Assai meno presto* is done the same way as before, the attack of the last *Presto* requires a preparation strictly in tempo. For this, insert an extra (preliminary) presto beat, which also cuts off the strings, giving them a chance to lift the bow quickly for the *ff*. To direct the concluding 5 measures with downbeats would be rather pedantic. You may use a vigorous gesture similar to a 4-beat: *One, Two, Three, Four,* ONE!

In conducting this movement from memory, it is helpful to have a clear picture of how the repetitions differ from one another:

Scherzo	1st section repeated
	2d section repeated
Trio	1st section repeated (repeat written out, orchestration changed)
	2d section repeated
Transition	
Scherzo	1st section repeated (repeat written out, dynamics changed)
	2d section not repeated (dynamics changed)
Trio	1st section same as 1st time
	2d section repeated
Transition	
Scherzo	1st section not repeated
	2d section not repeated
Coda	

Ex. A.1. Beethoven, Symphony No. 7, mm. 235–37

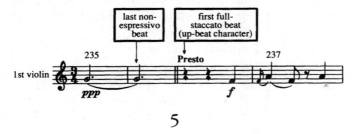

5

Johannes Brahms
Symphony No. 4 in E Minor, Op. 98—
First Movement

This *Allegro non troppo* requires flexible pacing, but tempo modifications should not exceed a span of about ♩ = 66–80. If handled skillfully and gradually, they will be hardly noticeable to the listener.

The tradition of a leisurely beginning goes back to the days of the composer. At one point, he intended to alter the start of the movement to prepare for an unhurried violin entrance. Later, however, he abandoned the idea. The four measures that he crossed out in the autograph are shown in example A.2.

Measure 1 For a well-coordinated and beautifully played beginning, the conductor needs the undivided attention of both violin sections. His gesture, 2-beat *espressivo*, must suggest a continual melodic line in which the half notes are fully sustained.

Ex. A.2. Brahms, Symphony No. 4, opening measures crossed out in the autograph

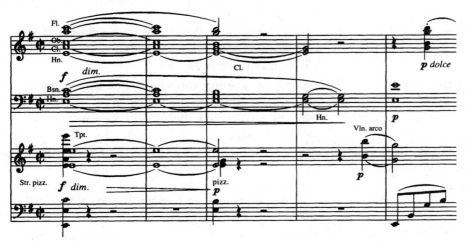

M. 4	The dynamic sign for the violins does not indicate diminuendo in the strict sense but is a phrase accent (see pp. 404 and 408). Use a larger gesture on *Two* for preparation.
M. 9	Emphasize *One* for the $<\;>$.
M. 12	After a minor crescendo, lead back to *p* .
M. 17	Do not use large gestures for the *f*. The oboe solo will not be heard sufficiently if the other players overdo the *f*. If necessary, change their markings to *mf*.
Mm. 19ff.	Lead the violins; the winds accompany *leggiero* and need no encouragement.
M. 26	*Two* is a staccato gesture.
M. 27ff.	Do not "work" for the crescendo too soon! The real crescendo is still to come in m. 33.
Mm. 37ff.	A staccato beat is needed for the syncopations. In m. 38, cue in the trumpets (their first entrance!)
M. 45	Resume a legato beat. At this point the tempo has increased to about $\downarrow$ = 80.
M. 50	Bring out the second horn pair.
Mm. 53ff.	Beat staccato. Even when the celli, later the violins, play the melody, the gestures retain staccato quality to control the rhythm of the staccato accompaniment.
M. 86	To make the crescendo more effective, mark the last quarter note in the strings *mf* .
M. 90	Change to legato beat. In mm. 91 and 92, the violins divide the bow. The second violins continue the same bowing in m. 93, but, for an effective diminuendo, the first violins should play mm. 93 and 94 in one bow.
M. 95	*Espressivo* beat.
M. 107	The *pp* and the rhythm in the trumpets is controlled by a light-staccato beat.
M. 110	For good ensemble, the strings must adjust to the articulation of the wind instruments.
M. 117	Quick and intense crescendo.
Mm. 119ff.	Use incisive gestures (also for the off-beat accents).
M. 123	If the trumpets sustain the D in *f*, they are likely to cover the woodwinds; their long note may have to be marked $>$ *mf*.
M. 136	Wait on *One* for a moment before a gentle legato beat on *Two*.
M. 139	If you have used very little forearm motion for the preceding measures, an increase in arm motion will lead the $<\;>$ effectively.
Mm. 153ff.	Maintain the flow of this passage while controlling the delicate dynamics with gentle gestures.

M. 168	Strong crescendo, especially in the winds. Change to *marcato* beat.
M. 183	A slight ritard prepares the *ff p* and the gloomy passage that follows. Use a small but precise beat beginning with m. 184.
M. 194	*Two* prepares the $<\ >$.
M. 206	The energetic downbeat that prepares the *ff* attack is a sudden change from the preceding neutral-legato. Beat staccato until m. 218.
M. 219	Use a legato beat from here on.
Mm. 227ff.	This passage is directed with subtle gestures that reflect the dynamics and, at the same time, secure continuity (no breaks between wind and string entrances!).
M. 239	The left hand helps to indicate the sudden *pp*. Keep strict time with small gestures.
M. 243	The double basses had a pause of no more than fifteen measures; still, cue them in for a very soft pizzicato.
M. 246	For the recapitulation, which begins here, the tempo will have slowed down to about ♩ = 72. Keep a steady pace for twelve measures.
M. 258	Hold back slightly to lead the melody in the violins (*p* after the *pp*!) in the mood of the movement's beginning.
Mm. 259–370	The comments on the performance of the exposition apply to the recapitulation.
M. 371	The Coda starts here; the conducting patterns are much the same as used for the preceding section.
M. 377	Reduce the size and intensity of the beat for the sudden *f* after *ff*. In order to build the final climax the orchestra must "start afresh." Note that Brahms asks five times for more crescendo or for *più f*, even within a *ff*. These markings, which defy logic, must be understood as a composer's request for undiminished intensity.
M. 388	According to the autograph the *f* in the timpani part is a misprint. Brahms clearly marked *ff* beginning with this measure. (Many conductors let the timpani make a crescendo of two measures, leading to the printed *ff*.)
M. 392	From here the momentum increases more and more. The pace may be accelerated to about ♩ = 88.
Mm. 422ff.	Lead the accents with forceful gestures.
M. 431	In this and the following measure bring out the first horn pair.
Mm. 436–437	Strong gestures must lead these very short chords.

M. 439

It has become a tradition to slow down the tempo for the 4 timpani notes. However, an exaggeration of this nuance would not be in line with the impetuous drive of the Coda.

6

Ludwig Van Beethoven
Overture to Egmont Op. 84

In the introduction the $\frac{3}{2}$ time is subdivided, and the tempo is generally taken ♩ = 72–76.

Measure 1

The opening chord, marked by a fermata and dynamics that do not exceed a single *f*, is in sharp contrast to m. 9 which calls for a sustained *ff* without a fermata. How to interpret the diminuendo sign is a matter of opinion. Some conductors let the *f* fade into a *p*. In any case, the hold should last for more than six quarter counts. For the initial attack, use a quarter note preparation (staccato). Release the fermata with a quarter beat, which serves as preparation for m. 2.

M. 2

Giving equal emphasis to each quarter beat would result in the rhythmic figure ♩ 𝄽 ♩ 𝄽, but the notation leads us to assume that Beethoven wanted ♩· 𝄾 ♩· 𝄾. Therefore, use the tenuto technique, with strong emphasis on the first and third quarters; the second quarter is used for a connecting gesture. The fourth is in the manner of a cutoff, and the fifth is relatively weak. The sixth is a strong preliminary beat.

M. 4

The sixth beat is done with a gentle staccato, now indicating *p*.

M. 5

Beat neutral-legato with clear subdivision; elaborate gestures would be out of place here.

M. 6

The sixth quarter may have a slight staccato quality to bring out the separation from the following note. Clear separations of this kind are typical of Classical style and should always be carefully observed.

M. 8

Indicate the expressive < > with the left hand; do not slow down the tempo, and use the accented upbeat on *Six*.

M. 9

Using *Six* for preparation would cut the players off and result in a quarter rest. To hold the *ff* unison as long as possible, you may use a shortened preparation for the next bar.

M. 14	Do not use too small a gesture for the **p** string entrance, since it is played with some vibrato. The **pp** must be still smaller.
Mm. 15ff.	An unobtrusive staccato beat on *Six* secures the rhythmic emphasis for the motive in the cellos and basses.

Beethoven's explicit dynamic markings must be carefully observed. There are no fewer than thirteen **pp** signs within seven measures calling for a subdued neutral-legato execution.

M. 22	The sudden appearance of *espressivo* for three wind instruments signifies a sharp contrast: The players must be encouraged to play their notes with an imploring expression. Obviously, Beethoven did not consider it necessary to add a **p** for these instruments, *espressivo* being sufficient, but he marked the horns and, in m. 23, the celli **p** to indicate the change, returning to **pp** in m. 24.
M. 25	The new tempo (♩. = ca. 54) starts without time for preparation, and therefore this bar requires an unmistakably clear beat (♩ = ca. 160). Indicate the crescendo by increasing the intensity, but not the size, of the beat. Throughout the *Allegro,* the beating pattern must remain flexible, from a straight 3-beat to a subdivided 1-beat or a regular 1-beat.
M. 28	The **sfp** is indicated by subdivision or by a sharp upbeat; legato beat follows.
M. 42	Change to staccato beat; no crescendo until marked in the score!
Mm. 47ff.	*Gradual* crescendo.
Mm. 58, 62	High rebound for strong preparation.
Mm. 74ff.	Beat marcato. By this time the tempo may have increased slightly, but the contrast to the second theme (m. 82) must not be too obvious.
M. 82	The tempo is slightly slower; the forceful chords on *One* and *Two* can be directed by using 3-beat, though not with the regular pattern, which would be too academic. Beat *Two* with a strong but quite small motion, carrying only slightly to the right. Also, *Three* should be comparatively small but incisive.
M. 84	1-beat legato.
Mm. 93ff.	Indicate the crescendo by intensity of gesture, saving the first large motion for preparation of the **ff** in m. 99.
Mm. 100ff.	The **sf** may be indicated by a sharp upward motion on *Three* or by the left hand.

M. 116	Sudden change to legato gesture, leading into the lyric episode.
M. 123	The *p* must not be disturbed by the way you lead the *f* chords. Use a sudden staccato gesture.
Mm. 153ff.	The beat remains small and steady.
Mm. 163ff.	Because of the changed orchestration (winds) it may be necessary to add some staccato to the beat.
M. 206	The wind chords are important for the modulation. A strong gesture should obtain the greatest possible volume from the winds.
M. 215	A strong *One* must be addressed to the first violins.
Mm. 259ff.	Use a small but extremely intense gesture. Many conductors rearrange the notes of the horn quartet in mm. 259–262 and 267–270 for a more balanced sound of the wind chords.
Mm. 263ff.	By contrast, the gesture must express the timid feeling of these four bars.
M. 266	Subdivide *One* (two), *Three*; *Three* prepares the *ff*.
M. 275	In this and the following two measures, the second horn pair can double the notes of the first and second horns (in Beethoven's time, the A was not available on horns in E flat). Note that clarinets and bassoons pause to allow the players to prepare for the *ppp* !
M. 278	Beat *One*, *Three* (*Three* with a sideways motion) and stop abruptly.
M. 279	After the pause use a 1-beat preparation or prepare with *Three*, in case you prefer to lead the wind passage with a small 3-beat.
Mm. 281ff.	Indicate the entrances very quietly.
M. 286	The cutoff is usually the preliminary beat ($\bullet$ = 168), which must express the subdued excitement of the beginning of the *Allegro con brio*.
Mm. 287ff.	Do not make the crescendo too early.
M. 294	Lead the trumpet (*p* $<$ *ff*) and beat a subdivided 2-beat as transition to . . .
M. 295	. . . *Alla breve,* but do not rush (not faster than $\bullet$=92).
M. 313	At this point the gesture should not be too emphatic, to allow for the crescendo that follows.
Mm. 317ff.	Use marcato beats.
M. 319	Bring out the trumpets.
M. 329	The downbeat is also the preparation for the *sf* on *Two*.

7

Johann Strauss
Overture to Die Fledermaus

Entrance cues will no longer be mentioned, since a thorough study of the score is presupposed and the techniques of cuing have been amply demonstrated.

Conductors differ widely in their interpretation of this work, there being no unanimity even among the Viennese. The following discussion is concerned mainly with baton technique.

The interpretation of this overture, whose entire thematic material is taken from the operetta, should reflect the relation between the music and the libretto to which it was written. Lack of familiarity with words and stage action accounts for frequent misjudgments in regard to tempi and expression. An authentic full score has been published; also, a facsimile of the overture's autograph is available.

Measure 1ff.	♩ = 132–138, full-staccato. Only the preparatory beat is large, as is *Two* in m. 2. In this way, you direct the motive ♩ ♩ ♩ 𝄾 strongly and indicate the rhythm for the run with a minimum of gesture.
M. 4	Here *Two* is *not* preparatory; the next preparation is in *One* in the next measure.
M. 8	Use the left hand for the ***p*** .
M. 12	The cutoff gesture should leave the baton at a medium height to allow a convenient preparation for the next tempo.
M. 13	♩ = 84 (*alla breve*), neutral-legato.
M. 15	The conductor may or may not lead the oboe solo; if the solo is conducted, any exaggerated gestures should be avoided.
M. 19	Address the first violins with an expressive-legato beat.
M. 21	*Two* is staccato to stimulate the piquant violin figure.
M. 22	Address the second violins; their staccato notes must be audible and played scherzando.
M. 27	Sudden change to light-staccato.
Mm. 31ff.	Some conductors make a transition back to the original tempo by means of a stringendo, although this is not recommended. In any event, an intensive gesture is needed for the ***p*** ⊂ ***ff*** .
Mm. 37ff.	Syncopation beat.
Mm. 41ff.	♩ = 58. Beat marcato on the ***fp***, then use tenuto. The tenuto pattern, with its connecting gestures, produces

a unified attack by flutes, oboe, and bell. They would not respond very well to a legato motion.

M. 47 ♩ = 100. Light-staccato. The first two beats in the *Allegretto* must be given so convincingly the tempo is clear to the cellos and bassoon and that the violas have no doubt about their sixteenth notes. It is possible to use the last eighth in the *Lento* to prepare the new tempo; in this case, the eighth beat must be lengthened so as to correspond to the following quarter beat.

M. 50 Change to *poco espressivo*.

M. 55 Light-staccato.

M. 58 Expressive-legato, stringendo to about ♩ = 112.

M. 69 Indicate a sharp *fz* (trumpets!) on *One* and do not fail to establish the slower tempo (♩ = 108) decisively.

Mm. 74ff. This passage is often taken slightly slower (♩ = 100), although no tempo change is indicated by the composer (a *meno mosso* would require a minor ritard on *Two* in m. 73). Lead the music with freedom of gesture and bring out the alternation of staccato and legato.

Mm. 82, 90 Many conductors hold back slightly on *Two*, but any exaggeration would be out of style.

M. 97 Lead the cellos with an *espressivo* gesture.

Mm. 99ff. The *poco rit.* is usually distributed over the next five measures and should not be overdone.

M. 104 A *tempo* (or *più mosso*, about ♩ = 116) is traditional here. Beat light-staccato.

M. 106 Prepare the pizzicato clearly.

M. 107 Change to an *espressivo* gesture suggesting vibrato for the accompanying strings. These instruments have a tendency to drag at this point unless led convincingly.

M. 108 According to the autograph, the *poco rit.* begins in this measure.

M. 109 Give the flute and violins time for the eighth note A.

M. 110 ♩ = 116. Observe that the first ♪ is still *p*, but beat it staccato.

M. 114 Use small gestures for the *p*.

M. 121 This bar can be held back slightly. The autograph leaves no doubt that the last note is D (some editions print C sharp).

M. 122 1-beat, about ♩. = 69 (*nicht zu schnell!*) In the autograph the *pp* is followed by a *crescendo molto* beginning in the next measure. Measures 122–25 have been subjected to various manipulations, none of which can claim authenticity. The frequently heard break before measure 126 is a mannerism.

M. 126	Address the double basses strongly.
M. 128	Beat a vigorous rebound for the accent on the third quarter.
Bar 131	The ♪♪ ♩ ♩ requires a dynamic preparation. The same is true for the trombone attack in mm. 141ff.
M. 165	The end of the musical thought is indicated by a strong marcato beat. Let a fraction of a second elapse before the next attack.
M. 166	The composer did not indicate a ritard or a fermata on the D. Nevertheless, three different executions of this measure can be heard. They are mentioned here, though not recommended.

1. 3-beat with ritardando

2. 3-beat with ⌒ on *One*, the two eighth notes still played with ritardando

3. 1-beat with ⌒ on the half note and repeated beat without ritardando; the two eighth notes are thus strictly in tempo.

M. 181	A tempo relation is possible ($\downarrow \cdot = \downarrow$), which means ♩ = 138. Use small gestures.
M. 200	Stop briefly on *One* to give the solo bassoon time to breathe. The fermata on *Two* is hardly needed.
Mm. 201ff.	♩ = 76. Start beating neutral-legato and develop gradually to *espressivo*.
M. 209	Change to staccato.
M. 210	Resume the legato beat, emphasizing *One* for the off-beat accents.
M. 215	A large gesture on *Three* brings the melody into sharper relief.
M. 218	According to tradition, the oboe plays *poco rubato*. The conductor may lead the accompaniment unobtrusively or direct the melody, depending on the personalities of conductor and oboist.
M. 224	An effect of comic exaggeration, intended by the composer, can be secured with an expressive tenuto beat on each count.
M. 225	*A tempo.*
M. 228	Usually a pause is made before the start of the new theme. For this, cut off the violins with the left hand so that the baton is spared for the preparatory *Two*. The last note is marked staccato at the corresponding place in the operetta (No. 4). It is a mannerism to use a special gesture for this upbeat staccato and to

	hesitate before attacking the next bar. The correct tempo marking is *Allegro moderato*. The accents in the melody always require an emphasized beat.
Mm. 248ff.	Use a light gesture to keep the playing from becoming too heavy. As a contrast, direct the motive ♪♪♪ ♪ (mm. 252 and 254) with a vigorous beat.
M. 260	Indicate the *fp* and bring out the horn.
M. 269	Precise upbeat so that the trumpet will not drag.
Mm. 278ff.	Except for the change in orchestration, this section is the same as when it occurred the first time (see m. 74).
M. 315	A smooth transition can be made by beating *Two* so as to equal the pulse of the waltz tempo (♩ = ♩.).
Mm. 351ff	If these measures are taken too rapidly, the double basses may produce disagreeable noises! The composer's mark is *Allegro moderato* (not faster than ♩ = 132).
Mm. 371ff	Some conductors make a ritard, with the theme slightly held back and speeding up until m. 380. However, it is at least as effective when played in tempo, accenting the octave jumps sharply and playing the theme with a sudden *p* .
M. 388	♩ = 160, with small gestures.
M. 395	Beat *One* sharply in case the brass instruments tend to fall behind.
M. 404	A definite indication is needed for this contrasting *p* subito.
Mm. 412ff.	Bring out the syncopated motive in the horns and trombones.
M. 419	Lift the baton for a strong preparation to direct the concluding measure with one energetic stroke.

8

Claude Debussy
"Fêtes"
(*No. 2* from Nocturnes for Orchestra)

When Debussy revised the score of the Nocturnes, he not only corrected wrong notes but made radical changes in regard to orchestration, phrasing, and dynamics. This version bears the mark "Edition définitive réorchestrée par l'Auteur." Right at the beginning of "Fêtes", the orchestration must include oboes, English horn, and clarinets; if it does not, the score is incorrect.

Measure 1	A speed of $\half = 88$ is in the best French tradition. Use a marcato gesture for the beginning with a straight or subdivided beat. Subdivision controls the rhythm more firmly, but it would stifle the flow of the music if applied continually.
Mm. 3, 7	There is a marked difference in intensity of beat between *ff* and *f*, especially in measure 3 where three woodwinds must be heard against the entire violin section.
M. 9	Light-staccato, wrist motion only!
M. 10	Use a slightly larger beat for the crescendo, then immediately indicate the *pp* (m. 11) with the left hand.
Mm. 13ff.	Indicate the accents.
M. 23	The tempo is twice as slow. Beat this bar with a strong marcato, using a regular 4-beat. Include in *Three* the preparation for the timpani.
M. 24	Sustain the *ff*.
M. 25	Cut off the wind chord sharply and keep strictly in tempo during the *p* $>$ of the timpani. Subdivide *Four* and use the last eighth beat to prepare the harp entrance.
M. 26	4-beat in the tempo of the beginning ($\eighth = \eighth$).
M. 27	The tempo is slightly faster ($\dotquarter. = 184$). The pattern is 5-beat, grouped into 3 + 2 by the composer. The *sfz* in strings and cymbal requires a sharp gesture on *One*, followed immediately by light-staccato.
M. 29	Same tempo in 3-beat. After the accented *One*, use small beats for a subdued accompaniment; the flutes and oboes play *f* on their own initiative.
Mm. 39ff.	Keep the tempo in hand.
M. 41	A slight $< >$ of this sort can be indicated effectively by adding a gentle motion of the forearm to the wrist movement.
M. 44	Keep the beat small and precise. The difficult passages of the English horn and oboes will suffer if the tempo has been hurried previously.
M. 46	Do not become so preoccupied with the main instruments that you forget the double bass entrance!
M. 49	The larger gesture on *Three*, which prepares the next measure, will not disturb the flute passage.
M. 52	Strong indication of the rapid diminuendo.
M. 55	A slightly emphasized *Two* helps the oboe with the phrasing.
M. 60	*Arco* for the basses is missing in the score.

M. 63	A definite *One* brings the trumpets in precisely.
M. 64	Weaken *Two* and *Three* so as not to conflict with the quadruplet.
Mm. 70ff.	Relax the pace slightly. Bring out the crescendo in the woodwinds by addressing only this group.
M. 82	Indicate the ***pp*** subito in the first violins with a sudden left-hand gesture.
Mm. 86ff.	For this passage, the beat must be sufficiently flexible to express both legato and staccato. Stress *One* slightly, the pattern being the subdivided 1-beat rather than actual 3-beat.
M. 97	The left hand may be used for the ***sfz*** on *Three*.
Mm. 102ff.	The crescendo in the winds needs no indication; save your gesture until m. 106. Do not rush, let the strings sing!
M. 116	♩ = 88 (twice as slow as the quarter beat in the opening). Light-staccato.
Mm. 124ff.	The gesture must reflect the correct phrasing. All triplets are slurred! (This was confirmed by Debussy when asked by the conductor Pierre Monteux.)
Mm. 138ff.	Do not speed up the tempo.
M. 149	Add $>$ to the horn parts, in this bar and in m. 151.
Mm. 151ff.	A well-balanced climax requires economy of gesture.
Mm. 170ff.	Use a heavy marcato gesture but without slowing down. (A steady tempo is necessary for the coming transition to *I° Tempo*.)
M. 174	If the tempo has been maintained strictly, the last measure in $\frac{2}{4}$ is exactly as long as two measures in the new $\frac{6}{8}$ (♪ = ♩. = 176).
Mm. 190ff.	The violins play three notes against two beats; therefore, weaken *Two*.
M. 202	Here, the faster tempo (♩. = 184) is established.
M. 209	Cue in the cymbal roll with the left hand.
M. 221	Indicate the crescendo strongly.
M. 233	Use a sharp wrist motion on *Three* for the pizzicato in the violas.
Mm. 236ff.	Small gestures with the utmost precision.
M. 252	Slower tempo immediately. Since no preparation is possible, the first and second beats must establish the new tempo very clearly.
M. 260	A well-prepared *Three* leads the pizzicato and the ***sf*** in the horns and brings in the English horn, clarinet, and first horn. Do this without slowing down.
Mm. 264ff.	The third beat must be flexible enough to allow the flutes and oboes time to play their triplet figure without rushing.

M. 266	Sudden a *tempo.*
Mm. 269ff.	Delicate handling of the baton and a clear mind are needed for directing the fleeting notes of the close.
M. 278	You may wait slightly before the final downbeat.

9

Béla Bartók
Concerto for Orchestra — First Movement

Bartók's sectional timings supplement his metronome indications as an additional guide for conductors. Right at the start, the first thirty-four measures (metronome ♩ = 73–64) are calculated to last one minute and thirty-eight seconds, including one acceleration and one ritard. The following section (♩ = 64) comprises sixteen measures without any printed tempo modifications and is given a duration of one minute. This estimate implies some liberty in pacing, because when played at metronome speed these sixteen measures last only forty-five seconds.

Here again, metronome markings, though no more than an approximation of the music's inner pulse, fulfill an important function (see chapter 32). Using the *Tranquillo* in measure 155 as an example, do not stick mechanically to the metronome's ticking (♩. = 70), but rather, while remaining close to the indicated speed, sing to yourself the oboe and harp lines. Yet, you must sense the eighth note units distinctly enough to apply them with certainty to the $\frac{4}{8}$ measures that follow.

Measures 1 ff.	Beat this *poco espressivo.*
Mm. 6ff.	The string tremolo must be played at the point of the bow. Note that only the violas, without mutes, play the tremolo near the bridge.
Mm. 23ff.	The tempo increases to about ♩ = 84, then slows down very gradually. *Three* in m. 29 prepares the flute entrance in the new tempo, ♩ = 64.
Mm. 39ff.	It can be assumed that the tempo modifications, implied in the composer's sectional timing, are related to the rendering of the trumpet passages; a hardly noticeable slowing down in the eighth note motion of the strings may result.
Mm. 51ff.	Although the beat retains the legato pattern, it allows for gestures that reflect articulation and phrasing.
Mm. 63ff.	The phrase groups for the accelerando are 4 + 3 + 3 + 3. Switch to 1-beat with the third phrase group. For a well-organized increase of tempo, "think" with the trumpets while speeding the quarter beats. The 1-beat in m. 70 starts at ♩. = 50–60. Note that the composer marked the final measure ♩. = 76, no faster!

M. 75   In this measure, use a quick and vigorous rebound for the short break. Having whipped up the baton, stop for a moment before bringing in the violins in the new tempo, ♩. = 83. This is a tempo change without a timed preparation (see chapter 22).

Mm. 76ff.   Beat full-staccato. To direct the interspersed ⅔ bars with authority, your feeling for lopsided rhythms must be unshakable.

M. 90   Incisive 3-beat. Cue in trombones and timpani.

M. 95   Use legato gestures.

Mm. 99ff.   In case the winds are not heard clearly, the strings make a diminuendo and resume *f* in m. 102.

M. 113   Address the second violins with an *espressivo* gesture.

Mm. 123ff.   Clarinets and bassoons may have to double in order to stand out sufficiently; the string accompaniment must not be too heavy. Alternate between legato and staccato gestures in line with the orchestra's playing.

Mm. 154ff.   The transition to the new tempo, ♩. = 70, works best when the 4/8 measure is directed with a 2-beat, ♩ = 105. This brings in the oboe securely and helps to establish the eighth note unit unmistakably. (Use a 2-beat also for the other 4/8 bars.) For this passage, apply a legato pattern that reflects the subtle nature of the music and still leaves no doubt about the rhythm. Note the temporary change of key in the clarinets.

Mm. 192ff.   A precise beat is needed to direct the strings (ten violins in all).

M. 206   The rallentando of two measures is a very minor slowing down.

Mm. 215ff.   Trombones, English horn, and trumpet must be cued in. The composer's tempo instructions for this passage are not clear. The mark ♩. = 69 in m. 229 seems to be in contradiction to the *sempre più tranquillo,* extended through thirteen measures. Many conductors take the liberty of beginning a minor rallentando with the trumpet solo, then slow down more noticeably for the expressive low string passage. Measures 229 and 230 are played at ♩. = 60 (with or without subdivision).

M. 231   Return to beating staccato and synchronize the *f* subito in the strings with the timpani cue.

M. 239   This is the first piccolo cue (the third flute had briefly participated in an earlier passage).

M. 240   Control the diminuendo in the brass.

M. 242   It is helpful to be aware of the phrase grouping: 6 + 6 + 4 + 3 + 4 + 4 + 3.

M. 248   Observe the single *f* after the *ff*!

M. 271	The *pochiss. allarg.* together with the trombone and timpani cues on *Three* is best directed by means of a quick 3-beat (♪ = 200, wrist motion!).
M. 272	After a brief stop, bring in the clarinet with a freely timed preparation. Use 1-beat, legato *poco espressivo*.
M. 284	Indicate the ***pp***, then slow down the beat slightly, without subdivision.
Mm. 300ff.	Cue in the wind players; English horn and piccolo should play very softly.
M. 313	Before resuming the quicker tempo after the ritard, stop for a moment on the downbeat in m. 312, then use a regular preparatory beat to attack the *Tempo I.* For the passage that extends from here to m. 396, analyze the phrase groups in conjunction with the orchestration.
Mm. 342ff.	Study the brass setting thoroughly. The third trombone has its first cue in m. 350.
Mm. 380ff.	Bring in the strings; the double basses enter ***f***!
M. 390	First percussion cue.
M. 396	Subdivide skillfully to bring in the violins (***p***) after a brief pause. Resume the 1-beat in the next measure.
M. 424	Direct the pizzicato together with the flute and oboe entrances.
Mm. 425ff.	Your gesture must remain clear to facilitate the coordination of the quadruplets in the harp and the quintuplets in the strings.
M. 438	Do not "beat forte" for the harps!
Mm. 456ff.	Throughout this passage keep the legato beat smooth and steady. Cue in the trumpets.
M. 468	Use a full-staccato gesture to prepare the robust ***f*** of the violas in the next bar, then immediately indicate ***p*** and resume beating legato while slowing the pace.
M. 474	Subdivide for the flutes in this and the next measure (♪ = 120).
M. 476	Having used the last eighth in m. 475 as a free preparation, return here to 1-beat at a speed of about ♩. = 60. Beat ***f*** staccato (disregarding the dynamics in the woodwinds as far as your beat is concerned) and increase the pace steadily so as to resume the *Tempo I* in m. 488.
Mm. 494ff.	Five phrase groups begin here, each consisting of three measures, with changing rhythmic patterns. Note that the first two groups end with a lopsided beat. The sequence of bars in the next two groups, however, is short, long, short, while the last group shows the pattern short, long, long. For perfect

coordination, the orchestra needs flawless direction by the conductor.

M. 509   The dynamics are reduced to a single *f* (*p* in the timpani) for a final intense crescendo.

10

Felix Mendelssohn
Violin Concerto in E Minor Op. 64—
Third Movement

Start practicing at the *Allegretto non troppo;* the metronome indication of ♩ = 96 was suggested by Joseph Joachim, who had studied the concerto with Mendelssohn. This short transition follows a fermata. Whether there is a pause, caused by applause or tuning, or whether the violinist proceeds directly, be ready for the solo entry. If you do not lift the baton until the soloist starts playing, you will not arrive at the first beat in time. Keep the baton in the position of attention, and just as the violinist attacks the upbeat, make the preparatory gesture without hesitation. Follow the traditional rubato in measures 9 and 10, synchronizing *Three* in measure 10 exactly with the A. In measure 13 the soloist is likely to slow down before the *pp*. Hence, delay the third beat and follow delicately. In the next bar, watch the violin bow so as to end the fermata with the soloist.

Allegro molto vivace (♩ = 92). Most of this movement is conducted with 2-beat, although in certain places a subdivided beat is used.

Measure 1	This is often done with 2-beat, using a half note preparation. The rhythm may be more incisive with a subdivided beat, in which case the preliminary beat would be a quarter note.
M. 2	Most violinists like to hurry this figure, but you keep the tempo.
M. 4	Use 2-beat from here.
Mm. 9ff.	Precision of gesture must be combined with lightness and elegance; too tense a beat would hamper the fluent movement.
Mm. 18, 20, 21	The entries after *One* must not be late; keep the beat moving to prevent any hesitation.
M. 23	Neutral beats on the rest.
M. 24	Be on the alert to catch the pizzicato exactly with the D sharp in the solo. The effectiveness of this depends on a skillful preparation on *One*.
Mm. 25ff.	*Two* in measure 25 prepares the next attack and may be slightly hastened by using a gesture that is not too sharp but rather flexible. This may seem to contradict

previous suggestions, but when such transparent passages occur in accompaniment, the conductor must rely to some extent upon musicians having an attentive ear. An academic beat would not arouse the "chamber music" participation of the individual players, a participation that is essential here.

M. 30	The best way to secure a perfect ensemble is to think with the solo violin. The clarinets will follow.
M. 35	Use a slight syncopation beat without delaying.
Mm. 41ff.	The soloist's freedom of playing should not be restrained by the accompaniment; pick up the beat when necessary.
M. 46	Address the second violins.
M. 55	For the handling of this passage, see ex. 26.5. In case you must subdivide to prevent rushing, return to 2-beat for Mm. 57 and 58 so as not to lose the *grazioso* quality of the music.
Mm. 63, 65	*fp* beat on *One*.
Mm. 71ff.	A lively gesture must maintain the swift pace of the movement and prevent the wind entrances from being late.
Mm. 75ff.	The beat must build the crescendo and prepare the bass entrance, leading to a strong *One* in m. 76. Change to legato in m. 77.
M. 80	A slight ritardando is traditional; follow the soloist.
Mm. 81ff.	The violin resumes the fast tempo; concentrate upon the runs to be with the soloist all the time.
Mm. 98ff.	Watch the runs again and do not let the wind entrances drag. The violins also need some indication in m. 100 so as not to be late after the sustained note. The pizzicato in the low strings, together with the entrance of the flutes, needs a clear upbeat.
M. 129	Slightly slower for the *tranquillo*. Beat *Two* exactly with the A in the violin to get the following pizzicato precisely in time.
M. 184	Beat the rests, following the soloist strictly.
M. 193	Follow the slight rubato which is customary and synchronize *Two* with the A, but catch up immediately in the next measure.
M. 198	The soloist usually speeds up at this point; be sure to follow.
Mm. 204ff.	Subdue the accompaniment by using a small gesture (the crescendo in m. 206 applies only to the solo). The *sforzati* in the orchestra must not be too heavy and need not be reflected in your beat.
M. 216	Address clarinets, bassoons, and double basses.

M. 218	Closely follow the soloist, who needs time to attack the high E.
M. 222	Indicate *fp* strongly, then go along with the rapid movement of the solo instrument. The violinist will be grateful for not being hurried in mm. 226–229. Trumpets and timpani should reduce the *ff* to *f*.

11

Wolfgang Amadeus Mozart
Recitative: "E Susanna Non Vien"
from Le Nozze di Figaro, Act III

The remarks made in chapter 16 are pertinent to this discussion. The words as well as the music of the vocal part should be studied so that the conductor knows on which counts the syllables fall.

No matter what liberties the singer takes with the rhythm, the conductor must always give a clear *One* in each bar. Whether or not to beat the other counts during sustained notes or rests depends upon the speed of the music. Beating on all counts is practicable in moderate tempo, using small and smooth gestures. In faster tempo or when the singer hurries, too many beats may become confusing, in which case it is advisable to skip all beats that are not necessary.

When the beat follows the singer's liberties, it is bound to become irregular and to affect the various preparatory beats. Therefore, since the conductor must be on time with the entrances, free preparations may have to be used.

Measure 1	Synchronize *Three* with the singer. Beat in tempo (♩ = 60) on *Three-Four*, no matter how fast the first two quarters were. A gentle syncopation beat on *Three* brings in the orchestra.
M. 2	Indicate the counts clearly with a slight gesture, unless the soprano rushes unduly so that you must hurry to the next downbeat.
M. 3	Use a clear downbeat and cut off quietly on *Four*, preferably with the left hand.
Mm. 4, 6	Procedure similar to m. 1. *Four* must be incisive to secure clear thirty-second notes.
M. 7	If the singer hurries, it is better to skip *Three* and *Four* so as to be ready for the sharp downbeat in m. 8.
M. 8	Do not beat *Three* before the singer reaches it. The tempo changes without preparation. Beat *Three* and *Four* clearly in the new tempo (♩ = 100).
M. 9	Wait on *Four*.

M. 11	Downbeat only.
M. 12	Use four beats, synchronizing *Three*.
M. 14	If the singer's tempo is steady, the preparation for the *fp* is easy; but if she hesitates, you must wait on *Two* and then give a quick free preparation. Beat *Three* and *Four* in rapid succession, to be ready for the next downbeat.
Mm. 15ff.	Here again, be sure not to fall behind the singer. The second beat in m. 16 must coincide with the soprano's C sharp (the violas change to A!).
M. 18	Beat the first and fourth counts only, following the vocal part.
M. 19	If necessary, wait on *Two* and *Four*.
Mm. 21ff.	The preparatory beats on *One* in each measure introduce contrasting accompaniment figures; the first is wistful, the second dramatic.
M. 23	The conductor takes the lead in this bar, the tempo being identical with the previous *Andante*.
Mm. 24ff.	Indicate *fp* strongly and follow the singer closely. A smooth and convincing gesture brings on the closing E-Major chord, helped perhaps by the left hand.

12

Ruggiero Leoncavallo
Prologue to Pagliacci

When the Prologue is performed on the concert stage, the orchestra begins forty-four bars before the first vocal entry (No. 8 in the full score). The numbering of bars in this discussion starts at that point.

Measure 1	1-beat ($\downarrow$. = 88), marcato gesture.
M. 3	Beat staccato.
M. 25	Beat this bar with a larger rebound so as to prepare the following *pesante* a trifle slower.
Mm. 29–36	Gradual increase in tempo. Use a strong gesture for the *secco* effect in m. 36.
M. 37	*A tempo.* Beat steadily in light-staccato.
M. 46	Synchronize a neutral downbeat with the vocal part.
M. 47	Give a clear staccato beat for the off-beat entrance.
M. 50	After the fermata, wait for the upbeat until the singer, after a short pause, attacks the next phrase. In a case like this, the simplest thing to do is to watch the singer take his breath, thus timing your preparation so as to arrive together with him on *One* in m. 51.

M. 51	4-beat, *poco espressivo.*
M. 53	Use a flexible gesture that allows for a possible rubato.
M. 54	A marcato third beat straight toward the right brings out the second half of the measure emphatically.
M. 55	There is not fermata in the full score. Follow the singer and stop on *Three*. Release the chord with the left hand, then beat *Four* to bring in the singer (together with the celli) after the count.
M. 56	According to the vocal score, the beginning of the vocal line can be performed half-spoken. Actually, this is never done.
M. 59	The vocal score does not conform to the orchestration: second violins and violas sustain their chord throughout the third count, which is treated as a fermata (*col canto*). The singer starts *in parte ei vuol* after flutes and harps have ended their passage. Beat *Three* with a short gesture to the left, wait, and repeat *Three* on the singer's F sharp to prepare the next bar.
M. 64	A tenuto gesture is best for this type of chordal accompaniment; the quick connecting gestures enable you to follow the singer from one chord to the next.
M. 65	Either separate cutoff and preparation or do both with the same gesture.
M. 67	Cue in the singer.
M. 74	*A tempo* here means maintain a steady tempo.
M. 88	The sudden change to slower tempo is accomplished by retarding the rebound.
M. 91	There is a pause on the eighth rest in the vocal part; beat tenuto, the upward motion leading into the next bar.
M. 92	Follow the singer.
Mm. 96ff.	If the singer is very slow, the 1-beat may be subdivided or changed to 3-beat.
M. 99	Cut the chord; for the execution of the pause see m. 50.
M. 100	The tempo is faster (1-beat). Follow the singer with sharp and distinct beats until m. 105, then stop as though there were a ⌢ over the rest, and wait. Watch the singer again.
M. 111	Use subdivision, if needed, to follow the singer.
M. 114	3-beat; prepare the entrance on *Three* carefully.
M. 117	Use a calm, flexible *espressivo* 3-beat.

M. 122	Change to a neutral-legato 2-beat.
M. 125	The vocal score is misleading: The first note (tied from the preceding bar) is an eighth note.
M. 128	*A tempo.*
Mm. 129ff.	In these bars the tempo increases gradually as more instruments enter, and the *espressivo* is intensified.
M. 139	Give the singer time for a good breath on the eighth rest.
M. 140	Use an energetic *marcato* gesture, but not so large that the orchestra will play too loudly and cover the voice.
Mm. 142ff.	Lead the heavy ritardando with clear beats, unperturbed by the syncopations! They can be controlled by decisive marcato gestures, without the need for subdivision, except perhaps at the end of the passage. Cut off the concluding A flat with a sideways gesture, saving the upward motion for the following attack.
M. 144	Here again the beat is very expressive but should keep the orchestra subordinated to the singer.
M. 151	Hesitate slightly before *One* to give the singer a chance to breathe, and attack the beat with him.
M. 152	The sudden *p* needs a definite indication.
M. 156	Beat tenuto on *One* and subdivide the other counts. A fermata is customarily made on the first eighth note of *Three* for a sustained "high note" (often changed to A flat). Keep the baton perfectly still and (watching the singer!) use a swift connecting gesture leading to the next eighth beat. These last three eighth beats should not be too slow.
M. 157	Only *Two* is subdivided; wait for the singer and use the subdivision to prepare *Three*, then proceed in tempo.
M. 158	There is no fermata in the full score. Cut the chord and use *Two* to prepare the F-sharp minor chord (three bassoons) on *Three*.
M. 161	Energetic full-staccato; beat the rests with small and relaxed gestures, except for the preparatory beats.
M. 162	After the chord on *Three*, do not beat *Four* until the singer is about to slur down to his concluding note, then use *Four* to prepare I° Tempo (1-beat).

APPENDIX *B*

Wagner's Instructions Regarding the Performance of Two of His Overtures

1

Overture to Tannhäuser

In August 1852 Wagner wrote an article "Über die Aufführung des Tannhäuser, Eine Mitteilung an die Dirigenten and Darsteller dieser Oper." This "message to the conductors and singers of this opera" included performance instructions for the overture. Two months later Wagner announced in a music magazine that conductors intending to perform the work in concert should ask him for special information. His concern was caused by his dissatisfaction with performances of the overture.

Wagner's remarks are here presented in code form. The comments that appear in parentheses are based on notes made by Felix Mottl during Wagner's rehearsals for a *Tannhäuser* production in Vienna (1875). They are believed to be authentic. For the tempo of the introduction, see p. 407.

Measure 1	(Not dragging, in walking motion.)
M. 2	The winds take a breath before the last quarter note; also in mm. 4, 6, etc.
M. 4	Bassoons: Change the dotted half note to a half note followed by a quarter note.
Mm. 38ff.	Trombones and tuba: Breathe whenever needed to sustain every note forcefully at full length.

	All instruments, except trombones, tuba, and timpani, play *ff* $>$ in each measure.
M. 81	(Allegro: begin very calmly, increase tempo only later.)
M. 94	*(Poco ritenuto.)*
M. 123	Increase tempo slightly.
M. 124	Only slight ritenuto without any noticeable change of tempo; sharply contrasting expression, languishing.
M. 132	Change the *fp* to *p* in all instruments.
M. 140	Do not speed up too much.
M. 142	This theme, although to be played with passion, must not be conducted too fast. An all-too-quick tempo would give it the character of levity which must be strictly avoided. (Do not rush; broadly.)
M. 195	For the eight-part divisi of the violins: The six lower lines of equal strength, the first line could be played as a solo, but the second line, beginning with m. 205, must be performed by the largest number of players.
M. 196	(Calmer.)
M. 202	Clarinet: separation between the long note and the triplet.
Mm. 212–19	The clarinet has the most important part and must be heard distinctly; the first violins must not cover it.
M. 219	*(Molto ritenuto.)*
M. 220	(Begin calmly.)
M. 228	Rather strong increase in tempo.
M. 240	· Hold back for the transition into the energetic tempo that is required here.
Mm. 301–08	With full and steady force; any decrease in strength is to be avoided.
M. 321	Violins from here on in utmost piano, like a whisper; the theme in the winds, though not played loudly, must catch the listener's attention immediately.
M. 369	Increase the tempo gradually, but with striking effect, to prepare for the *ff* entrance in m. 379 where the tempo must be sufficiently fast for the rhythmically enlarged theme in the trombones. In order to make the melody understood, their notes must not appear to be played as single tones. Conductor and orchestra must make every effort to maintain the *ff* with the utmost energy and force to achieve the intended effect.
M. 439	After the preceding renewed acceleration (mm. 433–38) the last four bars must be slowed down for a broad and solemn tempo.

2

Prelude to Die Meistersinger von Nürnberg

Wagner's comments are quoted, in free translation, from his essay "Über das Dirigieren." They begin with a discussion of the prelude's basic tempo.

The basic tempo *sehr mässig bewegt* would in older terminology equal an Allegro maestoso. No other tempo needs modification more than this one, especially when of long duration and marked by episodic treatment of the thematic content. It is a favored choice to combine a variety of motives because, with a regular $\frac{4}{4}$ rhythm, its broad structure permits modifications with great ease. At moderate speed this rhythm is highly flexible. When conducted in forcefully "moving" four beats it can express a real, lively *Allegro* (this is the intended basic tempo that appears most vividly in mm. 89ff.), or else it can be applied to measures 122ff. with the character of a lively scherzando [see ex. 2.5]. It can even be understood as an *alla breve* conducted with two moderately slow beats per measure, in the sense of a real, deliberate *Tempo Andante* of former times. This is to be applied to the passage beginning at measure 158.

The notes enclosed in brackets have been added by the author.

Measure 1	[*Sehr mässig bewegt = Allegro maestoso,* see p. 361; *sehr gehalten* does not refer to the tempo but indicates well-sustained notes in the winds.]
M. 27	[Wagner says that he marked this tempo change in the score; however, since the only marking is *ausdrucksvoll,* this term seems to indicate slowing down.]
M. 41	To be performed with vigorous, weighty quarter beats.
M. 58	Change to 2-beat in the sense of *Andante alla breve.*
M. 59	A *cantabile* passage begins here with increasing intensity resulting from the natural feeling for the music and the modulating harmony.
M. 85 (or 86?)	Return to 4-beat with the beginning of the new pattern—that is, when the harmony changes on each quarter note. [Wagner says that he marked this tempo change in the score; as the only marking is *ausdrucksvoll,* it is clear that the term indicates slowing down in this context.]
M. 89	Basic tempo in its most lively form.
M. 96	The *poco rallentando,* hardly noticeable, leads into the new tempo.
M. 97	*Mässig im Hauptzeitmass* [moderately fast within the basic tempo]. To be played in straight $\frac{4}{4}$ time. The tempo, together with an extremely tender expression,

assumes a passionate, almost hasty character, like a secretly whispered declaration of love. As passion and haste are clearly enough expressed by the lively figuration, the tempo must be held back somewhat, which means that the basic tempo is reduced here to its slowest *nuance* [italics added].

M. 105 The theme assures a more and more dominating restlessness, making it easy to lead the tempo eventually back to an *Andante alla breve* as previously explained. [Wagner's comments are by no means clear. Did he suggest a change to 2-beat at some point, or did he merely wish to indicate that the acceleration must lead to a lively *Allegro* in m. 118?]

M. 122 A lively scherzando; each bar consists of two measures in $\frac{2}{4}$.

M. 158 *Andante alla breve* in two moderately slow beats.

M. 188 With the return of the forceful, march-like fanfare, the broadening of the rhythm in $\frac{4}{4}$ is in clear evidence.

M. 196 The doubling in the figuration adds to the broadening of the tempo, so that it ends exactly the way it had begun. [If taken literally, this contradicts Wagner's initial remarks regarding the basic tempo. Traditionally, the tempo of the beginning is not resumed before m. 211, which is probably what the composer had in mind.]

Carl Maria von Weber
Overture to *Oberon*

This work, together with Weber's overtures to *Der Freischütz* and *Euryanthe,* can be called the prototype of a Romantic opera overture. No matter whether it begins with a slow introduction or starts with a rousing *Allegro,* its thematic material is invariably derived from tunes heard in the opera. Lesser composers have been content with putting together a potpourri, a loose sequence of what they believed to be "hit tunes." The great masters, however—Weber, Berlioz, Wagner, to mention the most prominent among them—created coherent musical structures of symphonic dimensions.

Nevertheless, a conductor studying these scores would be remiss in relying simply on experience in the symphonic field. Only by becoming familiar with the opera, its background, words, and music will the conductor become aware of the musical and dramatic significance of the themes incorporated in the overture. Especially in regard to the choice of tempo, it would seem unlikely that a composer would wish a certain melody to be played in the overture at a markedly different pace than it is being sung in the opera.

In the absence of metronome indications (which Weber had provided for the *Euryanthe* Overture), a meaningful pacing of the *Oberon* Overture certainly requires a study of the opera score. Its two tempo markings, *Adagio sostenuto* for the introduction, *Allegro con fuoco* for the main section, are hardly sufficient for an eloquent reading of the music's shifting moods. In fact, a degree of flexibility is expected as characteristic of this style—a flexibility, however, that must not disrupt the momentum inherent in an *Allegro* movement. In his essay "Über das Dirigieren," Wagner addressed this question at length (see Appendix B).

The following comments combine references, enclosed in brackets, to the seven episodes in the opera from which Weber drew the essential musical ideas for the overture, with general performance suggestions. The reader is advised that some editions of the overture have been subjected to changes whose origins are questionable. For these comments the first printed edition of the opera's full score has been used.

Measure 1

[The magic horn call is heard several times in the opera. First, it opens No. 3, "Vision," where it is written in $\frac{2}{4}$ time and marked *Andantino*. Next, it is inserted after No. 8, now marked *Moderato* in $\frac{4}{4}$ time. Finally, it appears in No. 14, again in $\frac{4}{4}$ time but marked *Andante con moto*. In all these cases the notation is in quarter notes with double-dotting.]

The pace should not be overly slow, about ♪ = 80–88. [To fit the *Adagio sostenuto* of the overture's introduction, Weber had to notate the horn call in eighth notes.] This metronomic speed can be applied, with minor modifications, to the entire introduction. Weber added to the tempo designation the words *ed il tutto **pp** possibile,* much in line with a subdued atmosphere in fairyland. Strangely, they are missing in many editions.

It would be pedantic to beat out the rhythm for the solo horn, but the player should be persuaded not to drag the solo and should release the fermata when the conductor lifts his stick to prepare m. 2.

M. 2

Beat in eight, but the subdivision must be subtle and unobtrusive (wrist!). Logically, the muted violins are marked ***p***, while violas and celli play ***pp***. All strings have an accent on the third quarter. Insert a brief pause after releasing the fermata.

M. 4

Only the celli have an accent on the fourth quarter.

M. 5

Continue subdividing without dragging.

M. 6

[Similar wind passages, played ***pp*** staccato, appear repeatedly in No. 1, "Introduction," where they are written in sixteenth notes with the marking *Andante quasi Allegretto,* $\frac{4}{4}$ time.]

The suggested speed of ♪ = 80–88 seems reasonable, although some conductors prefer to rush the winds for a showy effect. Note that the winds are marked ***ppp***, requiring discretion from strings and horn.

M. 9

Horn, second violins, violas, and celli should be marked with a diminuendo sign to let the first violins end their phrase audibly.

M. 10

[Measures 10–15 are taken from No. 22, "Finale," where they appear in the guise of a *Marcia maestoso* played ***ff*** first by the brass, then by the strings.]

For the introduction Weber transformed a bombastic march into an elfin procession played ***pp** possibile.* The speed of ♪ = 88 seems adequate. In the original score, timpani play throughout mm. 10–15.

M. 11

In the original score the celli's first note is played pizzicato.

M. 13	On the second and third quarter beats the violins do not have slurs in the original score. [Slurs are marked, however, for winds in a similar passage occuring in the opera's march.]
M. 16	The seven concluding measures that begin here are not found anywhere in the opera.
M. 19	cf. ex. 21.17.
M. 21	In the original score the divided violas are *not* tied to m. 22.
M. 22	In the original score the final tutti chord is marked *fff* and has a staccato dot for all instruments.
M. 23	[The principal theme of the *Allegro con fuoco* is taken, with minor alterations, from No. 11, "Quartet," with tempo designations that do not suggest an all too rapid pace. The beginning of the "Quartet" is marked *Allegro con grazia,* followed by *Animato* at the point where the first violins begin the sixteenth note passage that we know from the overture.]
	We must ask, did Weber intend, for the sake of brilliance, a tempo completely at variance with the manner in which the same music is performed in the opera? For the "Quartet," both the music's nature and the projection of the words seem to suggest a metronome speed not exceeding $\quarternote = 138$, convincing also as the basic pulse of the overture.
M. 30	In the original score the last three notes of the second violins are notated an octave lower than the same notes in the first violins.
Mm. 43ff.	Several accents printed in the original score are missing in modern editions. In m. 44, the sixth note in the second violins must read D.
M. 50	cf. ex. 21.9. The strings may have to add a diminuendo sign to the half notes to allow the woodwinds to be heard more clearly.
M. 55	It is advisable to shorten strings and bassoons to eighth notes. The horn call is played here almost at double tempo, whereas the staccato passages in bars 57 and 60 are unnoticeably slower than in the introduction ($\quarternote = 70$ vs. $\eighthnote = 80$).
M. 61	A very slight ritard in mm. 61–64 may serve as a "red-carpet" device to introduce the clarinet solo.
M. 65	[The new theme, the overture's second subject, is taken from No. 5, "Aria," where it bears the tempo marking *Andante con moto* and is sung by a tenor to the words "A milder light, a gentler beam is shining o'er life's broader stream." With emphasis on *con moto* the tenor performs this melodious line conveniently at $\quarternote = 116$–20.]

Unfortunately, a tradition adopted by many clarinetists and conductors asks for a drastic change of tempo, almost twice slower than the tenor sings his aria. A metronome speed of ♩ = 116 is suggested for the clarinet solo; this speed allows for an expressive presentation without upsetting the continuity of the movement. It should be noted that the original score indicates a crescendo for the clarinet in m. 69, a diminuendo in m. 70, and an accent on the downbeat in m. 71 (*not* on the third quarter note in m. 70!).

M. 73   With the first violins taking the lead the pace may be increased to ♩ = 120, thus gradually resuming the basic *allegro* tempo.

M. 81   [Here begins an adaptation of a passage in No. 13, "Scene and Aria," where it is notated in $\frac{12}{8}$ time with the tempo designation *Presto con fuoco*.]

For this theme, which gains more and more importance, the basic speed of ♩ = 138 is to be resumed, notwithstanding the soft dynamics in the strings.

Mm. 91–92   Timpani cues, played ***pp***, are found in the original score but are missing in some editions.

M. 101   Conductors who have unnecessarily slowed down their beat in the preceding measures are forced to return abruptly to the basic tempo, a mannerism frequently heard.

M. 103   The original score marks ***pp*** for first violins and violas (the ***p*** sign for celli and basses is wrong). The ***pp*** must be strictly maintained, with a sudden and impressive crescendo within one and a half measures.

M. 123   [The six bar passage that begins here is taken from No. 12, "Solo and Chorus," *Allegro Pesante*, $\frac{2}{4}$ time. The music accompanies Puck's exorcism and is sung to the words "Whether ye be in the cavern dark, [***pp***] lighted alone by the diamonds' spark."]

While the tempo remains unchanged, *pesante* suggests heavy accents in mm. 124 and 127. The ***fp*** for the fourth horn in m. 127 is a misprint; it must read ***pp***.

Mm. 132ff.   cf. ex. 26.6.

Mm. 139ff.   In the original score, the sixteenth notes in the first violins are slurred, all twenty-two notes.

M. 154   The overture's second subject is here recalled (as it was in m. 141 by the oboes). To let the violins sing, the trombones should play diminuendo after attacking each of the four chords.

M. 158   Careful balancing of the wind instruments is needed to let the two flutes dominate the overall sound.

M. 182	A widespread "tradition" calls here for ritenuto, no more than a meaningless "putting on the brakes," instead of letting the music's lively rhythm continue.
Mm. 189ff.	Here, a hardly noticeable broadening would make sense in order to bring out the accent on the diminished-seventh chord in m. 190.
Mm. 200ff.	cf. ex. 21.10. In m. 201, celli and basses must be brought out sharply.
M. 203	The wind chord on the downbeat must be attacked forcefully.
Mm. 209ff.	If the countervoice in the woodwinds is not heard sufficiently, the first horn pair can double (requiring some adjustment for the second horn pair).

The First Violin Part of Mozart's Symphony No. 35 in D Major (K. 385) Marked for Performance

The text of the first violin part of this symphony has been corrected to conform to Mozart's autograph (published as a facsimile). Bowings and some fingerings have been added. All other added markings, offered as suggestions, appear in brackets to set them apart from the original. When entered into orchestra parts for practical use, brackets would confuse the players and must be omitted.

First Movement

Measure 1	Most conductors use a 2-beat for the beginning. For this reason, the sign ₵ has been added to Mozart's **C** but put in brackets. A speed of ♩ = 144–52 is recommended, also alternating 2-beat and 4-beat for certain passages (see ex. 12.33).
M. 7	The added tenuto sign on C sharp prevents the players from "dropping" this note, a frequently heard habit in connection with appogiaturas, which can lead to rendering such notes almost inaudible, especially in large halls.
M. 10	The main theme consists of three motives: five bars (stately), four bars (songlike), and four bars (playful). The suggested bowing underlines the character of the third motive.
M. 44	Mozart's phrasing is essential for an incisive syncopation. The musical context suggests that, in

	this case, *tr* stands for an inverted mordent (*Pralltriller*).
M. 49	The marking (*save*) warns the players to be economical with the bow during the sustained F sharp.
M. 66	Mozart wanted the *p* to commence on the second quarter; for the added diminuendo, see pp. 392–93.
M. 74	The marking (*ten.*) reminds the players to sustain the A to its full value. Technically, this requires very quick, almost abrupt, bow action.
Mm. 77ff.	The suggested bowing, though different from the original, is recommended in the interest of correctly sustained eighth notes.
M. 80	The (*mf*) produces a better orchestral balance (see mm. 110 and 186).
M. 94	In general, whether or not to apply *divisi* to double and triple stops depends on intonation, articulation, and sound and is to be decided on the merits of each case. (Purists can rightly claim that in former times such chords used to be performed in unison.)

Second Movement

Measure 1	The authenticity of *Andante* is not proven.
M. 2	The players must lift the bow before the triplet.
M. 6	Dots have been added for phrasing.
Mm. 9ff.	Mozart's bowing secures a soft accompaniment (oboe and bassoon soli) and must not be changed. In m. 11 the violins can apply some vibrato.
M. 15	In the autograph, the first B is followed by a dot, but B and D are clearly thirty-second notes, as they are in m. 13 where there is no dot. Thus, it can be assumed that Mozart intended even notes in both instances, in contrast to the dotted rhythm in measure 14.
M. 23	A bow change on the second note would upset Mozart's logical phrasing. Besides, using the bow sparingly on the high C contributes to the beauty of the melodic line.
M. 25	Mozart wished to tie the sustained D to the grace note (see also m. 74!) and to separate the thirty-second note by marking it staccato. The short upbeat creates an element of surprise which would be destroyed by altering the original phrasing. (A different effect is intended in m. 74, another example of variety vs. analogy!).
M. 33ff.	Here, and in mm. 82ff., wedges indicate an accent (see ex. 34.9).

M. 43	Dots have been added (also in m. 45) to indicate the phrasing; a sustained legato would be contrary to the style.

Third Movement

Measure 3	Chords of this kind must not be routinely marked with successive down-bows!
M. 25	This measure is to be played on the string.
M. 26	Mozart marked the winds staccato; this probably also applies to the violins.

Fourth Movement

Measure 1	The autograph clearly shows ₵.
M. 9	Here, successive down-bows assure "clipped" chords to let the eighth notes in the low instruments stand out.
M. 32	The change of phrasing is optional. Yet the suggested slurs are so "violinistic" that Mozart would probably have approved.
M. 125	The violins must not play too heavily; a (repeated) p serves as warning.
M. 126	The original phrasing would create a problem within a passage that is performed off-string.
M. 137	Some editions print A as the last note for violas, cellos, and basses; the autograph has F sharp for all instruments.
Mm. 223ff.	This passage is distorted in printed parts by the omission of grace notes. Players unaccustomed to the original version may find them confusing, a problem that is easily remedied by some practice (slow!).
M. 240	The indication (*stay in middle*) is a warning not to use too much bow, neither here nor in the following measures. The entire passage, including m. 243, must be played softly and smoothly.

Ex. D.1.

Violino I

Trills begin on the upper note, unless marked * (= inverted mordent).

Ex. D.1.   *Continued*

(continued)

Ex. D.1.   *Continued*

Ex. D.1.   *Continued*

(continued)

Ex. D.1. *Continued*

Ex. D.1. *Continued*

Men. D. C.

(continued)

Ex. D.1. *Continued*

Ex. D.1.   *Continued*

(*continued*)

Ex. D.1.   *Continued*

Ex. D.1.   *Continued*

(continued)

Recommended Reading

Far from a bibliography, this list, limited in scope and intent, merely serves the author to recommend to his readers a number of books that have proven useful to his studies. Although the process of selection may have been affected by the author's proclivities, he trusts that all the titles listed here, even those that refer mainly to keyboard music, provide the kind of information that is appreciated by conductors. Only texts written in English or available in English translations have been included.

HISTORY OF CONDUCTING AND ORCHESTRAL PERFORMANCE

BERLIOZ, HECTOR. *Treatise on Instrumentation*. New York: Dover Publications, 1991.

CARSE, ADAM. *The History of Orchestration*. New York: Dover Publications, 1964.

————. *The Orchestra from Beethoven to Berlioz*. Cambridge: W. Heffer, 1945.

————. *The Orchestra in the Eighteenth Century*. New York: Broude Brothers, 1969.

GALKIN, ELLIOTT W. *A History of Orchestral Conducting*. New York: Pendragon Press, 1986.

KOURY, DANIEL J. *Orchestral Performance Practices of the Nineteenth Century*. Rochester: University of Rochester Press, 1992.

WEINGARTNER, FELIX. *On Music and Conducting*. New York: Dover Publications, 1969.

STYLE AND PERFORMANCE PRACTICE

Early Sources

BACH, CARL PHILIP EMANUEL. *Essay on the True Art of Playing Keyboard Instruments*. New York: W. W. Norton & Sons, 1949.

CZERNY, CARL. *On the Performance of Beethoven's Piano Works*. Facsimile, edited by Paul Badura-Skoda. Vienna: Universal, 1970.

MOZART, LEOPOLD. *A Treatise on the Fundamental Principles of Violin Playing*. London: Oxford University Press, 1951.

TÜRK, DANIEL GOTTLOB. *School of Clavier Playing*. Lincoln: University of Nebraska Press, 1982.

Modern Research

BADURA-SKODA, PAUL. *Interpreting Bach on the Keyboard*. New York: Oxford University Press, 1993.

BADURA-SKODA, PAUL, AND EVA BADURA-SKODA. *Interpreting Mozart*. New York: St. Martin's Press, 1962.

DANNREUTHER, EDWARD. *Musical Ornamentation*. New York: Novello, Ewer & Co. 1893–1895. (Reprinted by E. F. Kalmus [1961?].)

DEL MAR, NORMAN. *Orchestral Variations*. London: Eulenburg Books, 1981.

DONINGTON, ROBERT. *The Interpretation of Early Music*. London: Faber & Faber, 1974.

DORIAN, FREDERICK. *The History of Music in Performance*. New York: W. W. Norton & Sons, 1942.

EMERY, WALTER. *Bach's Ornaments*. London: Novello, 1961.

KELLER, HERMANN. *Phrasing and Articulation*. New York: W. W. Norton & Sons, 1965.

LANDON, H. C. ROBBINS. *The Symphonies of Joseph Haydn*. New York: Macmillan, 1956. 2d. ed., 1961.

MARTY, JEAN-PIERRE. *The Tempo Indications of Mozart*. New Haven: Yale University Press, 1989.

NEUMANN, FREDERICK. *Ornamentation in Baroque and Post-Baroque Music*. Princeton: Princeton University Press, 1978.

———. *Performance Practices of the Seventeenth and Eighteenth Centuries*. New York: Schirmer Books, 1993.

———. *Ornamentation and Improvisation in Mozart*. Princeton: Princeton University Press, 1986.

NEWMAN, WILLIAM S. *Beethoven on Beethoven*. New York: W. W. Norton & Sons, 1988.

ROSENBLUM, SANDRA P. *Performance Practices in Classic Piano Music*. Bloomington: Indiana University Press, 1988.

SACHS, CURT. *Rhythm and Tempo*. New York: Columbia University Press, 1988.

SCHLOTEL, BRIAN. "Schumann and the Metronome." In *Robert Schumann: The Man and His Music*. Edited by Alan Walker. London: Barrie & Jenkins, 1972.

TODD, R. L., AND P. WILLIAMS, eds. *Perspectives on Mozart Performance*. Cambridge: Cambridge University Press, 1991.

VINQUIST, MARY, AND NEAL ZASLAW. *Performance Practice: A Bibliography*. New York: W. W. Norton & Sons, 1971.

ZASLAW, NEAL. *Mozart's Symphonies*. Oxford: Clarendon Press, 1989.

Vocal Art

COLORNI, EVELINA. *Singers' Italian.* New York: Schirmer Books, 1970.

GRUBB, THOMAS. *Singing in French.* New York: Schirmer Books, 1979.

KAGEN, SERGIUS. *On Studying Singing.* New York: Dover Publications, 1960.

RUSHMORE, ROBERT. *The Singing Voice.* New York: Dodd, Mead & Co., 1971.

TOSI, PIER FRANCESCO. *Observations on the Florid Song. [1725]* London: W. Reeves, 1926.

Instruments

BOYDEN, DAVID D. *A History of Violin Playing.* New York: Oxford University Press, 1965.

DEL MAR, NORMAN. *Anatomy of the Orchestra.* Berkeley: University of California Press, 1983.

GALAMIAN, IVAN. *Principles of Violin Playing.* Englewood Cliffs, N.J.: Prentice-Hall, 1962.

PETERS, GORDON B. *The Drummer Man: A Treatise on Percussion.* Wilmette: Kempers-Peters Publications, 1975.

SCHULLER, GUNTHER. *Horn Technique.* New York: Oxford University Press, 1962.

SZIGETI, JOSEPH. *Szigeti on the Violin.* New York: Dover Publications, 1969.

For the past twelve years the author has contributed articles to *The Journal of the Conductor's Guild.* Back numbers are available by writing to The Conductor's Guild, P.O. Box 3361, West Chester, PA, 19381.

Some of these articles are listed below, since they might clarify and amplify ideas that are part of this volume.

"The Metronome Indications in Beethoven's Symphonies" (vol. 1, no. 1: 1980)

"Inner Repeats in the Da Capo of Classical Minuets and Scherzos" (vol. 3, no. 4: 1982)

"The Conductors' Dilemma" (vol. 8, no. 4: 1987)

"On or Before the Beat: A Matter of Fashion?" (vol. 9, nos. 3 & 4: 1988)

"Authenticity in Musical Performance" (vol. 10, nos. 3 & 4: 1988)

"Good Taste in Music and Related Matters" (vol. 11, nos. 1 & 2: 1990)

General Index

Index of Figures and Works

Page numbers in boldface indicate figures and music examples.

Figures

Works